The AllShihTzu Book-
Print Edition

AllShihTzu.com

ISBN: 153340903X
ISBN-13: 978-1533409034

DEDICATION

We wish to thank the readers and Members of the AllShihTzu site for politely yet persistently requesting for us to create a print version of this book. As our goal is to provide the most helpful information possible, we thank you for encouraging us to continually grow. Your loyalty means so much to us!

Table of Contents

Before You Begin

There is a big difference between owning a dog and having a canine family member. Anyone can do the former and it takes a kind, loving soul to do the latter. If you have this book, you no doubt know this as well and want to do all you can to raise your Shih Tzu well. We do hope that you find this book to be a helpful guide in navigating the path of nurturing your Shih Tzu to be the happiest, healthiest dog possible.

Our goal was to provide you with an extremely comprehensive book, yet at a reasonable cost. That is why it took us such a long time to figure out a way to produce this print edition book for you. As independent publishers, the elements that affect the printing cost (and therefore, the retail price) of a book are color and length. If we retained what the AllShihTzu Version 3 eBook offered (500+ pages, color), the price to print this book would have been astronomical and affected retail price in such a way that it would have been much too expensive for the typical Shih Tzu owner.

In regard to length, we refused to cut out any needed information, therefore we chose this large 8.5x11" size and worked tirelessly to format it to be as few pages as possible. We worked quite extensively on culling information and as to not repeat text, you'll find that we sometimes refer you to other sections in the book.

In regard to color, the print cost for a color book of this length would have been sky-high and for that reason, we chose the black & white format.

Please note that the information in this book is not intended to be a substitute for professional veterinary advice, diagnosis or treatment. Always seek the advice of your veterinarian with any questions about your dog's health. Do not disregard professional medical advice or delay seeking advice or treatment because of something you have read here.

During the course of this book, certain brand names are mentioned. This is because we personally like these items and we find them to be very helpful in caring for Shih Tzu. You do not have to use them if you do not wish to; if you have found something comparable that works well for you and your Shih Tzu, that's okay too! If you would like to see our exact recommendations, you can find them in the Shih Tzu Specialty Shoppe. This can be accessed from any page of the AllShihTzu website. Look to the navigation (it is in alphabetical order) and choose 'Shoppe'.

Love, Hugs & Shih Tzu Kisses,

The AllShihTzu Team

About the Shih Tzu

A Brief Recap of History

Origin Overview - You may already be familiar with the history of the Shih Tzu, however it is so interesting that we would be remiss if we did not cover this, at least in a brief summary.

The Shih Tzu is thought to have originated in East Asia (Tibet and China), being one of the oldest and smallest of the Tibetan holy dogs. The Shih Tzu therefore also has the nickname 'Tibetan Temple Dog'. This breed is also known as the 'Xi Shi quan' (西施犬), based on the name of Xi Shi, who was regarded as the most beautiful woman of ancient China. 'Chrysanthemum Dog' is another alternative name for this breed, due to the way in which the hairs grow around the face.

While it was long believed that the Shih Tzu was an old breed, recent DNA analysis *does* point to this. Tibetan dogs- such as the Shih Tzu – are thought to be the ancestors of the Gobi Desert Kitchen Midden Dog, dating back to over 10,000 years ago. A vast majority of dogs at that time were untamed. Eventually, a new breed evolved from the Gobi Desert Kitchen Midden Dog, which was called the Small Soft-Coated Drop-Eared Hunting Dog. The Small Soft-Coated Drop-Eared Hunting Dog then evolved into the Kitchen Midden Dog.

Though there are no written records, a popular assumption is that ultimately the Kitchen Midden Dog, through distinct breeding programs, was used to develop the Tibetan Spaniel, the Pekingese, the Japanese Chin, the Papillon, the Pug and the Shih Tzu. As you can imagine, the process of developing each dog breed was spread out over thousands of years.

During the time of later development, there is debate over which breeds were used to perfect the Shih Tzu. Some believe that this breed had Pekingese and Lhasa Apso influences.

The Move into England – Record keeping in the 20th century allows us to know more details about this breed's history. Two Shih Tzu were brought into England from China by General Sir Douglas (a senior British army officer who later became Military Secretary) and his wife, Lady Brownrigg. There is conflicting information regarding the date that this occurred. Some sources list it as 1920 and others say 1928. We do believe, however, that it was the more commonly listed date of 1930.

When brought to England, they were referred to as Tibetan Lion Dogs, which distinguished them from the Chinese Lion Dogs (the name for the Pekingese breed, at that time). In 1933 a few Shih Tzu were shown alongside Apsos at the Cheltenham show by the Apso and Lion Dog Club. However this did not last long as the show world quickly saw that they were a distinct and unique breed. The Shih Tzu were much smaller, with shorter legs and more compact faces and snouts. The following year in 1934, the Kennel Club permitted the Apso and Lion Dog Club to change its name to Shih Tzu (Tibetan Lion Dog) Club, ruling that the dogs from China were not Apsos, but were indeed Shih Tzu. By 1935 the 'Tibetan Lion Dog' part was taken out of the club's name and The Shih Tzu Club of England was born under the Presidency of the Countess of Essex, with Lady Brownrigg serving as Secretary.

The Move into America- Soldiers returning to the States from WWII, brought Shih Tzu with them and breeding programs were quickly established. The unique beauty and friendly temperament of this 'newly discovered' breed quickly led to a fast rise in popularity. The AKC (American Kennel Club) formally recognized the breed on September 1, 1969. The Shih Tzu were classified as non-working dogs, in the toy dog group. In 1969, a total of 2,811 Shih Tzu were registered. By 1978, the number of registered Shih Tzu grew to over 5 times that number: 14,894. Over the next 9 year period over 85,000 Shih Tzu were registered with the American Kennel Club, placing the Shih Tzu in the top 25 most popular breeds. The Shih Tzu has consistently been in the top most 20 most popular dog breeds in the United States for decades. The Shih Tzu placed at #17 in 2014 and at #19 in 2015.

Today's Shih Tzu - Not only is the Shih Tzu famous for its beautiful appearance, this breed is so popular because of its amazing personality. Shih Tzu are known for being brave, happy dogs that are generally not nervous, shy or overly 'yappy'. Though a toy sized breed, the Shih Tzu is relatively sturdy, which correlates to this breed's high energy levels. Though very active and therefore with a need for daily exercise, the Shih Tzu tends to do quite well in a wide variety of settings. This breed can be content in all sorts of households, from a single-dog small apartment to a multiple-dog larger home.

Many people choose to bring a Shih Tzu into their family to reap the benefits of having a dog that truly craves human companionship, is even-tempered and will indulge their owners by thoroughly enjoying being spoiled. Yet, the Shih Tzu also has an animated personality; they can be feisty, a bit mischievous and may try to see just what it is that they can get away with. One thing is sure, your Shih Tzu will always keep you on your toes and will be a loyal, loving canine family member.

Pronunciation

The pronunciation of 'Shih Tzu' is quite interesting. There are millions of people: owners, well-established breeders and even those in show, who do not pronounce this as it is meant to be. The most common *incorrect* pronunciation is: 'shit-zoo'.

Why do so many people say this? One reason is that like many other words in the English language, people often default to the easiest way to pronounce a word. A good example of a common word that is mispronounced quite often is the word 'Arctic', as in, "the Arctic Ocean that is located in the top northern hemisphere." The majority of people will say: Ar-tic; They leave off the first "c" in the word. The correct way to say this word is: Arc-tic. But many people have defaulted to the easier way of pronouncing it. And this is, partly, what has happened to the word 'Shih Tzu'.

Another reason why so many people say this dog's breed name incorrectly is because the incorrect way of saying it has become so popular. It is almost akin to peer pressure to say it incorrectly! Quite often, when one person says it inaccurately, another person does not correct them since the mispronunciation has become so common. In many cases, the person who *does* know the accurate pronunciation worries that they themselves are the ones who would be perceived as enunciating it incorrectly, so they don't speak up. And the endless circle continues.

There are other incorrect pronunciations of the word as well; some of these are: Shi –Doo, Sheet Zoo, She – Doh and just about any other mix of the vowel and consonants that one could imagine.

For the correct pronunciation of Shih Tzu let's look to the Oxford English Dictionary, which is the world's most comprehensive single-language print dictionary according to the Guinness Book of World Records. It is the premier dictionary of the English language. According to this trustworthy, reputable resource, the correct pronunciation is: (shē' dzoo).

> **shih tzu** 🔊 (shē' dzo͞o')
>
> *n.*
>
> A dog of a breed developed in China, probably from a Tibetan breed, having a long flowing coat, short legs, a square muzzle, and a tail that curls over the back.

The mark of ¯, shown above the first 'e' is called a diacritic mark. Specifically, it is a macron. Diacritic marks are used to show the sound value of the letter to which they are added. The macron of ¯ means that the letter is pronounced as a long vowel. The short vowel would be said as 'eh' and the long vowel that we are discussing here is enunciated as a long 'E', as in the word 'bee'. Therefore, the first syllable is pronounced as 'She'.

The dzoo may seem a bit trickier, however, it is a simple roll of the 'd' into the 'z' of 'zoo' (dah-zoo). There is heavy emphasis on the first syllable. The 'She'... followed by the second syllable, the 'dzoo'. When said as one single word, the 2 syllables flow together, thus making the pronunciation: Sheedzoo.

The American Shih Tzu Club and the American Kennel Club verifies this, as they have officially and publicly confirmed the pronunciation of Shih Tzu. Image below, you will see the introductory section of the AKC New Puppy Registration Paper that owners receive once a Shih Tzu pup has been registered with them.

Congratulations on your new
Shih Tzu

About the Shih Tzu

Lion-like dogs like the Shih Tzu (pronounced "sheed-zoo") existed in China for many centuries. In fact, the Chinese

We do encourage owners to pronounce Shih Tzu correctly as Sheed-zoo and to educate other owners to do the same. We give honor and respect to the breed when we speak its name properly.

Plural - The breed's name of Shih Tzu is both singular and plural; just as we do with the word 'fish'. Therefore, if a person had 5 dogs, they would say, "I have five Shih Tzu".

Nickname – Many owners refer to this breed simply as 'Tzu'.

The Breed Standard Explained

Pet VS Show Shih Tzu - The majority of Shih Tzu will not match the breed standard 100%, particularly when it comes to measurements; every dog is unique. In many cases, an owner will have purchased or adopted a pet quality Shih Tzu as show quality dogs are rare. Even if two champions were paired, there is no guarantee that the resulting litter will contain any show quality dogs. When a puppy displays promising qualities of being a show dog, often they are held onto by the breeder or sold at very high prices.

There is absolutely nothing wrong with having a pet quality Shih Tzu for a pet. The only thing that this means is that the puppy may not perfectly fit the very strict and very rigid guidelines of the AKC or other reputable kennel club. Additionally, owners should try to not compare their own dogs to those in show. You are not expected to keep your Shih Tzu in a long show coat nor spend hours each day meticulously grooming your dog. This said, some owners do enjoy keeping their Shih Tzu 'ready for show'; this is great for those that have time and for many it can be considered a hobby, as quite a bit of money and time is involved.

Overview In order for a dog breed to be an official dog breed, a standard must be set. These are guidelines which state in detail what the particular dog breed looks like. This includes size, type of coat, facial structure, body structure and so on.

The AKC follows breed standards that are set by the breed's parent club. Therefore, the AKC standards for the Shih Tzu are set by the American Shih Tzu Club. The CKC (Canadian Kennel Club), KC (The Kennel Club of the UK) and the FCI (Fédération Cynologique Internationale - which has over 80 member countries) all have very similar breed standards as the AKC. The wording may differ slightly, however all agree on all major facets of exactly how a Shih Tzu 'should' look. A breed standard has two purposes: It is a guideline for breeders in their attempt to produce dogs that best fit the standard and it is used by judges to assess dogs in conformation events (dog show events in which dogs are judged on how closely they match the official standard guidelines).

The AKC breed standard may be revised every 5 years; however, this does not mean that it will be. If revisions are made, most often the changes will be negligible.

Size: The Shih Tzu is in the Toy Group. The breed standard weight and height for well recognized kennel clubs is as follows:

AKC *Adult weight:* 9 to 16 pounds (4.08 to 7.25 kg). *Adult Height:* Ideally 9 to 10.5 inches (22.86 to 26.67 cm); not less than 8 inches (20.32 cm) and not more than 11 inches (27.94 cm).

CKC (Canadian Kennel Club) *Adult weight:* 9 to 16 pounds (4.08 to 7.25 kg). *Adult Height:* Ideally 11 inches (27.94 cm).

FCI and KC *Adult weight:* 4.5 to 8 kg (9.92 to 17.63 lbs.) with an ideal weight of 4.5 - 7.5 kg (9.92 to 17.08). *Adult Height:* Not more than 27 cm (10.63 inches).

So, as you can see, there is a general agreement on the size of the Shih Tzu. The FCI and KC allow for a slightly larger dog of almost 18 pounds, with the AKC preferring a dog not over 16 pounds. The AKC looks for a slightly shorter dog in show (ideally 9 to 10.5 inches), though all clubs agree that the ideal height should not exceed 11 inches.

Now, Let's Look at the Breed Standard Since we are based in the US, we will look at the AKC standard. The standard is similar for FCI, KC and CKC.

Per the AKC's most recent information (at the time of this writing) at: akc.org/dog-breeds/shih-tzu, based on the American Shih Tzu Club guidelines found at: americanshihtzuclub.org, the following is the breed standard. In alternate text we have added our explanations, as we interpret them:

General Appearance - The Shih Tzu is a sturdy, lively, alert toy dog with long flowing double coat [there is an inner and an outer layer]. Befitting his noble Chinese ancestry as a highly valued, prized companion and palace pet, the Shih Tzu is proud of bearing [the way in which the dog moves, stands and behaves] , has a distinctively arrogant carriage [the way in which the dog holds and moves the head and body] with head well up and tail curved over the back. Although there has always been considerable size variation, the Shih Tzu must be compact [limbs, head, tail, close to the body], solid, carrying good weight and substance [not a long dog; never considered to have a 'skinny' appearance].

Even though a toy dog [the AKC recognizes 21 toy breeds, the Chihuahua is the smallest, the Pug is the largest], the Shih Tzu must be subject to the same requirements of soundness and structure prescribed for all breeds [being classified as a 'toy' will not be an excuse for not meeting breed standards in show], and any deviation from the ideal described in the standard should be penalized to the extent of the deviation. Structural faults common to all breeds are as undesirable in the Shih Tzu as in any other breed, regardless of whether or not such faults are specifically mentioned in the standard [there are more faults that a dog can have other than what is listed in the AKC breed standard, it is important to understand that a whole array of things could deduct points aside from the few mentioned here].

Size, Proportion, Substance - *Size* - Ideally, height at withers [shoulder blades] is 9 to 10½ inches; but, not less than 8 inches nor more than 11 inches. Ideally, weight of mature dogs, 9 to 16 pounds.

Proportion - Length between withers [shoulder blades] and root of tail [where the tail meets the rump] is

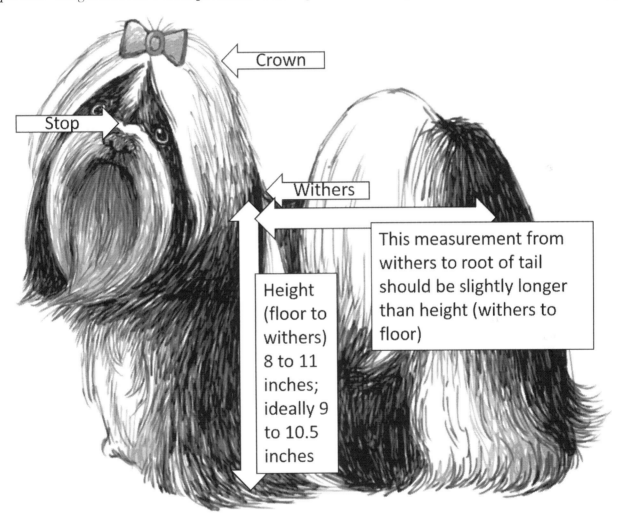

Crown

Stop

Withers

Height (floor to withers) 8 to 11 inches; ideally 9 to 10.5 inches

This measurement from withers to root of tail should be slightly longer than height (withers to floor)

slightly longer than height at withers. The Shih Tzu must never be so high stationed [where the body is, in relation to the floor, when standing] as to appear leggy [legs appear long], nor so low stationed as to appear dumpy or squatty [overly short or thick].

Substance - Regardless of size, the Shih Tzu is always compact, solid and carries good weight and substance [a heavier weight will not show via longer legs, it will be distributed; whether a Tzu is 9 lbs. or 16 lbs., the body shape will be the same].

Head - *Head* - Round, broad, wide between eyes, its size in balance with the overall size of the dog being neither too large nor too small. [No individual part should stand out over another. The individual parts of the head – nose, lips, eyes - should combine to produce an agreeable expression] *Fault:* Narrow head, close-set eyes.

Expression - Warm, sweet, wide-eyed, friendly and trusting [the dog has a natural, happy appearance]. An overall well-balanced and pleasant expression supersedes the importance of individual parts [if the expression is as explained, this is more important that perfect ear set, perfect nose, etc.] Care should be taken to look and examine well beyond the hair to determine if what is seen is the actual head and expression rather than an image created by grooming technique. [Since the coat of the Shih Tzu can hide so much, judges physically touch the dog to ensure that the hair was not styled in such a way as to hide faults].

Eyes - Large, round, not prominent [when looking from the side, do not bulge out], placed well apart, looking straight ahead. Very dark. Lighter on liver pigmented dogs and blue pigmented dogs [liver Shih Tzu will have brown eyes (paw pads, lips, nose and eye rims will be brown), blue Shih Tzu (blue is a diluted black); paw pads, lips, nose and eye rims will be a steely navy blue; eyes will have a lighter iris, sometimes with a tint of grey]. *Fault:* Small, close-set or light eyes; excessive eye white [small irises].

Ears - Large, set slightly below crown of skull [the upper back of the skull]; heavily coated [thick hairs; ears should blend into the head].

Skull – Domed [a curved top skull that is evenly rounded and not flat].

Stop - There is a *definite stop* [the stop is the distinct definition between the skull and the muzzle and should be clearly seen, but not as to cause wrinkles].

Muzzle – Square [when viewed from the front, the muzzle should form a square, being wide from top to bottom and from side to side – in order to have the desired 'square' shape, the jaw must be wide and strong], short, unwrinkled [skin is tight], with good cushioning, set no lower than bottom eye rim; never downturned. Ideally, no longer than 1 inch from tip of nose to stop, although length may vary slightly in relation to overall size of dog. front of muzzle should be flat; lower lip and chin not protruding and definitely never receding [when looking from the side, lips and chin are square; they do not stick out or slant inward].

Fault: Snipiness [a lack of substance to the underjaw, giving the head a pointy profile], lack of definite stop.

Nose - Nostrils are broad, wide, and open [no signs of stenotic nares (pinched nostrils), which this breed is prone to. Some outgrow this. For some, it can cause breathing issues and a procedure needs to be done to resolve the issue].

Pigmentation - Nose, lips, eye rims are black on all colors, except liver on liver pigmented dogs and blue on blue pigmented dogs. [Tzu that carry liver have brown paw pads, eye rims, nose and lips. Shih Tzu with blue have blue paw pads, eye rims, nose and lips; this often can appear to be black but upon close inspection it will be a diluted black that has a dark blue tint to it, often more noticeable when outside in bright sunlight]. *Fault:* Pink on nose, lips, or eye rims.

Bite – Undershot [the lower jaw juts out further than the upper jaw; more precisely with this breed, the ideal undershot bite for the Tzu is one in which the outer surface of the upper teeth engages *or* nearly engages, the inner surface of the lower teeth. This is also called a 'reverse scissors bite']. Jaw is broad and wide. A missing tooth or slightly misaligned teeth should not be too severely penalized. Teeth and tongue should not show when mouth is closed.

Fault: Overshot bite [upper jaw juts out further than the lower jaw].

Neck, Topline, Body- Of utmost importance is an overall well-balanced dog with no exaggerated features [all elements blend together, no one body part is more noticeable than another feature].

Neck - Well set-on flowing smoothly into shoulders; of sufficient length to permit natural high head carriage and in balance with height and length of dog.

Topline - Level [the topline is the visual line made by the spine when looking from the side, from the withers (top of the shoulder blade) to the base of the tail].

Body -Short-coupled [relatively short distances between areas, i.e. from withers to rump, etc.] and sturdy with no waist or tuck-up. The Shih Tzu is slightly longer than tall. *Fault:* Legginess.

Chest -Broad and deep with good spring-of-rib [the ribcage is not narrow when viewed from the top], however, not barrel-chested [though not narrow, not too round]. Depth of ribcage should extend to just below elbow. Distance from elbow to withers is a little greater than from elbow to ground.

Croup - Flat [where the back flows into the tail].

Tail - Set on high, heavily plumed [hair is thick and feathered] carried in curve well over back. Too loose, too tight, too flat, or too low set a tail [the set is the exact area where the tail meets the rump] is undesirable and should be penalized to extent of deviation.

Forequarters- *Shoulders* - Well-angulated, well laid-back, well laid-in, fitting smoothly into body [not slopping forward, no hunching].

Legs - Straight, well-boned, muscular, set well-apart and under chest, with elbows set close to body.

Pasterns - Strong, perpendicular [front pasterns are the equivalent of a human's wrists and rear pasterns are the equivalent of a human's ankles].

Dewclaws - May be removed.

Feet - Firm, well-padded, point straight ahead.

Hindquarters - Angulation of hindquarters should be in balance with forequarters.

Legs - Well-boned, muscular, and straight when viewed from rear with well-bent stifles, not close set but in line with forequarters.

Hocks - Well let down, perpendicular **[the top ankle joint]**. *Fault:* Hyperextension of hocks.

Dewclaws - May be removed.

Feet - Firm, well-padded, point straight ahead.

Coat - *Coat* - Luxurious, double-coated, dense, long, and flowing. Slight wave permissible. Hair on top of head is tied up. *Fault:* Sparse coat, single coat, curly coat. *Trimming* - Feet, bottom of coat, and anus may be done for neatness and to facilitate movement. *Fault:* Excessive trimming.

Color and Markings - All are permissible and to be considered equally.

Size Differences

Overview - The AKC standard for the Shih Tzu calls out for a dog that at full adult size will be between 9 and 16 pounds (4.08 to 7.25 kilograms). Males do tend to be larger than females, though either gender can be at the low or high end of this range. In addition, there will always be some Tzu that are slightly smaller than this and some that are slightly larger.

Smaller than Average Shih Tzu – In most typical litters there will be some Shih Tzu that are a bit undersized, maturing into an adult weight of 7 or 8 pounds. These dogs should be examined by the veterinarian to ensure that they are receiving enough nutrition, have enough muscle mass and are free of any health issues. In most cases, the 7 or 8 pound Shih Tzu will simply have smaller than normal bone structure.

Issues can occur, however, if a Shih Tzu is 6 pounds or under as an adult. Some owners will have specifically sought out a very tiny Tzu and others will be surprised that growth stopped at this weight. There are breeders who purposefully produce Shih Tzu that are much smaller than the standard. We believe this is unethical and can lead to that dog suffering from many size-related health issues.

Shih Tzu purposely bred to be smaller than the standard are often advertised as 'Teacup', 'Toy', 'Miniature' or 'Imperial' Shih Tzu. None of these terms are official; they are simply a marketing term. There is no accepted variation of the Shih Tzu.

The most common method of producing smaller Tzu are to pair together two undersized dogs. In laymen terms, the two chosen dogs are the 'runts of the litter'. Often, undersized puppies of that litter are then paired together to further create very tiny dogs. This means that inline breeding is occurring. Inline breeding is the pairing of closely related dogs: son and mother will be paired or father and daughter. We find this highly unethical. Supporters of this will argue that it "happens in the wild" and therefore it is natural. We do not agree. We are not living in the wild. Tzu that are home raised and bred by loving home breeders are not in the wild. We live in a civilized world and with proper breeding practices, inline breeding does not have a place.

The reason that inline breeding is done so often in the attempt to breed tiny Shih Tzu is because once a litter is produced, if they are smaller than standard as the breeder hoped, it is then easier for the breeder to pair together closely related dogs as opposed to finding other 'runts' from other litters.

If you are an owner of a smaller Shih Tzu, it is important to follow all care tips and guidelines with the greatest of care. While smaller Shih Tzu may be healthy, they are more prone to many types of injuries and health issues. The most common injuries to a smaller than standard Tzu are those that are related to body structure and body density. Risk of injury from jumping and from being on leash will be far greater. You will want to take care that your Shih Tzu does not injure himself by jumping up and down from heights. As we recommend with all Shih Tzu, a harness should always be put on instead of a collar when the dog is on leash to prevent stress on the neck.

Such issues as hypoglycemia, hip dysplasia, luxating patella and stenotic nares (just to name a few) are seen more often with undersized dogs.

Please note that trying to 'fatten up' a dog will not work to bring an undersized Shih Tzu to standard size if his size is due to bone structure. The best thing you can do is to be aware of possible health issues, follow all care guidelines, keep your Tzu on an excellent food and exercise program and take him for yearly health checks with the veterinarian.

Larger than Average Shih Tzu – There are many owners of large Shih Tzu who are concerned that their Tzu is 'too large'. There are a few elements to this:

1) Some first time owners may not realize just how large 16 pounds is. They may have seen several Shih Tzu that were in the 9 to 10 pound range and most likely they saw many Tzu puppies; this led them to believe that the Shih Tzu breed is tiny. While they *are* a toy breed dog, they are not very small dogs such as the Chihuahua (6 pounds or under) or the Papillon (7 to 9 pounds). In fact, the weight of a Shih Tzu is close to the largest of all toy breeds, the Pug (14 to 18 pounds). Therefore, many owners of 15 or 16 pound Tzu may be concerned about their dog being too big, when in fact the dog is the perfect, expected weight.

2) Another element is the possibility of the dog carrying excess weight. In general, this is not a major concern for the Shih Tzu breed. They are active dogs and are not known for being prone to weight issues. However, if a bit too much food (or table scraps) are fed and walks are a bit shy of what they should be, this can cause a gradual weight gain that eventually becomes noticeable.

3) The last element is that a Tzu may be naturally over the AKC standard of 16 pounds. There are a lot of dogs that fall slightly above or below the standard. A 17 or 18 pound Shih Tzu may be perfectly healthy and of proper weight for his bone structure. This is only 1 or 2 pounds over what is expected in the show ring and as long as the dog is not carrying excess weight, there is no reason to be concerned. The only factor that is affected by this is the possibility of breeding. Size is genetically passed down and oversized Tzu should not be bred as this goes against the goal of producing dogs that adhere to the breed standards.

A Note About Imperials – While 'Imperial' can be a marketing term in regard to size as we already discussed, there is another way in which this may be used. Because the Shih Tzu originated in China, some breeders will claim that they have puppies that carry the bloodlines of royalty. There is no such thing.

The Tzu's ancestors existed thousands of years ago. Dogs that were very close to the Shih Tzu we have today were not coming into their own until the 1930's. There are no written records of breeding that date back to the days of when Chinese royalty were developing breeding programs for the Shih Tzu and perfecting the breed. Therefore, it is impossible to know if a dog is a 30th generation dog from centuries ago and there is undoubtedly no method of knowing if a certain dog is a direct descendant of any one particular breeding program that took place in China or Tibet before the 20th century. This is most certainly a marketing ploy that potential puppy buyers should be aware of.

This said, because this is such a regal breed with an impressive history, some breeders tend to use the term 'Imperial' to signify the breed's reputation and may, in turn, also try to produce Shih Tzu that fall near the lower end of the 9 to 16 pound range. With good breeding practices, if the dogs matures to be 9 to 10 pounds, this fits the standard and there is nothing wrong with this. As with any litters, there may be some dogs that fall a bit under the weight goal. And as mentioned earlier, if these Tzu are 7 or 8 pounds, they may be perfectly healthy.

If you are thinking of purchasing a new Shih Tzu puppy from an 'Imperial' breeder, do question her to find out if the goal is the low end of the accepted weight scale or if the pups are expected to be significantly undersized. As a side note, some breeders are working toward having the 'Imperial' be an official dog breed; though this is something we highly believe will not come to fruition.

Shih Tzu Colors

Per the AKC breed standard, all colors and all markings are permissible and are considered to be equal. And therefore, the Shih Tzu is one of few breeds that can literally hold any possible color. A Shih Tzu may be solid, solid with a marking, be parti (two colors) or tri-color (three colors).

Unless a Shih Tzu is liver or blue, his nose (and eye rims, lips and paw pads) should be black. And unless liver or blue, the eyes should be very dark. Liver or blue does not need to be the dominant color on the coat to affect skin pigmentation or eye color.

There are 7 solid colors:

- **Black** – A true solid black with not have any other color showing. If a Shih Tzu does have a small patch of another color, he can still be a 'black', but will be a 'black with a marking', i.e. 'black with tan marking'. The nose will be black.

- **Blue** – Blue is a diluted black. While a blue Shih Tzu may appear to be black, the coat will be dulled and the skin pigmentation (nose, eye rims, lips and paw pads) will be a dark, steely navy. This may be most noticeable when outside in bright sunlight. Blue Shih Tzu may have lighter colored eyes than their counterparts.

- **Liver** – Livers will have some brown in the coat, which can range from very dark to very light. The dog may be solid, parti or tri-color. A Shih Tzu will be liver based on his skin pigmentation. This includes the nose, eye rims and paw pads, which will be a diluted brown. Regardless of the coat color, if the nose is liver, the dog is liver. The liver gene may affect the eyes, which would give you light brown, green or hazel eyes.

- **Brindle** - Despite this being listed as a color, this is actually a pattern of striped colors. The brindle (striping) may range from light to heavy.

- **Gold** - A tan /yellow, found commonly among Labrador Retrievers.

- **Red** - A very deep and dark orange. It's common for a red to be very dark red as a newborn and fade to a much lighter red just within the first few weeks.

- **Silver** - Gray with a deep shine.

There are also parti's. Most parti Shih Tzu will have white with another color. Possible parti coats include: White and Black | White and Blue | White and Brindle | White and Gold | White and Liver | White and Red | White and Silver.

And there are tri-coats: Silver, Gold & White | Black, Silver & White | Black, Gold & White | Black, Silver and Gold.

What About Chocolate? Many Shih Tzu are dubbed 'Chocolate' colored; however, this is not an official color. A chocolate - if he has a brown nose - is a liver.

Shih Tzu Intelligence

Overview As owner of a Shih Tzu you surely know that this is a quick-thinking and intuitive breed. The Shih Tzu is exceptionally aware of his humans (actions, words, even non-verbal cues) and his environment. And this breed will not hesitate to express how he is feeling, good or bad. The AKC breed standard for the Shih Tzu mentions 'lively',

'alert', 'friendly' and 'trusting', which suggests high intelligence.

Yet, with all of this said and undisputed by most owners, just how is it that the Shih Tzu breed is not known for his intelligence? In fact, if you go by one of the most commonly referred to sources, the Shih Tzu scores very low in intelligence, #70 out of 79. We will discuss this in an unbiased way, to look at all of the ways that intelligence is factored and what this means in regard to the Shih Tzu breed.

The Intelligence of Dogs in General- The low ranking that this breed is given does not take away any of the facts regarding how smart canines are in general. There are several factors that are looked at when theorizing the basic intelligence of canines:

- **Understanding of words -** This plays a huge role in canine intelligence. In general, dogs that live in households with plenty of interaction can understand an average of 165 words. So, if you thought that your Shih Tzu only understood a few commands and some basic greetings, think again! Some understand less and some more; breeds in the top 20% of intelligent canines know up to 250. Yet even at the average of 165, this is the equivalent of a two year old human.

- **Memory skills -** This goes much further than memorizing words. This relates to how a dog can see an object and remember it weeks later. And of course, this applies to remembering his humans as well. Stories about dogs that are separated from their owners for long periods of time but then are overjoyed to be reunited are true. It's a myth that dogs only have short memories. They have both short and long-term memories and all that is needed is repetition for something to move from short term memory into long-term.

- **Awareness** - This includes the intelligence to understand his environment and all that surrounds the dog. Your Shih Tzu is showing intelligence when he understands he is at the dog park that you took him to last week or realizes that you are driving him to the groomer when you head off in a certain direction. Such actions as when you take out a brush and your Shih Tzu runs away or you walk toward where his leash is hanging and he gets excited; these are signs of intelligence that your Shih Tzu is fully aware.

- **Perception** - This is similar to awareness, yet it involves how a dog uses all of his senses to understand any particular event. He'll use a combination of vision, hearing, smell, touch and sometimes taste to learn what something is.

You may be interested to know that using the earth's magnetic field is included in this as well. In fact, scientists know that many animals are able to sense this. It is called Magnetoreception. Studies of Magnetoreception in canines have proven that if a dog is off leash and without confining walls (able to make his own choices) and the Earth's magnetic field is calm (there are daily fluctuations as the earth rotates), they prefer to pee and poo with their bodies aligned on a north to south axis.

It is unclear why they prefer this, but they do. Over the course of 2 years, 70 dogs of 37 different breeds were studied. In total, they pee'd 5582 times and poo'd 1893 times. Without any impediments, they positioned themselves north-south instead of east-west.

- **Social cognition** - This involves a dog's ability to interpret subtle social cues. One of the most well-known studies of social cognition involved an examiner placing an object under 1 of 2 buckets and trying different things to let a dog know which one it was under.

Now, if you patted at a bucket, of course your Shih Tzu would be curious about that one and ignore the other. But what if you just nodded at it? Or even just looked at it? Well, in this regard, canines were found to be more intelligent than chimpanzees and even human babies. It's a good point to keep in mind; your Shih Tzu is picking up cues from you all of the time.

For example, how you move, the things you look at, tiny gestures that you're not even aware of, everything you do before you get ready to leave your Shih Tzu home alone is giving him clues about how you feel about it and what you expect from him. Knowing this can help in dealing with a dog's separation anxiety.

- **Problem Solving** - This involves how a dog can work out a problem, such as a treat hidden and only released with a series of manipulation tasks. For example, a button is pressed by the paw, a lid needs to be lifted up, a lever is moved aside. There are some great games meant for both owners and dog to play together to help a dog hone his skills with this. We'll have more on this in the 'Toys' section, page 36, so that you can practice with your Shih Tzu, if you wish.

Emotional Intelligence
- The range of emotions that an animal can feel is always take into account when looking at intelligence. And this is an interesting element as it also can help compare how smart a Shih Tzu is compared to a human. As a human grows, his or her capability to feel and express certain emotions expands. For example, excitement is there from birth. Yet contempt is not felt nor expressed until a child is about 5 years old. Numerous studies have shown that a canine is as intelligent, at least, as a 2 and 1/2 year old human.

The emotions that are proven to exist in dogs are: excitement, distress, contentment, disgust, fear, anger, joy, suspicion, shyness, affection and love. They develop in that order. And are fully intact by the time a toy breed like the Shih Tzu is 4 months old (with larger breeds it can be up until 6 months old).

It is a bit surprising that studies show a dog's development stops just short of feeling shame, pride or guilt. Shih Tzu can walk around very proudly (the AKC breed standard for the Shih Tzu mentions: "... proud of bearing, has a distinctively arrogant carriage.") and your Shih Tzu certainly looks guilty after having an accident or tearing apart your shoe. So how can this be?

Here's the thing: Pride develops at the 3 year mark in humans. Studies show that canines stop emotional development at 'about' the 2.5 year mark equivalent. The key here is the word 'about' and these figures are rough estimates. It is important to note that dogs are proven to feel shy (it is the 8th emotional intelligence to develop), which can be seen as the opposite of confident. On that vain of thought, if a dog is not feeling shy, one could say that he is feeling confident.

Also, there is a very fine line of distinction between confidence and pride, though many people use these words interchangeably. A dog may feel the first (if we agree that 'not shy' equals confident), but not the latter. With pride, a person crosses the line of feeling good about himself and ego starts to play a role in the subtext of how the brain works.

In regard to guilt, can it really be that your Shih Tzu does not feel guilty when all signs tell you otherwise? It's a controversial subject since so many dogs fully appear to show this emotional intelligence. One study tested the response of dogs that had been left alone to shred up objects. Then later, an examiner did the shredding, but left the dog to face his owner (who acted unpleased). The dogs displayed the same behaviors and facial expressions as they had when they themselves were the culprits. It is thought that our canine pets pick up on their owner's cues as to how to feel, behave and react during an event such as tearing apart a person's belongings.

Some researchers say that when a dog lowers his ears and positions himself a certain way and otherwise shows signs of feeling shame, this is actually the dog feeling submissive, fearful or a combination of both.

How Dogs Learn

How Dogs Learn - Dogs learn by rank. They most often ignore anyone (human or other dog) if the dog feels that he himself is superior. Puppies take cues and learn by observing older dogs. Dogs of any age, learn via instruction from their owners. There are instances of course, of dogs doing things when observing others that are thought of as subordinates. For example, an older dog may investigate something that a puppy is pawing at. However, in regard to a dog truly soaking in knowledge and learning something new (what is expected, a command, etc.) this is most effective when it comes from someone ranking higher than the dog.

This is why it is important for Shih Tzu owners to establish themselves as leaders (Alphas) before housebreaking or teaching a Shih Tzu commands. Little will be accomplished if your Shih Tzu doesn't see you are the one in charge. You may also wish to refer to 'Teaching Proper Hierarchy', page 108.

The Shih Tzu Intelligence Ranking- The Intelligence of Dogs - A Book from 1994. This book is a bit controversial, yet due to a lack of other sources, it is a very popular method of comparing dog breeds. Way back in 1994, a professor of canine psychology at the University of British Columbia in Vancouver named Stanley Coren published a book. He revised it in 2006. In his book, The Intelligence of Dogs, he published a ranking of 131 breeds in regard to how smart they were.

A huge issue with this is the way in which it was conducted. Here are some highlights:

- Only working and obedience intelligence was taken into consideration.
- He did not see or interact with any of the dogs.
- The ranking of intelligence was done only by trial judges from the AKC and CKC (Canadian Kennel Club), who based their opinions on what they witnessed in the show rings.
- It was a relatively small group of people. Only 199 of them responded to the written evaluation sheets.

It should be noted that later, dog owners were asked to rank their dog's intelligence and some of the breeds fell into the same ranking order.

Only based on command elements, 131 breeds were placed into 6 different groups of intelligence levels.

Many of the breeds tied.

- 10 breeds are listed under the 'Brightest Dogs'.
- The next grouping holds 21 breeds ranking in #11 though #26 and are labeled 'Excellent Working Dogs'.
- The 3rd grouping holds the next 29 breeds, ranking in place #27 through #39 breeds and are under the label of 'Above Average Working Dogs'.
- This is followed by 41 breeds at #40 through #54 which are, according to these findings, 'Average Working/Obedience Intelligence'.
- The 5th grouping is called 'Fair Working/Obedience Intelligence' which lists out the next 22 breeds, ranking in place #55 through #69.
- The last set are the final 11 breeds, taking the ranks of #70 to #80, labeled 'Lowest Degree of Working/Obedience Intelligence', with the Shih Tzu at number 70.

According to the judges involved, this breed did not do well with commands, and overall was ruled to need 80 to 100 repetitions of new commands given before following them…And only obeyed the first command 25% of the time (or worse).

So What Does This All Mean? It should first be mentioned 8 out of the top 10 breeds are in the Herding, Sporting or Hunting groups, which really gives them a good foundation for this particular type of testing. For many generations, specific and careful breeding was done to instill certain traits in particular breeds. Dogs that were used for herding cattle have strong, inbred traits to follow commands for the difficult and demanding tasks of controlling livestock. They are, by nature, very aware of their surroundings, taking cues from both humans and animals. This goes for those in the Working and Hunting groups as well.

If we look at the top 10 breeds, let's see what we have:

1. The Border Collie: Herding Group
2. The Poodle: This includes the Toy, Miniature and Standard; and while they are in the Non-Sporting Group, they were bred to be retriever dogs, mainly retrieving fish from rivers and other bodies of water.
3. German Shepherd: Herding Group
4. Golden Retriever: Sporting Group and bred to be excellent hunting dogs.
5. Doberman Pinscher: Working Group and bred to be superb guard dogs.
6. Shetland Sheepdog: Herding group, one of the most popular and widely used dogs for sheep herding.
7. Labrador Retriever: Sporting group, commonly used as water dogs.
8. Papillon: This is the only canine breed among this top 10 list of intelligence that was bred to be a toy sized companion dog, just like the Shih Tzu.
9. Rottweiler: Working Group, this breed is well known for its guard dog capabilities but had been used for generations as a cattle driving canine.
10. Australian Cattle Dog: Herding group, as the name implies, used extensively as a cattle herder and livestock guardian.

So, as you can see, 9 of the top 10 dogs that ranked the highest for intelligence, *again only based on ability to learn commands quickly*, have very strong inbred traits to take commands from humans and actually work side-by-side with them. In contrast, while the Shih Tzu breed was being perfected, great time and energy was devoted to developing a graceful, small lap dog that would be friendly, affectionate and a perfect companion. And this, of course, may explain why the Shih Tzu was judged to not take commands as quickly as some other breeds. Though, we must remember that obedience to commands is not the only method of measuring how intelligent a breed is.

Does Compliance to Commands Equal Intellect? As stated earlier, when Dr. Coren's book was released, many disagreed with it. However, over time it has been accepted as the guideline of choice with little competition. The definition of intelligence is: *The capacity for learning, reasoning and understanding.* Despite this, if a person was asked to perform a task and did not want to do so, he would not immediately be labeled as unintelligent. Most would describe him or her as being stubborn or of having independent thought.

Being stubborn and having independent thought are two traits commonly seen with the Shih Tzu breed. This does not make them inane or unthinking. Owners know that aptitude shows when their Tzu realizes that their human is sad and goes over to show affection…Or when a Tzu immediately runs behind the sofa, just knowing that grooming tends to begin when his human walks toward where the brush is kept. Intelligence can be seen and proven when a dog shows that they know certain toys by name, excels at indoor games or mouths a food dish to bring to their human when they want more food or remembers particular people who have visited the home before.

Being an essential member of the family, carefully keeping an eye on young children, responding to both unspoken and spoken communication and displaying effort in regard to command training are also ways in which intelligence can be seen.

How to Help Your Shih Tzu Reach His Potential

- A dog needs to be *allowed* to learn. For example, a neglected dog that lived in a crate would, sadly, have few skills. He would have the capacity to learn, but without being allowed to, he would not gain any knowledge. The key to allowing your Shih Tzu to be as smart as possible is to give him the opportunity to develop his intelligence. *There are things that you can do:*

1. Allow your Shih Tzu to use his canine senses. Bring him to a new environment or stay out with him in the yard to let him smell, hear and explore. Hide a special treat in the house and encourage him to find it by smell alone. Now hide a treat and see if he can learn to find it by reading your cues of shakes or nods. Every chance to do these sorts of things allows the gears in a dog's mind to work.

2. Teach your Shih Tzu words. This can go so far passed just commands! A dog can easily understand 165 words on average and that is a lot. It is as much as a two year old toddler. Children of that age understand most of what their parents say (and also speak sentences of three or four words). Your Shih Tzu is ready and able; you just need to teach him.

How can you do this? Choose3 objects. Hold up each one, saying the corresponding word out loud. Do this over and over, helping him learn what those 3 things are. Once you think he's ready, line up all 3 and command him to grab one of them. Did he do it? Great! Give him a treat and tons of praise. Practice a lot, so that there's plenty of repetition (dogs are great with long term memory, not short, so you need to keep going so that the information stays in his long term memory). The next week, teach 3 more. Life is fun (and easier) when a dog is allowed to be as smart as he is capable of. You may want to keep a list of the words your Shih Tzu understands, it's a blast to actually see it and know how smart he is.

3. Play learning games. Playing fetch is great since it helps grow the bond between human and dog and it can be a good exercise workout. However, games that engage the mind are just as important. You can hide a treat under 3 overturned cups, teaching your Shih Tzu to learn which one holds the reward. As he catches on to what you're doing, slide the cups to make it more difficult. ***There are some great interactives toys you can use as well.*** *** Please do note that these are NOT for dogs to play with alone. These are intelligence building games that require the owner to be involved.

Beginner Level: Outward Hound Kyjen Paw Hide Treat Toy - This is a good game to choose as a beginner step for a Shih Tzu that is not used to these sorts of challenges. Shaped to look like a big paw, there are 6 small holes that you place kibble down into. After you demonstrate how the lids are lifted, your Shih Tzu will learn to do this as well. To make it challenging, do not use all of the holes. Only hide food in 1 or 2, allowing him to have to use his sense of smell.

Medium Level: Trixie Flip Board, Level 2 - For Shih Tzu that are smart enough to know how to sniff something out and move a simple lid, this is a great game that helps a dog go up another level of learning. Treat lids need to be opened using various knobs and slides. It's colorful, fun and can really help a dog use his brain to gain understanding and perception.

Expert Level: Dog Twister - This is a great game, designed to really stimulate a dog's mind. It is very challenging and is meant for dogs that have practiced enough to easily play the beginner and moderate games. It is a fun, intricate sliding puzzle toy that comes with complete instructions on what to do and different steps you can take as your Shih Tzu progresses.

 If you are interested in seeing these puzzle games that you can play with your Shih Tzu, look to 'Toys- Owner & Shih Tzu Together' in the Shih Tzu Specialty Shoppe. You can reach the Shih Tzu Specialty Shoppe by entering any page of the AllShihTzu website. Look to the navigation; it is in alphabetical order. Choose 'Shoppe'.

A Final Word - To allow a dog to live a full life and truly be happy, we must understand just how intelligent our dogs are. They read our nonverbal cues with incredible accuracy. They understand a lot of what we are saying (even if they just overhear us). They have real emotions ranging from excitement to shyness. And they are proven to feel love. Isn't it great to know that the love you feel for your Shih Tzu is returned in the same way? Show how much you care by doing everything you can to keep the emotions of fear and suspicion at bay to let contentment and joy shine through.

Bringing Your Shih Tzu Puppy Home

Puppy Supplies to Have

Things will run much smoother if you plan ahead and have most, if not all, of your puppy care items already in your home.

1 Gates or canine playpen. A lot of new owners think that putting a puppy in a crate, at all times that the pup is not being closely supervised, is what is 'normally' done. However, there are serious downsides to this. If a crate was very small, we'd actually consider this to be neglect. Being in a confining, claustrophobic space can cause a dog to feel exceedingly stressed. In turn, stress can cause a pup to bark/whine/yelp/cry more or even become depressed.

In addition, it does nothing at all to stop a puppy from going to the bathroom; puppies will urinate and eliminate when their bodies have to regardless of where they are. So, we highly suggest a gated area or canine playpen. Inside this, you will want to have: a quality dog bed (resting on floors can put wear on the Shih Tzu's elbows, not to mention that it is not a warm, comfortable place for a puppy to be), toys (more ahead on great toys), water & food and pee pads.

2 Perhaps a carrier crate (ask the vet). Sometimes veterinarians will ask that puppies be brought to the office in a carrier crate. This is done to help control the spread of infectious disease (such as Kennel Cough or Dog Flu) and to keep all of the animals under control. Once you locate an excellent vet for your puppy, ask ahead of time what the protocol is for bringing your puppy to the office.

3 Puppy food. This includes both the 'old' food that the puppy has been eating and the 'new' food if you do decide to change brands. Most puppies do not do well with quick changes in diet. For this reason, you'll want to have enough of both 'old' and 'new' to make a gradual changeover. Many breeders offer samples of puppy food to new owners. However, most samples only last for 1 or 2 days. Find out the exact brand and variety that the puppy has been eating. Having enough for 2 weeks is usually sufficient to make the switch. We will discuss much more about this ahead in the Feeding and Nutrition Chapter.

4 Honey. Hypoglycemia is a fast and dangerous drop in blood sugar. Without quick treatment, this can be fatal. Toy breed puppies from the age of 2 to 4 months are most vulnerable to this, though it can happen to older pups. Feeling the stress of a new home and/or not eating on a regular basis are two common triggers for this to develop. At the 1st signs of hypoglycemia, a dollop of honey should be put on a fingertip for the puppy to lick off or gently rubbed on the roof of the puppy's mouth or gums. Many sources list Karo syrup as a quick source to level out blood sugar, however it can have laxative properties. For this reason, we always recommend using honey instead. In severe instances of Hypoglycemia, urgent vet care will be needed. We discuss this ahead in the 'Puppy Care' section, page 27.

5 Collar, Leash & Harness. This is not a breed that should be leashed to a collar. Doing so can cause injury that, for some Shih Tzu, can have life altering consequences. Since choosing the correct accessories is vitally important for Shih Tzu of all ages, for full details please refer to the 'Care Items – Shih Tzu of All Ages', 'Collars & Harnesses' section for details, page 34.

6 Grooming supplies. This should include: Quality shampoo, conditioner, leave-in coat spray, paw wax, nose balm, brushes, combs, canine toothbrush, canine toothpaste, body wipes and eye wipes. For full details please refer to the 'Grooming' section, page 76.

7 Food and water dishes or food dish and water dispensers. For puppies, it is best to use dishes that are shallow. This is so that the puppy does not bang its head against the rim of the bowl when eating or drinking. For dogs of any age, food and water dishes made of ceramic or stainless steel are recommended. Why? Some puppies and dogs are allergic to plastic dog bowls. Heavy dyes used with plastic can leak into food. Plastic scratches very easy, which can cause tiny nicks where bacteria begins to grow. Colored plastic bowls can discolor facial hairs over time and cause the nose to gradually lose color. Finally, plastic bowls are much lighter than steel or ceramic and can more easily be pushed across the floor or tipped over. For these reasons, ceramic or stainless steel bowls/dishes are best. If your Shih Tzu will be home alone, a canine water dispenser is a great idea. It can't spill and good ones will come with filters to clean out the nasty chemicals that can be found in tap water.

8 Dog bed. You may wish to have your new puppy sleep in your bed; however, remember that this can very quickly become a habit that will be very hard to reverse. Therefore, think carefully about this and if you want your Shih Tzu to sleep in your bed for the next 14 or 15 years. While adults *can* safely sleep in an owner's bed, due to his small size and the fact that your puppy will not yet be housebroken, it's best for him to sleep in his own bed in his own area. Once your Shih Tzu is older, if you want him to sleep with you and it fits your lifestyle, there is nothing wrong with this. Either way, you'll want a quality dog bed for your puppy to rest/sleep on for naps and for when you are not home.

9 Toys. The toys that you choose for your Shih Tzu puppy will have a major effect on how well he copes with teething, his ability to learn to self-soothe when alone, his quality of sleep and the level of boredom that the pup experiences. Since choosing the right toys is applicable to Shih Tzu of all ages. for full details please refer to the 'Care Items -Shih Tzu of all Ages', 'Toys' section, page 36.

10 Car Seat. Deep down inside, many owners know that a car seat is the safest option for when they have their dog in the car, but for one reason or another, do not follow through. We strongly encourage all owners to learn about why this is so vital and how to choose the best one not only for safety, but to help keep a Shih Tzu comfortable and lessen motion sickness as well. For full details please refer to the 'Care Items – Shih Tzu of All Ages', 'Car Seats' section for details, page 40.

11 A good veterinarian. While not a 'supply', we are listing this here, since it is so vitally important. Most breeders, as stated in the sales contract, will ask that you bring your new puppy to a veterinarian within a certain amount of time from the day that you bring your Shih Tzu home. This is generally within 24 to 72 hours. This protects:

a. *The breeder* - Since most breeders guarantee against genetic health issues, having your veterinarian confirm that the puppy is healthy gives the breeder proof that the pup did indeed go home to you without issues.

b. *The puppy*- Although the puppy most likely had a 'well puppy check' right before coming home to you, it is best to have this complete medical exam to be sure of the puppy's health.

c. *You -* Having a puppy is a big responsibility; you will want to make sure that you start off with a healthy puppy so that you can work at keeping him that way!

The best veterinarian may not be the closest one to your home. It is suggested to interview with at least 3 veterinarians within reasonable driving distance. You can ask to set up an appointment specifically to meet the veterinarian and spend time getting to know about him/ her and their practice.

You will want to ask:

• How many Shih Tzu they currently have as patients. Ideally, you will want a veterinarian who has experience with the Shih Tzu breed.
• If they take calls after the office has closed. You will want this answer to be "yes".
• What is their backup for weekends/after-office times. You will want to know that if something happens on a Saturday morning at 2 AM that someone will be able to help you.
• If they ever perform house calls and under which circumstances they do so. There may be instances in which you deem your Shih Tzu too sick to travel.
• How long they have been in practice. While a new veterinarian may be wonderful, we do recommend choosing someone who has been in practice for at least several years.
• Their rules for bringing in a sick puppy. You will want this answer to be that the sick puppy is crated and even perhaps brought in through a separate door; as if you are ever there for a simple checkup you will want your own Shih Tzu protected from potentially very contagious diseases.

12 **Yogurt**. Yogurt may help with stress that a puppy experiences. Puppies being brought to a new home can (and often do) experience stress. Even if the home is very loving and the new owners are trying to do everything perfect, the puppy can experience stress simply from the situation. The pup is leaving the only home that he knew. He is taken away from dam and siblings. It can be very overwhelming. While a pup is making the adjustment, his body can react to all of this with stomach upset and intestinal issues, as stress can disturb the balance of good VS bad bacteria in the G.I. tract of the dog. The 'good' bacteria in the G.I. tract are needed for the body to function in a healthy way. Plain yogurt culture can help put the good bacteria back into the puppy's body. For this reason, speak to your vet about feeding a new puppy 1 to 2 teaspoons of plain, whole white yogurt each day. This should be in addition to normal meals and not as a meal replacement.

Note: Take care to feed the correct type. Any yogurt that has Aspartame is toxic to a dog. The ingredient that you DO want is acidophilus culture. The yogurt should be PLAIN whole white yogurt, **not** with fruit or fruit flavors added. If you opt for drinkable yogurt, normal dosing is 4 ounces a day for the first 2 weeks in a new home in order to help keep a puppy's digestive tract healthy.

Puppy Proofing Your Home

Bringing home a puppy or dog is very much like bringing home a baby. You must make your home safe. Shih Tzu puppies and dogs are very curious. It will surprise you just how curious your Shih Tzu can be! It only takes one moment for you to lose track of where your Shih Tzu is and for your dog to be injured or be poisoned. For this reason, puppy-proofing should be done before you bring home your puppy. It is important to note that while this type of organizing of the home and yard is called 'puppy proofing' it should be done on a regular basis to keep adults and seniors safe as well. Dogs - no matter the age- love to mouth things. It is how they figure out what something is and if it is or is not worth their attention. A dog is capable of mouthing just about anything. And if certain substances or items are swallowed it can lead to poisoning or partial or full stomach or intestinal blockage. These are very serious and potentially life threatening issues. Never assume "Oh, my dog won't have any interest in that"; because a dog will mouth something first and *then* decide if he has interest in it.

Both Indoor & Out - **Plants.** This is a concern for puppies and dogs alike. Whether you garden indoors (preparing seedlings, etc.), have houseplants or your yard has a garden or landscaping, keep in mind that many flowers and plants are poisonous. There are 100's that can cause a dog to become ill or worse, so in the home keep things up high and out of reach. Outdoors, erect fencing or never fail in your supervision. It only takes a moment for a puppy or dog to take a nibble on something toxic. Some of the most common plants in or around homes that are toxic include: Azalea, Boston Ivy, Carnation, Daffodil, Delphinium, Easter Lily, Gladiola, Iris, Ivy, Marigold, Mistletoe, Peace Lily, Poinsettia and Tomato plant (entire plant except the ripe fruit).

Indoors - **Medications.** Keep all medications, including any dog supplements, in a safe area the puppy cannot access. Do not leave vitamins or other pills in reach or on a coffee table. A determined Shih Tzu can quickly chew through a plastic container. Puppies are surprisingly quick at pulling things off of end tables or other low surfaces.

Trash. Shih Tzu can tip over small trash cans. Put these up high where your dog cannot get into them. Sanitary supplies and used razors are the most common trash dangers.

Bathtubs and Toilets. Bathtubs or toilets with open lids can be a drowning hazard. If you have a youngster in your home who uses a step to reach the toilet, your Shih Tzu may find a way to use it also.

Cleaning Supplies. Keep cleaning supplies in high cupboards or use childproof latches to secure lower cupboards. Remove the puppy from the area when you are using liquid or spray cleaners. Chemicals can get into the eyes of a curious puppy and the vapors can be harmful to lungs and eyes.

Electrical cords. These are a big danger to puppies; the shape and texture often lures a teething puppy to want to chew on these. This can cause burns in the mouth, electrical shock, or death via electrocution. Tie up loose electrical cords with wrap ties and keep them out of sight. You can also run cords through purchased spiral cable wrap, cord concealers, or even PVC pipe to keep them safe from your puppy.

Small Objects. Keep small objects (coins, jewelry, needles and thread, straight pins, yarn, dental floss, rubber bands, paper clips, tiny children's toys, etc.) out of your puppy's reach. Jewelry and coins are easily swallowed and can contain metals that are toxic. We know of an adult dog that got into a lower bathroom cabinet, swallowed a small chunk medical tape and barely survived after 3 operations and $4500 later. Remember to not just do this when about to bring your Shih Tzu home, a check should always be made. Look on the floors each day and immediately pick up any small objects.

Stairs. Close off stairs with a baby gate.

Cat Litter Boxes. Many dogs will eat cat feces from the litter box if given the chance. This can be a dangerous health hazard. Cat litter can cause an intestinal obstruction, and in addition, intestinal worms the cat may have may be passed on to the dog (if the cat is in the process of being de-wormed, eggs and worms can be shedding into the feces). One solution may be to put the litter box up high. Many owners choose the top of the dryer or washing machine.

Tobacco products. Cigarettes, cigars, nicotine gum and patches, contain substances that can be toxic or fatal to dogs. Keep these out of reach of your Shih Tzu.

Outdoor Dangers - Chemicals. Make sure all gasoline, oil, paint, lawn fertilizers, insecticides, and auto supplies are placed into secure containers, out of reach. Be especially careful with antifreeze and rat poison; both taste good to dogs and can be deadly if ingested.

Water. Pools, ponds and hot tubs should be covered or fenced off. Drainpipes can also pose problems.

Sharp Objects. Walk around your property and look for items that could be a hazard to your puppy, such as broken glass, exposed nails, or other sharp objects. Plan how you will restrict your puppy's access to these areas if sharp objects cannot be removed.

Naming Your Shih Tzu

Overview Naming your Shih Tzu may involve a bit more than simply choosing a name that sounds cute. The name you choose will decide how well your Shih Tzu recognizes that name. This is a huge element in training your dog. In addition, if the name does not fit certain elements, other animals in the home and your Shih Tzu may become very confused. Both the number of syllables in the name and the beginning consonant sound will play a major factor. Dogs do learn to know their names; however dogs generally only pay attention to the first syllable of the word. That is why dog commands are very short. For example, "Sit" instead of "Sit down now". When an owner does say, "Sit down now", the dog is listening to and noticing the first syllable: "Sit". Therefore, if you name your Shih Tzu "Jumping Jack Jelly Bean", your Shih Tzu will respond to "Jump" as his name.

This does not mean that you need to choose a name with only one syllable. However, the name should have a strong sounding 1st syllable; as you will want your new Shih Tzu to have an easy time learning his name. This, of course, is very important in regard to training your dog. If you have other pets in the home, it is best to not choose a name that begins with the same syllable as another pet. For example, "Rocky" and "Roxanne" as this can be very confusing for both of your pets. It will be best to choose a name that begins with a different sound than any other pets and any human family members for that matter too.

Based on the registration of dogs in the US, the most common names for male and female dogs include:

Male dogs: Max, Jake, Buddy, Bailey, Sam, Rocky, Buster, Casey, Cody and Duke

Female dogs: Princess, Molly, Lady, Sadie, Lucy, Daisy, Ginger, Abby, Sasha and Bella

No matter what you decide to name your Shih Tzu, you will want to use the name as much as possible. Each time you wish to get your Shih Tzu to pay attention to you, say his/her name first. This should be said in a happy, yet confident tone. In time, this will help greatly as calling out your puppy's name can stop him right before he is about to have an accident or is walking too far away from you. If you have an opportunity to know in advance which puppy you will be purchasing, you can ask the breeder (or other person who owns the puppy) to begin to say the chosen name to your pup while he is still there. This will give a Shih Tzu puppy a jump-start on knowing his name.

Giving Your Shih Tzu More Than One Name - You may decide that you want your Shih Tzu to have more than one name; you may opt for a first name and a middle name or you may wish for him or her to have a regal sounding name consisting of 4 words. The options are almost endless. When you register your pup, he or she does not need to have just a first name, for example: Tiger. There is much more that you can do and there are several ways to do it.

For AKC registration, you can give your puppy a name that is very long, up to 50 characters. However, the standard registration of a name (and ownership) is up to 36 characters; therefore, if you choose to go beyond that and up to the maximum of 50, it will cost $10 more to do so (current fee, as of the time that we are writing this). Keep in mind that the space between each name does count as a character. For example: Bouncing Baby Boo Boo has 18 actual letters; however there are 3 spaces between the 4 words, giving you a total count of 21 characters which is under the 36 or 50 limit so you would be fine.

Option A: You can choose one name of 1 or 2+ words. It can be any names in any order and many owners will make sure that the common name that they call their dog is in there. For example, the name that your puppy is registered as may be: Rowdy Rocking Cowboy; and then Cowboy would be the name that you commonly call your pup.
Option B: You may choose to have an 'also known as' in the official registered name. This is shown as the common 'AKA'. An example of this would be: Living Life To the Limit AKA Cuddles.
Option C: You can have numbers in the name if you choose. These can be Arabic numbers such as 1, 2 or 3 or you can spell them out. The first option would look like this: *Smiling Each Day AKA Smiles 5*. The other option would look like this: *Smiling Each Day AKA Smiles Five*. When numbers are used, it is most often done by breeders who will choose similar if not exact names for each Shih Tzu puppy, but then change the number that follows.

Words that are Not Permitted - One of the most important rules is that you may not put the word 'Champion' in the name. This is reserved for dogs that have won at AKC show events.

• A Shih Tzu's name cannot be simply 'Shih Tzu'. No dog may be registered as the name of the breed that they are, or any other official breed for that matter. Therefore, a Shih Tzu cannot be registered as 'Beagle'.
• Swear words are not allowed.
• The following words are not allowed to be any part of a name (no matter how long or how short): Male, Female, Bitch, Stud, Dam or Sire.
• You may not have a registered Kennel name in there. Only breeders can do this, and they can only do so once they have proven to the AKC that they have had an established program for at least 5 years.
• You *can* use the terms: Sir or Lady and this is done a lot. For example, for a male one may choose something like: Sir Isaac of New ShihTzuLand AKA Nippy and for a female: Lady Rose Petals AKA Flowers.

Changing Your Shih Tzu's Name - If your Shih Tzu is registered under a name and you decide to change that name, you may (for a small fee). One may wish to do this when ownership changes. Or, if you have previously chosen a simple name such as "Tiger" you may later decide to change the official name of your Shih Tzu to "Sir Tiger of the Terrain", for example. If you decide to do this, we do suggest still using the 'common' name that you use for your dog at home.

Name information for Breeders - If you have had your first litter of Shih Tzu, you may feel proud and with ethical breeding, you should be. However, in regard to the AKC, you will not yet be able to register those puppies with your kennel name. There is a program called the Registered Kennel Name Program. Here are the guidelines as to what a person needs in order to qualify:
1. Be a breeder in good standing with the AKC, with a record of breeding and registering purebred dogs in conformity with AKC registration rules & policies.
2. Have a documented background of involvement in AKC events.
3. Meet 1 of the following breeding requirements:
o   Have bred at least 5 registered litters in the past 5 years
o   Have owned stud dogs that have produced at least 40 registered litters in the past 10 years

Note: A breeder, who has bred at least one AKC registered litter, may be granted a registered kennel name on a temporary basis for 5 years. The requirements must be met during the five-year period to be eligible to renew the kennel name. If you qualify to register a Shih Tzu with your chosen kennel name, here are the rules:

• You may only have up to 2 registered kennel names
• It does not need to be a 'real' word. It may be a unique word that you created all by yourself. Example: 'ShihTzuCastle'.

• The name may contain a maximum of 2 words and a maximum of 15 total characters and spaces. Example: 'ShihTzuCastle Exceptional'.
• The name may not have been used more than incidentally and rarely by other breeders in the naming of dogs in the past 10 years. Therefore, if the name was used on a fairly regular basis, even 1 time every 4 years this would be considered a' 'taken' name and you would not be allowed to use it. If someone used your chosen name only 1 time and another person used it another time just once with a few years in-between, that would be considered coincidental and you would be allowed to use it.
• Ineligible words would include, but are not limited to, conflict either phonetically or in spelling with the name of a breed (such as "Shetzhoo"), AKC titles, names of cities, family names, corporations or trade names or names of famous and universally recognized persons (Bill Gates, etc.).
• A kennel name may not contain any offensive or bigoted words.
• You cannot be associated with a pet store that sells dogs.

How The AKC Protects the Kennel Name that You Choose - When a kennel name is registered, the AKC Club will take care in protecting it. Currently, an AKC name is protected in all positions of a dog's name. For example, if the name "Singleton" was the name of your kennel or was 1 of the words in the name of your kennel, then that word could not appear anywhere in the name of a dog without your written permission. Also, a dog or litter can only be registered with a kennel as its 'owner' if the kennel is registered with the AKC.

Introducing your Shih Tzu to Family & Home

While we do use the word 'puppy' in this section, much of this will apply to an adult Shih Tzu new to a home as well; after all, he is starting off somewhere different too! When you bring a new Shih Tzu home, this is going to be a huge change; for both Shih Tzu and all members of your family. The addition to your household can affect other pets that you may have as well.

Overview - A young Shih Tzu puppy needs a careful and planned introduction into your home. Without this, a new pup may become very stressed and overwhelmed. Stress on a dog of any age can and usually does cause not only emotional issues, but also physical health problems. In addition, stress on a very young Shih Tzu can cause hypoglycemia.

As a loving owner, you should take charge to gently show your new puppy his new world, make a smooth introduction to all the people and/or animals that will be his new family and help him feel comfortable and welcomed.

Preparation - Before you bring your new Shih Tzu puppy home, do prepare. Things will be quite exciting and you do not want the additional chaos of putting out the water bowl, setting up sleeping quarters or running out to the store for forgotten items. Have all items set up where you wish for them to be and plan to have the house as neat and calm as possible. All of your friends and extended family may wish to be there for the arrival of your new Shih Tzu; however it is best for the Shih Tzu if he meets his immediate new family first and then is introduced to friends, neighbors and other family members at a later date.

Introduction to Human Family Members - If you have other immediate family members, you should ask them to be sitting quietly in a room, for your arrival back with your Shih Tzu puppy. A pup will feel very overwhelmed if everyone rushes to him. A sudden barrage of loud voices, pats and hugs from a bunch of people can frighten a small puppy, even though all intentions are good.

In whatever method you obtained your puppy, he will most likely already have a sense of you. He will know your smell, your voice and your touch. When you arrive home, an introduction should be made to each individual person, one at a time, so that he can get to know them as well. Have each person say hello in a calm and pleasant voice. Allow your puppy to smell them and get a sense for who they are. Each person should have a *small* treat. Too many treats and your puppy's tummy may be full by the time he meets everyone.

Children and adults alike should be asked to sit down to be at the puppy's level and gently pat the pup to say hello. While a Shih Tzu puppy is so cute it is expected that everyone will want to pick the puppy up and hug him over and over, this can be too overwhelming on the first day.

Introduction to the Home - After taking 5 - 10 minutes to meet each person, you can then give your new puppy a tour of the home. He will need to get a good and solid sense of his surroundings. Be sure to show him where he can always depend on the water bowl to be and where he'll be given his main meals.

Note: It is suggested for all members of the family to take rotating turns in feeding the pup. This teaches hierarchy. If only one person does all the feeding and all the care, the Shih Tzu may only recognize *that* person as his 'leader' and this can cause issues later when the other people find that their commands are not being listened to. In addition, encourage your puppy to get to know his dog bed; he will need to know it is his own special place to retreat too if things get too stressful.

It is best to allow your new Shih Tzu to have several weeks at home with you and your family before you allow neighbors, friends and extended family over. Once your puppy has adjusted to his new home and family, you can then begin a slow introduction to other people. This should be done at home; you will not want to bring a puppy out to public places until he has had all of his puppy shots.

Walk your puppy throughout each room of the home. As you do this, point to his important items, saying "Water", "Toys", "Bed", etc. Doing this for the first two weeks will help your new Shih Tzu gain a sense of security. Once you decide on where to place the water dish, doggie bed, toys and more, do not change the locations if at all possible. Your Shih Tzu needs to know exactly where to go for what he is in need of. You will also want to walk your Shih Tzu around the perimeter of your yard. While you should always have your Shih Tzu on a harness and leash when outside, training your puppy where his 'territory' ends will be important in case your puppy gets loose.

Introduction to Other Pets - If you have another dog or any other pets, this will be a very important aspect to bringing your new Shih Tzu home. One cannot expect current pets (dogs and/or cats) to suddenly be socialized in the acceptance of a new dog and at the same time expect a new Shih Tzu puppy to suddenly know how to get along with other animals. It is unwise to assume that because a pet has a wonderful personality that they will become instant best friends with the new arrival. A sudden change of having a new puppy in the home can trigger quite a mess of chaos if your pets are not ready.

Whether you have cats, dogs or both, you should take time well before you bring your new puppy home to make sure that the cat/s or dog/s will get along well with a new dog. You can do this by having a friend, family member, neighbor, coworker or other who has a dog come over for a visit. Ideally, it is best if you can find someone who has a Shih Tzu. If not, the 2nd best option would be to have someone come over who has a dog in the same class (toy breed dog).

When testing your current dog's behavior to a new dog, allow the animals to feel each other out. Keep a careful eye out for any trouble. If a dog stares at another, in almost a frozen state, this can be the posture that is shown before a dog attacks. If you already have a cat, keep an eye out for his/her behavior also. If your current cat does not tolerate a small dog, your new puppy could be very injured in a fight. It is not a bad sign if the animals ignore each other. This means that they do not see the other as a threat. In time, a dog or cat will get to know your new Shih Tzu and they can then become best friends. If you are sure that your current pet/s is tolerable of another dog in the home, all should be fine when you bring your new puppy home.

An owner must keep watch when the young, new puppy is eating; an older dog may try to show dominance by taking his food. Your current pet/s may feel jealousy if you lavish all of your attention on the new puppy. Hopefully, you have estimated the time that you have in one day, to make sure that you can give care and attention to all animals on an equal basis. Before you know it, your new Shih Tzu puppy will become a happy and wonderful addition to your family.

Falling into a Schedule

Please be sure to always have a good daily schedule and certain times set aside for:

Grooming - It is very important that a puppy learns right away that being touched will be a normal part of the day. He will need to get accustomed to grooming elements such as brushing, wiping of the face, eyes, and genital area (if urine splashes or there are small bits of feces), dental cleanings and more. Each day, take 5 to 10 minutes to brush the entire body. Don't forget all legs, armpit area and even the tail. Run your finger over a puppy's gums and teeth. This prepares a pup to get ready for dental brushings. Wipe the eye area in the morning, after each meal and once again before bed. This will help avoid tear staining. We highly recommend using quality canine eye wipes, which will help prevent the development of tear stains. Tushie wipes are also very helpful to swipe the bum and genital area after a Shih Tzu goes to the bathroom; even small bits of urine or feces can smell quite terrible and when clung to fine hairs, can be very uncomfortable for a Shih Tzu.

Walks - A puppy will need to have all puppy shots complete -and then for 2 weeks to pass - before being taken out in public. When reaching this point, twice a day walks are important for health and for releasing pent-up energy. They help a Shih Tzu learn about the world; Repeated exposure to traffic, other dogs, people, etc., will teach a dog to not bark at these elements or fear them. Try to keep walks at the same times each day.

Commands - 8 weeks old? Time to begin command training! The sooner you begin, the sooner you will have a well behaved, well-mannered dog.

Play time - Social interaction is very important. Plan at least 2 sessions a day of play and *focused* interaction, lasting 15 to 20 minutes. This can be doing a puzzle game together, teaching commands, playing hide n' seek, etc.

Quiet, relaxation with the family - Of course, we do not get puppies and dogs just to have them in the background...The goal is to have a canine family member. So, this means that you and your family should plan 'relaxation time'. This usually occurs after dinner... The family sits around the TV, talking about the day, etc... And this is when a puppy should be with all of you, as a member of the family unit.

How to React to Whining and Crying

Do be aware that it is normal for young puppies to cry when first in a new home. It is a big adjustment to go from the dam and littermates to a new environment. It is hard to not take it personally and to wonder if you are doing something wrong. However - barring any medical issues - you are not doing anything wrong; your puppy just needs a bit of time to adjust. Crying may be normal, even if the breeder raised the puppy with good socialization skills. This phase will pass and usually only lasts a week or so. You can help by offering all of the comforts needed (including a soft baby blanket and soft toys. If the breeder gave you a toy or blanket with the scent of the puppy's littermates and/or dam, this will help as well.

Owners can become confused about when to go over to a crying puppy and when to ignore it. Human instinct tells us to rush over and offer comfort. However, in some instances you will want the puppy to learn to self-soothe. If you go to a puppy each time he cries, he will 'learn' and 'be taught' that crying equals attention.

Instead of outgrowing this phase, a puppy may continue on for life! Attention given to a puppy should be at certain intervals so that a puppy does receive a message that he is not truly alone, but does not think that each time he cries someone will come running. With the schedule of grooming, walks, command training and family time… along with potty training and feeding, a puppy's day has meaning. A puppy will have a schedule of things that happen each day. Soon, his inner time clock will tell him when an event is to happen. With all this in place - and with the puppy warm, safe and comfortable- it is alright if a puppy whines a bit when alone.

During the day - Do let a puppy know that you hear and acknowledge his communication. During the day, if possible, every 15 to 20 minutes (if he is whining/crying), walk over to say hello (not in a soothing way, but in a matter-of-fact way) and offer a pat and a smile. Then, if you are busy, move on to what you were doing. So again, not every time a puppy cries, but at intervals so that he learns that he has a loving family, but that crying does not equal instant attention.

At nighttime, (more in the 'Housebreaking' section, page 43) , you do not want to respond to crying unless you feel there is a legitimate bathroom need. If so, with lights as dim as possible and with making as little noise as possible, bring your Shih Tzu to his designated bathroom area. Only speak to say, "Good, dog" and no more. This must be a serious time and not a time for any sort of interaction or play. Quietly bring him back to his area and leave it at that.

It may seem cruel in a way, *however* never teaching your Shih Tzu to self-soothe is even worse. You want him to grow to be a confident, emotionally strong dog. Now, this is not to say that he can't have a bit of help! One of the more effective methods is to obtain a companion toy. The ones we recommend, SnugglePets, are a good size, made of quality material, are super soft, emit a soothing heartbeat and if you wish, can emit a warmth as well.

 To see all recommended companion toys, look to 'Toys – Separation Anxiety' in the Shih Tzu Specialty Shoppe. You can reach the Shih Tzu Specialty Shoppe by entering any page of the AllShihTzu website. Look to the navigation; it is in alphabetical order. Choose 'Shoppe'.

Puppy Care

Vaccinations

Vaccinations are a crucial step in making sure that a puppy will be protected against dangerous and often fatal canine diseases. An owner should never believe, "I keep my puppy clean, well fed and do not expose him to other dogs, so I do not need to have my puppy vaccinated". All puppies should be vaccinated or their lives will most likely be very short.

A newborn puppy is not naturally immune to diseases. Though, the puppy will have some antibody protection which comes from its mother's blood via the placenta. The next level of immunity is from antibodies in the mother's milk. This milk, actually called colostrum, only gives a puppy antibodies for a short time. Those antibodies will begin to lose effectiveness when the pup is between 6 to 20 weeks old. It must be noted that the puppy will only receive antibodies against diseases for which the mother had been recently vaccinated against or exposed to. As an example, a dam that had not been vaccinated against or exposed to parvovirus, would not have any antibodies against parvovirus to pass along to her puppies. The puppies then would be susceptible to developing a parvovirus infection. **Photo courtesy of Serendipity Shih Tzu**

The age at which a puppy can effectively be immunized is proportional to the amount of antibodies in his system (what he received from the dam). High levels of maternal antibodies present in the pup's bloodstream will block the effectiveness of a vaccine. When the maternal antibodies drop to a low enough level in the puppy, immunization will be sucessful. This is why a series of shots are given.

There is a period of time from several days to several weeks in which the maternal antibodies are too low to provide protection against the disease, but too high to allow a vaccine to work. This period is called the'window of susceptibility'. This is the time when despite being vaccinated, a puppy can still contract a disease. Consequently, any puppy that has not yet had his shots must be kept away from other animals and it is best to limit the number of people who have contact with such a young pup.

While each veterinarian may have their own vaccination schedule, vaccinations should always fall close to the following schedule. When you are obtaining a new puppy, you should be sure to have proof that the puppy is up-to-date on his shots before you bring that puppy home. Some of these vaccinations will (or certainly should) be given before you obtain your puppy. Although currently 15 states in the US have laws regarding the age limit on which a puppy may be sold, the average age in which a Shih Tzu puppy is ready to go to a new home is between 8 and 10 weeks old. Therefore, your new puppy should have at least 2 or 3 vaccinations when you obtain him. Once your puppy has had all of his puppy shots, you can then allow him to meet other people, go to parks, accompany you to stores and explore the world!

Typical Vaccination Schedule

5 weeks
- Parvovirus: For puppies at high risk of exposure to parvo.

6 weeks
- Combination vaccine* without leptospirosis.
- Coronavirus: where coronavirus is a concern.

9 weeks
- Combination vaccine* without leptospirosis.
- Coronavirus: where coronavirus is a concern.

12 weeks or older (sometimes as old as 16 to 26 weeks)
- Rabies: Age at vaccination may vary according to your local laws.

12-16 weeks
- ** Combination vaccine.
- Leptospirosis: this will be included in the combination vaccine where leptospirosis is a concern, or if traveling to an area where it occurs.
- Coronavirus: where coronavirus is a concern.
- Lyme: where Lyme disease is a concern or if traveling to an area where it occurs.

Adult ***(boosters)
- Combination vaccine.
- Leptospirosis: this will be included in the combination vaccine where leptospirosis is a concern, or if traveling to an area where it occurs.
- Coronavirus: where coronavirus is a concern.
- Lyme: where Lyme disease is a concern or if traveling to an area where it occurs.
- Rabies: Time interval between vaccinations may vary according to local law.

*A combination vaccine, often called a 5-way vaccine, usually includes adenovirus cough and hepatitis, distemper, parainfluenza and parvovirus. Some combination vaccines may also include leptospirosis (6-way vaccine) and/or coronavirus (7-way vaccine). The inclusion of either canine adenovirus-1 or adenovirus-2 in a vaccine will protect against both adenovirus cough and hepatitis; adenovirus-2 is highly preferred.
**Some puppies may need additional vaccinations against parvovirus after 15 weeks of age. You will want to talk to your veterinarian about this.
***According to the American Veterinary Medical Association, dogs at low risk of disease exposure may not need to be boostered yearly for most diseases. Speak with your veterinarian to determine the appropriate vaccination schedule for your Shih Tzu. Remember, recommendations vary depending on the age and health status of the dog, the potential of the dog to be exposed to the disease, the type of vaccine, whether the dog is used for breeding, and the geographical area where the dog lives or may visit.

Bordetella and parainfluenza: For complete canine cough protection, some veterinarians will also give vaccinations of: Inra-Trac III ADT. For dogs that are shown, in field trials, or are boarded, it is often recommended to have vaccinations every six months.

Reactions to Vaccinations - Immunizations are intended to stimulate the immune system to then protect the dog against a specific infectious disease. It is very important to have your Shih Tzu receive all needed vaccinations.

However, this stimulation of the dog's immune system may cause some minor symptoms that you should be prepared for. All dogs, regardless of breed or size, receive the same vaccine dose. When testing was done to ensure that vaccines could be considered safe, this was done using 'average' sized dogs. Over time, with millions of innoculations having been given, this has shown that the 'one size fits all' dose is generally considered safe. Smaller dogs, however, do have adverse reactions more often than larger dogs. You may wonder if being given a 'half dose' is an option; there have not been enough studies yet to prove if this would be effective.

Your Shih Tzu may react to immunizations in ways that range from soreness at the site of injection to mild fever to allergic reactions. The allergic reactions can range from mild to severe:

• **Mild.** Mild reactions include fever, sluggishness and loss of appetite. These reactions usually resolve without any treatment needed.
• **Moderate.** The dog's skin may show a reaction. This is called Urticaria. It may show as hives or bumps. There can also be swelling that happens very quickly, redness on the dog's lips, around the eyes, and in the neck region. It is usually extremely itchy. Urticaria may progress to anaphylaxis, which is considered life-threatening. However, Urticaria is the most common reaction in dogs if a reaction is to happen.
• **Severe.** The most severe reaction is anaphylaxis. This is a very sudden, severe allergic response that causes breathing difficulties, collapse and possible death. This is very rare. Symptoms usually include sudden vomiting, diarrhea, staggering, rapid drop in blood pressure , swelling of the larynx leading to airway obstruction (and inability to breathe), seizures and cardiovascular collapse or death.

Both anaphylaxis (serious) and urticaria (moderate) are reactions that are triggered by antibodies that the immune system has made to some portion of the vaccine. If this is to happen, it usually happens after the 2nd particular vaccine.

Diagnosis - There is no diagnostic test for anaphylaxis or urticaria, however a quick physical exam will allow your veterinarian to immediately know the signs of an allergic reaction to a vaccine.

Treatment- Anaphylaxis (the severe reaction) usually occurs soon after vaccination, often while the dog is still in the veterinary clinic. Anaphylaxis is an extreme emergency. Your veterinarian will begin immediate emergency life support including establishing an open airway, oxygen administration, intravenous fluids to increase blood pressure and medications such as epinephrine, diphenhydramine and corticosteroids. Dogs that survive the first few minutes usually return to normal health.

Urticaria (the moderate reaction) occurs soon after vaccination, often shortly after a dog gets home. Your veterinarian will recommend immediate return to the clinic for treatment. Urticaria is usually treated successfully with injectable corticosteroids like dexamethasone or prednisone. Antihistamines such as diphenhydramine (Benadryl®) do little to help with acute allergic reactions but may be given by injection to help prevent recurrence of symptoms after steroids wear off.

Mild vaccination reactions usually require no treatment. However, if the symptoms persist for more than 10 hours, call your veterinarian.

Home Care and Prevention - Be sure to schedule vaccination appointments when you will be available to monitor your Shih Tzu after the vaccine is administered. Do not hesitate to call your veterinarian with any questions or concerns. Severe vaccination reactions are very rare and the benefits of vaccines are life-saving. Reactions are more commonly associated with vaccines for leptospira, rabies and parvovirus. Your veterinarian is the best judge of what vaccines are needed to protect against the diseases in your area. While the veterinarian will record any adverse reactions to vaccines to help prevent those vaccines from being administered again, it is a good idea to keep a record for yourself.

A Note About De-Wormings – Parasites are a major concern for pets. We cover the details of this in the 'Worms' section, page 249. Just as with vaccinations, puppies need to be de-wormed on schedule (and then as an adult). Many of the de-wormings will be done before you bring your new Shih Tzu puppy home. For others, this will be done when you bring your puppy to the vet. The normal schedule is to have this done at 2, 4 and 6 weeks old. It should be done again at the 6 month mark and then again (at a minimum) at the 1 year mark.

Hypoglycemia

Shih Tzu, like many other toy breeds, are susceptible to a form of low blood sugar called hypoglycemia. This happens when the sugar level in a dog's blood quickly drops. In moderate to severe cases, treatment is needed right away. While this *can* happen to Shih Tzu and immediate treatment is necessary, this does not mean that a Shih Tzu puppy will develop this. The majority of puppies will glide through the young puppy stage and be just fine. However, since this can be fatal without treatment, it is very important to know the signs of hypoglycemia. Taking action right away can help you quickly restore your puppy back to health.

The Age this Most Often Happens- This is most common with puppies from birth to 4 months of age.

What Causes this to Happen - The Shih Tzu (like other toy breed dogs) has a very small fat reserve that surrounds their liver. Changes in this reserve may happen when a Shih Tzu:

• Becomes stressed (going to their new home, having too many people greet them if they are not socialized yet, etc.)
• If the puppy uses up a lot of energy in a short amount of time (playing very hard when they are very young)
• If the puppy misses a meal (we suggest free-feeding a Shih Tzu until the puppy is 3 months old. After this, meals should be on time, all of the time.)

The effects- When these things happen, that small fat reserve may be quickly used up and the Shih Tzu's body will then begin to take its blood sugar for energy. It is at this time that hypoglycemia may set in.

Prevention - Keeping stress at a minimum will help. A young puppy already has enough to handle. A newborn to 8 week old Shih Tzu puppy will already need to handle: • Being weaned from the dam • Being de-wormed • Having dewclaws removed • Having vaccinations • Learning about baths and grooming

At 8 weeks to 10 weeks old, the puppy has the stress of entering a new environment. The puppy must then become accustomed to: • New voices • New scents • New noises • New sleeping area • A change in diet - a sudden change to a new food can trigger hypoglycemia, so be sure to keep feeding your new puppy the same food that he ate while with the breeder and do a gradual change over the course of 3 to 4 weeks.

Signs of Hypoglycemia - An owner should be aware of the signs in order to give treatment immediately.

Puppies may: • Have a sad look on their face • Become weak and listless • Stagger when trying to walk • Fall down • Appear 'drunk' • Bump into walls

Without treatment, the progressive signs will be: • Fainting • Coma • Seizures.

Not all puppies will show all of the signs if they do develop hypoglycemia. If your puppy shows signs of being very sleepy or uncoordinated, do the following : • Stand your puppy up • See if he or she can walk normally

Treatment - If your puppy cannot walk normally or shows the other signs of entering hypoglycemia, you should immediately try to raise his blood sugar level. You can do this in several ways: • Rub a dab of honey on the puppy's gums or roof of his mouth • Have the puppy drink water with sugar mixed in • Offer a children's sugar-coated breakfast cereal if you do not have sugar or honey.

Notes: Be sure to only use one method. And also please do not use Karo syrup; many sources list this but it can have a laxative effect.

Veterinarian Care - If this does not restore your puppy to normal or if the puppy is unable to be roused or unable to swallow, you must bring the puppy to the veterinarian right away. The veterinarian can then use IV intervention to try to correct the puppy's blood sugar level. Remember, not all Shih Tzu puppies will develop hypoglycemia, however all toy dog breeds are susceptible to this. Keeping an eye on your young puppy, knowing the signs and taking quick action will keep your Shih Tzu healthy and able to live a long and happy life.

Growth Charts

Expected Weight Per Breed Standards – The AKC breed standard calls for a Shih Tzu to be 9 to 16 pounds (4.08 to 7.25 kg).

How Much Adult Shih Tzu Really Weigh - Despite the 'ideal' standards for show dogs, a Shih Tzu can be slightly under the expected weight (7 or 8 pounds, often without health issues related to being undersized) and others will be slightly larger at 17 or 18 pounds and not considered overweight or 'unnaturally large'. Some breeders strive for the high end of the weight scale in order to produce Shih Tzu of substance that will have fewer health problems than their tiny counterparts may endure. Opposite to that, some breeders do aim to produce smaller than average Shih Tzu (often labeling them 'toys' or 'Imperials', though these are not official, accepted terms) and these very small dogs will need some extra TLC. A Shih Tzu that is only 5 lbs. or so fully grown may have trouble regulating body temperature and often will be more vulnerable to both injury and illness.

Puppy Growth - *Newborns* - Born only a few ounces, a Shih Tzu puppy will have the most rapid growth during the first month, doubling in size within just days. *Puppies* - It is during the first year that a Shih Tzu puppy will grow to his full adult size. However, there will be times of rapid weight gain and times of stalls. From age 2 months and on, it is a good idea to check for weight gains twice a month. If there is no gain at all for 2 weeks, it is suggested to bring him in for a checkup. *9 Months to 12 Months* - This breed finishes growing to its adult size between the 9 month and 12 month mark, though a few will continue to fill out just a bit up until 15 months.

Body Shape Changes - You will notice that Shih Tzu puppies are quite round. They have extra fat on the body that is needed to provide warmth and fuel reserves. As a Shih Tzu matures into an adolescent and then an adult, he will have a bit of a sleeker, leaner appearance. There will be a gradual slimming around the up-tuck of the flank (sides of the body) and the ribs as the fat layer thins out. While it is rare for adolescents or adults to be overweight, health issues that impede a dog from being active can cause unhealthy weight gain. This is true for senior Shih Tzu as well; if exercise decreases but calorie intake remains the same there may be weight problems.

About charts – One issue with traditional weight and growth prediction charts is that many do not take into account that growth is much more rapid when the pup is young and each month as he matures his growth rate slows. Also, most do not take into account spurts and stalls, which are natural.

About the 'Rules" - The general 'rules' for growing puppies do not often apply to this breed. The first rule being to take the 8 week old weight, multiply that by 3 and then add 1 pound. The next 'rule' is to take the weight at 3 months old and double it. If owners do this, many will find that the predicted weight is very far off, often under by several pounds.

About our 'Rules' – We've found that the most accurate adult weight predictions for Shih Tzu can be achieved if you take the 8 week old weight, multiply that times 4, and then add between .25 and 1 pound. In the majority of cases with Shih Tzu puppies *2.25 pounds or under* at 8 weeks old, adult weight is normally the puppy weight multiplied by 4, with .25 added. And with Shih Tzu puppies *2.75 pounds or higher* at 8 weeks old, adult weight is normally the puppy weight multiplied by 4, with 1 pound added.

In regard to making predictions at 3 months old, we instead prefer to look to 4 months old. Growth is much more predictable at this age. Our rule is to take the weight at 4 months old and double it.

About our data – Using our own rules, we predicted the weight of over 100 Shih Tzu. We have 2 diferent charts to show you the results. This information has been compiled over a period of 4 years, using weights from 74 to 103 Shih Tzu puppies at any one given time, with data from 129 Shih Tzu in total.

Over the course of time, we were unable to continue collecting data for some Shih Tzu (were taken in by a new owner, owner stopped reporting data, etc.). In those cases, we made contact with another owner as soon as possible and continued the data collection from that particular starting point with a new Shih Tzu. For this reason, the pool of Shih Tzu, fluctuated between 74 and 103 over the course of those 4 years.

Please keep in mind that this is for reference only. At the time that you look to these charts, your Shih Tzu may be having a growth spurt or a pause.

8 Weeks old. As you can see, the majority of Shih Tzu pups were between 2.5 and 3.5 pounds at the 8 week mark. We predicted the adult weights, using the 'multiply by 4, add .25 for smaller Tzu and 1 pound for larger Tzu rule'. That led to accurate predictions (within .25 pounds) an average of 80% of the time, which is quite good.

Weight in pounds of Shih Tzu puppy at 8 weeks old:	1.75	2	2.25	2.5	2.75	3	3.25
Percentage of puppies that were this weight:	5%	8%	8%	15%	12%	14%	11%
Predicted adult weight (in pounds):	7.25	8.25	9.25	10.25	12	13	14
Percentage of Shih Tzu that did reach the predicted weight:	75%	90%	75%	80%	80%	85%	75%
Actual adult weight range of the Shih Tzu (in pounds):	7 - 8.5	8-9.5	9-10.5	9.5-12	11.75-14	12.78-15	14-16.5

3.5	3.75	4
14%	5%	8%
15	16	17
95%	85%	70%
14.75-16	15.5-17	16.5-18

4 months old. As we move into the 4 month mark, and the Shih Tzu pup is closer to his adult weight and growth is slowing down a bit, predictions are even easier and, as you can see, slightly more accurate. The majority of Shih Tzu pups were between 5.5 and 7 pounds. Here, the predictions were correct 85% of the time (within .25 pounds).

Weight in pounds of Shih Tzu puppy at 4 months old:	4	4.5	5	5.5	6	6.5	7
Percentage of puppies that were this weight:	5%	10%	11%	17%	13%	14%	12%
Predicted adult weight (in pounds):	8.25	8.75	10.25	11.25	12.25	13.25	14.25
Percentage of Shih Tzu that did reach the predicted weight:	80%	90%	85%	85%	90%	85%	80%
Actual adult weight range of the Shih Tzu (in pounds):	7.75-9	8.75-9.5	11-Oct	10.5-12	11.5-14	13-15.5	14.5-16

7.5	8
10%	8%
15.25	16.25
90%	85%
16-17.5	16-25-18.5

Care Items – Shih Tzu of All Ages

Collars & Harnesses

Choosing the right accessories for a Shih Tzu is vitally important.

The collar - For the majority of dog breeds, the collar serves as the apparatus to attach the leash. However, collars are not appropriate for brachycephalic breeds such as the Shih Tzu and they can cause injury to toy breeds.

When a leash is connected to a collar, top concerns include:

• Compression and constriction whenever the Shih Tzu pulls ahead and the leash goes taut, causing breathing difficulties.
• Injury to the windpipe if the Shih Tzu lunges to the side or jerks his head. This includes the very serious issue of collapsed trachea in which rings of cartilage surrounding the windpipe collapse inward.
• Increased risk of disc disease and neurological problems.

For these reasons, the collar should only be used to hold the Shih Tzu's ID tag (your name & contact info), and in areas that require it by law, proof of rabies vaccination and/or registration information.

Choosing a Collar for Your Shih Tzu - There are many different types of collars and there are only a couple that are ideal for this breed. For this breed, the two best options are:

•*Flat collar, quick release* - This consists of one flat, adjustable strap that fits around the neck. It closes with a clasp that is ideal for fast removal. You'll want it to be lightweight yet sturdy, weather resistant and with stitching only on one side to prevent irritation.

•*Flat collar, break away* - Similar to the quick release collar, this is a flat, adjustable collar in which the clasping mechanism will break apart if excessive force is placed upon it in emergency situations. An example would be if the Shih Tzu's collar was accidentally caught on an object such as fencing, a part of a safety gate or even a chair leg, in which the dog would otherwise be strangled.

Choosing a Collar - Weight and Sizing- Now that we have it narrowed down to only a flat collar with either a quick release or breakaway clasp, you'll want to choose one that correctly fits your Shih Tzu in regard to both weight and diameter.

Material - The material that the collar is made of along with its thickness will determine how heavy it is and therefore how much weight will be placed on a Shih Tzu's neck. Flat collars (the type we recommend for this breed) can be found in an array of materials that include leather, polyester or nylon webbing. Let's look at the choices:

• Polyester - This is a cheap material that is made from synthetic polymers. This low quality fabric wears out extremely quickly, absorbs and holds body oils that can lead to terrible smells and is not a good choice.
• Leather - These collars can look very stylish though the downsides are that these are not waterproof and some cheaper leathers can stretch out over time.
• Nylon (webbed nylon) - Flat collars with a quick release or breakaway clasp are the best choice for most Shih Tzu. A quality collar made of nylon webbing will be weather resistant, washable, resistant to odors and sturdy.

Size - The general rule of safety and comfort is that once the collar is on, you can easily slip two fingers between it and your dog's neck. This allows it to be loose enough to avoid any type of constriction but be tight enough that it cannot slip off or be easily snagged onto something. While the collar for your Shih Tzu will be adjustable, you'll want to make sure that as your puppy grows, it can be sized to still fit those two fingers underneath. Check for an adjustment need every 2 weeks for growing pups.

How Many Collars You Should Have for Your Shih Tzu - You'll want to have at least 2 quality collars so that if one is taken off your Shih Tzu and misplaced, you'll still have one on hand. The collars should be periodically checked for any wear and tear. Depending on their use (if you always use one and the backup one is rarely used), if your Shih Tzu is still growing and the quality of the collar, you may need to replace it anywhere from every 1 to 5 years.

Times to Remove the Collar - Many owners wonder if it is okay to keep the collar off of a Shih Tzu when the dog is at home inside the house. One element that you'll want to be exceedingly aware of is the chance of the door being opened and the Shih Tzu darting outside. If you do take the collar off when at home, it can help to have a rule that even household members knock on the door to announce their presence so that the dog can be held while the door opens.

Keep in mind that while it can be freeing for a dog to be collar-free while sleeping and playing inside of the house, for some this can cause intolerance for times that it must be placed on (when outside, for ID purposes only). It is recommended to take a Shih Tzu's collar off when brushing the coat, since the collar can impede proper grooming. You'll want to be able to do long strokes down the back of the head, over the neck and along the back, in addition to the front of the neck and down the chest. It should also be removed during baths to properly scrub and rinse the coat; keeping in mind that a wet dog is quite slippery and all exit points of the house should be secured to prevent an unplanned escape. For Shih Tzu that have breathing problems due to tracheal collapse or other medical issues, the veterinarian may recommend that the collar be kept off while the dog recovers.

The harness - A proper harness should be the apparatus that is used any time that a Shih Tzu is on leash. As opposed to a collar, the harness will distribute pressure, force and tension across the dog's shoulders, chest and back, freeing the neck from possible injury. The chest, shoulders and back are much sturdier since they are comprised of bone and muscle as opposed to softer cartilage and ligaments of the neck. Using a harness frees the Shih Tzu's neck from potential injury and does not impede breathing as a collar may do. Also, this is a curious breed that often tends to want to lead while on walks. A harness allows an owner to better keep a Shih Tzu on course, without having to worry about causing any type of neck injury.

Choosing a Harness for Your Shih Tzu - Some owners shy away from harnesses due to a bad experience of the Shih Tzu resisting or showing intolerance for it; however, in most cases this is just a matter of the dog needing time to become accustomed to it and having one that is comfortable. The best type of harness for a Shih Tzu will be easy to slip on and can be adjusted to fit nicely without pinching the skin. Let's look at some things to keep in mind:

1) A comfort wrap harness is a good choice for Shih Tzu as these are designed for small sized dogs. The width of the straps should be 1/2 inch for puppies and 1/2 to 1 inch for adult Shih Tzu, depending on his/her overall size and weight. If the straps are too thin, they will pinch and cut into the dog's skin, causing discomfort, redness and even sores.

2) While harnesses can be found in leather, the best material will be nylon or poly air mesh, as these are sturdy, resistant to odor, weather resistant and lightweight.

3) Since it can be difficult to get a Shih Tzu to step into a harness and trying to do so can cause the dog to become frustrated, you may wish to obtain one with easy 'quick-snap' buckles on the shoulders and/or belly. This way, it's super easy to put on and off within seconds. Some have Velcro closures, which is fantastic as well.

4) Stretch mesh harnesses can work well for puppies; they slip on similar to a shirt. However, adult Shih Tzu are more powerful and this type of harness may not work well for an adult Shih Tzu.

5) While wearing a quality harness will not have any adverse effects to the coat during short term use, it should be removed when the leash is taken off. Leaving it on can cause body oils to accumulate under the strapping, blocking healthy air circulation to both skin and coat.

The Puppia harness is one of the most popular ones for Shih Tzu:

• It is made of polyester air mesh (for breathability) that is sturdy but soft to the touch (won't chafe a Shih Tzu's skin)
• It has quick-snap buckles (making it very easy to put on)
• It has an adjustable chest belt
• It has hook straps to provide adjustability, which makes it able to perfectly fit a Shih Tzu of any size

For all recommended collars, harnesses & leashes, look to 'Accessories' in the Shih Tzu Specialty Shoppe. You can reach the Shih Tzu Specialty Shoppe by entering any page of the AllShihTzu website. Look to the navigation; it is in alphabetical order. Choose 'Shoppe'.

Toys

Many owners find that they've stocked up on toys that do not hold the Shih Tzu's interest for long, are subpar for their intended purpose or are being outright ignored. There are tons of cheap dollar type stores that sell dog toys in bulk, but you'd be better off buying nothing. Since toys are a vital part of caring for a Shih Tzu of any age, this section will explain how to choose the best ones.

The 4 Types of Toys for Shih Tzu - Let's look at what a typical Shih Tzu requires:

1) Teething & Chewing Toys - Puppies need to have the right toys when they are teething and the urge to chew does not stop when teething is done. Adult Shih Tzu and even some seniors enjoy chewing.

Why these are important - Shih Tzu start to teethe at about 4 months old and as soon as it begins, their gums become exceedingly itchy due to teeth loosening and adult teeth slowly erupting. This lasts for several months. Many will be done by the 8 month mark. During this time, having the best teething toys possible is important to both ease your puppy's discomfort and protect your home from destruction. Without toys that are sized appropriately and offer the texture that is needed to soothe soreness and relieve itch, a puppy may mouth and chew anything he can access.

Aside from this, essential chewing toys are needed for every Shih Tzu of any age, with the one exception of some seniors that may not have interest in chewing or may not be able to chew due to tooth loss, etc. Dogs do not just chew for teething needs, they also chew as a form of entertainment. When a dog finds that something is pleasurable, he will repeat the action as much as possible. So if you have great toys, using them will become habit. If, however, your Shih Tzu's toy collection is lacking and he has to resort to other things (furniture legs, your shoes, etc.) then going for *those* things may become habit.

The qualities of a great teething or chewing toy - There are 4 elements that you'll want to look for when it comes to chew toys for your Shih Tzu:

1. Textures. What pleases a dog of any age and what helps puppies whose gums are itching like mad, is a toy that has certain textures that feel good on the gums and feel good when his jaws chomp up and down. If the toy is boring or brings little pleasure, the dog has no motivation to use it. You'll want to look for toys that have various textures of different sizes so that a Shih Tzu can choose which parts he'd like. If the toy is made of just one material, it needs to be the right consistency to feel good in the dog's mouth. Cheap plastic toys can often be too hard, which doesn't feel good and then are disregarded.

2. Cooling. While certain fabrics, material and textures are needed, another element that makes a teething toy great is temperature. Toys that can be frozen to send out soothing coolness to sore gums should be part of a teething Shih Tzu puppy's toy collection.

3. Size. Some dog toys are made generically in one size. If a Shih Tzu becomes frustrated trying to get a toy into his mouth or finds it too uncomfortable to play with it or chew it, he will disregard it and it will end up in the pile of toys that he doesn't care for. So, making sure that it is appropriately sized for toy breed dogs (often an extra small or small, depending on the actual toy itself) is a must.

4. Durability. If you find a toy that your Shih Tzu simply loves but it only lasts a week, it'll be hard to judge who will be more upset, you or your dog! Dogs become attached to favorite toys very quickly, so if one is torn apart or can no longer be used, this can present a problem. It's much better to spend a bit more for a quality toy than to have to buy a cheap one 10 times.

2) Fundamental Toys – These are also referred to as 'boredom reducing' toys or as 'basic' toys, but they need to be far from basic, if you want your Shih Tzu to actually like them. Dogs' lives are rather uncomplicated and they do not have much to keep themselves busy. They are walked, they play with you, they eat, they sleep… and their only real possessions that they have are their toys. Having the right ones is an essential part of proper care.

Why these are important- When there is not much going on at home, a Shih Tzu will do 1 of 3 things: Rest, become restless (pacing, barking, etc.) or stay busy (playing with a toy or chew, paw, scratch or otherwise 'play' with objects in the house if the right toys are not accessible). And without the right toys to serve as entertainment, boredom can quickly develop. Dogs that spend the day in what seems like an endless loop of boredom can become depressed, sullen and then act out when they finally have the chance. Toys will fill your Shih Tzu's day with 'something to do' and in a way, a dog's toys are his hobby (both what he collects and what he does to stay occupied).

The qualities of a great fundamental toy - There are 3 main elements that make a toy a great one for a Shih Tzu:

1. It calls for attention. In order for a toy to cure boredom, it first has to gain a dog's attention. If a dog fails to notice a toy or has no motivation to even check it out, it will do little good.

Long ago, it was thought that canines only saw in black and white; however you are probably aware that dogs see color. It is a bit different than how we see and can be compared to how things look at technicolor time (when the sun is getting ready to set). So, it is important that a Shih Tzu has toys that draw him in with color. If you take a look around at cheap $1 toys, these are often faded greys and browns or pastels; they don't do much. And if they *do* look bright, sadly that may be due to inexpensive dyes that fade fast. Therefore, color is definitely a factor in choosing toys; having some in a variety of hues will help keep things interesting.

Toys can also *literally* call out for attention. Some of the best toys to encourage a Shih Tzu to interact are quality stuffed animals that either sing, make animal noises or speak in voices. These can be tremendously helpful in keeping a Shih Tzu busy. And these are also fantastic for when a Shih Tzu is home alone, since feeling isolated is a major factor in separation anxiety. When toys speak, this can really take the edge off a puppy or dog's feeling of seclusion.

2. It provides incentive. A dog has no reason to play with or chew a toy if he receives nothing in exchange for doing so. Trying to buy as many toys as possible but without carefully choosing which ones will actually be of interest to a dog is the #1 mistake that owners make when buying toys. You'll end up with a huge pile of toys that are ignored and that only takes up room in your house and leaves your Shih Tzu with nothing to do. It's better to have 8 to 10 excellent toys that are put to use than 20 toys that are ignored or do little to keep your Shih Tzu busy.

3. Quality. As with teething toys, making sure that fundamental toys are durable and last for a good amount of time is crucial. When a dog latches on to 'favorites' it can be heartbreaking if the toy breaks, falls apart or otherwise becomes so worn out that it can no longer be used. If the manufacturer isn't making it anymore or it can't be found in the same color, this can be upsetting to a dog. In fact, once you obtain some excellent toys and find that your Shih Tzu simply loves a certain one, you may want to order doubles so that you always have one on standby should the first become lost or eventually wear out (since no toy can last forever).

3) 'When Alone' Toys - There are 2 situations when a Shih Tzu will need some extra help and the right toy can provide this for him:

1. Puppies at night. Until a new puppy becomes completely used to his new environment and is able to sleep through the night, he may cry, whine or whimper for hours. Owners can become stressed as they are not sure what to do. You want to teach a puppy to learn self-soothing techniques but at the same time, it's awfully hard to just let a puppy cry himself to sleep. Therefore, one of the best toys that you can obtain for a puppy is a comfort/companion toy that can help a Shih Tzu have a sense of wellbeing when he is not near his owners. This in turn, also helps prepare him for times during the day when he may be alone as well. Companion toys come into play here (more ahead).

2. When home alone. There are many things that you can do to help your Shih Tzu if he is suffering from separation anxiety. Having the right setup (a properly sized indoor canine playpen or gated off area), making sure that lights are kept on (in case it becomes stormy or you get home after dark), leaving on pleasant noises, experimenting with a window view vs non-window and more. And which toys are available to a Shih Tzu when the dog is home alone is a crucial part of helping him cope. You may also wish to refer to the 'Separation Anxiety' section, page 170.

There are 2 types of toys that will help: 1) Those that keep him busy & 2) Those that provide comfort.

1. The qualities of the best 'stay busy' toys: These are treat-release toys that offer a reason to work at them for long periods of time. This reduces the amount of time that the dog realizes that he is alone as he focuses on the toy. You'll want one that *slowly* dispenses the food and can stand up to a lot of use.

While you can simply add kibble, a more effective alternative is to add a blend of foods that have a consistency that is thick and emits a strong and tempting aroma. Peanut butter (creamy not chunky) with can be mixed with kibble pieces and usually works well. You can also try a blend of: mushed banana, small kibble pieces and even some crumbled, crisply cooked bacon.

You will also want to obtain a quality toy brush that can appropriately clean the inside of these types of toys, as old caked on food can lead to a buildup of bacteria.

2. The qualities of the best comfort/companion toys: When you get right down to the basics of why dogs struggle when alone, it is because they are *well aware* they are completely alone. They are isolated from contact with *anyone*. So, the answer to this is to help the dog feel that he is with someone (or something) and that being with this other entity provides a feeling of safety, security and companionship. Touching or being near this other entity must provide warmth, comfort and be physically pleasing. It may sound like we are explaining another dog, but there is no reason to bring another pet into the house when there are effective toys that do this task. The best companion toys will be soft stuffed animals that are appropriately sized that do 2 things: Provide soothing warmth and emit a soothing heartbeat.

We're good size, are soft & emit a soothing heartbeat

We can also emit warmth for extra comfort!

These are often super effective to help Shih Tzu with separation anxiety and to relax and sleep well at night.

4) Owner & Dog Together Puzzle

Games – There are some fantastic puzzle games that encourage a dog to think, help a dog learn how to focus and are a wonderful way for you to bond with your Shih Tzu. While you do spend time with your Shih Tzu taking walks, when grooming him and even just relaxing together, choosing a puzzle game to play together is a great way to add some fun to his day. Since you will be working together as a team, this is conducive to creating a great relationship. These sorts of games have flaps, sliding doors and latches that hide treats. It will be your job to teach your Shih Tzu how to move the parts to reveal the goodies.

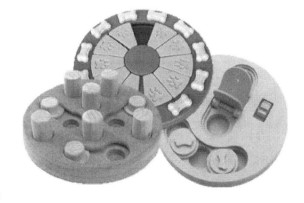

Agility Equipment – You don't need to sign your Shih Tzu up for an AKC agility event in order to have fun with these! While the typical Shih Tzu will be too small for much of the equipment that you can find online, both weave poles (you teach your Shih Tzu to weave left and right around poles) and chute tunnels (your Shih Tzu enters one end and zips out through the tunnel to find you at the other end) are both ones that work well for this breed. Do note that the agility equipment does tend to run a bit on the expensive side.

Top 3 Toy Tips   **1) Have more than 1 toy bin.** Have at least 2 separate bins of toys and if you bring your

Shih Tzu into the car a lot, have 3. The minimum of 2 is to be able to switch out the bins, essentially offering 'new' toys every 2 to 3 weeks. While you will always want to let a Shih Tzu keep his favorites at all times, tucking one bin away and bringing out the other can give a dog the excitement of having a 'new' collection and can bring about renewed interest. If your dog is in the car with you a lot, having a small supply in the car that is only used when driving can help a dog look forward to car trips and stay busy with 'new' toys when on the road. Raised canine car seats are best for this breed, so that they can be high enough to look out of the window (which cuts back on motion sickness) while staying safe and additionally, these have plenty of room for toys.

2) Perform a 'keep and don't keep' every so often. Things accumulate; it's a fact of life. One problem with dog toys is that if you have too many, the good ones can get lost in a pile of worthless ones, making it more difficult for a Shih Tzu to see and find the ones that will do their job the best. Throw away or donate the ones that your dog has no interest in (or that don't even do their job in the first place) and only keep the ones that are actually beneficial. Also be sure to throw out any toys that are worn out or ripped, as small pieces can present choking hazards.

3) Don't buy for you, buy for your Shih Tzu. Sometimes dog toys can look very fun to us humans... we see something cute and assume that our dog will love it too... and then we are taken back a bit when the dog doesn't seem to like it at all. When you are buying toys for your Shih Tzu ask yourself "What is the purpose?" (to help with teething, for chewing, to fix boredom, a fundamental toy, to stay busy or to provide comfort) and then keeping in mind the elements discussed here, ask, "Does this fulfill that purpose?"

 All recommended toys can be found in the Shih Tzu Specialty Shoppe under the 3 'Toy' sections. You can reach the Shih Tzu Specialty Shoppe by entering any page of the AllShihTzu website. Look to the navigation; it is in alphabetical order. Choose 'Shoppe'.

Car Seats

Though it is very clear that having your puppy or dog sit in your lap while in the car is extremely dangerous, many drivers do not ever think about the possibility of an accident until it happens. After all, that is why it is called an accident. It is an unplanned, negative event that causes damage and injury. But what you can plan for is the safety of your Shih Tzu by using the best car seat for this breed.

Facts to Know

1) 8% of owners do not use a car seat. Out of the remaining 92%, over half of those owners (55%) felt unsure if they were using the best seat possible or if they were using it in the right way.

2) Dogs that are unrestrained in the car will be thrown even with a slow-moving impact. With a vehicle that is traveling at 35 mph when hitting an stationary object, a Shih Tzu that weighs 10 pounds will be thrown with the force of a 400 pound object. This can cause severe bodily injury including broken bones, fractured neck, severe internal injury to vital organs and brain damage.

3) Improper canine car seats that are too large or those in which the Shih Tzu is not properly fastened can bring about the same results. Studies estimate that a puppy or dog, improperly secured, will be thrown in any accident in which the car is traveling over 15 mph.

Elements of a Good Car Seat for Your Shih Tzu

There are several qualities that a proper seat will have that will all work together to keep your Shih Tzu safe and happy:

1) Sizing - Car seats are available for all dog breed sizes from the smallest toy dog to the largest of the giant breeds (though large dogs are usually are secured with belts or a hammock). The Shih Tzu should be in a seat specifically for toy breeds. Problems can arise if an owner borrows a previously used seat made for different breeds or simply obtains a generic one. If the seat is too large - even if the belt and buckles can be adjusted - this removes the safety barrier that the walls of the seat provides. While you will want there to be room for your Shih Tzu's favorite toy and perhaps even a small blanket to keep him comfortable, you'll want a car seat that is specifically for his size.

2) Material and Comfort - The material that a car seat is made out of will have a big impact on whether or not a

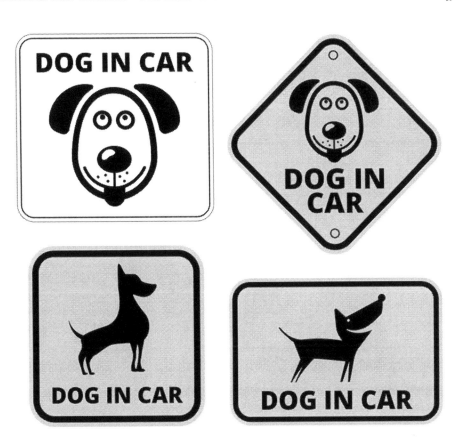

puppy or dog tolerates it. You'll want a durable outer casing that is sturdy and inner padding that offers comfort to the entire body without being abrasive to the coat. Those with padded foam work well and those with covers made of cotton or other washable fabric are great so that you can keep it in good condition. Most quality car seats will be made of environmentally friendly materials that are free of hard dyes and are made with Velcro strapping; this ensures that any chewing of the seat will not result in adverse effects of ingesting potentially allergy-causing elements.

3) Height - While large dog breeds have the nice benefit of being big enough to stick their noses out of the window, the Shih Tzu must struggle against the feelings of confinement when safely seated in a car. This can be resolved by obtaining the proper booster seat.

A booster seat - and do make sure it is a safe one - will keep the Shih Tzu raised enough to see out of the window. This is so important to help the puppy or dog fight the common issue of motion sickness. When a dog's body is feeling one thing (movement) but his eyes are telling his brain something different (the inside of the car is not moving!) this causes a problem in the inner ear which can make a dog very ill with dizzying motion sickness. A dog may quickly develop a queasy stomach, vomit, become restless, whine and essentially suffer while the car is in motion.

When a Shih Tzu has a bad experience like this, it makes him far more likely to put up a fight the next time the owner wants or needs to take him for a drive. Therefore, the best car seat for your Shih Tzu will also have the element of being a booster seat so that your Shih Tzu's face can be closer to a window (opened to varying degrees according to speed and weather conditions).

Tips - Even once you obtain the right seat for your Shih Tzu, these following tips may help make the riding experience safer and more tolerable:

1) If your car has a front passenger airbag that you cannot manually shut off, the safest place for your Shih Tzu's seat is in the back. Some owners choose to move the front passenger seat as far back as possible - and this may help to some degree since the airbag deploys from the dashboard. While meant to protect occupants of a car during an accident, an air bag shoots out in 1-30th of a second at an amazing speed of 200 mph (320 km/h), which can cause traumatic injuries if a dog is situated too close.

2) Even when in a car seat that is just perfect for a Shih Tzu, most dogs cannot put up with long rides. There will be a tipping point at which a dog simply cannot take the confinement and motion any longer. The best thing to do is to give your Shih Tzu a break before he reaches this point. Each dog is different, however for most a break every 20 to 30 minutes is best. Find a safe area- away from traffic - where you can allow your Shih Tzu to stretch his legs, go to the bathroom and have a nice drink of cool water and perhaps a small snack.

3) If your Shih Tzu has trouble tolerating the car, having the right car seat will help. But additionally, you may need to help your Shih Tzu become accustomed to being driven. Start with small drives with your Shih Tzu securely fastened in his seat. Offer a favorite toy and a small blanket (a baby's swaddling blanket works good in the car). For those that really put up a fuss, just go up and down the driveway. Over time, increase the distance to one time around the neighborhood. Then twice and so on, making each week a drive that lasts slightly longer. Most Shih Tzu do well when they are allowed to gradually get used to something. You can read more in the 'Traveling with your Shih Tzu' section, page 278.

4) Be aware of the danger of a car seat & a collar - A canine car seat for toy breeds works by having a safety strap that is attached to the dog's collar or harness. NEVER attach it to your Shih Tzu's collar. Even in the event of a small fender-bender, this can severely injure your Shih Tzu's neck. Always place a comfortable harness on your dog and then attach the seat's safety-strap to that.

 If you need help choosing the best car seat for your Shih Tzu, if you are not happy with the seat that you are using or if your Shih Tzu does not tolerate it well, you may wish to look to 'Car Seats' in the Shih Tzu Specialty Shoppe. There is a great list of the top recommended seats, along with reviews. You can reach the Shih Tzu Specialty Shoppe by entering any page of the AllShihTzu website. Look to the navigation; it is in alphabetical order. Choose 'Shoppe'.

Housebreaking

Step-by-Step

Overview It is very important to remember that puppies have absolutely no idea that they are supposed to urinate or eliminate where you want them to. The area that you choose, whether pee pads or an area outside, has no meaning to your Shih Tzu until you train him; until then, that pad is just another object in the home and the area outside is just a place to run around and play or sniff at things. It will be your job to show your Shih Tzu the meaning of the area and what is expected.

Housebreaking in and of itself, is not extremely difficult; it does however take a bit of time. Some owners give up too early. It's vital to remember that it normally takes several months for a puppy to be fully trained. The more times you break from the training rules, the longer it will take him. For this reason, how well you perform as a trainer directly correlates to your Shih Tzu's success. Puppies struggle to keep information in their long-term memory. Most 'live in the moment'. For housebreaking to work, you must follow the rules to such an extent, that the information transitions from a pup's short-term memory to his long-term memory and that going to the bathroom in a certain area is 'reflex'.

Note: The actual fundamentals of housebreaking are not overly complicated and will work **IF** you follow all of the guidelines, all of the time. Owners struggle the most whe 'hiccups' occur. For this reason, we will first do a detailed overview of all the steps you need to abide by. Once you have that down pat, we will then dive into some of the most common hiccups that can occur and exactly how to deal with them. Never label a Shih Tzu as 'untrainable'; there is always an answer!

Some elements that are needed are:

•**Consistency -** Showing your puppy what to do every *other* day will severely limit your puppy's success. Puppies need consistency. For any time that you are home, stick with the training rules. Be sure that all members of the household know the rules, so that when you are not home but someone else is, that consistency can remain.
•**Praise** – Puppies and dogs love praise more than anything else. Your praise will give your Shih Tzu self-confidence and a confident dog is a happy dog. Praise reinforces and shows a puppy that they did a good thing. When praised for doing expected actions, your puppy will want to continue pleasing you, to receive the best element in the world: your love and attention.

'Papertrained' New Puppies - It should also be noted that some breeders will claim a puppy is successfully 'paper trained'; this is often nothing more than the puppy being limited to a small area and peeing and pooing on newspaper since that is the only option; this does not count as being trained. Therefore, even if a puppy is 'paper trained' by the time you become his owner, you will need to begin training in a way that fits what you expect.

Reversing Previous Training – If a Shih Tzu is coming to you having been previously trained for indoors (*actually* trained for this and not just due to the scenario listed above) and you wish to make the switch to outdoors, this can be done. You just need to start fresh, as if housebreaking for the first time. It will, however, be easier as the dog will have the general knowledge; you just need to teach him where the designated area is and allow him time to become accustomed to things. Do follow all of the guidelines in this section.

Also, if your Shih Tzu comes to you already trained to go outside, you may still need to follow most if not all of these guidelines. He will need to learn where the designated area is, get used to his schedule, receive reinforcement praise & reward to learn that you (his new owner) *also* expects bathroom compliance and you will need time to learn his signals.

Your choices for Housebreaking- It is a popular notion that toy breed dogs can easily be trained to use pee pads. While this is possible, this is not as easy as it sounds. A puppy may resist or have a hard time using pads because dogs have a natural instinct to want to 'choose just the right spot' to urinate or eliminate. Earlier we talked about the studies that have proven that canines are very in touch with nature; when uninterrupted, they will align their bodies with Earth's magnetic pole when urinating or eliminating. So, training your Shih Tzu to use an outdoor bathroom area is your best bet for success. This said, indoor training can be done if you are persistent and you have a puppy that is cooperative.

It is important to choose one housebreaking method and then stick to that training. For example, if you want your dog to use pee pads in the winter but to go out in the yard in the spring, your puppy will become very confused. It is almost impossible for a dog to know that he is supposed to use different methods depending on the weather. Therefore, one method should be chosen and then implemented all the time until your dog knows exactly what to do.

The only exception is when your Shih Tzu is home alone. You will leave him in a safe area with pee pads; this does not 'count' as using two methods; because as he matures he will be able to hold his needs for longer and longer, until those pads are no longer required (though they may be placed there 'just in case'). Do not worry that the pads will confuse him; when you are home and you take him outside, you will be there to give tons of praise & a reward, so it is *those times* that will become ingrained in his memory.

Should you Choose the Indoor Method or the Outdoor Method?

While we *highly* recommend the outdoor method, the indoor method is best if you live in a home in which the outside yard area is not easily accessible or, for personal reasons, you are not able to easily bring your dog outside. Also the number of hours that the Shih Tzu will be home alone comes into play. If the maximum time home alone is 7 or 8 hours, then training him to go outside is best, since by one year old or so, he'll be able to hold his needs while home alone. To summarize this:

If the Shih Tzu will be alone for more than 8 hours, say 9 or 10 hours on *most* days, no dog will be able to consistently hold his needs for that amount of time. It is then that you would want to train for the indoor method, since no matter his age, the indoor method will be used on most days.

If the Shih Tzu will be alone for 8 hours or less: Train outside. Soon you will have a 1 year old dog that is able to hold his needs for the 8 hours and will only go to the bathroom outside.

5 Tips to Keep in Mind

1. It will be your job to always supervise your Shih Tzu when outside. Training will not work if you simply let your Shih Tzu out into the yard. You need to be there to give praise as soon as the deed is done. Not to mention that being outside alone, even in a fenced-in yard, can be quite dangerous. A puppy can try to dig under a fence, find a small hole to crawl through or another animal may find their way into your yard. In some locations, there are known reports of hawks swooping down, picking up and carrying away toy breed dogs. One must remember that these things do happen; therefore your dog should always be supervised.

2. If you will be gone for some days (work, school, etc.) your puppy will need to eliminate indoors (hopefully on pads) but do not focus on this too much. As your puppy matures, he will be able to hold his needs for longer periods of time, finally reaching a point where he eliminates in the morning before you leave and then again as soon as you get home. Don't expect a puppy to perfectly 'hit the mark' on pee pads when home alone. The goal is to instill strong housebreaking habits of going in a designated outdoor area when you are home to bring him there.

3. The time that a puppy can hold his needs will increase as he matures. A good rule of thumb is 2 months old = 2 hours, 3 months old = 3 hours and so on, up until about the 8 hour mark. When you are home with your Shih Tzu you will need to take him to his designated bathroom spot at those intervals (and other times as discussed ahead). However, keep in mind that you need to increase the intervals as your Shih Tzu grows. If your Shih Tzu is 2 months old and you take him out every 2 hours and then you are still doing that when he is 4 months old, his bladder and bowel muscles will not have a chance to strengthen as they would otherwise.

4. You cannot usually control when a pup pees & poos. In regard to morning pee & poo times, this may be able to be adjusted slightly for some dogs (more ahead), however let us note that if water is limited in an attempt to limit the amount of times a puppy must urinate, this is extremely dangerous to the pup. It can even be fatal. A constant supply of fresh water is necessary.

5. Walks. A huge mistake that owners make is allowing their dog to pee or poo when out on walks. If you do this, you miss a huge opportunity to house train. You will want to bring your Shih Tzu to his designated area before you bring him for a walk. Follow the rules regarding how long to stay with him there. Also, once the walk has ended, do not go right inside. Bring him back to his bathroom area to see if he needs to go. Ideally, your Shih Tzu will *never* pee or poo when out on walks. He will always do so in his designated area.

Outside Training – Choosing an area. One of the most important aspects will be to choose one area for your puppy to use the bathroom. Simply bringing your Shih Tzu 'outside' is not sufficient. One area should be designated for bathroom needs. If you bring your puppy to a new spot each time, this will confuse him. Being consistent and always going to the same area will make this much easier for both of you. When you are choosing the area, keep the seasons in mind; a location easily accessed in the summer may be impossible to get to in the winter.

How Often a Puppy Must be Taken to the Designated Bathroom Area - No matter if you choose the pee pad method or the outside method, your Shih Tzu puppy should always be taken to the designated area:

• When waking up
• Immediately after being let out of a gated area or pen
• Right before bedtime
• Several times throughout the day (every 2 hours for a 2 month old, every 3 hours for a 3 month old, etc. until the adult Shih Tzu is taken out every 5 or so [when you are home]). Increase the intervals as your Shih Tzu matures, so that he learns to hold his needs.
• 15 to 20 minutes after eating
• Any time your puppy makes a motion of going to the bathroom
• Right before walks & right after a walk is complete

Rules for the designated area -

1) Choose an area, but allow your Shih Tzu to choose the exact spot by himself. This can be done by standing in the exact center of your chosen area, having your Shih Tzu on a 6 foot leash and allowing your puppy to roam around in that entire diameter.

2) Be very patient. All dogs are different. Some will only take a minute to choose a spot and then want to run back inside the home. Other dogs will take 5 to 10 minutes to choose the spot to urinate and 15 to 20 minutes to choose the spot to eliminate. One of the most common issues that owners complain about is that a puppy goes to the bathroom as soon as he comes back into the house. This is because:

A: The puppy was taken outside *before* the need to pee/poo…time was taken to allow the pup to find the right spot, but not needing to go, nothing was done…*so much time was taken*, that the urge to pee/poo happened *after* coming back inside the home…**OR**

B: The owner was too impatient. Standing there, a bit bored, 5 minutes can feel like 20 minutes. It is important to give your Shih Tzu plenty of time to choose the perfect spot, for bladder/bowel muscles to relax and for the dog to release. If it helps, keep an outdoor chair in the center of the designated area; Sit, read, check emails, etc. Keep track of the time to be sure that 20 minutes goes by before you decide that you were outside long enough. And don't worry, as your Shih Tzu grows, bathroom times will be quick and fast, perhaps lasting just a minute or so.

Note: One very common reason an owner becomes impatient is due to the weather. If you are cold, you may not want to remain outside long enough & if you feel that your Shih Tzu is cold, you may want to get him back inside ASAP. This goes for rainy days too. Therefore, to resolve this issue, please dress appropriately for the weather. If it is very cold, place a warm vest or lined hoodie onto your Shih Tzu; *that*, along with doggie shoes or paw wax to protect the paws, will help him tolerate cold weather and be able to concentrate on bathroom needs. If it is raining, use an extra-large umbrella to keep both you and your Shih Tzu dry.

When You are Home; Tethering Your Shih Tzu VS Confining

Confining - If you are very busy and cannot keep an eye on your Shih Tzu, place him into his canine playpen or gated off area. If he is allowed to roam the house, he will pee and poo everywhere and anywhere. A crate is not recommended, as living in a crate all day and only coming out to urinate or eliminate is not much of a fun life for your puppy. Placing your puppy in a playpen or in a gated off area of the home allows you to keep checking on your puppy while offering your Shih Tzu plenty of room to play and to be part of the household – hearing noises, seeing people and being involved in the home environment.

Tethering - Anytime that you can, keep your Shih Tzu right near you, so that you can 'catch him' when he makes a motion to pee or poo. You can keep an eye on your puppy by using the Umbilical Cord Method. With this method you will attach a leash to your puppy's harness. Using a collar is not recommended. Why? Because if you are not careful at every moment, you may walk too quickly or turn a corner before your puppy can keep up with you… when a Shih Tzu is connected to a dog collar and leash and there is a sudden 'jerking', this can cause injury to the neck, including collapsed trachea – a very serious condition in which the cartilage in the dog's trachea literally collapses inward and causes serious breathing problems and pain.

With this method, your puppy will be connected to you with a leash approximately 6 feet long. This allows you to walk around the home while keeping your puppy close enough to notice if he is about to have an 'accident'.

The Importance of Praise

– Praise and reward are what makes it possible for a dog to truly learn what is expected of him. Sure, if you always take your Shih Tzu outside every few hours he will pee and poo out there. However, he will not be learning; he will be going simply because he happens to be standing there. But, when you offer enough praise and a small reward, your Shih Tzu will start to make a connection; he pees in a certain spot and he hears super excited words and gets pats, he made his owner happy and oh, he gets a tasty treat too! Now, he has a reason to try and repeat that action that brought about so many good things. Whenever your Shih Tzu pees or poos where you want him to, act as if your Shih Tzu just did the most wonderful thing in the world.

In regard to reward, keep it very small so that he does not fill up; just a tiny morsel of something yummy (small pieces of microwaved bacon works wonderfully) and have the treat be right in your pocket (place it in a zipped plastic baggie) so that you can give it to him immediately.

To Recap

• Choose a designated area
• Allow your Shih Tzu plenty of time to choose a spot and relax his bladder and bowel muscles. Sit in a chair if you must.
• Take him to the designated area at all recommended times
• Take him to the designated area any time that you see your Shih Tzu is making a motion to pee or poo
• Take him to the designated area right before his walks & as soon as a walk is complete
• Offer tons of happy praise as soon as he is done peeing or pooing & give him a small taste of a yummy treat
• As your Shih Tzu matures, gradually stretch out the time intervals of when you bring him out, so that he can learn to hold his needs longer and longer.

Having the Right Setup For When Your Shih Tzu is Home Alone - When you leave your Shih Tzu home, do remember your puppy's limits (a 3 month old can only hold needs for 3 hours, a 4 month old for 4 hours, etc., up until the age of 1 year with a maximum time of 8 hours). Knowing this limit, it is unrealistic to assume that if you leave your Shih Tzu in a pen for the day, that your puppy will be able to hold his needs if you are gone for 8 hours.

The best method to use if you will be gone for an extended time is to gate off an area or to place your puppy in a canine playpen. Your goal will be to have your Shih Tzu urinate or eliminate on newspaper or pee pads. The area that you choose should have different locations for your puppy:

• A quality dog bed
• An area for toys
• An area with water
• An area with food (if you will not be there to feed your puppy at designated times)
• An area with newspaper to urinate and/or eliminate (more ahead on the issue of missing the pads)

Nighttime - Have the last meal of the day be about 2 hours before bedtime. Bring your Shih Tzu outside about 20 to 25 minutes before bed. Again, be sure to give him enough time to relax the bladder and bowel muscles. If you know that your Shih Tzu is safe, warm and comfortable do not respond to barking/whining/yelping unless you feel that a bathroom need is legitimate. If so, bring him to the designated area however keep lights low, do not speak except for saying 'good dog' and quietly bring him back to his sleeping area when done. The goal will be to keep this a very serious time. At night, play time should never be a reward for housebreaking. If so, a Shih Tzu will try to get you to interact with him, perhaps even forcing some urine out, just to gain your attention.

At night, when whining/yelping/barking noises to get attention are ignored and a puppy is only attended to for bathroom needs, the puppy will soon learn to self-soothe himself back to sleep, waking only if there is a urination or elimination need. You may also wish to refer back to 'Bringing Your Shih Tzu Puppy Home', 'How to React to Whining and Crying', page 25.

The 'Puppy Pees' - It is normal for some Shih Tzu to urinate when excited. This is most common with puppies that simply become overwhelmed with attention or with the expectation of attention. The puppy will then have excitement urination behavior. Most puppies will grow out of this phase. However, in the meantime, you may find a couple of things helpful:

1. Try to play with your puppy *outside*.
2. Bring your puppy to the designated bathroom area to urinate before playtime.
3. For dogs that are simply over-excited, whether young puppies or older adult dogs, it is best to approach the dog from the side and slowly introduce play time.
4. Puppies that display this behavior should not be directly picked up. It is best to kneel beside your puppy, pat him a bit and then gently roll him onto your lap. This eliminates the sudden excitement of being picked up and hugged.

Accidents - How you respond to accidents will have a huge impact on housebreaking success.

1. If you catch your Shih Tzu in the act of eliminating in the house, do something to interrupt him like clapping loudly (don't scare him). Immediately take your Shih Tzu to his bathroom spot, give lots of praise, and give a treat if he finishes eliminating there.

2. Don't punish your dog for eliminating in the house. Do nothing but clean it up. Rubbing your dog's nose in it, taking him to the spot and scolding, or any other type of punishment, will only make your Shih Tzu afraid of you or afraid to eliminate in your presence. Dogs do not understand punishment after something happens, even if it's only seconds later. Punishment will do more harm than good.

Housebreaking Basics Checklist

√ Have ONE designated area

√ Puppy is taken out on schedule & whenever he makes a motion to pee/poo

√ Pup is always taken there on leash

√ Be patient; sit in a chair if it helps

√ Great praise is given when the pup pees/poos

√ Remain calm and do not scold for accidents

√ Accidents are cleaned with an enzyme cleanser

√ If you can't keep a close eye on the pup, have him behind a gate or in a canine playpen

√ Try to avoid any pee/poo'ing during walks; visit the designated bathroom area BEFORE & AFTER walks

√ Handle nighttime bathroom needs to show it is a serious time

√ Time the last meal of the day for 2 hours before sleepy time

3. Cleaning the soiled area properly is very important because dogs are highly motivated to continue soiling in areas that smell like urine or feces. It's very important to use a quality enzyme cleaner. If you just use paper towels and dish soap (or something to that effect), it will not eliminate trace odors that linger behind. Those odors send a very strong signal to a dog that essentially yells out "This is the bathroom area!", and a dog rarely ignores that. He will then want to go to the bathroom in that spot again as opposed to signaling that he wants to go outside.

Medical Issues - If your dog is having a lot of training accidents, this can point to medical issues, such as a bladder infection. Therefore if your Shih Tzu is having a lot of accidents, despite proper training, be sure to bring your Shih Tzu to the veterinarian to check for any medical issues which may cause your puppy or dog to lose control of their bladder or bowels.

Most Common Housebreaking Hiccups

My dog pees or poops as soon as I bring him back inside! It is important to make sure that the dog is focusing on the task and to allow enough time. In regard to focusing, make sure that your dog is not multi-tasking. There should be **no** playing or roaming around the yard. Keeping your dog on a 6 foot leash, stand in the middle of the designated area and allow him to circle within that spot. While he may sniff and look around, do not engage in any play or talk to disturb him.

In regard to time, while it would be great if dogs went on cue, some need up to 20 minutes for bowel muscles to relax and then push out the fecal matter. With urination, a dog may release half the bladder and need a bit more time to release the rest. Set up an outdoor chair, bring your phone or flip through a book, but give him enough time. If a Shih Tzu truly pees *right after* coming back in, a good trick is to come in and then hold your Shih Tzu in your lap. A dog will not pee on his owner when held this way. Keep him on your lap for about 10 minutes and then carry him right back to the designated bathroom area. Most likely, he will pee at that time.

My dog can't hold his needs for more than an hour! The first thing to look at would be any health issue that was causing this. With a full and complete checkup to ensure that there are no medical issues, an owner can then look to other reasons.

This can often be a matter of needing to strengthen bladder and/or bowel muscles. Here's how it works: Very young puppies have very little control over holding their needs. As pups grow, bladder and bowel muscles grow stronger but the degree to which they strengthen depends, in part, on your actions. If you took an 8 week old pup outside every 2 hours and once he turned 3 and then 4 months old, you did not extend that time, his body will still be used to going every 2 hours. The key will be to gradually let there be more time in-between taking the dog outside. Aim for 15 minutes longer than normal and slowly work out from there. A dog that is used to going every 3 hours cannot suddenly learn to hold on for 8 hours; however if this is done in 15 minute intervals over the course of days and weeks, he can certainly work his way there.

My dog pees or poops at night when I'm sleeping! He didn't even wake me up! Barring any health problems, this is not uncommon with young pups. And while most dogs will alert owners to a need, some are very quiet and will just do the deed silently. You'll want to make sure to bring him outside 1 hour and then 20 minutes before bed, giving him those 20 minutes we spoke about earlier. In addition, 2 hours before sleep time, no more food should be fed. Do not, however, limit water. You'll also want to make sure that the sleeping area is big enough. If a dog needs to go, he will indeed go even in a small confined space. For this reason, it is best to create a gated area that can hold a bed and pee pads. This way, if you are not alerted, there is a good chance that the pads will be used. Finally, making sure that your dog gets enough exercise and activity during the day can help the dog sleep better through the night. Two daily walks are best and some play time (fetch, etc.) along with some command training all work together to provide enough stimulation to help a dog stay asleep at night.

My dog is peeing everywhere in the house! Be sure to have all health issues ruled out (bladder infection, urinary tract infection, etc.). If the Shih Tzu is fine and peeing/pooing everywhere, is it because he has access to 'everywhere'? The Shih Tzu needs to be confined to one spot (his gated off area or his canine playpen) until he is fully trained. If this is done due to marking, information regarding marking is ahead. With the Shih Tzu's access to other areas of the home under control, begin 'do-over' in regard to housebreaking. Start at the beginning, following all of the rules and steps.

My dog's pee is uncontrollable! This may be a urinary tract or bladder infection, so this needs to be checked out by a veterinarian. If this is due to marking behavior, information is ahead.

My Shih Tzu pees or poos very early in the morning, is there any help for this? This happens a lot. There are several things you can do:

1) Change your Shih Tzu's last meal of the day to be 1 or even 2 hours earlier. By doing this, there is a better chance that he will pee and poo when taken outside in the evening for his last bathroom trip before bed.

2) Alternatively, the opposite may work. If you feed your Shih Tzu 2 hours later than normal, he may not need to eliminate until 2 hours later than normal the next morning. If doing this creates a very early dinner time (3 or 4 PM), you can give your Shih Tzu a small snack, if needed, at what used to be his dinnertime.

3) Exercise your Shih Tzu more in the evening. While you don't want to exercise a Shih Tzu too close to bedtime, taking a longer walk than normal or playing an exciting game of fetch about 2 hours before bed can help tire him out so that he sleeps longer in the morning.

4) In some cases, some type of noise is waking the Shih Tzu. This may be birds chirping, a neighbor closing his car door, etc. Moving your Shih Tzu's sleeping area to one that is more insulated from outside noises may help. Another option is to use a white noise machine to block out noises that may be disturbing your Shih Tzu's sleep.

5) Sometimes, a Shih Tzu will wake up and bark because he is bored; an owner may mistake this for a bathroom need. The owner takes the Shih Tzu out, and since he is outside, he does let out some urine. But, if the Shih Tzu was able to keep himself occupied when he woke, he may very well stay busy for a while before barking to gain an owner's attention. For these cases, you will want to sneak a treat-release toy into his sleeping area once he is out for the night. When he wakes, he'll discover it and may remain happily quiet.

My Shih Tzu rips apart/moves his pee pads! This is also common. The best solution is to duct tape the pads into place. Since the residue from the tape may ruin your flooring, we suggest obtaining a large piece of linoleum (you can get this at your local home supply store) and place this under his gated area.

My Shih Tzu keeps missing the pee pad! If the dog's area is too large, this can happen. We do NOT suggest leaving a Shih Tzu in a small area, since a confined space can bring on feelings of claustrophobia, causing stress and increasing separation anxiety. However, the area should be only big enough for a bed, food & water, a toy area and pee pads. A dog will not pee on his bed. He will also not pee on his food & water. Rarely will he pee on his toys. Therefore, the only area left would be the pee pads. You can place down 1, 2, 3 or more. As just discussed, tape these down if you must. Once he has better control, you can increase his area as you see fit.

How should I scold my Shih Tzu? Yelling at or punishing a puppy in any way will not help with training. Your Shih Tzu will have no idea why you are upset. Being scolded can cause a dog to feel belittled and lead to him becoming skittish. If things are going terrribly wrong, reassess how many of the rules you are following consistantly. Scolding never, ever works. When all rules are followed, the only reaction from you that will help with his training, is when you offer tons of attention and praise when the pup does go in the correct spot.

Tips for Indoor Pee Pad Training

If choosing this method, do remember that it goes against a dog's urge to 'choose just the right spot' to do his business. Therefore, some extra patience on your part will be needed. The pee pads should be placed in the area that your Shih Tzu will be when home alone (gated off area or canine playpen). When you are home, keep the entry to that area open. At each designated time and any time your puppy makes a motion of needing to urinate or eliminate, bring your puppy to the newspaper or pee pads. Each and every time that your Shih Tzu does use the paper or pads, give tons of reward. Be sure to act extremely excited. Give great praise; happy excited words, a small treat, hugs, kisses and pats.

If your Shih Tzu misses the pads, move the feces onto the pads for a small amount of time. Just long enough to put a bit of the scent onto the pad. If your puppy misses the pad when urinating, before you use your enzyme cleaner (explained in the 'Accidents' section, page 47), wipe up the urine with paper towels and place those onto the pads for just a bit of time to allow the scent to linger on the pad.

Tip: Learning to go the bathroom on a pad can be confusing for a puppy. A cardboard box can be the answer. With the use of a box, you can make the pad more of a 'designated area'. The box can be removed once a puppy is fully trained. **Here is what you can do:** Obtain a good sized, sturdy cardboard box without a top. The open-ended top will face up (think 'no roof'). It works best to have this in the corner of the gated off area (or your Shih Tzu's spot for when he is home alone), since it will need stability, as we continue on. Cut a 'doorway' on one of the sides. Have the doorway cut all the way down (you don't want your puppy to have to step over to get in).

So, essentially, the box will surround the pad. It will have no top. There will be a doorway for the puppy to easily enter. The pad will be surrounded by this cardboard to give it a feeling of being more of a designated area than just a pad that is placed down on the floor. When you bring your Shih Tzu to pee or poo, have your puppy on leash and keep him on leash for the entire potty time. Lead him over to the designated area. Guide him in through the 'doorway'. Using the leash, keep him in that area, not allowing him to exit. It can take a puppy anywhere from 10 seconds to 15 minutes to go to the bathroom, so give him time to go potty. If he goes, give great reward. As time goes by, you can cut all sides of the box down in height. Then, with more successes, you can cut the sides of the box even further down in height. Once your puppy has shown that he fully understands his bathroom area, the box (which is now only small pieces of cardboard) can be removed. This also works for those who have an outside deck but not a backyard and want their puppy to go potty in one corner of the deck.

Tips for Adults & Seniors

You may have gotten an adult Shih Tzu for many reasons and your adult may have come from a breeder, rescue or other previous owner. In some cases, this adult Shih Tzu will already be house trained. In other cases, the dog may need to be reminded or may need to learn from the beginning. If your adult is not house trained, ignore the expression that "you can't teach old dogs new tricks", because of course you can!

Many adult dogs adopted from animal shelters may not have gotten enough opportunities to eliminate outside, and as a result, they may have soiled in their kennel areas. This tends to weaken their housetraining habits. In addition, scents and odors from other pets in the new home may stimulate some initial marking (see next section for marking). Remember that you and your new adult Shih Tzu need some time to learn each other's signals and routines. Even if your Shih Tzu was housetrained in his previous home, if you don't recognize his bathroom signal, you might miss his request to go out, which leads to him eliminating indoors.

Therefore, for the first few weeks after you bring your adult Shih Tzu home, you should assume your new dog isn't housetrained and start from scratch. If your Shih Tzu was housetrained in his previous home, the re-training process should progress quickly. The process will be much smoother if you take steps to prevent accidents and remind your Shih Tzu where he is supposed to eliminate.

Follow all of the advice for housebreaking a Shih Tzu puppy. In addition, adult senior dogs, will be more prone to accidents as they age. Handling accidents the right way is very important and seniors with weak bladder muscles may need to wear doggie diapers. You may wish to refer to the 'Senior Care' section, page 270.

Marking

Overview A Shih Tzu of any age may mark; this is not technically a housebreaking issue, it is a behavioral issue.

Both male and female dogs mark. Dogs do this to mark their territory, not because they do not know where to eliminate or they do not understand the rules of housebreaking. Marking is not a method of emptying the bladder; it is a process of spraying out a bit of urine to mark territory. This is more common in households that have more than 1 dog. You will know that this is territorial marking behavior if:

• The dog only urinates a little bit; he will not release his whole bladder; he will urinate just enough to mark the spot
• The dog keeps urinating in the same spot
• The dog is house trained and does not eliminate feces in the home, but only urinates inside.
• This is more common if a female is not spayed or a male is not neutered. However, even if the dog is spayed or neutered, if there is another dog in the home that is not, this can prompt this behavior.

How to Stop Marking Behavior

1) Clean the area, but not with a strong smelling cleaner. This can trigger your dog to try and mark again to cover that scent. You'll want to use a quality enzyme killing formula that breaks down the tiny particles found in urine so that no trace amounts linger behind.
2) Try to not allow your Shih Tzu to see other dogs walking near the home - just seeing another dog may trigger your dog to mark. Depending on the layout of your home, curtains can be closed, etc.
3) Try to make the area in which your dog is marking, into a play area. Play with your dog there, give a treat, have him lie down and pat his tummy.
4) Spay or neuter **all** pets. Dogs that are spayed or neutered are less likely to do this. Even if your Shih Tzu is

Marking Basics Checklist

√ Urine indoors is cleaned with an enzyme cleanser
√ Block visuals to other dogs, if possible
√ If the dog marks one specific area, turn that spot into a play area
√ Keep a close eye on your dog & use distraction if he/she starts to urinate
√ If you can't keep a close eye on the pup, have him behind a gate or in a canine playpen
√ Reassess if proper hierarchy is in place
√ Consider neutering/spaying all pets

spayed/neutered, another pet that is not can trigger this behavior.

5) As soon as you see your Shih Tzu get into position to do this, make a loud noise to distract your dog and then immediately bring him to his bathroom area. Give enthusiastic praise and reward if he urinates there.

6) Marking may be done to show dominance. This can happen if a Shih Tzu mistakenly believes that he is the leader of the house or if he is unsure & is 'fighting' to take his place as leader. So as not to repeat text, please refer to the 'Teaching Proper Hierarchy' section for the details on teaching proper hierarchy to a Shih Tzu, page 108.

* Until this is under control by following this advice, do not give the Shih Tzu free reign in the house. Keep him in his area (gated off area or playpen) when you cannot keep a close eye on him.

Marking Behavior with More Than 1 Dog – In a house with proper hierarchy, the humans are the leaders (Alphas) and the dog is the Beta. However, in multiple dog homes, within the group of the Betas, there is *also* a leader: the Beta Leader. In other words, there is always an 'Alpha Dog'. If it is not clear (in the Shih Tzu's mind) who the Beta Leader is, he may 'fight it out' and marking is one way that a dog will do this.

He may try to show that *he* is the dominant one by marking the territory. You can help by establishing which dog is the Alpha Dog, so that the dogs do not have to figure it out or fight for the position. It is *usually* the older dog. However, you can take notice when the dogs are playing. Is one of them more outgoing? Is one dog more pushy when it comes to choosing toys? Which dog runs to their food first? Noticing this, will help you know who is trying harder to be the Alpha Dog.

Once you know, you can then help both dogs. Remember that the dog that is *not* the Alpha Dog is just as important and loved as the other dog. Not being the Alpha Dog is not a negative thing. Both dogs will be less stressed and happy, knowing their place in the 'pack'. Essentially, you will do everything for the Alpha Dog first. When it is time to feed your dogs dinner, give the Alpha Dog his food first. When handing out treats, the Alpha Dog gets his first. When it is time to take the dogs outside for a walk, put the harness and leash on the Alpha Dog first. These small gestures help the dogs feel secure that you- the main leader- are showing them that you understand the 'pack'. In addition, follow all of the general rules of marking (previous section).

Feeding and Nutrition

Water

While giving your dog water may seem like one of the easiest items on the care checklist, there are actually several elements that owners should be aware of. When we think about our Shih Tzu having a balanced diet, we don't always think about the fact that what they drink plays a huge role in this. Just as for humans, water has many purposes. It

helps the body absorb nutrients and carries those nutrients through the cells of the body. It aides in the digestion of food. Adequate amounts will allow the intestines to work as they should to produce healthy stools. It lubricates everything from joints to the spinal cord to internal tissues. And it also serves to help regulate a dog's body temperature. Essentially, water is the life force of all living mammals and a dog can only last 2 to 3 days without it. The amount that a Shih Tzu drinks along with the quality of that water will have a huge effect on his health.

Photo courtesy of Puppies on the Prairie

How Much Water a Shih Tzu Needs - The amount of water that a Shih Tzu puppy or dog needs will vary depending on several factors including his activity level, age and the weather (both temperature and humidity). In *general* it is safe to say that a 5 lb. Shih Tzu. (2.26 kg) needs at least 1 cup (.23 liters) per day and a 10 lb. Shih Tzu (4.53 kg) needs at least 2 cups (.47 liters) per day.

Note: This amount can vary by up to 30%. Dogs that ingest foods that have high levels of water may drink a bit less. Dogs that are active and/or live in areas of warm/hot weather may need more.

Health Issues that Cause Increased Thirst - If a Shih Tzu seems desperate for more water or makes attempts to drink from other sources such as puddles in the yard, etc. this can point to a medical condition. It is important to note that many of these health issues can strike puppies. Owners often overlook these possible health concerns since there is a belief that only older dogs are at risk. However, excessive thirst (Polydipsia) on a continual basis despite being given an adequate amount of water often points to one of the following conditions:

• *Diabetes* - Increased thirst is often the very first symptom. Others signs include: change in appetite, weight loss, fruity smelling breath, weakness, a thinning or dullness of the coat and/or vomiting. Left untreated there may be UTI's, skin infections, eye problems including cataracts and blindness. This disease strikes 1 in 500 dogs. This is not just a concern for senior Shih Tzu; puppies can develop this as well and it is often referred to as juvenile diabetes mellitus.

• *Liver disease* - Increased thirst for water is among the leading signs of liver disease. Other symptoms include loss of appetite, confusion, vomiting, diarrhea, dizziness, a yellowing of the eyes, weakness and/or blood in the urine. Left untreated there may be fluid buildup in the abdomen (Ascites) and/or seizures.

• *Kidney disease* - Increased thirst is one of the first signs of problems with the kidneys. Other signs include change in urination (with an increase or decrease), urination at night, uncontrolled dribbling of urine, blood in the urine, decreased appetite, dulled coat, weakness, diarrhea and/or vomiting. Left untreated, it will lead to kidney failure at which time there may be a buildup of waste products in the body that manifests as uremia (a distinct ammonia smell), mouth ulcers, severe weight loss, loss of muscle mass, anemia (a deficiency of red blood cells presenting as pale skin and weakness), dangerously high blood pressure, difficult breathing and/or seizures.

• *Cushing's disease* - The most prominent signs of this in dogs is drinking excessively which leads to excessive urination and also incontinence issues; a Shih Tzu may urinate at night in his bed or have trouble holding his bladder during the day. Over time, approximately 90% of all dogs with Cushing's will develop a pot-bellied appearance which is due to a redistribution of body fat coupled with a breakdown of abdominal muscles, caused by hormone fluctuations. Left untreated, there may be hair loss, a darkening of the skin (most often seen on the underbelly) and/or skin infections.

• *Cancer* - Many types of cancer can cause a dog to drink more water than normal, including adrenal and pancreatic cancer.

• *Stomach / Intestinal ailment* - Any time that a Shih Tzu is eating less than normal due to illness, the body may try to make up for this by drinking more. In addition, any sort of stomach ailment that causes vomiting and/or diarrhea will cause a puppy or dog to quickly become dehydrated. Some dogs need encouragement to rehydrate - and may need a supplement such as Pedialyte, while others will actively seek out more water.

Why Tap Water is Terrible for Your Shih Tzu - What is actually in most tap water is shocking and it's amazing that it's legal. The federal law regarding tap water in the States is outrageous. Only 91 contaminants are regulated - and even many of those are allowed to be in the water in 'small' amounts. There are over 60K contaminants that aren't regulated at all. Scientists agree on one thing: The elements in tap water can cause cancer and a wide range of disease and ailments even with minimal consumption. If a Shih Tzu is allowed to ingest tap water for weeks, months and years this will have a huge effect on his health and can even lead to disease that cuts his life span short. Many of the dangerous elements in water are deemed 'safe' because that label is given to one glass. The toxins are only considered dangerous if ingested for years. Since you'll be giving water to your Shih Tzu for over a decade, this can't be ignored.

We don't have much info regarding tap water in the UK or other European countries, however if it even comes close to what's in the US and Canada tap water, you'll want to make some changes if you currently allow your Shih Tzu puppy or dog to drink it.

The United States Environmental Protection Agency and Health Canada's Water Quality and Health Bureau tell the public exactly what we can expect our tap water to contain:

Fluoride - This is exceedingly toxic to dogs (and also proven to be unsafe for humans). Why is it bad? You may be surprised to know that this chemical that was originally used to kill rats causes tooth disease, bone loss and deformities, can lead to kidney disease, causes hormone problems and can even lead to cognitive damage. Additionally, it is proven to cause Osteosarcoma which is the #1 cause of bone tumors in canines, developing in over 8000 dogs each year in the US.

Barium- This is a metal that comes from the erosion of natural deposits in the earth and is also a run-off from metal refineries. This is shown to cause unsafe elevations in blood pressure.

Beryllium - This comes from many sources including metal and coal factories and aerospace, defense and electrical companies. It causes intestinal lesions with long term consumption.

Chlorite - Possible long-term health effects are anemia and central nervous problems. This is a by-product of water disinfectant.

Chloramines- This chemical is purposely added to tap water to control microbes. It can cause eye and nose irritations, stomach problems and anemia.

Antimony - This can increase bad cholesterol and decrease healthy levels of blood sugar. It comes from the discharge of petroleum refineries, fire retardants and electronics that cannot be fully filtered out.

Trichloroethane (1, 1,2) - This harmful chemical can lead to liver, kidney, or immune system problems. It is a waste product from the discharge of industrial chemical factories.

Note: Keep in mind that our list is a short sampling of what you can expect to be in every bowl of tap water that a dog drinks.

What to do - There are 3 good choices that will ensure that the water your Shih Tzu drinks will be safe and only serve to be a part of a healthy diet.

1) Use a water filtering device that connects to your kitchen tap. These are relatively inexpensive and easy to attach. Once in place, you'll only need to replace the filters every other month or so.
2) Use a canine watering system that filters the water as it is being dispersed.
3) Offer bottled spring water. An adult Shih Tzu needs 1 to 2 cups per day. Going by the '2 cup a day' requirement, one gallon (16 cups) will last a Shih Tzu for 8 days. This equals less than 1 gallon per week. In many supermarkets, you can purchase a gallon for less than $1.

If you'd like to see recommendations for both bowls and water filtering devices, look to 'Bowls' in the Shih Tzu Specialty Shoppe. You can reach the Shih Tzu Specialty Shoppe by entering any page of the AllShihTzu website. Look to the navigation; it is in alphabetical order. Choose 'Shoppe'.

Nutritional Needs

If you are feeding your Shih Tzu a high quality manufactured food or are home cooking with healthy ingredients & are offering a full and complete vitamin & mineral supplement, you do not need to fixate on the *exact* ingestion of protein vs carbs vs fat, etc. However, here are the most important nutritional elements to know about:

Protein (and Amino Acids) - Dietary protein contains 10 amino acids that a dog cannot make on his own. They provide the building blocks for many important biologically active compounds and proteins for a dog. Also, they provide the carbon chains needed to make glucose for the dog's energy. The 10 essential amino acids found in meat protein are: arginine, histadine, isoleucine, leucine, lysine, methionine, phenylalanine, threonine, tryptophan, and valine. Studies show that dogs can sense when their dog food lacks a single amino acid and may even avoid eating it.

Carbohydrates - Dogs need a certain amount of energy to sustain the normal activities of their daily lives. Growth, pregnancy, lactation, and exercise all increase these normal energy requirements. This energy comes from 3 major dietary components: carbohydrates, protein and fats.

Healthy Fats – Dietary fat is the most concentrated source of energy for a dog. It also provides essential fatty acids (important for skin & coat health) and aids in nutrient utilization and transportation. Fat is involved in cell integrity and metabolic regulation.

Vitamins & Minerals- These are vital for the body to function properly. Vitamins that dogs need include:

Vitamin A - For healthy vision and for bone, skin & immune function
Vitamin B1 (Thiamine) - For energy metabolism; important to nerve function
Vitamin B2 (Riboflavin)- For energy metabolism; important for normal vision and skin health
Vitamin B3 (Niacin) - For energy metabolism; important for nervous system, digestive system and skin health
Vitamin B6 (Pyridoxine)- For protein metabolism; helps make red blood cells
Vitamin B12 (Cobalamin) For making new cells; important to nerve function
Vitamin C (Ascorbic acid) An antioxidant (which can help prevent disease). Is part of an enzyme needed for protein metabolism; important for immune system health; aids in iron absorption
Vitamin D - Helps the body absorb calcium.
Vitamin E – Is an antioxidant
Vitamin K - Activates bone proteins
Beta-carotene (Is not the same thing as Vitamin A; about 3% of this gets *converted* in Vitamin A) – Important for eye health and a strong immune system. Keeps skin healthy.
Biotin - Needed for energy metabolism
Calcium – For strong bones and teeth. Helps blood clot and helps nerves send messages. Also aids in muscle contraction.
Folic acid - Helps with protein synthesis
Phosphorous – Works with calcium to keep bones and teeth healthy
Omega 3, 6 and 9 - Fatty acids play a role in cell structure and function. Essential fatty acids are needed to keep your dog's skin and coat healthy. Puppies fed ultra low-fat diets often develop dry, coarse hair and skin lesions that become increasingly vulnerable to infections. Omega 3 and Omega 6 are most crucial.
Magnesium – Helps the body absorb other vitamins, is needed for proper bone growth and is used in the production of protein.

Calorie Requirements

Many owners want to know how many calories a Shih Tzu needs. And this sort of question can be answered; however you should know that you do not need to stick to any exact numbers when feeding your Shih Tzu nor should you bother yourself with daily calorie counting. The only time that you may want to do this, is if a Shih Tzu is deemed underweight or overweight (very uncommon but more likely with seniors). There is no need to be fanatical when it comes to calories. It is MUCH more important to focus on feeding your Shih Tzu the best food possible. With that said, we will continue on to look at how many calories a Shih Tzu needs, if you are indeed curious about this.

The amount of calories that a Shih Tzu puppy needs to fuel his growing body or an adult needs to maintain weight depends on a few different factors:

Activity level - This is one of the most significant factors. There are surprisingly very few studies that have been done in regard to how many calories canines burn when walking or doing other activities. However, two different studies have both suggested the same essential findings that a typical canine will burn 65 calories during a 1 hour walk. A Shih Tzu, we estimate, due to his size, would burn about half of this, perhaps 35 or so.

This may not seem like a lot, since humans can burn anywhere between 200 and 400, depending on their pace, weight and so forth. Nevertheless, since a dog requires much less calories per day than his human family members, those 35 or so calories are going to count against a much smaller number. The rate of 65 calories per hour (for a typical dog) was determined to be the average number if a dog walked at a pace of 3.8 to 4 miles per hour - which means that a mile would be covered in 15 minutes. For a Shih Tzu, walking at this fast pace is not reasonable. A 20 to 25 minute walk to cover 1 mile may be more typical for a Shih Tzu and therefore, a slightly lower number of calories would be burned; somewhere in the range of 35 calories.

Age is another important aspect to factor in when figuring out calorie needs. Puppies have a higher metabolism than adult dogs. The 1st year is one of rapid growth, which requires nutrients and calories to fuel a growing body. This evens out around the age of 10 to 12 months. Then, as a dog matures into a senior, the metabolism slows down even more. Senior Shih Tzu 8 years and older may burn anywhere from 50 to 100 less calories per day. On top of this, activity for the senior dog often decreases as he may suffer from arthritis or other age related medical issues that affect mobility.

Medical Issues - There are some health conditions that may affect a dog's metabolism and therefore his calorie needs. This includes but is not limited to:
• Hypothyroidism
• Heart problems
• Medications - some medications may cause weight gain even if a dog is not eating more food (usually water retention) and others cause increased appetite so that a dog will consume more food and calories.

Spayed/ Neutered Dogs – Despite many assumptions about this, in most cases a spayed or neutered Shih Tzu (or any other dog breed for that matter) does not need fewer calories than those that are not fixed. Of course, a spayed female puppy will need fewer calories as she matures into an adult- just as a non-spayed female would- and a neutered male will need fewer calories as he matures into a senior- just as a non-neutered male. For the small percentage of dogs that *do* gain weight after being fixed, it is theorized that this may have to do with the fact that the dog is calmer; he is not pacing all day rearing to find a mate or acting hyper due to hormones. While pacing and other such actions do not count as 'exercise', this *does* fall under the category of NEAT (Non-Exercise Activity Thermogenesis), which is the energy (calories) expended for everything one does aside from sleeping. So, a calmer dog equals a dog that is burning less calories and therefore that dog does not require as many. The figures involved here are *very* tiny; however over the course of a year or two, this can add up.

Calories in the Food You Feed Your Shih Tzu
- Home cooking is one of the healthiest choices in regard to feeding a Shih Tzu nutritious, high quality food since you know each and every ingredient and there, of course, will be no fillers, by-products, artificial colors or preservatives. With wholesome ingredients such as no-skin white breast chicken meat, fresh vegetables and fruits, meals will be calorie dense. While you will have many choices of ingredients, here are the counts for some of the most popular foods:

White breast chicken (no skin) = 124 calories for 4 ounces
Sugar snap peas = 10 calories per 1/4 cup
Yams = 39 per 1/4 cup
White rice = 66 per 1/4 cup

Carrots = 14 in 1/4 cup (chopped)
Blueberries = 21 per 1/4 cup
Raspberries = 17 per 1/4 cup

With this said, many owners do choose a commercial dog food. Please be careful to choose wisely. The cheaper the food, the cheaper the ingredients and this can greatly affect the health of your Shih Tzu. Inexpensive food can cause a Shih Tzu to be hungry all of the time, be malnourished, have digestive problems, allergies and other issues. With manufactured brands, the choice will be dry or wet. Both have their pros and cons. Most brands have nutritional labeling that shows you all of the facts you need to know, including calorie count.

One of our top recommended commercial brands, Orijen, is tightly packed with quality nutrients and therefore has a high calorie count per cup. (Cheaper brands will fill out the kibble with fillers and low nutritional foods that keep the calorie count down, thus causing a Shih Tzu to require a larger amount of that kibble to receive a comparable amount of nutrients).

Orijen for puppies has 490 calories per cup (37% from protein, 19% from fruits and vegetables and 44% from healthy fats - puppies need to ingest more fat than adults).

Orijen for adults has 478 calories per cup (38% from protein, 21% from fruits and vegetables and 41% from healthy fats).

Our 2nd top recommended brand, Whole Earth Farms, is also tightly packed with quality ingredients including chicken and white fish. There are no by-products, corn, glutens, soy, artificial preservatives, artificial flavors, coloring or dyes. The average calories per cup are 450 (depending on the flavor and variety).

Low Quality brands (per cup) - Alpo has 375 calories, Artemis ranges from 308 to 348, AvoDerm ranges from 298 to 430, Beneful ranges from 306 to 392, Breeder's Choice has between 365 to 400, Diamond falls between 338 to 419, Eukanuba contains between 396 to 457 and Iams has 341 to 421.

Snacks - Remember that if you are counting calories for your Shih Tzu, you will want to add in any snacks that you are feeding your dog - and they can add up quickly. We recommend healthy treats such as raw baby carrots which have 35 calories in a 1/2 cup or raspberries (32 calories per 1/2 cup) and plain white yogurt (75 per 1/2 cup).

How Many Calories a Shih Tzu Puppy Needs - Please keep in mind that 'puppy' refers to a Shih Tzu from the age of 2 months to 1 year and therefore these numbers are a general guideline only. There will be starts and stops to growth; during growth spurts there will be a need for more calories. Varying activity levels will also affect these numbers. Therefore, you can use this as a general guideline but there is no need to be fixated on the number or work hard to meet it exactly. Your best guideline for a puppy's calories needs will be that he is gaining weight steadily. Puppies should be weighed every month to look for increases. In addition, your veterinarian will be able to tell you if your Shih Tzu is gaining as needed. If you think that there is a stall or a loss, this should be reported to the vet ASAP.

Note: When people say that puppies need more calories than adult dogs, this means that they need more calories per pound of body weight than adults.

For example, a Shih Tzu puppy needs roughly 55 calories per pound of body weight, while an adult needs approximately 40 calories per pound of body weight, if an active dog.

The following numbers are based on a healthy puppy that is fairly active (play, running around the house, etc.) and is taken for daily walks of 20 to 40 minutes. Please keep in mind that due to growth spurts and stops, these numbers are very general and should not be strictly adhered to; remember that a healthy, gradual weight gain is what will be your guide that you are feeding your Shih Tzu enough, along with recommendations from the veterinarian. Variations in metabolic rates can alter these numbers by as much as 20 percent.

Weight 2 lbs. (0.90 kg) = approx. 110 calories

Weight 3 lbs. (1.36 kg) = approx. 165 calories
Weight 4 lbs. (1.81 kg) = approx. 220 calories
Weight 5 lbs. (2.26 kg) = approx. 275 calories
Weight 6 lbs. (2.72 kg) = approx. 330 calories
Weight 7 lbs. (3.17 kg) = approx. 385 calories
Weight 8 lbs. (3.62 kg) = approx. 440 calories

As you Shih Tzu matures from puppy to adult (the 1 year mark), you can then refer to the guidelines below for the calorie needs for an adult Shih Tzu.

How Many Calories an Adult Shih Tzu Needs to Maintain Weight - The following is a general guideline only, as each dog is an individual. These figures are for adult Shih Tzu that are done growing and have reached their full width and height. Variations in metabolic rates can alter these numbers by as much as 20 percent.

Weight 7 lbs. (3.17 kg), exercise 1x per day = approx. 245 calories
Weight 7 lbs. (3.17 kg), exercise 2 x per day plus extra time playing fetch, command training, etc. = approx. 280 calories
Weight 8 lbs. (3.62 kg), exercise 1x per day = approx. 280 calories
Weight 8 lbs. (3.62 kg), exercise 2 x per day plus extra time playing fetch, command training, etc. = approx. 320 calories
Weight 9 lbs. (4.08 kg), exercise 1x per day = approx. 320 calories
Weight 9 lbs. (4.08 kg), exercise 2 x per day plus extra time playing fetch, command training, etc. = approx. 360 calories
Weight 10 lbs. (4.53 kg), exercise 1x per day = approx. 355 calories
Weight 10 lbs. (4.53 kg), exercise 2 x per day plus extra time playing fetch, command training, etc. = approx. 400 calories
Weight 11 lbs. (4.98 kg), exercise 1x per day = approx. 385 calories
Weight 11 lbs. (4.98 kg), exercise 2 x per day plus extra time playing fetch, command training, etc. = approx. 440 calories
Weight 12 lbs. (5.44 kg), exercise 1x per day = approx. 420 calories
Weight 12 lbs. (5.44 kg), exercise 2 x per day plus extra time playing fetch, command training, etc. = approx. 480 calories
Weight 13 lbs. (5.89 kg), exercise 1x per day = approx. 455 calories
Weight 13 lbs. (5.89 kg), exercise 2 x per day plus extra time playing fetch, command training, etc. = approx. 520 calories
Weight 14 lbs. (6.35 kg), exercise 1x per day = approx. 490 calories
Weight 14 lbs. (6.35 kg), exercise 2 x per day plus extra time playing fetch, command training, etc. = approx. 560 calories
Weight 15 lbs. (6.80 kg), exercise 1x per day = approx. 525 calories
Weight 15 lbs. (6.80 kg), exercise 2 x per day plus extra time playing fetch, command training, etc. = approx. 600 calories
Weight 16 lbs. (7.25 kg), exercise 1x per day = approx. 560 calories
Weight 16 lbs. (7.25 kg), exercise 2 x per day plus extra time playing fetch, command training, etc. = approx. 640 calories
Weight 17 lbs. (7.71 kg), exercise 1x per day = approx. 595 calories
Weight 17 lbs. (7.71 kg), exercise 2 x per day plus extra time playing fetch, command training, etc. = approx. 680 calories

Senior Calorie Needs - Older, senior Shih Tzu will often need fewer calories than their active, adult counterpart. The number of calories needed per day will vary greatly from dog to dog (because health and activity levels vary so much), yet may be in the 33 calories per pound of body weight range. Malnourishment at this stage in life can affect life span and exasperate any medical issues, so you'll want to make sure that your Shih Tzu is eating a bit less due to normal decreased appetite and not due to another issue. The senior dog may have trouble eating due to tooth loss, loss of appetite due to health conditions or side effects of medication. While the following can be used as a general reference point, it is highly recommended to discuss calorie and nutritional needs with your Shih Tzu's veterinarian. These figures are for Shih Tzu 8 years and older that are fairly inactive. Variations in metabolic rates can alter these numbers by as much as 20 percent.

Weight 7 lbs. (3.17 kg) = approx. 231 calories
Weight 8 lbs. (3.62 kg) = approx. 264 calories
Weight 9 lbs. (4.08 kg) = approx. 297 calories
Weight 10 lbs. (4.53 kg) = approx. 330 calories
Weight 11 lbs. (4.98 kg) = approx. 363 calories
Weight 12 lbs. (5.44 kg) = approx. 396 calories
Weight 13 lbs. (5.89 kg) = approx. 429 calories
Weight 14 lbs. (6.35 kg) = approx. 462 calories
Weight 15 lbs. (6.80 kg) = approx. 495 calories
Weight 16 lbs. (7.25 kg) = approx. 528 calories
Weight 17 lbs. (7.71 kg) = approx. 561 calories

Always use common sense over charts if you are keeping track of calories, and in most situations calorie counting is not needed when a Shih Tzu is healthy, eating quality meals and receiving regular exercise. If you notice any losses, unexplained gains or signs of eating problems, do bring this to the attention of the vet since many issues are best resolved when detected early.

All Meal Feeding Details

We will go over the most important elements of feeding and then follow with the most commonly asked questions regarding feeding.

Free Feeding VS Scheduled - Free feeding is the method of leaving out food all day long and allowing a dog to eat whenever he wishes. Scheduled feeding is the method of choosing certain times throughout the day to offer full meals. When a Shih Tzu is under 3 months old it is recommended to free feed. However, a schedule should be put into place right at the age of 3 months (unless otherwise directed by your dog's veterinarian) since studies show that scheduled feedings translate to a more well behaved dog. When a dog has a daily schedule, including meal times, this creates a structured environment and makes a dog feel safe and secure. Also, doing this will make it clear that you are the one providing the food (by having your Shih Tzu first obey the 'Sit' command before the bowl is placed down- refer to 'Teaching Proper Hierarchy', pg 108), therefore leading to a dog that is more well-behaved and listens to commands on cue.

When you do scheduled feedings, it is very important to choose times and then stay with those times. Your Shih Tzu will certainly remember when it is dinner time and an owner must remember also. If you are very busy and seem to keep forgetting, even if you are 10 minutes late, it may help to set a timer to ring that will remind you that your Shih Tzu is expecting their food.

Manufactured VS Home Cooking - **Manufactured food** can vary from downright horrible to fantastic. The range of what is offered is mindboggling. Some foods (brands you see commercials for all of the time) are filled with all sorts of disgusting things such as animal by-products (parts of an animal that are not deemed fit for human consumption such as undeveloped eggs, genitals, feet, brains, lungs and spleen. Yuck! They can also be packed with chemicals, which include artificial coloring, artificial flavoring and a high amount of chemical preservatives.

In addition, low-quality food is often packed with fillers. Fillers are just what they sound like. They contain zero nutritional value, they 'plump out' the food and they fill up your Shih Tzu's stomach. While it will appear that your Shih Tzu is full after eating, 1/10 to 1/3 of what he ate was not actual food (depending on the brand of dog food that you use). These fillers are not absorbed into the Shih Tzu's body, since they are basically 'nothing'. The body knows that they have nothing of value, so they quickly pass through and come out the other end. Owners are misled to believe that their dog ate enough, when in fact those fillers are just a waste. Since the Shih Tzu did not receive a full, healthy meal, his body may crave more food & nutrients, leading to possible issues such as eating grass and ingesting feces. So, in summary, feeding a low-quality food to a Shih Tzu can be terrible for his health; not only will he be malnourished, he is more prone to have allergic reactions to those chemicals, causing everything from upset stomach to skin & coat problems.

Manufactured foods are rated 1 through 5 stars. Some of the most well-known brands such as Beneful, Kibbles n' Bits, Pedigree, Alpo, Hill's, Eukanuba, Regal, Purina and Iams are only 1, 2 and 3 star foods. Do look to 4 or 5 star foods. We highly recommend Orijen or Whole Earth Farms. In regard to Orijen, it does not contain nasty fillers and ingredients are promising: boneless chicken, chicken meal (type of 'condensed' meat very high in protein), boneless salmon, turkey meal, herring meal, russet potato, chicken fat, sweet potato, peas, fresh boneless turkey, fresh whole eggs, fresh chicken liver, carrots and fresh boneless lake whitefish are the main ingredients.

The senior formula also contains salmon and anchovy oils, which is an excellent source of needed omega-3 fatty acids and low amounts of mercury. It also offers a Shih Tzu omega-6 fatty acids and monounsaturated fatty acids.

We really like that they add healthy herbs, botanicals and probiotic microorganisms; this shows that they go above and beyond to offer a truly healthy food choice. Most local supermarkets and local pet supply stores do not carry Orijen. They boast that they offer 'premium' brands, but you'll most often see these 1, 2 and 3 star foods we are talking about. You can obtain Orijen online at places such as Amazon or the Orijen site itself.

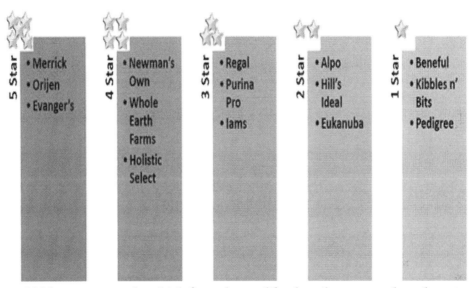

If you would like to see exactly which formulas we like, based on age and needs, you can see our recommendations in the Shih Tzu Specialty Shoppe. You can reach the Shih Tzu Specialty Shoppe by entering any page of the AllShihTzu website. Look to the navigation; it is in alphabetical order. Choose 'Shoppe'.

Home Cooking – Home cooking can be a great option because the Shih Tzu can tend to have digestive issues as well as food intolerance and food allergies. Even for those who are not great cooks, it is very easy. Most of the ingredients are ones that you would normally purchase. You can usually save money by home cooking, as well. For example, a family usually buys lean hamburger, chicken, fish and vegetables; all ingredients in many healthy recipes. Since manufactured brands add vitamins & minerals to their mix, it will be vital to add a high quality dog food supplement, given once per day (or as recommended on the particular brand you choose to use). A dog also needs fat. Some of this will come from fish that you offer and meats have some fat. However, your Shih Tzu's daily supplement should contain Omega 3, Omega 3, 6 or Omega 3, 6, 9.

Here are some ingredients you can choose from:

40% meat/fish: White chicken meat (de-boned, no skin, boiled, baked or broiled), liver, lean hamburger, mackerel or tuna. Other sources of protein include beans such as kidney beans.

25 % vegetables, a mixture of at least 2 of the following:

• Butternut squash

- Baby carrots
- Beets
- Spinach
- Zucchini
- Cauliflower
- Sweet peas
- Green beans

25% carbs:

- Oatmeal
- Plain white or brown rice
- Plain potatoes
- Sweet potatoes
- Plain pasta

10% fruit:

- Blueberries
- Raspberries
- Strawberries
- Banana
- Mango
- Pear

Added extras:

- Cottage cheese
- Plain whole white yogurt
- Eggs

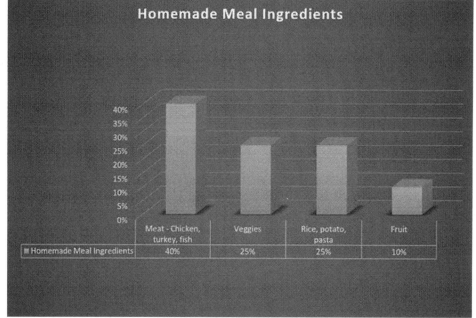

All food should be mixed very well and served warm. When you refrigerate extras, be sure to put the food in good Tupperware type containers.

Here is a meatloaf recipe that many Shih Tzu love:

Max's Meatloaf

Ingredients:
- ¾ cup water
- 1 egg, slightly beaten
- 1/4 cup baby peas
- 1/4 finely chopped carrot
- 1/2 pound of mixed ground pork, chicken and veal
- 1 cup plain oatmeal
- You will need a frying pan, a strainer, a mixing bowl, a baking sheet, aluminum foil and non-stick cooking spray

Directions:

1) Bring water to a boil in a small frying pan. Add the carrot and peas. Reduce heat to medium and cook for 5 minutes. Drain in a strainer and then allow to cool slightly.
2) Place all ingredients in a large bowl (egg, peas, carrot, meat & oatmeal) and mixed very well to combine them.
3) Place this on a foil lined baking sheet with a touch of non-stick spray on it. You can shape this into a bone shape

(just for fun) or a long meatloaf shape.

4) Bake in a preheated 450° F oven for 30 minutes.

5) Remove from oven when done and allow to cool for 10 minutes.

And here is a recipe for a hearty stew:

The idea behind this recipe is to cook a large quantity, that will last for several weeks.

Ingredients:

- 4 pounds ground turkey, frozen
- 6 medium sized potatoes
- 1 pound broccoli florets
- 1 15-ounce can of kidney beans
- 1 15-ounce can of lima beans
- 1 14-ounce can of cut green beans (no salt added)
- 1 can of leaf spinach
- 1 can diced tomatoes (tomatoes are just fine for dogs to eat, it is the tomato leaf that is toxic)
- 1 cup of sliced carrots (or canned, if you prefer)
- 1 15 ounce box of plain instant oatmeal
- 1/4 cup canola oil
- 7 cups water
- You will need 1 big pot (18 quart), use of a microwave, a knife, a stirring spoon and containers to hold extras.

Directions:

In the big pot, add the canola oil to the water and heat. Before it even starts to boil, add the frozen turkey and all of the vegetables except the potatoes (add the broccoli, kidney beans, lima beans, green beans, spinach, tomatoes and carrots).

Wash the potatoes and bake them in the microwave. First poke holes in them with a fork, wrap each one in a paper towel and place in a circle on the microwave tray. Microwave for 16 minutes on high. Once they have cooled, dice them up. You may include the skins if your Shih Tzu likes potato skins. Add to the pot.

Keep an eye on your pot of turkey and veggies. When it comes to a boil, lower the heat to 'low' and stir in the oatmeal. The mixture will be thick at this point, stir well. If not thick, slowly add more oatmeal. Simmer on a low heat for 20 minutes before turning off the heat. Allow this to cool very well, at which time it will thicken up even more. Spoon the mixture into smaller containers for refrigerator storage. You can refrigerate for up to 6 days and be sure to freeze all of the leftovers- for up to 3 months.

Switching Foods - If just obtaining a new 8 week old puppy, you should feed your Shih Tzu the same food that he has been eating. A sudden change in diet can cause upset stomach and other issues. If you wish to change over to a different brand of dog food or to homemade food at any time in your Shih Tzu's life, slowly make a change over the course of 4 to 5 weeks as not to disrupt a Shih Tzu's digestive tract.

This is one of the most common methods:

- Week 1 and 2: ½ old food and ½ new food, mixed together
- Week 3: 1/4 old food and 3/4new food, mixed together
- Week 4: 7/8 old food and 1/8 new food, mixed together
- Week 5: Fully eating new food

Dry VS Wet - Both have their pro's and con's. Dry kibble is great for the teeth. And some of the highest quality manufactured foods are dry foods. Wet food (both canned and homemade food) is often more appealing to a finicky eater. No matter which you choose, be sure to offer some quality dental treats for snacks (this will be even more important if you offer wet food).

How Often to Feed Your Shih Tzu - Until a puppy is 3 months old, he should be free fed (food is kept out at all times so that the pup may eat whenever he wishes). After 3 months old, 3 meals a day plus snacks (reserved for reward) is best. As an adult (starting at 1 year old), a Shih Tzu should have 2 meals per day, plus snacks reserved as reward for reinforcing good behavior. While many adult dogs can eat just 1 meal per day, this does not often apply to toy breed dogs; 2 meals is best.

How Much to Feed Your Shih Tzu — As you've seen in the previous 'Calorie Requirements' section, the amount of calories found in different foods varies wildly. For this reason, it is impossible to simply say, "Give your Shih Tzu 1/2 cup of food per meal/day." It really all depends on what type of food you feed him. If you are opting for a manufactured food, the feeding labels are pretty spot-on. If you are feeding homecooked food, one meal can vary from 1/4 cup to 3/4 cup depending on the exact ingredients and your Shih Tzu's age, activity level and metabolism. The best way to know how much to feed your puppy or dog is to allow him to eat for 15-20 minutes at each of the designated times. What he has not eaten in that amount of time, he does not need.

Snacks, treats and chews should be reserved for rewarding good behavior. In this way, training will be easier. If snacks and chews are given to a dog all of the time (good behavior or not), they will lose important meaning when you are attempting to train your Shih Tzu.

Vitamins & Supplements - A pet supplement is a product that is intended to complement the diet and help support and maintain normal biological function. There are 'basic' supplements that work to round out the diet, making sure that a dog receives the full daily requirement of vitamins and minerals. There are also supplements that can help with specific health issues that a dog is facing - whether due to medical conditions or age.

While home cooking has many benefits - and this is why we recommend home cooking - we recommend that if you offer homemade meals that you also offer a full & complete vitamin and mineral supplement each day. This is because just about all high-quality manufactured dog foods have these vitamins and minerals pre-mixed into the food. So, it is not a matter of commercial food being healthier or 'better' in this reagard, it is simply a matter that the companies add the vitamins & minerals to whatever base they use.

In regard to supplements for specific issues, there are literally hundreds: Some to improve concentration, some to help calm a dog, others to give energy and so forth. And of course, you can't give a dog all of them. Issues that owners face is that there are far too many to choose from and only some of them actually do as they say. Here's a list of some supplements that we recommend for certain issues/conditions:

• For arthritis, joint issues and range of motion issues; most often seen with senior dogs but also for Shih Tzu recovering from hip/knee problems: Glucosamine or Glucosamine combined with green lippid mussel.
• For healthy skin and coat: Omega 3 or Omega 3,6,9
• For anxiety, stress, nervousness: Colostrum Calming Complex
• For proper absorption of nutrients, digestive health, to help a pup gain weight, gas issues and to help stop coprophagia (eating feces): Prozyme
• For coprophagia: A brewer's yeast, Cayenne, Biotin & vitamin mixture that tastes good going in, but causes feces to taste really bad.

For other health conditions, your vet may recommend other, specific supplements.

 To see our list of recommended supplements, look to 'Supplements and Treats' in the Shih Tzu Specialty Shoppe. You can reach the Shih Tzu Specialty Shoppe by entering any page of the AllShihTzu website. Look to the navigation; it is in alphabetical order. Choose 'Shoppe'.

Most Common Feeding Problems

I'm not sure what the rating is for the food I feed my Shih Tzu. There is a great website called 'Dog Food Advisor' that lists out just about every brand of dog food, gives you its rating (1 through 5 stars) and tells you exactly why it was rated as so.

My Shih Tzu never eats/doesn't eat enough! While it may seem that your Shih Tzu never eats, if your puppy is gradually growing or your adult Shih Tzu is maintaining, this means that your Shih Tzu is indeed eating exactly as much as he needs to. Remember, what may seem like a very small amount of food to you, is often appropriate for a toy breed dog. If your Shih Tzu puppy is not growing or if your adult is losing weight, there may be a serious health issue at play. Loss of appetite is a sign of many health conditions; do have your Shih Tzu checked by the veterinarian ASAP.

Another issue of why a Shih Tzu may be reluctant to eat is if the bowl is not in correct proportion to a Shih Tzu's body. Sometimes if the bowl is too deep, the dog can bump his forehead on the edge of the bowl or have a hard time reaching the food or your dog may otherwise have a hard time eating in a comfortable position. This can cause a dog to avoid eating or he may carry the food to a different area and eat it there. You may wish to experiment with different sized bowls.

My Shih Tzu is picky. I can't find a food my Shih Tzu likes. While all owners have an urge to give their Shih Tzu something that the dog finds to be absolutely scrumptious (the canine equivalent of lobster in butter with a side of steak sirloin), the most important thing is that the food is healthy for the Shih Tzu. With manufactured brands, it's not good for a Shih Tzu to have changes in his diet every other week, as an owner searches for a food that will taste 'perfect'; the changes can cause stomach upset. For this reason, we suggest trying no more than 2 manufactured brands (4 or 5 star); as long as your Shih Tzu's digestive system tolerates the food, stick to your guns. With home cooking, you can experiment with the ingredients; perhaps your Shih Tzu prefers carrots to peas, or pasta to rice. You can make kibble more appealing by adding low-sodium chicken or beef broth (stir well, so that the Shih Tzu does not just eat off the top) and warming it in the microwave (just until it is warm, do not over-heat). And remember, if your adult is maintaining, he is eating enough.

My Shih Tzu only likes freeze-dried food, is that okay? Yes, as long as it is a 4 or 5 star food.

My Shih Tzu only eats if I hand-feed him. This can become a trap for many owners. You hand-feed your Shih Tzu just a few times and he expects it all the time. In fact, he demands it and refuses to eat unless you do this. Of course, you must stop this habit and get things back on track. Do reassess your Shih Tzu's bowl to make sure it is one that he is comfortable with. Many Shih Tzu that love being hand-fed do better with raised bowls. If his bowl *is* raised, he may prefer a floor bowl or a flat plate. Then, place his food in/on his bowl/plate. While he will resist at first, at some point he will become so hungry that he *will* eat the food. You will need to wait him out. It is canine instinct to survive. No dog will refuse to eat when it comes down to it.

Note: If a Shih Tzu has collapsed trachea or another health issue in which moving his neck causes pain, this can be one rare but possible explanation for a Shih Tzu only eating when hand-fed. If you suspect any such thing, bring your Shih Tzu to the veterinarian ASAP.

My Shih Tzu literally only eats one food (just chicken, nothing else, etc.)! This can be a matter of an owner giving in too quickly. You gave your Shih Tzu one particular food and now, he refuses to eat anything other than that. An owner will try to offer the Shih Tzu's 'normal' food to him, the dog will sniff it and back away… and within a minute the owner will say, "Well, my dog is a picky eater, I guess he refuses to eat his normal food now!" But, this only reinforces the behavior. Barring any health issues, when a dog is hungry, he will eat. If you want your Shih Tzu to eat a certain food or a mix of food, offer it and leave it there. If he is used to you caving in quickly, he'll test you a bit. He'll expect you to sigh and offer that one food he loves the most. But if you hold steady, he will eat the 'normal food' you offer, if there is no other choice. If he's been particularly stubborn, you can take that one food and blend it very well into his 'normal' food. Also, picky eaters often do best with warmed food and/or with food that has low-salt chicken or beef broth drizzled over it.

My Shih Tzu hides his food/brings it to a different spot. The most common reasons for this center around a dog having a need to 'protect' his food. The 3 most common reasons are:

1) If the dog was the runt of the litter (the smallest puppy) this could have reinforced this type of behavior. The smallest dogs are commonly pushed aside by littermates. A puppy that had to fight for food may have an urge to hide and run with their food to 'protect' it.
2) Rescue dogs are also known for this behavior, as many have gotten used to always being hungry and when given food, they feel that they need to protect it.
3) Dogs that do not feel secure that their food is safe will move it to another room, one where they feel that their food is protected. This can happen if the kitchen is a very noisy room, if there are other dogs in the home and the Shih Tzu feels as if they need to compete for food or if people sit or walk too close to where the dog food dish is.

Be sure to offer a nice quiet area for your Shih Tzu to eat. This should be an area with no one walking by, without loud noises and without people talking to your Shih Tzu or trying to pat or play with your dog while he eats. This will help make your Shih Tzu feel that his eating area is indeed a place where his food is safe. When your Shih Tzu takes any food out of the dish, immediately take the food and put it back. Get ready for your dog to test you; he may try to move it 10 times before giving in to your request. It will be worth it.

While this can seem like a game, it is not. Keeping a very close eye on your dog and not allowing your Shih Tzu to eat outside of the designated area will show your dog that if he wants his tummy full, he must eat where you ask him to. Never give in and always stay consistent. Also, think about snacks. Do you give your dog treats in other areas of the home? In order for this training to work, a dog must learn where he is and is not allowed to eat. If your Shih Tzu has this behavior, even small dog treats should only be given in the designated eating area (unless you are outside of the home, of course).

My Shih Tzu eats too fast! Some dogs do wolf down their food as if they think it's their last meal and this is not good for the stomach or the digestive system. This can be resolved by using a slow-feed dog bowl (be sure to choose stainless steel) or by placing slow-feed stainless steel balls into the dish that you already have. Both work to displace food so that it takes longer for a dog to eat his meal.

My Shih Tzu is underweight, how can I get him to eat more? There are a lot of owners that are concerned about their dog being underweight. The good news is that in most cases the Shih Tzu is actually at his correct weight; this is a toy dog breed after all. With that said, if a Shih Tzu has lost weight or if a veterinarian has told you that your dog is underweight, you'll have a valid reason to be concerned and take some steps to encourage some weight gain. There are a vast array of medical issues that can cause weight loss or will prevent a puppy from gaining. The #1 most important step before helping your Shih Tzu gain weight is to have any and all medical issues ruled out.

With health issues ruled out and your vet's approval for at-home weight gain, you can then do the following:

1) Keep up with exercise. Though daily walks do burn some calories, it will be the food intake that matters here and you don't want to cause additional health issues that can arise from being sedentary while you are working to help your Shih Tzu gain a bit of healthy weight. Exercise can also trigger the appetite to kick in.

2) With your vet's approval, aim to add about 150 calories more per day. This can be accomplished by having your Shih Tzu ingest 1 tablespoon of salmon fish oil (123 calories) along with 1/4 cup of whole cottage cheese (55 calories) per day. This will be 178 calories more per day. Both foods are easily tolerated by most Shih Tzu and are healthy additions. The fish oil can be blended into meals (1/3 tablespoon if you feed 3 meals per day… 1/2 tablespoon in each meal if you feed twice per day). The cottage cheese can be blended into meals as well.

Weigh your Shih Tzu once per week to check for an increase. For very small Shih Tzu this can be done on a kitchen scale. For larger Shih Tzu, you can place a basket on a scale, place your Shih Tzu in it and then check the increase. With the plan we have discussed, if there is no weight gain after 3 weeks, you will want to reassess things with your veterinarian.

Snacks

Just as much thought should go into what you give your Shih Tzu for snacks as it does in regard to main meals. Snacks given in-between meals and treats given for reward, can account for 10 to 20% of a dog's calories for the day. When you look at the overall nutritional needs for this breed of lean protein, healthy fats, carbohydrates, vitamins and minerals, what you offer your Shih Tzu for snacks will play a huge role in his overall health and well-being.

First, Let's Look at Which Snacks are Bad for a Shih Tzu

Rawhides - It's amazing that these are even still on the market as rawhide should never be given to a Shih Tzu or any other dog. These are made from the inner layers of cow or horse hides and then artificially flavored. They have a vast array of quite terrible risks:

1- Contamination - With these snacks there is a risk of E. coli and salmonella poisoning. Over the years, many brands have been recalled but not before hundreds of dogs became dangerously ill. There was even a case of hides being recalled due to arsenic contamination.

2- Digestive problems - Some rawhides are not digestible at all and others cause problems as the body is only able to partially digest them. This causes a range of problems that include stomach and intestinal distress and diarrhea.

3- Blockage - This is one of the most severe risks when giving rawhide to a Shih Tzu. These are notoriously hard to chew and break apart which makes these a serious choking hazard. In addition, chunks of rawhide can become stuck in the Shih Tzu's throat or digestive tract. Signs of blockage include: Dry Heaving, Vomiting, Repeated swallowing, Distress that manifests as panicked pacing, Pain that causes the dog to have trouble sitting, lying down or finding a comfortable position, Diarrhea, with or without blood and/or Refusal to eat or drink. This is a serious medical emergency that often needs to be treated with expensive surgery and not all dogs survive.

Pig Ears - The dry, brittle texture of these snacks makes it a bad idea to give a Shih Tzu pig ears. The shards can cause tooth breakage when being chewed and shards can cause injury to the throat. Once swallowed, improperly chewed pig ears can cause blockage to the intestinal tract.

Bones - It is not safe to feed a Shih Tzu real bones from ham, chicken, turkey, duck, roast or any other meat. Cooked bones are the biggest danger, though raw bones can cause problems as well. When bones are cooked - regardless of their size - they become brittle. When they are chewed, sharp splinters can break off. This can cause injuries and serious health issues including: Chipped teeth, Mouth injuries, Splinters in the lower jaw, Blockage to the esophagus, Inhalation of a bone splinter into the windpipe, Blockage in the stomach or intestines and/or Bone fragments causing injury to the rectum.

Raw bones are a bit safer, but still pose some risks that do not make them the best snack for a Shih Tzu puppy or dog. The problems with bones include over consumption of marrow (raw bones contain marrow which can cause diarrhea and for some dogs that are prone to pancreatitis, it can cause a flare up) and splinters (raw bones that are cut are more likely to crack which can cause all of the same dangers of those that are cooked).

Brightly colored snacks – Treats that are red, orange or otherwise brightly colored are often packed with heavy dyes that can cause an allergic reaction. For times that you do give a manufactured treat, it is best to stick with those that are white or lightly colored.

Wholesome Snacks for a Shih Tzu

Commercial treats *do* have their place; those that double as dental chews can play a role in good dental hygiene including removal of some plaque and to freshen breath and some wholesome made in the USA snacks can be part of a healthy diet; however adding in some veggies and fruit can make a big difference in a Shih Tzu's overall health. Do note that healthy food is only healthy when given in moderation. **Why Fruit and Vegetables?** These treats are great for many reasons including:

1- Studies show that diets rich in both fruits and vegetables reduces the risks of many types of cancer
2- They are packed with essential vitamins, minerals and fiber
3- They offer a good amount of nutrients in a small package; which is perfect for this toy breed

Best Fruits for a Shih Tzu- You'll want to stay away from the cores of fruit and there are some fruits such as grapes which must be avoided. However, the following are extremely safe and healthy without super high levels of natural sugar or sodium:

Pear slices - Given without the core, pear slices are an excellent snack for a Shih Tzu. You'll want to keep the skin on, since it is proven to have antioxidant and anti-inflammatory properties. The skin also has phytonutrients, which are a potentially anti-cancer acid. Health benefits include decreased risk of both stomach and esophageal cancer. This fruit is a great source of fiber, Vitamin C, copper, iron, potassium, manganese, magnesium and B-6. There are approximately 100 calories in a whole fruit. A good serving size is 1/4 of a pear, cut into slices.

Banana - Peeled banana slices are a great snack for a Shih Tzu. This can be given at room temperature or as frozen treats. This fruit is considered to be a very heart healthy food that is low in saturated fat and cholesterol. Studies show that it may reduce the risk of heart disease. Bananas are good for Shih Tzu because they have zero sodium and are packed with dietary fiber, Vitamin 6, Vitamin C, manganese and potassium. There is about 100 calories in a whole piece; 1/4 of a banana, given in slices is a good serving size with 25 calories.

Blueberries - A handful of blueberries are a terrific, healthy snack for a Shih Tzu puppy or dog. These have very high antioxidant properties. Antioxidants can prevent a wide range of illness, chronic diseases, boost the immune system and keep skin healthy. They are a great source of Vitamin K, Vitamin C, manganese, fiber and copper. Cold, fresh blueberries can be given to a Shih Tzu for a treat and they can be frozen as well (which can make them less messy). There are 85 calories in one full cup. A good serving size is 1/8 to 1/4 cup for a puppy and up to 1/3 cup for an adult. Also, this is a great ingredient to mix into whole, white yogurt which is super good for a Shih Tzu as well.

Raspberries - This fruit has antioxidant properties like that of the blueberry which can help prevent disease, keep the immune system strong and aid in keeping skin healthy which helps avoid skin problems. Raspberries contain good levels of Vitamin C, manganese, fiber, copper, Vitamin K, biotin and Vitamin E. Given fresh or frozen (which helps to hold the juices in) this healthy snack has 65 calories for one cupful.

Mango - As with all fruits, you will want to make sure that your dog does not ingest the seeds, as they are toxic. However, pieces of fresh mango are an excellent, healthy snack for Shih Tzu. These are considered to be a 'super fruit' with outstanding nutritional qualities. Mango can help protect dogs (and humans) from many cancers including breast, colon and prostate. It has antioxidant compounds that protect the body's immune system and skin. This snack is packed with Vitamin-A, B6 (which can reduce the chance of strokes), C, and E. It also has beta-carotene, alpha-carotene, and beta-cryptoxanthin and potassium (important for heart rate and blood pressure). One cup of mango chunks has 99 calories. A good serving size is 1/4 cup for puppies and up to 1/3 cup for adults.

Do NOT give: Grapes, raisins, current berries (or current jam) or cherries. These are toxic.

Best Vegetables for a Shih Tzu - Veggies are an important part of a dog's diet and you do not need to limit this to small pieces mixed into main meals. Offering a vegetable as a snack is a great habit to get into. Let's look at some good choices:

 Carrots – This is one of the healthiest foods for a Shih Tzu that is easy to serve as a snack and packed with flavor that most dogs love. This is a 'super food' that reduces cholesterol, can prevent heart problems and some cancers, helps with vision, boosts the immune system, helps with digestion and aids in clearing toxins from the body.

While you can give cooked carrots to a Shih Tzu, for snacks it is best to stick with raw ones which are easy to hand out and the crunchy texture is good for the teeth. Carrots are a great snack with beta-carotene, potassium, carbohydrates (the main source of energy for both canines and humans), fiber, Vitamin A, B6 and C. Shih Tzu love these so much that you'll have to show some restraint to keep your puppy or dog from eating too many! There are 25 calories in one medium carrot. A good serving size is 1/2 carrot for a puppy and 1 full carrot for a full grown adult Shih Tzu.

 Green beans - Whether you personally like these or not, many Shih Tzu love this as a healthy snack and offering this as a treat is a great way to help keep your dog in good health. This veggie has Vitamin C, beta-carotene, manganese and a wide range of flavonoids which all serve as antioxidants to help keep a Shih Tzu's immune system strong and ward off disease. In addition, studies show that eating green beans can have cardiovascular benefits. While you can cook them, raw green beans are a great snack for Shih Tzu and are easy to hand out. A serving of 10 has 17 calories. A good serving size for puppies is 3 to 4 and 5 to 7 for adults.

 Other veggies - There are some other vegetables that a Shih Tzu can safely eat, though they do not make for good snacks on their own. The following are best when mixed into the main food that you are feeding your Shih Tzu for meals: Cauliflower, celery, lettuce, cucumber, pumpkin, potato, sweet potato and spinach.

How Often to Give a Shih Tzu a Snack - **Puppies** - You'll want to give snacks to Shih Tzu puppies for 2 reasons: As reward for good behavior including housebreaking and obeying commands and for teething issues. If treats are given at any other time, they will lose their meaning and will no longer be helpful when you are training your puppy.

In regard to teething, frozen toys work well at most times, however offering frozen fruits or veggies or flavored ice cubes can be good when a puppy tires of his chew toys and needs a new distraction. You can flavor ice cubes by mixing some apple juice (real juice, not 'flavored') or low salt chicken broth. **Adults** - While it's hard to resist giving your Shih Tzu a snack every time he looks at you with those dancing, gorgeous eyes, it's best to reserve snacks for rewarding good behavior. As an adult, your Shih Tzu will be house trained and will follow commands; however dogs are happy when we reinforce the idea that they are doing well.

Give your Shih Tzu a healthy snack of a fruit or a vegetable whenever he goes to the bathroom in the designated area, listens to the 'Sit' command, does well on a walk by putting effort into heeling or otherwise displays good behavior.

The Best Manufactured Treats – There are oodles of treats to choose from and just like manufactured kibble, there are some horrible ones and some wonderful ones. The bad ones will be packed with chemicals (coloring, flavoring and preservatives) that can cause a dog to have reactions ranging from upset stomach to itchy skin. It is wise to stay away from snacks made in China; treats made in that country are connected to thousands of cases of illness with dogs (gastrointestinal disease, liver disease, kidney disease and urinary disease) and even deaths. One issue is that the labeling on snacks can trick you. You must take note of where the treat is *sourced from*, not just where it is packaged. Some brands try to deceive pet owners by having 'Packaged in the USA' in prominent lettering with 'sourced from China' in very small print. Look for made in the USA wholesome treats made with all-natural ingredients and no additives.

Two of the snacks we highly recommend are: Wellness WellBites Soft Natural Dog Treats (these are made in the USA, have no corn, soy, artificial colors or flavors and are made with real lamb, salmon, ground brown rice, oatmeal) and Mac & Buddy Mini Bones (some also double as dental treats; these are made in the USA with no by-products, artificial colors or flavors)

 For a full list of all recommended treats, look to 'Food and Snacks' in the Shih Tzu Specialty Shoppe. You can reach the Shih Tzu Specialty Shoppe by entering any page of the AllShihTzu website. Look to the navigation; it is in alphabetical order. Choose 'Shoppe'.

Teething, Chewing, Tugging, Nipping

Teething

The teething stage is perhaps the most challenging phase for a puppy owner and it certainly is not fun for the pup either. Teething is the process when a puppy's milk teeth fall out and new, adult teeth grow in. There is no way to avoid this stage; it's an inevitable part of growth. You can, however, take some comfort in the fact that it only lasts a few months.

During this time, a puppy's gums are intensely itchy. They are so itchy that the pup can be in a frenzied state with super strong urges to chew. And a pup may need to chew so badly to help relieve the itch, that he will chew anything. Nothing is off limits: Your shoes, your wallet, the carpeting, your pillow. Every single item that is within reach is fair game. It is also during this time that a puppy can learn terrible habits. If chewing is not redirected in a healthy way, a puppy can be 'taught' that he may chew what he desires. This can be dangerous for the Shih Tzu and can be destructive for your home.

While there are early bloomers and late bloomers, the typical age of teething starts between 4 and 6 months. Puppies almost always lose their teeth in a specific order: First the smaller front teeth come out, then the premolars, molars and finally the canine teeth. Frequently, the puppy's teeth will fall out while eating or playing, so they are often swallowed and you may not notice that it has happened. If at the age of 6 months, if your Shih Tzu puppy is still holding onto his puppy teeth, you should have a veterinarian perform a dental checkup.

The growth of adult teeth normally happens in this order:

- 4 Months old - the incisors begin to grow in
- 5 months old - the canine teeth begin to grow in
- 6 months old - the molars begin to grow in

Typically by 8 months old, all teeth have ascended and teething stops for most puppies. Do keep in mind that some puppies are late bloomers and teething may last a bit longer.

When an Adult Tooth Grows in Before a Puppy Tooth Falls Out - Sometimes, an adult tooth will begin to drop down while the puppy tooth is still in place. A puppy may then have a double row of teeth. This can happen with one tooth or with several. With the milk tooth in the way, the adult tooth may grow in crooked. This can cause:

- Discomfort

- Cuts to the inside of the puppy's mouth
- Eating and chewing problems

Therefore, if you notice this, you will want the veterinarian to take a look at your puppy's teeth. Most likely, the puppy tooth can be pulled out by the vet without the need for sedation. It is small and not anchored in deeply like adult teeth are. Even if an adult tooth began erupting out of place, with the milk tooth out of the way, it will often gradually migrate to where it should be.

How to Help Your Shih Tzu with Teething Discomfort - When a puppy is teething, he has a strong, uncontrollable urge to chew on anything and everything. This is one reason why an owner must puppy-proof the home, to keep any dangerous items away from the reach of a Shih Tzu puppy, such as electrical cords. Your puppy will not understand the difference between chewing on your favorite shoes and chewing on a teething toy. All the puppy knows is that chewing makes him feel better and helps to relieve the discomfort that his teeth are causing. There are some things that you can do to get through this phase without your puppy chewing up the house that will help your Shih Tzu at the same time.

• **Teething toys.** When given the right type of toy, a puppy will want to chew on that toy as opposed to household objects that do not offer the same type of relief. This is why having a good supply of quality teething toys can go a long way in stopping a puppy from destructive chewing. A teething toy is much different than a regular dog toy. And there are some really effective teething toys out there; you just have to know what to look for. A good teething toy will have one or both of the following elements:

1) Textures and projections to reach and soothe gums. Good teething toys will be made from quality materials that will massage the gums while not causing damage. Others will have soft projections – appropriately sized- so that a puppy can work the toy just the right way to reach a particular itch.

2) Designed to be frozen. When a puppy is teething, having a cold toy to chew on offers a lot of relief. Many teething toys are meant to be chilled. It is suggested to keep several in the freezer. A puppy will happily chew on these for a while. After an hour or so, you can swap a warmed one out for another frozen toy that is waiting in your fridge.

 If you are not sure which teething toys are best for your Shih Tzu, you can see the ones that we recommend in the Shih Tzu Specialty Shoppe. You can reach the Shih Tzu Specialty Shoppe by entering any page of the AllShihTzu website. Look to the navigation; it is in alphabetical order. Choose 'Shoppe'.

•**Ice cubes.** This will not only entertain you, but will help make your Shih Tzu puppy feel better. Most puppies find it amazingly fun to chase an ice cube around on a slippery floor, such as one made of linoleum or hardwood. The ice cube's cold temperature will offer relief to the puppy's gums.

Stopping the Destruction of Your Home - Since a teething puppy will mouth anything that he can, it is very important to go over the entire house at least once per day to remove anything that is within reach. Here are some things that you will want to do, to prevent damage to your belongings and to help prevent injury/choking hazards for your puppy.

1) All shoes, gym bags, purses, clothes, keys, books, remotes, etc. should be put out of reach during this 3 month phase. If it is not on the floor, your puppy can't chew on it. It's best to find new homes for any items normally left on floors, coffee tables or any other place that a puppy could reach. Keep in mind that a motivated puppy may be able to reach and jump higher than you think. Items can be placed on shelves, in closets and other high areas.

2) If your puppy needs to be left home alone during the day for a certain amount of time, you can do a couple of things to help:
•Obtain a small plastic cooler; the type that one may use to bring lunch to work. Be sure that there are no small pieces that the puppy can chew off. Leave the cooler in the puppy's area with the lid completely off. Place 4 to 5 frozen teething toys inside. The insulation of the bottom and sides of the cooler, along with the coldness of the frozen toys

will keep those toys cold for many hours.
•Be sure to confine your puppy to a gated off area or place the puppy inside a playpen; where the environment is safe and there is nothing dangerous that the puppy can chew on except for his teething toys.

3) Finally, do not allow a teething puppy to have access to the entire house. That is just asking for trouble. Keep your Shih Tzu near you via the umbilical cord method (one end of the leash connected to his harness and one end to you) or have him in his canine playpen or gated off area when you cannot keep an eye on him.

The Distract & Switch Technique - Whenever you see that your puppy is chewing on something other than his teething toys:

1) Make a loud noise, clap your hands or call out his name loud enough to get his attention.
2) Hand a teething toy to your puppy in exchange for the object that he is chewing on.
3) When your Shih Tzu puppy does begin to chew on his teething toy, be sure to give him praise – happy excited words and pats to show the puppy that he is chewing on something appropriate.

Deterrent Sprays -With your home properly 'puppy proofed', your Shih Tzu not allowed to roam the house at will and with a fantastic collection of teething toys, there still may be times when your Shih Tzu reaches something that you could not move out of the way, such as the legs of a table. In these cases, an apple-bitter deterrent spray may work. It is often only needed for a week or so; most puppies will learn to stay away from something after reaching it and tasting the detterent spray 3 to 4 times. Be sure to choose a non-toxic, non-chemical, natural bitter apple spray that is safe for canines.

Chewing

While much of the same can be said for 'chewing' as 'teething', it is a bit different since chewing habits can develop at any age and unlike teething, can last essentialy forever if an owner does not take steps to correct the behavior.

The #1 rule to remember is that a Shih Tzu cannot chew on things that he does not have access to. If you leave your shoes within reach and then are frustrated that your Shih Tzu keeps chewing on them, it's time to get into the habit of keeping your shoes out of reach. If you are terrified that your Tzu will electrocute himself by his habit of chewing on cords, those cords should be tucked away or encased with a cord protector. With this said, there are some things that a puppy may chew on that cannot be moved. This includes carpeting, the edge of a sofa, etc. There are some things that you can do:

1) When you are home with your puppy, keep him leashed to you by looping the end of the leash through a belt loop, if doing so will not hinder your activities. This way, you can catch your Shih Tzu right when he starts and correct the behavior.

2) If you are busy and not able to do this, you can gate off certain rooms and/or keep your Shih Tzu in his area (the gated off area or canine playpen that holds his bed and toys).

3) Any time you see your puppy start to chew on a non-toy item, clap your hands loudly; loud enough to startle him. You won't want to call out his name, because you'll want your pup to associate his name with good things. So clapping very loud usually works best.

4) As soon as he stops - wondering what in the world that loud noise was - offer a chew toy. Entice him with encouraging words and temptingly wave it in front of him. The moment he mouths the toy, praise him enthusiastically.

5) If a Shih Tzu is determined to keep chewing on a specific non-toy item and distraction does not work, it will be time to use a deterrent spray to spritz onto items that a Shih Tzu normally goes after. A deterrent spray can work well, but do keep in mind that oddly, some dogs – particularly older ones - do not mind the taste. Also, if it works, you must reapply it to maintain its effectiveness until the dog has learned to avoid the object. Be sure to choose a non-toxic, non-chemical, natural bitter apple spray that is safe for canines.

 If you would like to see recommended, quality, safe sprays, look under 'Toys – Chew | Teething | Boredom' in the Shih Tzu Specialty Shoppe. You can reach the Shih Tzu Specialty Shoppe by entering any page of the AllShihTzu website. Look to the navigation; it is in alphabetical order. Choose 'Shoppe'

Nipping

There are few things that are more frustrating than when a puppy - that is just so cute and adorable - nips at you. Whether or not it breaks the skin, this very serious behavior that needs to be addressed in a serious way. This is a behavior that often begins when a puppy is a newborn and is playing with his littermates. Sibling puppies will play and nip at each other. If a puppy nips too much or too hard, the 'victim' lets out a loud yelp. If the nip was strong enough, the puppy that was bit will ignore the offender. In many cases, the dam will also exclude him for a while.

Dogs - from birth - understand that they live in a pack. When the pack (siblings and sometimes the dam) ignores him - essentially banishing him - he quickly learns that it was wrong to nip. The banishment is temporary of course and after a few minutes he is allowed back in to play. If he nips too hard again, he is banished again and it continues this way until he learns that nipping simply will not be tolerated.

When a puppy transitions from his old home (dam and littermates) and moves to his new home, his 'pack' changes. However, it takes him a little while to figure this out. Within a few weeks, he learns that his humans and any other pets in the house are his pack. You will want to teach him to stop nipping in the same way that he learned before. Therefore, if he nips and his 'pack' ignores him and temporarily banishes him - or more specifically the leader of the pack (you) does so, he will get the message loud and clear. Here are some methods to send the message that it is not acceptable:

1) Say 'No!' loudly and firmly.

2) Immediately move yourself into a position of authority. If you were both sitting on the sofa, place your puppy onto the floor. If you were both sitting on the floor, immediately rise and either sit on the sofa or stand. The idea is to show that you are the leader and the one in charge by being physically superior.

3) You'll need to 100%, absolutely and without wavering, completely and utterly ignore the puppy. Any other humans in the house must join in as well because he won't learn a thing if he nips you but can move on to play and interact with another human. This type of ignoring must be very clear. Everyone must act as if the puppy is invisible. No speaking (it's suggested to not even speak with other people, in case the puppy thinks you are speaking to him), no looking at him…nothing.

4) It will take a puppy anywhere from 1 to 10 minutes to actually understand that he is being temporarily 'banished'. When he realizes it, he will become a bit nervous. He may whine for attention, bark and/or pace around. *Only then* will you know that it is working.

5) After a full 5 minutes of time in which the pup *knows* he is being ignored, speak to him but do not pick him up.

6) After a minute or so, only if he does not try to nip again, return to the exact same positioning as you both were when the first nip occurred. For example, both on the floor or the sofa, etc.

7) Do not act overly happy, but interact as you were before the nip. Only if he does not nip again, rev things up a notch by petting him and offering words of praise.

8) If at any time he nips again, immediately start over by physically positioning yourself higher and everyone ignores him.

9) Most puppies need to have this done 4 to 5 times to start to really believe that banishment happens due to nipping.

10) In extreme cases if an ignored puppy continues to nip at ankles, etc. and is really out of control, he should be placed into his area (gated off area, etc.) for a 'time out'.

Tugging

Some puppies grab onto their owner's clothes (normally the socks, sleeve or pants leg), hang on tightly with their teeth and tug. Even when told 'no', they may slink away only to return moments later and start again. It can become a bad attention-seeking habit and it is best to stop this behavior as soon as it starts. It should first be mentioned that some puppies do not know how best to communicate needs and may do this if they are hungry, thirsty, sleepy or need to go to the bathroom. Therefore, you should first check to see if all needs are met. Only if they are and a puppy still does this on a consistent basis, can you then feel confident that it is done to get your attention. Here are some things that will work in combination to help a puppy break this habit:

1) Completely 100% ignore him. You'll want to make tugging at your clothes as boring as possible for the puppy. If nothing at all happens, he will most often find something else to do. This means no talking, no looking, not even peeking at him from the corner of your eye. Now, many puppies will not immediately realize that they are being ignored. But, since puppies do crave attention, if they receive none, they will notice after 5 to 10 minutes. An owner must be 100% consistent…and even then, it may take 1 to 2 weeks for a puppy to 'get it'….there will be a moment when the dog metaphorically thinks, "Ah, ha!"… After that it may be hit or miss for a while. Some days (or times) a puppy will remember and behave as expected and other days (or times) a puppy can regress back into the behavior and he will need this training to be reminded what is expected of him.

2) The other method is to offer a distraction. You need to be careful, because you don't want your puppy to think that he is being rewarded for tugging at you. It's best if you can have another family member call the puppy away. If you are alone with your Shih Tzu, slowly walk to a toy, show it to your Shih Tzu and then toss it several feet away.

Grooming

Choosing Your Products

The products that you use to clean the coat will have a significant impact on the health of the hair and the skin. Shampoo can completely change how a Shih Tzu looks (either for the good or for the bad) and his ability to grow out his hair in the future. Choosing your shampoo, conditioner and coat spray is a vital part of grooming.

The wrong product can strip off the protective cuticles from the hair shafts and leave the

hair exposed. This will lead to breakage, static and dry hair that can make a Shih Tzu's coat look just terrible. The right shampoo will cleanse the coat of debris without damaging the cuticles of the hair and a great conditioner will moisturize. It will also not weigh down the coat. This will give your Shih Tzu beautiful, shiny, silky soft hair.

How Cheap Dog Shampoo Ruins the Coat - Inexpensive, generic shampoos are abrasive with improper PH balance. Each strand of hair is made of 3 parts: the inner fibers, the middle layer and the outer layer called the cuticle. The ingredients in inferior shampoos often clean so harshly, that the outer layer of the hair strands will be damaged (vulnerable to be utterly ruined the next time you bathe your Shih Tzu) or the outer protective coating will be stripped away that first time, leaving the coat dry & frizzed. In this weakened state with the outer layer partially or fully gone and the middle layer left partially or fully raw, the coat is then vulnerable to the sun, the wind, dry air, cold air, static and contact friction. Split ends can occur; once damaged hair has a split end, it will run up the length of the shaft. It will then either break off as it travels up or the hair will snap off at the root. Therefore, with inferior products, the hair will be exceedingly unhealthy.

Why You Shouldn't Use Human Shampoo - Human products are often just as bad as cheap canine products; even if they work great on human hair because a canine's needs are entirely different. It cleans the hair based on the thickness of human hair shafts and therefore can be detrimental to a Shih Tzu's coat. Just because the Shih Tzu breed has hair instead of fur does not change this fact. Some owners use baby shampoo, believing that it is gentle. While it may be a *tad* milder, it certainly does not moisturize as a quality canine shampoo can. Some owners use dandruff shampoo; this is not good for the Shih Tzu because the way it works is to strip the scalp of tiny pollutants (dirt, debris) and then scrubs off the skin flakes. A Shih Tzu needs a shampoo that is gentle to the skin - since skin health greatly affects hair health - while protecting the integrity of the hair.

The Best Shampoos for Shih Tzu – An appropriate, effective shampoo will work in many ways. It will:

1) Gently remove dirt and debris.
2) Gently remove body oils that have accumulated on the coat since the last bath.
3) Moisturize the skin without leaving a heaviness that can block skin pores.
4) Moisturize the hair without weighing the coat down.
5) Effectively prep the coat for the next product, which is the canine conditioner. It will rinse off well without leaving residue behind so that the Shih Tzu's hair can soak in the nutrients and moisture of the conditioner.

The Conditioner - Choose your Shih Tzu's conditioner with as much care as you choose the shampoo. The conditioner will surround each hair strand, placing down a layer of protection. A great product will do this without clogging the skin and without being heavy. Heavy conditioners will cause the coat to look greasy within a day or two, once body oils mix with the product. An effective, superior conditioner does its job and is rinsed out, leaving behind only its benefits and nothing else.

The Leave-in Product - Aside from the shampoo which is really the foundation of a healthy coat and the conditioner that comes after it, a good leave-in spray is highly suggested to spritz the coat each time you are going to brush it and to give it a light misting to protect from the damaging rays of the sun during hot weather and the harmful arid air of wintertime. Be sure that the product is effective, yet light since you will use it many times in-between baths and you do not want it to be a product that ends up clogging pores and making the coat oily with heaviness. An extra bonus will be if you choose one with a light, pleasant fragrance that keeps your Shih Tzu smelling nice.

Special Shampoos- If your Shih Tzu has exceedingly dry skin or has dandruff, you'll want to use shampoo that is designed to meet the needs of repairing these issues. Some owners hesitate to give baths when there is a problem or if the coat is not looking so great… they don't want to make things worse. However, if you feel confident that you have a great shampoo and aftercare products, you can then relax and feel confident about bathing your Shih Tzu, cleaning the coat and seeing the results.

 If you are not happy with what you are currently using and would like to see all of our recommended shampoo and grooming products, look to 'Grooming' in the Shih Tzu Specialty Shoppe. You can reach the Shih Tzu Specialty Shoppe by entering any page of the AllShihTzu website. Look to the navigation; it is in alphabetical order. Choose 'Shoppe'.

Baths

The Timing of Baths - A bath should be given every 3 weeks and any time that your Shih Tzu has gotten very dirty, for example if the dog runs through a muddy puddle, etc. This is not an arbitrary time frame. Even if a dog does not appear to be dirty, there will be a slow accumulation of body oils. These oils pick up tiny debris particles over the course of several weeks. At about the 3 week mark, the oils will need to be cleaned off of the dog. If a bath is not given, oil will clog skin pores and block proper air circulation. This leads to an oily coat, it affects skin & coat health and in time, becomes quite smelly. (The reason why you don't want to give too many baths (once a week) is because even with quality products, excessive bathing can dry out the skin. This can lead to itchy skin and other skin issues that can also affect the coat). Therefore, regardless of how clean a Shih Tzu looks, a bath should be given every 3 weeks.

Sink or Tub? Young puppies often do best in the kitchen sink. It is not so overwhelming and if a puppy can have good bathing experiences when young, he will be more prone to accept baths. If a puppy has a bad and frightening experience, this can lead to a dog that is fearful of water and makes giving baths exceedingly difficult. For these reasons, it is suggested to begin by giving baths in a clean kitchen sink and as your Shih Tzu grows and becomes accustomed to the water, the bubbles, the scrubbing and all that is involved, he can graduate to the bathtub when he is larger and used to bath time.

Steps for Bathing a Shih Tzu

1) Have all your needed items right by your side, so that you don't need to leave your Shih Tzu alone. This will include a comb & brush, a small wash cloth, cotton balls, shampoo, conditioner and a quality towel.

2) First comb (to check for tangles) and then brush the coat. The goal is to remove any dead hairs and to have the hairs of the coat separated in preparation for the bathing process.

3) Place a bath mat or towel in the base of the sink/tub to prevent the Shih Tzu from slipping.

4) Have the tub/sink filled with water before you place your Shih Tzu in, as running water can scare a dog. Take care that the water is warm; not too cool and not too hot. Test it with your inner wrist. Cool water will give your Shih Tzu the chills and hot water not only can scald your dog but also triggers the hair cuticles to close, which means that your quality products cannot work as effectively.

5) You can place cotton in your Shih Tzu's ears to prevent water from entering the ear canal. You will tear away some cotton from a cotton ball to do this. Do not place the cotton deep.

6) Wet the coat by using a small container to scoop water onto all areas of the body or by using a nozzle. At first, water may roll off the coat and body oils may prevent water from getting through the coat, so you will need to make sure that the hair is thoroughly soaked before adding any shampoo. *Jiggermeister aka Jiggy, getting a warm & sudsy bath in the kitchen sink. Photo courtesy of Shih Tzu Garden, Where Exquisite Puppies are Grown!*

7) Do not be shy when using the shampoo. You want to use enough so that every area of the Shih Tzu is cleansed in the same way. Go over every single area of the body including arm pit area and paws. For the underbelly and genital area, use your soft washcloth.

8) Scrub well and down to the skin. During the 3 weeks or so that you last gave your Shih Tzu a bath, body oils have been slowly accumulating. You will want to scrub those away so that you can 'start fresh'. When they are not removed, this is when pores become blocked and a bad smell can develop.

9) Rinsing is very important. Even with a terrific shampoo, soap residue left behind will cake on the skin. It will then mix with body oils and begin to clump. Using a nozzle works well to reach down through the coat to make sure all the shampoo is properly rinsed out.

10) Using a wash cloth, you will want to go over the Shih Tzu's face, carefully wiping around the eyes.

11) Now it is time for the conditioner. Use a generous amount. The goal will be to cover all areas, from root to tip. Massage this in for several minutes (2 to 5). When you rinse, do rinse well.

12) Remove your Shih Tzu and wrap him in a quality towel.

13) Remove the cotton from the ears. Using a thin, clean washcloth, dry the outer ears and the inner ears (as far in as you can comfortably go).

* Aside from baths, we also recommend daily touch-ups. You will want to use canine tushie wipes to 'spot clean' the genital area and surrounding hair if there is any back-splash of urine, as this can make the coat quite stinky, discolor the hair & be very uncomfortable for the Shih Tzu. Also, quality canine body wipes can be used to touch-ups areas that are a bit dirty (anything from muddy paws to bits of food on the chest). And to prevent tear stains, wipe the eye area at least once per day with a quality canine eye wipe. **So, 3 types of wipes:** Tushie, body & eye. This, along with your brushings (and using a leave-in spritz) will keep your Shih Tzu looking great & smelling fresh for those 3 weeks between baths.

Jiggy dried and looking adorable, right after his bath. Photo courtesy of Shih Tzu Garden, Where Exquisite Puppies are Grown!

Drying the Coat

Short coats – You are lucky, the drying process is very easy. Towel dry your Shih Tzu by scrunching and not rubbing. Then, spritz the coat lightly with your leave-in product (or spray some into your hands) and tossle this through the coat. You can allow your Shih Tzu to air dry from this point.

Medium coats – The process is very similar, except that you should run a comb through the coat to ensure that there are no tangles after the bath. Next, towel dry by scrunching and not rubbing. Then, spritz the coat lightly with your leave-in product. Spray this about 1 inch from the roots, and using your comb distribute this to the tips of the hair. You can allow your Shih Tzu to air dry.

Long coats - It is *crucial* to dry a long coat in the right way. While we do not recommend it with any length coat, for long coat especially, **never, ever scrub** with a towel to dry the Shih Tzu. It can completely ruin a coat. Always srunch, dab, pat and blot to soak up excess water. You will then want to spray with a leave-in conditioner and comb through the coat. The steps are:

1.   Dab and blot the coat.
2.   Mist with detangler/leave-in conditioner. Spray this 1/2 inch from the roots of the hair and use your comb to distribute the product down to the tips. You may want to spray some leave-in into your hand and 'scrunch' the tips to moisturize them.
3.   Comb through the entire coat, separating hairs so that they dry quicker.
4.   Allow to air dry for 5 to 10 minutes
5.   Blow-dry on a *very low* setting to finish things off, misting a bit as you go and using a quality pin brush, as you

go….Lift the hairs with the brush to blow dry to dry the underneath hairs, then brush down in long motions. If the setting on the blow dryer is too high, it can severely dry out the coat and the skin. Additionally, if set too high, it can cause burns to a Shih Tzu's sensitive skin. Done this way, you should be done in about 3 to 4 minutes. Do NOT over blow-dry.

Brushing

There are 3 reasons why you want to brush a Shih Tzu on a regular basis:

1) To prevent tangles (also called mats or knots). This can be an issue for all but the shortest of coats. Once a tangle forms, it can be extremely difficult to remove without doing some sort of damage to the coat. If a tangle is not removed it can twist tight and pinch the skin. It can also grow, pulling in surrounding hairs. There is no end, really, to how large a tangle can get. Dogs that are neglected and find their way into shelters often have their entire coat tangled into one matted mess, which then needs to be completely shaved off. The more often you comb & brush the coat, the better the chances will be that you can discover a tangle while it is still tiny and easy to take care of. Do note that you may not see tangles and may not know a tangle exists until you are combing and find one.

2) To pull out dead hairs. It is not true that the Shih Tzu does not shed. All dogs shed. All humans shed! The hair growth cycle is a continuous one. Each hair has a phase of: grow, rest, fall. There will always be at least 1/3 of the hairs that are nearing or are in the 'fall' stage. Only a portion of those will fall off the dog and onto the floor. A certain amount will fall back into the coat. When *this* happens, the dead hairs will either get weaved into other hairs or will end up near the skin, which blocks proper air circulation. So, a huge part of brushing is to pull out those fallen hairs.

3) To keep skin and coat healthy via massage, debris removal and spritz addition. Though you will brush your Shih Tzu to keep the hairs separated to avoid tangles and to keep the coat clean of fallen hairs, the very act of brushing has *these* benefits as well. As the brush glides over the skin, it stimulates hair follicles and distributes natural body oils which is great for both skin and coat. It also removes all sorts of very tiny debris that you really can't see but is there. These will be miniscule particles that the coat picks up over the course of the day(s). Finally, since using a light mist of a leave-in product is *so* vitally important to coat health (it protects the hair from split ends, summer sun & winter cold, contact friction and arid air) and since it only lasts for 2 to 3 days, brushing is your opportunity to refresh the coat with the spritz.

So for these reasons, we highly recommend brushing your Shih Tzu every other day. At the very minimum every 3 days. And brushing every day (using the right products of spray, comb & quality brush) can only be beneficial. The more you brush, the cleaner the coat, the fewer tangles, the healthier the skin and hair.

Note: If there was just **one** 'brushing rule' it would no doubt be: Do not brush a dry coat. In some steps, you will mist the tool and in others you will mist the coat. Brushing a dry coat *one time* won't ruin a Shih Tzu's coat, but doing this on a regular basis can do quite a bit of damage. The hair can get static problems, which creates split ends. This in turn, causes the coat to look frizzy and hairs will break off.

To keep the hair healthy and looking as it should, use a *lightweight* leave-in conditioner spritz each time you do a full body brushing. Do NOT spray a ton of product on your Shih Tzu or on the grooming tools. A very light misting is all that is needed. With leave-in spritz, it is not 'the more the better'. Have you ever walked outside on a warm summer day and it was just *barely* raining? There was a mist, so slight, that it refreshed your face but did not make your hair wet? That is what you should envision when using your leave-in.

The Best Combs & Brushes – There are 4 that you will want to have:

1. A 2-level steel comb (7 and 1/2 inch is a good size). For all but very closely shaved coats, you'll want your first step to be a combing over the entire coat. Use the side with the wider teeth for going over the coat and use the side with the closer teeth for the facial areas.

2. A mat-remover tool, if you do find a tangle. While you can work some tangles out with your hands (and a lot of conditioner – details at the end of this section), a mat-removing tool can be a great help to easily remove a mat that would otherwise send you rushing to the groomer's.

3. A pin brush. The best brush for a Shih Tzu will be a quality pin brush and please note that in general pin brushes can range from terrible to fantastic. ***Qualities of a great pin brush:***

- *High quality pins* – Pins on inferior brushes will bend and/or recess back into the cushion. Once either of these two things occurs, the brush will no longer be effective.
- *Superior pin heads* – A huge factor is the quality of the tips of the pins. This is the element that makes contact with the skin and hairs of the Shih Tzu.
- *Tension* – Too strong of tension in a brush can cause discomfort and irritation to a Shih Tzu's skin. Yet, if the brush tension is too weak, it will not offer proper pressure as you brush down the coat.
- *Sizing* – You will want the brush to be sized correctly to effectively reach all areas of the body, gliding from one spot to the next. You'll also want it to feel good in your hand.

4. Boar Bristle Brush - While a superior pin brush will do everything you want it to do, if your Shih Tzu has a long show coat and you want to make some finishing touches, you will find that a quality boar bristle brush is just the tool for that final sweep around the coat. You will still do element 1 (comb), element 2 (brushing with the pin brush) and element 3 (the spritz we will discuss next), but the boar bristle brush (which we will call 'element 2.5') can have a smoothing effect which adds a nice, finishing touch.

Brushing & Combing Instructions

1) Be sure to remove the collar and/or harness before doing a full-body brushing. You won't want these accessories getting in the way of being able to do nice, long strokes over the coat.

2) Choose a location in which both you and your Shih Tzu will be comfortable. You want to feel relaxed and make this a nice bonding experience for you and your Shih Tzu. Many dogs simply love being brushed & combed, it is like getting a massage! So, if you send out the right vibes, your Shih Tzu will pick up on that. Brushing can be those 10 minutes or so every other day that you and your Shih Tzu have special 'we' time.

3) First, mist the comb using your leave-in. (do not spritz the hair yet; as it will be more difficult to do the next step with moist hair). Comb through the coat. Go slow if you are not 100% positive that the coat is tangle free. The goal with this first combing is to check for tangles and also to separate the hairs to prepare them for being brushed. Do not ignore any areas. Comb through the entire body, including the tail. Use the wide half of your steel comb for the main body and the finer side for more delicate areas like the paws and face. Every 10 swipes or so, re-mist your comb.

4) It is now time to do a thorough brushing with your quality pin brush. This is the fun part, because you will see the coat gradually coming to life, looking luscious and more beautiful each moment. It is now that you will mist the coat itself with your leave-in product. Spritz near the root and brush that down to the tips. Go section by section.

5) You are almost done! Use the comb to make any final touches or the boar bristle brush for long-coat final touches.

Removing Tangles

A tangle should never be left alone; things will quickly turn from bad to worse. If you find a tangle (mat, knot) you have 2 choices: You can try to work it with your hands to see if you can untangle the knot or you can clip it off with the proper de-matting tool. You may hesitate to clip it off, and that is understandable. You may worry that clipping off too many will ruin the coat. If you are trying to grow a long show coat, you are right. However, if you routinely brush your Shih Tzu, his tangles will be few & far in between. Clipping off one tiny knot will not even be noticeable.

In regard to a 'detangler spray', this is the same thing as a leave-in conditioner and the terms are interchangable. A product labeled as a 'detangler' is simply a coat conditioner spritz. There is no product that will magically loosen a knot. Nothing will work better than the quality leave-in conditioner that you already have for your Shih Tzu. There is no need to buy any additional 'detangle' products.

Therefore, if you want to attempt to work out a tangle by hand, cover both of your hands – liberally – with your Shih Tzu's leave-in . Just as you would try to work out a shoelace knot or work out a piece of gum from your child's hair, with your hands and the tangle super slippery, do be patient while you try to untangle the mat. It will be up to you regarding how long you work to try to remove a tangle. Just remember that you have nothing to feel bad about if you are a conscientious owner who brushes on schedule and every now and then (twice per year, perhaps), you need to snip off a tiny tangle.

Coat Length/Hair Styles

While a Shih Tzu certainly looks elegant with a long show coat, most pet owners opt for a short to medium puppy cut. Show coats are notoriously difficult to keep 'perfect' and taking care of such a hairstyle is often too much work for a typical owner to keep up with. While we do focus on pet Shih Tzu rather than show dogs, we can tell you that 95% of our Members have Shih Tzu with puppy cuts or 'medium' cuts in which the coat is moderately long, but not so much that it reaches the floor.

When you don't shave the coat short, you can experiment a lot...And if you have shaved it close, the coat will grow relatively quickly, thus allowing you to try out different styles soon after. Many choose a style based on the home environment and the normal day to day activities of the family.... For example, longer styles will need more grooming. They will also need more upkeep with trimming done more often. This is a good choice if you want the hobby of grooming your dog, which some people find to be rather fun; and of course, it's needed for show. Though it's time consuming, no one can argue how beautiful the dog looks in a longer cut. With this said, it really is an option for those who have consistent, long-term time to put into it.

For those with active dogs that play outside a lot or for owners who do not have the time to devote to longer styles, a shorter Shih Tzu haircut may be in order. Close puppy cut options will not develop as many tangles and the dog will stay cleaner, in general. A puppy cut can start to grow out and need some shaping every 4 to 5 months.

Since this breed can have very short hair, long hair and every length in between, you may wish to opt for a unique style that shows off all of these possibilities. Image below, the body is shaved short, legs are flared and crown and ear hairs are allowed to remain long. We should note that while this looks adorable, the tips of the flared legs of this cut tend to get dirty rather quickly.

Cuts, Clips & Trims - Unless you have a LOT of experience in grooming and cutting, it is highly recommended to have a professional dog groomer do this. It is always best to shop around first. You have every right to have a short interview with the groomer before any decisions are made.

It will be helpful to ask him or her if they have any experience in giving Shih Tzu the haircut that you have chosen...If they have not, try to judge their confidence in being able to do so. While they may not have given the cut to a Shih Tzu, they may have done so to a different breed, so it can be helpful to ask about that if they do not offer the information....and certainly ask to see pictures.

Speaking of pictures, it is always highly recommended to bring in a photo of the desired cut...As much as you can explain it to the groomer, a photo speaks 1000 words...and it will make this a much easier job for him or her if they have a clear photo to go by.

Another thing to remember is to always get a style for your dog not only based on what looks beautiful but also based on what you can afford to maintain...and how much time you have to properly groom if it is to have pieces of longer hair that will need to be brushed out to avoid mats and tangles. Keep in mind that squared off or layered styles will need more upkeep with more touch-up trims...while simple Puppy Cuts can be left to grow out for quite a while and will still look nice as long as proper combings are done to keep it tangle free and baths are given.

Age of a Shih Tzu's First Haircut - We recommend waiting until the adult coat has grown in. When this breed is very young, it will hold a puppy coat, which is composed of finer, thinner hairs. The changeover to adult coat happens gradually, an owner may not notice until one day they suddenly notice that the dog has a thicker coat. The Shih Tzu will eventually have a nice, full coat of hairs, thicker and with more follicles per square inch than when younger. By the 7 or 8 month mark, you should start to notice a change in the coat. By 10 months, a puppy cut can start to be grown out with the goal of a long show coat. It is at this 10 month mark that you may wish for your Shih Tzu to have his first hair cut to tidy up the puppy cut.

Touch-ups – Check for hairs that grow out passed the paw pads and trim these as needed.

Topknots & Bows

By Wendy Wu, Founder of NYBowtique

Introduction to Dog Bows - Aside from clothing, a great way to accessorize your Shih Tzu is with dog bows. This is a quick and inexpensive way to give your pooch some much needed style, especially during the summer months, when clothes aren't an immediate option. Unbeknown to many dog owners, dog bows can come in many different styles, shapes and materials. There are single loop bows, double loop with flag back bows and bows that display Swarovski crystals, gem stones, mini roses, rhinestones or even diamonds! And of course, bows come in many different sizes; for larger dogs, double loop dog bows work well. For petite dogs, single loop dog bows are ideal.

There are many places where you can get your hands on some dog bows. Pet boutiques usually carry a limited number of them, while groomers might even provide you with bows for free after an appointment. There are many online shops selling custom hand-crafted dog bows, specifically for long haired Shih Tzu. One site that stands out is NYBowtique. Our inventory consists of a wide range of designs to choose from including casual to glamorous and everything else in between.

Step-by-Step Instructions –

1. Start by gathering the hair right above the temple of your dog's eyes toward the middle of the scalp, be careful not to pull too hard as that could stretch your Shih Tzu's eye area. If a dog feels comfortable with his bow, sturdy but not overly tight, he will be more accepting when you wish to place a bow on him.

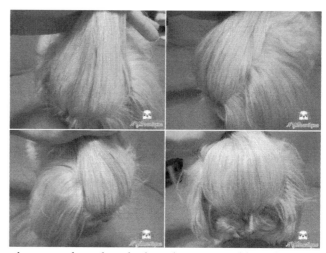

2. Tie the hair with a snag-free elastic band so it won't hurt your Tzu when it's time to take off the band. You can purchase these bands at beauty supply stores. This will keep the hair in place and technically can be worn alone; but the bow is to cover this and add a pretty touch.

3. You can now create either a flat or puff ball look. If your prefer your Tzu to have a flatter look, use the snag-free band to tie her hair and pass the band through as many times as it takes until it stays in place. If you prefer your Tzu with a puff ball look, tie the hair and pass the band through as many times just up until the last pass. At this point leave the band mid-way to create a puff ball look. Adjust the ball as needed.

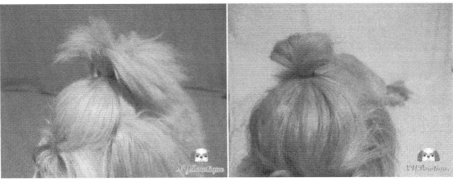

4. Now it's time to place the bow.

5. When you have chosen the dog bow of the day, slip your index finger and thumb inside the latex-free bands of the bow and gently place over the tied hair.

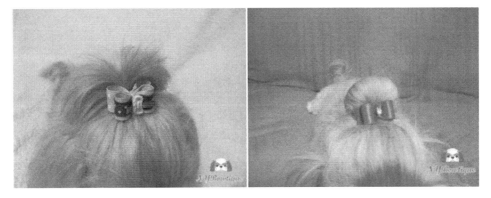

Tips for bows on puppies - One strategy to get your pup to enjoy wearing a bow is to put it on right before you take him for a walk. He will be more interested in seeing and sniffing the earth than to pay attention to the new object on his head. Using classical conditioning is a great way to teach puppies. They will associate a bow on their head with fun in the sun!

A word about bow safety- While there are many dog bows to choose from on the market today, we have to be careful to choose bows that are made of high quality material, are latex-free and do not contain wire-framed ribbons. It is also important to be cautious when buying bows with barrettes. While they may seem convenient, barrettes can be a choking hazard if your Tzu enjoys chewing on things. NYBowtique carries a full line of bows that fit all of these criteria's and can help accessorize your Shih Tzu in a safe and stylish way. We even take custom design orders!

Nails & Dewclaws

Nails Nail trimming needs to be done - on average - every 3 months. Some Shih Tzu have nails that grow faster and some slower. However, it is important to be aware of this grooming need. If nails are left to grow they can become ingrown or they may be filed down when the dog walks, which will cause uneven, unhealthy nails. You may wish to have a dog groomer take care of this or you may wish to do this at home. Many owners shy away from this task as it can be tricky for a dog to sit still and others are afraid of cutting into the quick. The quick is a vein that runs down the center of each nail; if it is accidentally cut it can cause quite a bit of bleeding. Having a solution such as 'Quik-Stop' can stop bleeding in most cases.

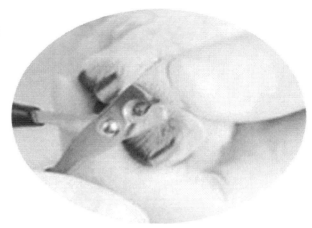

Many owners find grinders much easier to use than clipping tools; they work as mechanical files that quickly grind the nail down without having to cut it at all. The pros are that this is less invasive and very fast. The con is that it can be noisy and some dogs do not like the sound. All in all, we do recommend grinding as opposed to cutting since the benefits outweigh the cons.

If your Shih Tzu runs when it is time to trim the nails, you can begin by just training your dog to get into the position of trimming, without actually doing so. You should begin by training your Shih Tzu to lie still in the position needed to best trim the nails.

This can be done by laying your dog on his side and leaning over his body. Gently hold his paw and touch the nails. If your dog lies still, give lots of praise to let him know that he is being a good dog. As time goes by, and your Shih Tzu seems comfortable with lying down and allowing you to touch his nails, you can then carefully trim them.

You will want to cut/file right were th 'nail hook' appears (the area where the nail begins to slightly curve). Only cut/file very small bits at a time, 2 millimeters or so. Each time you trim a piece, stop to take a look at your Shih Tzu's nail. As you slowly cut/file away small pieces, you will eventually see a gray or pinkish oval of color in the nail. This is your sign to stop.

If you find that your Shih Tzu just won't sit still or that you dread filing or clipping the nails, it is best to bring your Shih Tzu to the groomer for this 4-times-per year grooming task. If you think that you may want to try a grinder instead of clipping, we highly recommend the Dremel 7300-PT 4.8-Volt Pet Grooming Kit. It is sized nicely for a toy breed, has 2 rotation speeds so that you can file in stages and the sanding band that comes with it is perfect for most Shih Tzu. If you have a smaller Shih Tzu (6 lbs. or under), you may want to additionally obtain the 100 to 120 grit sanding band.

Dewclaws - Dewclaws are the extra nails that are located very high on the side of the dog's paw. They are so high, that you could describe them as being located on the dog's ankle. With young puppies, these are simply very small, soft nails. As the Shih Tzu grows older, these slowly grow into what can be described as an extra thumb.

Breeders often have a Tzu's dewclaws removed to help prevent issues that they can cause. Because of where they are located, a dog can easily catch the dewclaw on fabric, the sofa, carpeting, etc. This can cause a lot of pain and it takes a long time for the claw to heal if it is ripped in this way. If dewclaws are not removed, in time they may begin to grow jagged and crooked. This, also, can cause discomfort to a dog.

When removed at a very young age, dewclaw removal is a simple process. It is often done by the veterinarian at the very young age of 3 or 4 days old, when it can be easily slipped out of the paw. When an adult Shih Tzu has his dewclaws removed, they are not soft, pliable nails any longer. What can be described as an extra 'toe' actually grows in the area of the dewclaw. The 'toe' is made of flesh, muscles, ligaments and tissue just like any other part of the Shih

Tzu. Therefore, removal is considered an amputation. The dog is put under anesthesia to have this done. Since the Shih Tzu is very sensitive to anesthesia, it is best to avoid having this done unless the benefits of surgery outweigh the discomfort a Shih Tzu is having with a dewclaw.

If you are planning on showing your Shih Tzu in a conformation event and the dewclaws are intact and not causing problems, this is just fine. For AKC show, there is no preference; dewclaws may or may not be intact.

However, 2 elements should be noted:

1- When you are trimming the nails, do not forget about the dewclaw. If left to grow, it will often grow very long and back into the dog's leg. This will be painful for the Shih Tzu and even worse having it removed.

2- Be careful when brushing your Shih Tzu if dewclaws remain. Sometimes it is easy to forget that a dewclaw is on the hind legs and can be caught in the brush. Always take care to go around this. Hairs right around the dewclaw can be carefully combed.

Dental Care

Overview Taking proper care of your Shih Tzu's teeth, will without doubt, extend his life span. This breed is prone to tooth decay. Chewing on treats – even dental treats – is not sufficient to keep teeth clean. A buildup of tarter and plaque can lead to very serious issues. Tooth decay can cause:

• Bacteria to build up and enter into the bloodstream - it can reach the liver, heart and brain. Tooth infection can kill!
• Loose teeth
• Pain and eating problems
• Infection that spreads up into the sinus cavities

While some dental chews will remove a small amount of plaque, it is nothing compared to what a quality brush and paste will remove. *Puppies* need to have their teeth brushed to keep gums healthy and to prevent decay and infection from spreading down deep to where adult teeth are waiting to erupt. *Adults* need routine brushings to keep plaque from building up. Once it does, it becomes hardened into what is normally called tarter or calculus. This then forms an impenetrable layer on the tooth, allowing bacteria to eat away underneath.

When Dental Care Should Begin - Dental care should begin the moment you bring your puppy home. However any dog of any age will benefit from having routine at-home brushings and cleanings. When an owner cleans a puppy's teeth, this sets up a good foundation for a lifetime of good dental hygiene and allows the pup time to become accustomed to having teeth cleaned. If you bring home an older Shih Tzu, one of the first things that you should do is to bring your dog to the vet. Not only for a medical checkup, but for a dental checkup. It does not matter if you received your Shih Tzu from the best breeder in the world or rescued your dog from a shelter...you will have no idea of the status of the dog's teeth and what type of dental care was previously given.

How Often To Brush a Shih Tzu's Teeth -To ensure excellent health and to avoid health issues to the best of your ability, a Shih Tzu should have their teeth brushed 1 time per day. Dogs behave better when they have schedules. Therefore, it will help to choose a certain time of the day which will be 'Brush the Teeth Time'. Please do not make the mistake of thinking that brushing your dog's teeth once a day is 'overkill'; it is not. It will save a dog from years of pain, infections, tooth loss and can extend your dog's life span.

Professional Cleanings - When you brush your Shih Tzu's teeth at home, this will remove plaque. A professional cleaning done at the veterinarian's office will remove tarter, calculus and other elements that could not be cleaned at home. This is known as a 'Full Dental'. This is usually done with the dog under anesthesia. Dogs are pre-screened to make sure that they are healthy enough for anesthesia, and depending on how susceptible they are to plaque buildup and decay, will need this type of cleaning every 12 to 24 months. The veterinarian will:

• Take x-rays to assess the health of all of the teeth and bones of the mouth.
• Flush the mouth with a solution to kill the bacteria.
• Clean the teeth with handheld and ultrasonic scalers. All calculus is removed from above and below the gum line.
• Use a disclosing solution to show any areas of remaining calculus which are then removed.
• Polish the teeth to remove microscopic scratches.
• Inspect each tooth and the gum around it for any signs of disease.
• Flush the mouth, again, with an antibacterial solution.
• Optionally, apply a dental agent to impede plaque buildup.
• Record any abnormalities.
• Determine the best follow-up and home dental care program for your dog.

How Effective are Dental Wipes? If it is your only tool available, wipes are certainly better than nothing.

However, nothing can beat a quality toothbrush and the right paste to effectively clean a dog's teeth and gums. Wipes are good for supplemental cleanings, however they will not have the abrasive quality that is needed to actually scrub away the particles that will develop into plaque.

What About Finger Brushes? Similar to wipes, if this is your only means of brushing, it is better than nothing. However, it will not have the density that a good brush will have. Additionally, the bristles are only on one side, which will lead to longer sessions to properly reach all surfaces. These can be very helpful for dogs that need to slowly become accustomed to cleanings. These small plastic coverings with imbedded bristles (usually very short and not effective for long-term use) slip over your index finger, allowing you to then 'brush' the teeth. These can be a good starting point for some dogs that need time to get used to having their teeth touched.

Toothbrushes When you are choosing a toothbrush, you'll want to keep a few things in mind:

1) Size - One of the most common issues that prevents an owner from being able to properly brush their dog's teeth is wrong sizing of the brush. You'll want a handle that allows you to have a solid grip and importantly, the size of the head which holds the bristles will need to fit inside your Shih Tzu's mouth with enough room for you to maneuver it over and around his teeth. Since brushing all exposed sides of the teeth and angling down toward the gum line is important for proper cleaning, you'll want a bristle head that is shaped and sized for toy breed dogs.

2) Firmness - Another common element that gets in the way of a brush doing its intended job is that over time, it becomes soft from use. Even if you chose the best brush for your puppy or dog, every 3 to 4 months, it should be replaced. If you use 3 to 4 new toothbrushes each year (a very small expense, relatively speaking), you'll be using a brush with proper firmness.

3) Shape - Your Shih Tzu probably doesn't have tons of patience while you brush his teeth. Therefore, the best toothbrush will be one that does the job as fast as possible. Brushes that have 3 sides (the bristles will scrub over all 3 exposed sides of the teeth simultaneously) work excellent. In addition, if you obtain the right one, these heads will be angled at 45 degrees, which is optimal for correctly cleaning the gum line.

Toothpaste Choosing the right toothpaste for your Shih Tzu is a vital part of dental hygiene. Using human products is a serious misstep that can cause dangerous toxicity. And using a cheap paste can greatly decrease the effectiveness of the brushing. **Why human toothpaste is so bad** - Some owners make the mistake of thinking that warnings to stay away from human products is part of a marketing plan to see more canine-specific products; however this is not the case at all. There are 2 ingredients in human toothpaste that can cause terrible poisoning with dogs and for toy breeds like the Shih Tzu, not much is needed:

X Fluoride - This chemical was first used mainly as an insecticide to kill bugs and as a poison to kill rodents (mainly rats). As preposterous as it may sound, it is a by-product of manufacturing (chiefly of the aluminum, copper and iron industries) and in the 1930's when governments did not have a good idea how to possibly dispose of it, they decided to add it to water supplies and toothpastes since in low quantities it appeared to help with tooth decay. During the 1970's and 80's dentists would put gobs of fluoride in mouth-guard type devices and have children sit for 30 to 60 minutes to allow the fluoride to sink into the teeth.

Studies have proven that when you consume too much it has devastating consequences. *Two things to note: #1,* Dogs swallow toothpaste, thus they WILL ingest it and **#2** the line of 'how much is too much' is blurry at best. It can cause teeth to weaken to the point of crumbling away, it can damage the musculoskeletal and nervous systems and for humans, it causes close to 10,000 bone cancer deaths per year in the US. Shocking? Yes. A reason to never brush your Shih Tzu's teeth with human toothpaste? Absolutely.

X Xylitol - If reason #1 was not enough, the other ingredient that can be harmful is xylitol, which can cause dangerous drops in blood sugar levels and can cause liver disease.

What makes a certain toothpaste good for a Shih Tzu? You might be wondering if brushing with water would do the same thing as using some paste and if dogs really need canine toothpaste. The answer is that the correct paste does serve a few important purposes. **1)** It will have mild abrasives that will work in conjunction with the brush to remove tiny particles of debris and bacteria. 2**)** It will work to remove staining from the enamel of the teeth **3)** It will have a pleasing taste (to a canine) that will play a huge role in how accepting the puppy or dog is to having his teeth brushed. A nice added bonus is that quality toothpaste will also temporarily freshen a Shih Tzu's breath.

 If you would like to see our recommendations for toothpaste, toothbrushes & dental treats, look to 'Dental Care' in the Shih Tzu Specialty Shoppe. You can reach the Shih Tzu Specialty Shoppe by entering any page of the AllShihTzu website. Look to the navigation; it is in alphabetical order. Choose 'Shoppe'.

How to Brush a Shih Tzu's Teeth - For dogs that are not used to this, you may wish to begin by allowing your Shih Tzu to become used to having your finger in his mouth. For the first week, set aside 10 minutes per day to have your dog sit down with you. Rub your finger all along his teeth. Be sure to touch all of them. When your Shih Tzu sits still and behaves, reward with happy praise, hugs and a small treat. You may find that a young puppy is very hyper and will not want to sit still. However, if you remain consistent and do this each day, your Shih Tzu will learn that when you say "Tooth Time" or whatever cue you do use, that it is time to sit close to you and have his teeth touched.

After a week or so, begin using the tooth brush. You will put a small dab of canine toothpaste on this (about the size of a penny). Be sure to brush all of the teeth and all sides of them. A good scrubbing takes about 2 to 3 minutes. This is such a short amount of time for such huge health benefits. While it is perfectly safe for a Shih Tzu to swallow quality canine paste, you may wish to wipe excess paste away with a clean piece of gauze.

Scraping a Shih Tzu's Teeth - You may wish to scrape your Shih Tzu's teeth yourself, instead of having this done at the veterinarian's clinic. Many breeders opt to do this at home due to the cost of having 5 to 10 dogs professionally done. You may choose to do this anywhere from once every month to every six months; the more often this is done, the easier it is, as there is less buildup.

The process of scraping is very similar to when humans use a plaque scraper. Some owners actually opt to use a human plaque scraper on their dogs, which can be purchased at any store in the dental care section. However, there are scrapers made specifically for toy breed dogs. This is recommended, since it will be sized correctly for the Shih Tzu. The dog should sit down (and should already be used to having his teeth touched from the daily tooth brushings). As you carefully scrape each tooth (be sure to get as close to the gum line as possible), use a paper towel or gauze to wipe the plaque from the scraper. Since your Shih Tzu will be trying very hard to behave and sit nicely while you do this, when your dog sits still for this, give a small treat as a reward every few minutes.

Once the teeth are scraped, you should follow up with a brushing. And then of course, with a yummy dog treat to reward your Shih Tzu for being so good. Even if scraping at home, do be sure to bring your Shih Tzu for dental checkups with the veterinarian on a regular basis, suggested at least once every 2 years.

A Word on Food & Treats - Long ago, it was thought that feeding a dog dry dog food or hard dog treats was sufficient for cleaning the dog's teeth. We now know that this is not true, they can *help* but brushing still needs to be done. Quality dental treats will also encourage strong teeth and jaw bones. We recommend routinely giving your Shih Tzu dental treats. Some taste just as yummy as a 'real' treat and your Shih Tzu will look forward to receiving it. One that we love is Old Mother Hubbard Mother's Solutions Minty Fresh Breath Natural Crunchy Dog Treats, and you can see all recommendations in the Shih Tzu Specialty Shoppe.

Hair and Coat

General Hair Growth Help

Please note that this section refers to general hair growth help. If your Shih Tzu has large balding areas and is completely losing his coat, refer to the next section, 'Serious Hair Loss'.

Overview Many Shih Tzu that are shaved or trimmed too extensively deep may have difficulty growing out the coat. Additionally, a Shih Tzu may struggle a bit to gain his full, adult coat.

The 7 elements that will help with Shih Tzu hair growth are:

1. Massage the skin when bathing. While shampooing your Shih Tzu, you will want to give his body a good massage. This stimulates blood flow to the hair follicles. Most dogs enjoy this when done in a quiet, relaxed atmosphere. Be sure that there is not a lot of foot traffic or distracting noise. The water should be lukewarm and you should test the water with the inside of your wrist before placing your Shih Tzu in the bath. He may feel more comfortable and safer if this is done in a clean kitchen sink, as opposed to a bath tub which may seem intimidating. During the shampooing, massage the coat for 10 minutes. With the next step of conditioning the coat, massage for an additional 10 minutes, for a total massage time of 20 minutes. This will stimulate blood flow, which in turn helps feed the hair follicles.

2. Take care of any mat immediately. Tangles can disrupt any coat, however if a Shih Tzu is having trouble re-growing his coat, this takes more importance than ever. As discussed in the 'Removing Tangles' section' page 81, work the tangle out or use the mat remover tool if you do find a tangle.

3. Use a high quality and proper canine shampoo and conditioner. You simply cannot expect the coat to look nice or be full and healthy without using quality products.

4. Let the coat air dry. While you are in the process of trying to help the coat grow, you will not want to use a blow dryer since this can add stress to an unhealthy coat.

5. Use a leave-in conditioner. This step should not be over-looked. The leave-in spritz will protect the coat from static, contact friction (the continual wear & tear on the coat when the Shih Tzu rubs against any surface), arid air, cold weather, sun exposure and split ends. Without protection from these elements, the coat not only can look terrible, but it can have trouble growing as well.

6. Use a rescue lotion for any balding spots or spots that were shaved too close. Barring any health issues (allergies, etc.) that may be causing skin issues and hair loss, thinning or balding areas can be helped with the right rescue lotion.

While this is used for 'hot spots' the right one will also promote hair growth by making skin and hair follicles as healthy as can be. Depending on the severity of the issue, this may need to be used as much as twice per day or as little as 1 time per week.

7. Provide cushioning. If your dog likes to lie down on the floor, whether it is carpeted or is hardwood, you will want to place a soft, clean baby blanket down first. Be sure that it has been washed with hypoallergenic laundry detergent. If your Shih Tzu has several areas in the house that he generally lies down to rest, have blankets there already in place for him. This will provide him with a soft, gentle surface during the time that his coat is not thick enough to provide proper cushioning.

Note: Any Shih Tzu- even one with a full healthy coat – can start to have thinning issues, particularly on the elbows, if they lie down on hard surfaces too much. Encourage your Shih Tzu to rest in his doggie bed or supply a pillow or small blanket.

For major cases, continue on to the next two sections, where more advanced care and treatment may be needed.

Serious Hair Loss

Please note that this section is a general overview regarding health issues that can cause hair loss. Alopecia X (unexplained hair loss) is covered in the next section.

The 3 most typical elements associated with a thinning coat are:

• **Irritated skin** - Once the coat thins down enough for owners to have a close look, you are often able to notice that the skin underneath the affected balding area is pink, swollen and/or has a rash. This is not always the case, however in most instances hair loss and skin problems go hand in hand.

• **Scratching** – In some cases, when a Shih Tzu scratches & chews at himself, it will cause hair to fall out. In other cases, thinning or bald areas may cause the skin to itch, which in turn prompts the Shih Tzu to scratch.

• **Odd patterns of hair loss** - There may be circular patterns of thinning hair or other unusual shapes where the coat is becoming bald.

The 8 Top Reasons a Shih Tzu may Have Hair Loss - There are many reasons why a dog's coat may thin and become bald in some spots, however we are going to discuss the most common reasons seen with the Shih Tzu breed.

1) Skin Problems -If a Shih Tzu is having issues that affect the skin, this will have a direct impact on the health of the hair follicle. In turn, the strength and integrity of hairs can weaken to the point of falling out. (You may also wish to refer to the 'Skin Problems' section, page 240, which prompts you to other areas of this book will be most helpful depending on what type of skin issues your Shih Tzu is experiencing).

2) Parasites - The most common parasite that causes hair loss with Shih Tzu is demodectic mange. These 'follicle mites' cause hair loss around the eye area, paws or other parts of the body. In some cases, the balding areas will begin to crust over. (For more regarding demodectic mange, you may wish to refer to 'Skin Problems' page 240). Ringworm (which is a fungus) is also a possibility. The telltale signs of ringworm are circular bald spots that appear on the head, paws, ears or limbs. They may have a red spot in the middle and the area may or may not crust over (for ringworm, you may wish to refer to the 'Worms' section, page 249).

3) Thyroid Issues - Both a low level of hormones (hypothyroidism) or high levels (hyperthyroidism) can cause hair loss. With this issue, problems are often seen over larger areas of a dog's coat and are not concentrated in one area. If this is the cause, the hair is often dry and brittle.

4) Stress - This is an intuitive, emotional breed and for that reason the Shih Tzu is highly susceptible to stress related conditions. Major changes such as a loss of a family member (human or pet), moving to a new home, severe levels of separation anxiety, etc. can really throw the body off kilter.

When a Shih Tzu is highly stressed, a condition called telogen effluvium may develop, in which a large number of coat follicles are forced into a prolonged resting phase. One to two months afterward those hairs may then fall out, especially after a brushing or a bath. Since this is a delayed reaction, a Shih Tzu that suffered through a bout of stress may only show this symptom of hair loss a couple of months afterward once things have settled down. For these instances, the coat often grows back to its normal dense and shiny state of health. If you suspect severe stress due to separation anxiety, you may also wish to refer to the 'Separation Anxiety' Section, page 170.

5) Allergies - Either seasonal, contact or food allergies may affect both skin and coat. Many allergens cause itchiness and in turn the Shih Tzu may scratch to the point of hair loss. Other allergies can cause the coat to become so dry and brittle that there is significant breakage, leading to a thinned down coat. We estimate that at least 25% of all thinning hair issues are due to allergies. For some reason, many dog owners do not look into this or perhaps procrastinate in getting treatment… whatever the reason, the dog sits at home suffering, when testing and treatment for allergies could effectively resolve the issue. (You may also wish to refer to the 'Allergies' section, page 215).

6) Diabetes - Seen in both adolescent and adult Shih Tzu, most owners first notice the signs of increased thirst, weakness and weight changes. A thinning or dulled coat is also a sign.

7) Cushing's disease - This is a disease in which the adrenal glands over-produce too much cortisol hormone. This most typically affects dogs over the age of 6 but can be seen in younger dogs as well. Other signs of this include: Bruising, increased thirst, increased urination and weakness.

8) Folliculitis - This is an infection of the hair follicles that may be accompanied by areas of pus, crusting on the skin where the coat is thinning. In some cases, spots may become bald and weeks later the sores and blisters of pus will appear. This is typically treated with a round of antibiotics.

Note: As we move forward into Alopecia X, please note that all of the listed conditions must be ruled out by a veterinarian before a Shih Tzu is diagnosed as having Alopecia X.

Alopecia X

Alopecia X refers to 'unknown hair loss' and can strike any dog breed. The coat will thin and/or have bald spots; this is either in circular patterns or an all-over thinning. In severe cases, the dog will become completely bald. There is a particular type of Alopecia X that is seen with dogs that carry the blue gene and therefore, can be seen with the Shih Tzu breed. It is called Color Dilution Alopecia. Dilute coats are affected by abnormalities in melanin transfer and storage of melanin. Color Dilution Alopecia often develops between the ages of 6 months to 3 years old. Whether it affects the whole coat or just the 'blue' color sections, affect hair becomes very dry, hair shafts break, patches of baldness appear and for most, a major thinning or complete loss of coat (though the face is not often affected). There can be scabs and scaling as well. Shih Tzu suspected of having Color Dilution Alopecia should still be tested for all possible health issues that could be causing hair loss & treatment is the same as it is for 'regular' Alopecia X.

If You Suspect Alopecia X - The first thing to do is to have all other causes of hair loss ruled out. Typical testing should include a blood panel, a urinalysis, thyroid testing, adrenal hormone testing, a skin biopsy.

Treatment

What we DO NOT recommend - There are some rather drastic treatments (not proven to work) that can really do a number on a toy breed dog. Though available as a treatment by some vets, we do **NOT** recommend:

X Growth Hormone – Given as an injection over the course of 6 weeks, this can cause diabetes, be toxic to the liver and cause aggressive behavior.

X Lysodren (also called mitotane) is normally used in the treatment of Cushing's disease. It can *cause* a dog to develop Cushing's disease because it can lead to a cortisone deficiency. Furthermore, this drug can lead to Addison's disease. It can also cause vomiting and diarrhea.

X Baby oil – We've seen this listed by some sources. Do not use this, it will clog the skin pores and it does not work at all.

Treatment we DO Recommend - There are a few things that can work quite well. Please keep in mind that these do not work for every dog. You should discuss these with your veterinarian.

Spaying and Neutering –Alopecia X, in *some* cases, can be related to a hormone imbalance. For this reason, the first step in treatment that a vet may recommend is to sterilize the Shih Tzu; un-spayed females should be spayed, intact males should be neutered. There are health benefits to sterilization regardless of whether or not there is a hair loss issue and some Shih Tzu will grow their coat back (though possibly not permanently).

Melatonin - Melatonin (considered a safe supplement) can prompt a coat to re-grow. Please note that in many cases, it is a combination of melatonin AND rescue lotion, shampoo, conditioner (see ahead). The proper dosage of melatonin for Shih Tzu coat loss is 1 mg per day. Approximately **30%** of dogs will show some response **within 12 weeks**. This is given for *at least 3 months* to see if it is helping. If hair regrowth occurs, one continues the melatonin until hair growth seems to have plateaued.

After maximum hair regrowth has been achieved, the dose is gradually tapered down to a weekly dose over several months. Some dogs can ultimately discontinue this; however if it is discontinued and the hair falls out again the condition may not be melatonin responsive a second time.

Note: Since this can have some side effects as shown ahead, you will want to first discuss this with your veterinarian.

Things to know about Melatonin:

• Melatonin is also used as a sleep aide. Your Shih Tzu may get drowsy when taking this.
• It can interfere with certain medications, including medications that suppress the immune system (immunosuppressant) and diabetes medications.
• There is no difference between melatonin packaged for humans and those packaged for pets. However, there can be a huge difference in the quality. Please obtain a quality brand; the one we recommend (Spring Valley) is packaged for humans and is one of the very few that offer low-dose 1 mg tablets.

Omega 3,6,9 may help. We recommend the type that comes in capsule form that can be broken open and sprinkled on food. Look for one that is derived from non-GMO natural oils from borage seed, flaxseed and/or fish. It can help in many ways including decreasing inflammation, decrease shedding and adding moisture to dry, irritated skin.

Special Shampoo, Conditioner & Massage Rescue Lotion - Some dogs have responded surprisingly well with dramatic results after owners have used a line of products that consists of a shampoo, conditioner and then a rescue lotion (sometimes in conjunction with melatonin). Please keep in mind that all dogs are different, so of course each Shih Tzu will respond differently.

The 3 products we recommend:

1) The shampoo. DERMagic's Peppermint and Tea Tree Oil Shampoo. This is an amazing formula with a unique blend of restorative and conditioning properties: peppermint, melaleuca (tea tree oil), lavender, chamomile, rosehip seed oils, aloe vera, vegetable glycerin, oat and wheat proteins. Shampoo with this liquid shampoo 1 time every 4 weeks.

2)The conditioner. DERMagic Rosemary Mint Conditioner Bar. Following the shampoo, while your Tzu is still in the tub and the coat is wet, gently yet firmly stroke this bar over the coat. Once you have covered the entire body, go back and stroke over thinning/balding spots 5 to 6 times. Condition with this 1 time every 4 weeks.

3) The *most important* element, the healing crème - DERMagic Skin Rescue Lotion. This will work best if you follow these directions:

1. Massage this into the skin (wherever the coat is thinning) **2 times each day for 7 straight days**. Take your time and massage for at least **5** minutes.

2. After this 1st week is complete, massage it into the skin (wherever the coat is thinning) **1** time each day. You can safely use this non-toxic product for months. If this does work for your Shih Tzu and you reach a point where the coat has grown back in, continue to use every other day for a few weeks. Keep a close eye on the skin & coat to spot any future issues.

Note: You will want to make sure that once applied and massaged onto the skin that the cream does not rub off. Slipping a cotton shirt on your Shih Tzu will be important- you may want to go 1 size up from the size your Shih Tzu normally wears so that the fabric covers more of the lower back and/or rear legs.

 For both our recommended melatonin, Omega 3, 6, 9 and hair loss shampoo, conditioner & the all-important rescue lotion, look 'Hair Growth Help' in the Shih Tzu Specialty Shoppe. You can reach the Shih Tzu Specialty Shoppe by entering any page of the AllShihTzu website. Look to the navigation; it is in alphabetical order. Choose 'Shoppe'.

Additional/concurrent steps:

1) Keep your Shih Tzu warm and comfortable by slipping a soft shirt or hoodie onto him. Shih Tzu can start to feel very vulnerable when the coat is very thinned.

2) Reassess everything that comes into contact with your Shih Tzu's coat. If he lies on your bed, tends to rest on a pile of your clothes… on blankets or pillows or has a doggie bed with a washable cover, wash these with a gentle hypo-allergenic laundry detergent. If he lies on the floors, immediately place down blankets for him (that have been washed with a gentle hypo-allergenic laundry detergent). If you opt to *not* try the DerMagic *and* you are *not* using high-end bath products on your Shih Tzu, immediately throw away what you have. In some cases, the harsh chemicals of cheap shampoo are worse than if you didn't wash your Shih Tzu at all. Please invest in a quality shampoo and conditioner.

3) Supply your Shih Tzu with extra padding to cushion parts of the body where the coat is thinner. Place an extra blanket on his bed - first washed with hypo-allergenic detergent – as this will offer an extra level of protection for tender areas.

Dandruff

The medical term for dandruff is seborrhea. While this problem is very common among humans, although it does affect dogs as well. It is most commonly seen with Shih Tzu that have dry skin, though there are other issues that may come into play. Dandruff refers to the shedding of dead skin cells from the skin, which flake off onto the hair. The element of flecks of skin dying off and then releasing from the body happens to all dogs (and all humans). This officially becomes known as the issue of dandruff when a larger than normal amount of cells die and then flake off.

One flake is too small for the human eye to see, however when a large amount sheds off at one time, they tend to clump together which produces the cumulative effect of larger flakes that one *can* see. Therefore, while the evidence of this can be seen on a Shih Tzu's coat, it is *actually* a skin disorder.

Like humans, the canine body is constantly renewing itself. Each day thousands of microscopic cells die and fall off of the skin. When a Shih Tzu suffers from dandruff, the amount ranges from triple to 10 times the normal number. It should be noted that dandruff is different than dander. Dander is also the flaking of dead skin cells; though they are infinitesimally smaller- often drifting through the air- and it does not lead to any substantial amount that would be mistaken for dandruff.

Why Shih Tzu May Develop Dandruff - Elements that can cause dandruff are:

• Dry skin - Dry skin in itself does not always cause dandruff; however when a Shih Tzu develops this disorder, dry skin will cause the problem to worsen.
• Food intolerance - Certain food ingredients may trigger dry skin, which leads to increased flaking of the skin.
• Age - As dogs grow older, they are more susceptible to developing dandruff. Therefore, this is much more common in senior dogs than with puppies.
• Cold weather - The condition may worsen in the wintertime, when temperatures plummet and the air is dryer. In these cases, while it may appear that the condition is improving during spring or summertime, it actually is still ongoing - just to a lesser degree - and should still be properly treated.
• Low humidity - If you live in an arid region, this can make a Shih Tzu's skin more prone to dryness and dandruff.

Other Signs & Symptoms that Can Accompany Canine Dandruff Are:

• Itchiness - A Shih Tzu may scratch at his coat, may chew on areas that he can reach and/or rub his body against the carpeting or another surface
• Redness - If you were to lift the hairs on the coat, you may spot areas of irritated, red skin.
• Thinning of the coat - In severe cases that have not been properly treated, repeated scratching to parts of the dog's body can cause the coat to thin in certain areas (and even develop bald patches)
• Oily skin - Some dogs may overproduce body oils as skin cells slough off which can create oily skin.
• An odd odor - When a Shih Tzu has the previously mentioned overproduction of body oils, this mixes with the dead skin cells and can produce an unpleasant, musty type smell.

Making Sure That it is Indeed Dandruff - Before treating your Shih Tzu for this issue, you should make sure that it is indeed a common case of dandruff. Random patches and small areas of dry skin can be treated in much the same way, but will not need to be treated with specialized shampoos for this skin disorder. You'll want to look for clear signs of white specks. If your Shih Tzu has the signs listed that include dry skin, an oily smell, itchiness and/or irritation, do take time to inspect the coat and lift sections of the hairs to look at the roots. While belly skin is easily accessible, skin that is flaking will generally be that which is under the coat - so check the back, the flank and the legs.

The 1 condition that is most often mistaken for common dandruff is Mites:

There is a canine condition commonly referred to as Walking Dandruff. Though, it is actually a skin parasite: Cheyletiella mites (Also called Cheyletiella mange). The presence of these mites will appear to be dandruff, but if you look for a long enough time you will actually see movement, letting you know that your Shih Tzu has a much different issue. In some cases, the mites themselves will be seen moving around; in other cases, the presence of the mites causes skin to flake off. The mites live under those skin flakes- when they move, the tiny specks of skin flakes wobble around or are carried on the backs of the parasites.

There is a rise in this parasite, and one of the main reasons is that most owners use some sort of flea control and most flea control products have no effect on Cheyletiella mites. This can affect dogs of any age, though most cases are seen with young puppies. These types of mites jump from host to host and can be found on dogs, cats, many wild animals, rabbits and even sometimes on humans. Therefore, if a Shih Tzu has mites, they can jump to his owner. Aside from the obvious movement that you will see when you look closely, the only other sign that differs from real dandruff is that with many dogs, the mites tend to nest on the main trunk of the dog (keeping away from the head, legs, etc.) Your vet will diagnose this by taking a small skin scraping or by simply applying a small piece of adhesive tape to the coat to lift off specimens. Under a microscope, 4 legs can clearly be seen, along with eggs that have been hatched and sometimes tiny bits of fecal matter.

If you suspect that your Shih Tzu has mites, you may be tempted to give him a bath; however this can wash off quite a few of the pests which can make the veterinarian's job just a tad harder. If the appointment is soon, hold off on baths, as you will be given prescribed medication to apply. There are several treatments for this: Pyrethrin shampoo, lime sulfur dips, Fipronil spray, Selamectin solution and Ivermectin (not always tolerated well). Depending on which type of treatment the vet prescribes, the coat will need to be treated anywhere from 3 weeks to 45 days. All pets in the house will need to be treated. Additionally, since the mites can jump to other surfaces and lay eggs all over the house, everything will need to be treated (carpeting, bedding, clothing, etc.) in the same way that one would treat for fleas. Once a mite has left its host, it can live for up to 10 days.

Treatment for Genuine Dandruff on a Shih Tzu Puppy or Dog - When the right product is used consistently, most Shih Tzu respond so well that flaking is drastically reduced and after a short while (2 to 3 months) you may never spot dandruff again - though it should be noted that some dogs have an overactive Keratinocytes process (skin renewal process) that may always cause some dandruff. The #1 most important element to treating this will be to use a quality canine dandruff shampoo. These are much different than 'normal' shampoos, as they will contain either specialized ingredients such as chlorhexidine gluconate, miconazole nitrate or have a blend of natural ingredients that work together to treat dandruff (Aloe vera, almond oil, collagen, coconut, apple, and lemon).

It is important to note that the use of human dandruff shampoos is not recommended, as they are extremely harsh on a dog's skin and may cause additional issues. The best dandruff shampoo for Shih Tzu will do several things:

• Descale the skin (Remove any bits of skin that have died but have not yet fallen off)
• Calm and soothe (relive itchiness and any irritation)
• Add moisture (which will then cut down on flaking quite a bit)
• Work as a degreaser (this refers to the removal of the oily greasy like substance that can be found on the coat along with dandruff)

Our recommended dandruff shampoo of choice is Furrever Medicated Shampoo. While you understandably may be in a hurry to rid your Shih Tzu of the dandruff, it is best to take things slowly and patiently. Don't overdo baths - Instead, increase bath time to 1 time per week until you see that it is clearing up. You will also want to use a good leave-in conditioner to aid both skin and coat between baths. After 1 to 3 months, you will see an improvement. At that time, you can switch to a high quality, canine shampoo that will keep the skin properly moisturized and combat dryness.

Note: Proper grooming will work well to decrease or essentially remove dandruff (though remember that the underlying cause may never go away), and this is the most important element. However another step that plays a role to ensure excellent skin health, is feeding your Shih Tzu the best food possible, as intolerance to certain ingredients often triggers skin issues. Artificial coloring, nasty additives and chemical preservatives can all exasperate dandruff problems. If you follow the steps that we have listed and your Shih Tzu's dandruff problem has not cleared up within 3 months, do please make an appointment with your dog's veterinarian. Underlying causes such as a thyroid imbalance or a different issue such as fungal infection may be at play.

Exercise

Requirements & Restrictions

Most dog owners will agree that one of the most enjoyable parts of having a dog is being able to do activities together. Having a walking partner is just one of the great benefits of pet ownership. With the Shih Tzu, exercise is an

important part of maintaining health and is a vital part of overall care; though too much exercise can cause a Shih Tzu to overheat or have too much stress put on the joints. The key is to find a good balance of offering enough activity to stay fit & release pent-up energy without overtaxing the dog.

A Note About Puppies – While of course you never want to

push a Shih Tzu of any age to his limits, you want to pay particular attention to not allowing young puppies to overextend themselves during the age of 8 weeks to 10 months. This time is one of rapid growth; and very excessive exercise can affect growth plates. Growth plates are somewhat soft areas at the end of bones; the cells there are constantly dividing, which allows those bones to properly grow as the pup matures into his adult size. Once that growth is done, the plates close. If a puppy is put under too much physical stress, there can be damage to those plates (what would be a sprain or pull for an adult dog). This can lead to malformed or shortened limb(s).

Walking - Going for a walk is the most traditional method of offering daily exercise for a dog and studies show that this routine activity makes owners healthier too. While running around and playing does count toward activity, nothing beats walks! There is always a Point A and a Point B, which helps ensure proper duration of exercise. And unlike free-running, speed can be adjusted by you, as you see fit. By following some easy guidelines, you can allow your Shih Tzu to reap the benefits of exercise while doing so in a healthy, safe way. There are several important benefits to walking your Shih Tzu:

1) It helps a Shih Tzu maintain muscle tone which helps maintain good posture and allows the muscles surrounding the hips and knees to be strong and supportive.
2) It is good for the heart and reduces the risk of heart disease.
3) It keeps the metabolism functioning properly.
4) It allows a release of pent up energy, which in turn gives you a more well-behaved dog. Dogs that receive regular outdoor exercise display less destructive behaviors at home.

Guidelines and Requirements - Keeping a routine is helpful for both owner and Shih Tzu. When walks are incorporated in the daily schedule, owners are more prone to follow through and dogs- with their incredible inner time clocks- quickly learn to look forward to this time. We recommend two 20-minute walks per day. If this is not feasible, the next alternative would be one 30-minute walk. The benefit to exercising a Shih Tzu in shorter intervals is that he can receive a higher amount of exercise over the course of a day, yet will be less prone to overexertion since the sessions are kept short. Here are some tips to keep the walks safe and fun:

1) Do take this time to teach your Shih Tzu to heel. Once this lesson is learned, it always makes walking more enjoyable for both owner and dog. Walking in tandem, without a dog pulling on the leash or stopping every few moments, makes this moderate exercise something to look forward to (see 'Heeling', page 108 for full training details).

2) During warm to hot weather, head out before 10 AM and/or after 5 PM, avoiding the hottest times of the day.

3) If you couldn't get out early enough to beat the heat and if the temperature is over 90 degrees F (32.2 C), it is best to skip that session as overheating may be a problem. Instead, opt for an indoor exercise activity (suggestions are ahead in this section) or plan to go later when the sun is lower in the sky.

4) Always bring a collapsible bowl and a chilled water bottle for your Shih Tzu. Even if you do not see signs of over-heating, take a break 1/2 way through the walk. It is best to rest in the shade, offering a nice break out of the sun and a cold drink of water.

5) Be aware of how hot walking surfaces can become in the summer. Recently, a news story in Nevada focused on the sudden surge of dog owners who obtained doggie shoes for their pets as temperatures soared into the 100's. And doing this saved many dogs from discomfort and/or injury. Paws are made of skin, albeit thick skin, and are vulnerable to cuts, scrapes and burns. If your Shih Tzu resists outdoor exercise, it just may be that he has an intolerance to the walking surface. If your Shih Tzu does not like shoes, a high quality paw wax can be just about as good as shoes, offering a layer of protection from the outdoor elements.

6) Try out different routes (if possible). There are so many triggers that can make a Shih Tzu jumpy, scared or otherwise problematic while out and about. What looks like a quiet road to you may have swarms of wildlife teeming in the background that causes the puppy or dog to have trouble staying by your side or can make a dog bark. Experimenting with different walking routes can allow you to see which one your Shih Tzu does best on.

7) Be aware of ground surfaces in the winter. Ice melt chemicals are very damaging to paws. Thawing snow can create puddles that are a mixture of water and these damaging chemicals. Ice, snow and frozen ground surfaces can prevent a dog from having stable traction. When temperatures drop to below 30 degrees F (-1.1 C), a sweater and booties or quality paw wax can be just the thing that turns an unenthusiastic Shih Tzu into one that is eager for some outside exercise.

8) While it may indeed happen, it should never be your plan to allow your Shih Tzu to poo or pee along the walking route. This can disrupt a dog's understanding of his housebreaking rules. Always take him to his designated bathroom area both before a walk and after returning.

Dog Parks

It'd be nice to believe that all parks specifically for pets would be a great place where our Shih Tzu could romp around and maybe even make friends with other dogs. At the very least, it sounds like a good method for a Shih Tzu to have a place to run freely and gain some socialization skills. However, there are some real concerns about the safety of dog parks. *Not every dog park is set up the same, so it's a good idea to investigate if your local park could have one of the following hazards.*

1) Being attacked by another dog. This is a sad topic, because the main reason owners bring Shih Tzu to dog parks is to allow their dog a nice environment to meet and greet other dogs. In theory, this is a great idea because once a Shih Tzu is exposed to any trigger over a period of time- including other dogs - he is much more likely to act calm and not bark during future encounters.

But the startling fact is that dog parks have been the scene of terrible and even deadly attacks: In Wauconda, IL at the Cook Memorial Park , a Shih Tzu named Shibui Fong killed when he was attacked by a Pit bull. At the Curtis Hixon Waterfront Park in Tampa, Florida, a Shih Tzu named Moby was killed by a 110 pound Rhodesian ridgeback dog. The larger dog sniffed the Shih Tzu twice and then seized his neck. Moby's owner tried to help, but was bit on the hand. Not giving up, he jumped on the back of the Rhodesian ridgeback and was dragged 5 feet before being bit on the leg. And while a tad unrelated, we must mention a shocking attack that happened at the Grape Street Dog Park in San Diego, California where a Shih Tzu named Frankie Bones was surrounded and killed by three coyotes.

It happens to other small dogs… For example, at the Simmonds Family Dog Park in Ohio a 6 lb. Miniature Pinscher was killed by a German Shepherd. At a dog park in South Euclid, Ohio a Husky killed a Chihuahua. It even happens with two larger dogs; a Golden Retriever was killed by a Great Dane at a dog park in Missouri. And the list goes on. All these attacks happened in dog parks that did not have separate areas for small and large dogs.

How to keep your Shih Tzu safe - Look for a dog park that has separate sections for large and small dogs. Many parks are adopting this method to avoid tragedies. Unless a park has separate, enclosed areas for dogs based on size and has a rule that all dogs walked on trails must be on leash, keep away from that area.

Side note of interest — Which dog breeds are most likely to attack?

DOG ATTACKS - US & CANADA 1982 TO 2014

	Breed Type	Attacks doing bodily harm	# of Child Victims	# of Adult Victims	# of Deaths	# of Maimings
Med/Lg Dogs	Pit bull	3397	1355	1312	295	2110
	German Shepherd	113	65	41	15	73
	Husky	83	51	8	26	27
	Chow Chow	61	37	18	8	40
Toy Breed Dogs	Shih Tzu	5	2	3	0	5
	Pomeranian	1	1	0	1	0
	Chihuahua	1	1	0	1	1
	Pug	1	1	0	0	1

Even if your Shih Tzu is running around only with other toy breeds, you'll still want to keep an eye on things since a toy dog may be aggressive as well. Though this is less likely to result in a fatal attack it can emotionally scar a dog for quite a while. Warning signs are that the other dog will have a frozen stance, raised hackles and may bare his teeth.

By no means should you let this scare you from bringing your Shih Tzu to a dog park as long as he is in an enclosed area with small dogs; however it is something to be aware of. Most often, the benefits of playing with other dogs and the socialization skills that come from that far outweighs any small chance of issues, if you play it safe.

Another option is to bring your Shih Tzu to a park that is not necessarily labeled a 'dog park' but rather is a park that does allow dogs if on leash. Many parks do not advertise that dogs are allowed; instead you will see signs posted regarding rules that explain about needing to keep the dog on a leash and to pick up any poo. In these types of parks, there will be far fewer dogs and can be better for shy Tzu that don't do well in large groups of dogs.

2) Catching parasites - There are several ways that a Shih Tzu can catch fleas or roundworms from other dogs.

With fleas, these can jump up to six feet from one animal to another. And in regard to worms, a puppy or dog can become infested with parasites by eating the feces of other animals.

How to keep your Shih Tzu safe - Using year-round flea protection is the best way for you to keep your Shih Tzu safe from fleas not only when at parks but any time your puppy or dog is in the same area as another animal. Eating feces is always a tricky thing because when at a park, a dog may eat it before an owner can intervene. Of course, any time your Shih Tzu is on leash, do not allow him to even sniff any feces. If off leash, keep a close eye on your Shih Tzu as you may need to move quickly to interrupt him.

3) Communal drinking water hazards
- Many parks have public fountains for dogs to drink from. And many owners wonder if it is safe for dogs to share water in this way. There are a couple of diseases that can be transmitted via shared water including the papilloma virus (which causes painful warts to grow in a dog's mouth) and respiratory diseases.

How to keep your Shih Tzu safe - It can help to make sure your Shih Tzu is fully hydrated before you leave for the park. Bring along your own supply of water in a travel jug for your Shih Tzu. Every 30 minutes or so, before your Shih Tzu becomes thirsty, have him take a break with you to rest and drink the water that you brought.

Another good reason to bring along your own fresh water is that a park's water supply may be shut down for maintenance at any time or during colder months so that pipes do not freeze in the winter weather. So bringing your own water for your Shih Tzu will ensure that your dog stays hydrated and can help prevent possible diseases spread by a shared water source.

Things to Bring to the Dog Park
- Here are 5 things that you should always bring with you when you take your Shih Tzu to the park:

1- Poo bags - Since you expect other owners to pick up their dog's poo, you won't want to forget to bring bags for your Shih Tzu. It's also a good idea to bring some extras in case someone else wasn't as prepared as you are.

2- Water with collapsible bowl or travel container - You may opt for a bottle of spring water with a collapsible travel bowl or there are water containers in which the cover doubles as the bowl. Either way, it's a good idea to bring about twice the amount that you think you'll need. Anything can happen, from the water being tipped to your Shih Tzu overheating and if it does, you'll be happy that you brought extra.

3- Additional collar/harness and leash - While the collar, harness and leash you have is no doubt sturdy, no one plans on that one moment when these accessories snap due to being old or worn. While this most likely won't happen, it can't hurt to either bring along extras or to just keep extras in the car for emergency situations.

4- Wipes - Canine paw wipes (or even just baby wipes) can come in handy in a number of ways when you bring your Shih Tzu to a dog park. There are several things that can stick to a dog's paws including lawn care chemicals, pollen and other allergy triggers, bits of feces from other dogs (even if an owner picks up the poo in a bag, there will be some feces left on the grass that dogs can step in) and small pebbles that can get wedged between paw pads. You'll want to wipe your Shih Tzu's paws before you put him back into your car. Use one wipe for each paw. If possible, rinse your dog's paws off with a hose (if the weather permits) or in the kitchen sink once you get him back into the house.

5- Hand sanitizer- Due to the #4 suggestion above, you'll want to be able to sanitize your hands once you've cleaned off your Shih Tzu.

When to NOT Bring Your Shih Tzu to the Park
- Not every dog should be brought to the park. Here's when to avoid this type of setting:

1- If your un-spayed female is in heat. Every single un-neutered male dog will try to mount her. This is unsafe for both your Shih Tzu and for you as you try to break them up. The tricky thing is that your Shih Tzu may be entering heat before you notice the signs. For this reason, if your female dog is not fixed, keep her on leash and watch how she reacts to other dogs. If she raises her tail and tries to present herself, that's your clue to pick her up and head back home.

2- If your puppy has not yet had all of his puppy shots. It's always a good idea to wait 2 weeks after the last round before bringing your puppy out to any public places and certainly to a park that is filled with dogs.

3- An overly shy Shih Tzu. You'll definitely want to work on training your Shih Tzu to be well-socialized. However, it never works well to move quickly from zero to one hundred. Dogs that have trouble being in social settings will need gradual, incremental exposure and suddenly being put into such an overwhelming situation is never a good idea.

Outdoor Alternatives to Dog Parks

1- Hikes. While a Shih Tzu's hiking pace will be a lot slower than yours, going for hikes can be exhilarating for both of you. It offers a bit of a fun challenge and beautiful views (and scents for your Shih Tzu) that isn't found in your neighborhood. Look for 'easy' trails and be sure to keep your Shih Tzu on a harness and leash.

Follow the same rules as you do for regular walks, taking breaks for rest and water. If the trail will be sandy, you may want to place shoes on your Shih Tzu for both good traction and to protect the paws from tiny pebbles that can irritate paw pads.

2- A dog friendly beach. Beaches are not just for the summer months! Off season is often the perfect time to bring a dog to the shoreline. There are less people and it's easier for a Shih Tzu to have fun near the water without distractions. Most dogs are enthralled with waves and taking a walk along the beach can be a fun way to get some fresh air and activity. Even winter can be a good time to go since in many areas it will snow inland but not near the water. Just check to see what the temperature will be along with the wind chill, which is often stronger right on the coast. If it calls for it, bundle your Shih Tzu up in a warm parka and shoes and let him see how much fun it is to explore the area.

3- To a dog friendly store. You may be surprised how many stores allow dogs, especially toy breeds and especially if the dog is in a carrier sling (or even a canine stroller). This is particularly a great idea during cold months when you and your Shih Tzu may both be experiencing cabin fever. While you'll want to call ahead to make sure, there are many chain stores that generally allow dogs including: Macy's (a huge pet supporter), just about every pet supply store including Petco, Bass Pro Shop (even if you're not into hunting and fishing gear, it can be fun to walk around there), Barnes and Noble bookstores, Bloomingdales, Anthropologie, Bebe , Foot Locker, the Gap & Bed Bath and Beyond.

Dressing for the Weather

A Shih Tzu should be protected from the outside elements during certain weather conditions. Being cold, or cold & wet, interferes with house training and with important daily exercise. Unless there is an icy blizzard or torrential rainfall, please do not skip daily walks. When dressed appropriately (both you and your Shih Tzu), he'll still appreciate being brought out to release pent-up energy. If owners only walked their dogs on nice, sunny 70 degree days, dogs would be very unhealthy! There is a saying that goes, "There is no such thing as cold weather, there is only such a thing as being inappropriately dressed."

Here is a good guideline to follow:

Temperature: 32 degrees or colder (1.1 Celsius): A Shih Tzu should have protection to the body (sweater, vest or coat) at all times. And on particularly windy days, this is even more crucial, due to the 'wind chill factor'.

Precipitation:

Snow: Any time that the ground has ice or snow on it, your Shih Tzu will better tolerate being outside if you use a good, quality paw wax. Booties can work as well, however paw wax will also protect the pads from wintertime issues like dry air, etc. *Note:* If ice-melt chemicals have been sprayed onto the streets, it may end up being in the puddles created by melting snow. If you will be walking your Shih Tzu in these conditions, please wash the paws off well after entering back into the home.

Rainy: Allowing a Shih Tzu to become wet from the rain, if the temperature is warm, is not a bad thing. It is part of socialization to events and to different elements. After all, you don't want your Shih Tzu to cower every time it sprinkles. Dogs do just fine in light rain, if the time is limited to normal walk times (20 to 30 minutes) and it is above 60 degrees (15.5 Celsius). However, if the temperature is 60 degrees or colder, a Shih Tzu should be protected from the rain with a rain coat, as a soaked coat in lower temperatures can lead to a bad chill.

Dogs that are Intolerant to Cold Weather Even with a Sweater On - Shih Tzu can get chilled very easily. While some conditions like hypothyroidism or other medical conditions can cause cold intolerance, most often it is only a matter of offering warmer clothing. Here are 2 tips if you have a Shih Tzu that is chilled quite often (and has no health conditions that would cause cold intolerance)

1) Just like for us humans, layering is what works best to keep warm. We would suggest a shirt and then a jacket, sweater or coat. Make sure that the fabric is not 100% polyester, which is terrible for keeping warm.
2) Ground surfaces hold in the cold. It is a myth that paw pads are "indestructible". Paw pads will feel and absorb the cold. So we would suggest quality paw wax to provide a layer of protection.

 Not sure exactly which clothing, booties or paw wax is best for your Shih Tzu? We've taken the guess work out for you! All top-rated, personally recommended items that you need for your Shih Tzu can be found in the Shih Tzu Specialty Shoppe. You can reach the Shih Tzu Specialty Shoppe by entering any page of the AllShihTzu website. Look to the navigation; it is in alphabetical order. Choose 'Shoppe'.

Fun Indoor Games to Play

If bad weather is keeping you at home, both you and your Shih Tzu may be in need of some indoor fun. While we always recommend keeping up with daily walks unless weather conditions are severe, we have some tips for indoor play. We'll go over 4 fun things to do with a Shih Tzu when inside. There will be some that you've heard of before, but may have never tried due to them sounding too basic. So, we have the details of exactly how to play the game to build up a challenge and make it more interesting.

Indoor Game #1 - Increasingly Challenging Hide and Seek - This is always on the list of games to play with a dog because at its core it's very basic; yet when played correctly and with lots of enthusiasm, it can be super amusing to owners and an interesting challenge for dogs. One of the best cures for a bored or restless dog is to offer a task that leads to self-confidence. Some sources list hiding an object for this game, however we are going to talk about the game of *you* hiding and your Shih Tzu finding you.

The basic rule of play is that you will have your Shih Tzu stay in a 'Sit' or have a helper hold him while you hide.

Note: If your puppy or dog has not yet mastered the 'Sit' command and/or you don't have a helper, don't worry you can still play! You'll want to set up a gate (or other similar object) across a doorway, leaving a very small opening. Plan your hiding spot. Place your Shih Tzu in the room that is 95% gated off. Distract him by throwing an item of interest toward the back end of the room and make a dash for your hiding spot. (See also, 'Commands', page 112)

You might worry that your Shih Tzu will catch on to this method of distraction rather quickly and that's okay because he will also be learning that this is a signal that the game is about to begin and many dogs will voluntarily be 'distracted' so that you can hide.

How to play with increased difficulty level:

1) Always plan your hiding spot so that your dog doesn't catch you standing in a room, wondering where to stash yourself.
2) Have treats in your hand or pocket, so that you can reward your Shih Tzu as soon as he finds you. Later, once he learns this indoor game, he won't need a treat at all, he'll just want another round to play.
3) The first time you hide, choose an easy spot in the next room over. Behind a sofa or behind a door is a good choice.
4) When you're ready for your Shih Tzu to begin searching, call out his name one time, in an eager 'come and find me!' tone.
5) As soon as he finds you, offer the treat and lots of enthusiasm as if he did something truly marvelous.
6) As you keep 'resetting' the game, by placing your Shih Tzu in the 'starting area', choose a slightly more difficult spot. By the 5th or 6th time, you should be a couple of rooms away, completely out of view. Some good places? The bathtub with the curtain drawn, in various closets with the doors open only enough for your dog to fit through and underneath blankets.
7) A session of about 10 'finds' is usually perfect, because you want to end this indoor game when your Shih Tzu is feeling good and hasn't become tired of it. This leads to wanting to play again the next day.

Indoor Game #2 - Which Box? This is a super fun indoor activity to play with a Shih Tzu in which you will help your puppy or dog build on his 'search and seek' skills. Dogs really love to play this and it not only gets them moving around but also builds up their confidence levels. The basics of this game are that you will have 5 to 10 cardboard boxes and only one of them will hold a treat. It's best if all of the boxes are essentially the same size - though they can vary somewhat so that it's easier to store them, one inside the other, for when you're not playing. You'll want the largest one to be only slightly larger than your Shih Tzu.

You can search your house for what you need or when out food shopping, ask the store manager for boxes; many grocery stores have tons of them right in the back and don't mind when people ask (it saves them from having to break them down). All boxes should be opened at the top. You can either fold the flaps down into the box or cut them off (which also makes storing them a bit easier).

How to play with increased difficulty level:

1) Choose the biggest room in your house for this fun indoor game and set things up while your Shih Tzu is behind his gated area or otherwise unable to watch what you are doing.
2) Choose a super yummy treat that has a strong scent.
3) When first playing this game, use 5 boxes. Spread them with the open top facing up, all across the room. With this game you will not hide the boxes at all; you'll want your Shih Tzu to be able to easily see all of them. Place the treat in just one (not the first one that he'll see when entering the room).

4) Allow your Shih Tzu into the room. Teach him how to play by leading him from one box to the other, asking in an excited tone "Where's the treat? Can you find the hidden prize?" Watch his nose go to work as you bring him from one box to the other.

5) His nose should tell him when he's found the correct box and you can help him by acting happy and helping him reach the reward.

6) As you continue to play, add more boxes. Once your Shih Tzu has mastered how to play this indoor game make it more challenging by placing the treat on the floor and cover it with a box; making sure that all boxes are turned over. Now he's really going to have fun using his sense of smell!

7) Make sure that the bits of treats are small enough so that your puppy or dog can play several rounds and still be hungry enough to want to search. End on a good note, with your Shih Tzu wanting more play; this makes a dog more likely to really look forward to playing the game on another day.

Indoor Game #3 - Adventure Box - This is a fun indoor activity for Shih Tzu that they can play on their own, once you have created it. Essentially, you will create a box that is filled with items that your dog has to rifle through to find the one prize that is hidden in it somewhere. Some owners make these out of primarily cardboard and paper items that include paper towel tubes, cereal boxes and newspaper. You can do this, however your Shih Tzu should be supervised when playing so that cardboard and paper items cannot be chewed.

We would suggest using non-chewable items that include empty plastic soda bottles (cleaned and closed), small plastic measuring cups, kitchen funnels, etc. Instead of using newspaper, you can use an array of different sized washcloths, hand towels and dishwasher rags.

How to set this up:

1) With a good sized box (roughly twice the size of your Shih Tzu).

2) The idea is to place the treat inside one of the washcloths (or newspaper if you closely supervise your dog).

3) Layer all the items on top of that. When you first play this game with your Shih Tzu, you'll want to pack the objects loosely. Once your Shih Tzu learns how this works, you can really pack them tight.

4) As your Shih Tzu becomes wise to how this works, you can become creative in how you hide things and what other objects you use. Treats can be placed inside an open water bottle or in a cleaned out margarine container that had holes poked through the top to allow the scent to be picked up.

Indoor Game #4 - Mind Challenges - Many owners know that their dogs are clever… they can sense when

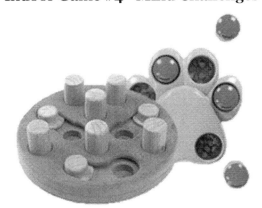

we're even thinking about leaving and they know exactly where we keep their food. They know how to tug at our heart strings and which facial expressions will get them what they want. Many owners do not give their Shih Tzu enough credit for really being able to solve puzzles or figure out games that involve sliding, working through mazes or flipping lids open. But know that the Shih Tzu breed is very intelligent and able to solve games.

They just need 2 things for this to happen: 1- the chance to do so and 2- an owner who is a patient, enthusiastic teacher. Indoor interactive games will have a particular maze or puzzle in which pieces must be moved a certain way to reveal a treat. Teaching a Shih Tzu how to nudge elements with his nose and how to search is a great bonding experience for a human and her canine family member. And most owners never knew how clever their dog was until given the opportunity to excel.

If you would like to see our recommended interactional games to play with your Shih Tzu, look to 'Toys - Owner & Shih Tzu Together' in the Shih Tzu Specialty Shoppe. You can reach the Shih Tzu Specialty Shoppe by entering any page of the AllShihTzu website. Look to the navigation; it is in alphabetical order. Choose 'Shoppe'.

Heat Stroke

Overview Always be aware that exercising in hot weather or exercising for too long poses the risk of heat stroke. Exercise is very important for your Shih Tzu and being afraid of your dog getting heatstroke should not stop you from exercising your dog. It's just something to be mindful of. It is a good idea to know the signs of heatstroke, should this occur, so that you can properly treat for it. Heatstroke occurs when normal body mechanisms cannot keep the body's temperature in a safe range. Dogs do not have efficient cooling systems (like humans who sweat) and get overheated easily.

A dog with moderate heatstroke (body temperature from 104° to 106°F) can recover within an hour if given prompt first aid and veterinary care (normal body temperature is 100-102.5°F). Severe heatstroke (body temperature over 106°F) can be deadly and immediate veterinary assistance is needed.

The Signs of Heatstroke in Dogs - A Shih Tzu suffering from heatstroke will display one or more of the following signs:
- Rapid panting
- Bright red tongue
- Red or pale gums
- Thick, sticky saliva
- Depression
- Weakness
- Dizziness
- Vomiting - sometimes with blood
- Diarrhea
- Shock - If it progresses without treatment
- Coma - If left untreated

What You Should Do - It's important to treat your Shih Tzu before bringing him to the vet. Once your dog is stable, he should then be brought to the closest veterinarian or animal hospital. Rushing to the vet, without first cooling down your Shih Tzu, can be fatal.

1) Remove your Shih Tzu from the hot area immediately. If you are outside and cannot make it inside to a cool room, seek shade. If you are outside and going indoors to a cool room is possible, do this immediately.
2) Work to lower body temperature. You can lower your Shih Tzu's body temperature by wetting your dog thoroughly with cool/lukewarm water. (Do not use cold water; this will be too much of a shock for the body). Soak towels and place them on his body.
3) Increase air movement around your dog with a fan.
4) Encourage your Shih Tzu to lap at water or a 50/50 blend of water and plain Pedialyte, but do not try to force-feed cold water; a dog may inhale it or choke.
5) Once your Shih Tzu has cooled down and he seems more stable, you should *then* bring him to the vet right away.

What Your Veterinarian Will Do - The veterinarian will continue to work to lower your dog's body temperature to a safe range (if you have not already) and continually monitor his temperature. Your Shih Tzu will be given fluids, and possibly oxygen. Dogs with heatstroke will be monitored for shock, respiratory distress, kidney failure, heart abnormalities, and other complications, and treated accordingly. Blood samples may be taken before and during the treatment. The clotting time of the blood will be monitored, since clotting problems are a common complication.

Aftercare- Dogs with moderate heatstroke often recover without complicating health problems. Severe heatstroke can cause organ damage that might need ongoing care such as a special diet prescribed by your veterinarian. Dogs that suffer from heatstroke once increase their risk for getting it again and steps must be taken to prevent it on hot, humid days.

Prevention - Any dog that cannot cool off is at risk for heatstroke. Following these guidelines can help prevent serious problems.

• Keep a Shih Tzu with conditions like heart disease, obesity, older age or breathing problems (stenotic nares, elongated palate) cool and in the shade when outside. Discuss with your vet how much exercise your dog can handle.

• Provide access to water at all times.

• Do not leave your Shih Tzu in a hot parked car even if you're in the shade or will only be gone a couple of minutes. The temperature inside a parked car can quickly reach up to 140 degrees.

• On souring hot days, restrict exercise and don't take your dog out with you.

• On hot days, avoid places like the beach and especially concrete or asphalt areas where heat is reflected and there is no access to shade.

• Wetting down your Shih Tzu with cool water or allowing your dog to swim can help maintain a normal body temperature.

Training

Teaching Proper Hierarchy

Overview In regard to any sort of training at all (commands, heeling, even housebreaking to a certain extent) and to stop *many* behavioral issues (begging, jumping, barking, general 'acting crazy' behavior, etc.), for your dog to listen to you at all, he first needs to see you as leader. All dogs – even cute little toy breeds like the Shih Tzu – live by canine instinct. A dog lives within his den (the house) and all members under the roof (both humans and animals) are his pack. The pack has a leader. This is the canine way and there are no exceptions. You may assume that you are the leader. However, in many cases, a dog has no idea that you even consider yourself to be in charge. Unless you make this clear, he will either struggle to understand who the leader is, try to take on the role himself (most dogs will step up if no one does) or he will mistakenly believe that he himself is the leader.

Teaching a dog that you are the leader (teaching proper hierarchy) is not all that difficult. The problem is that many owners do not do this consistently. You – and everyone in the house – must follow the rules every day. If you stop, a dog may begin to believe that his leader is weakening. And in the canine world, a weak leader is not a good one; the dog may then step forward to take on the leadership role.

So, again, these steps are not difficult, but it will be up to you to follow them exactly and at all times.

1. Make it clear that you provide the food. If your Shih Tzu arrives to his dish and finds food there, he will not know that you are responsible for it being there. For this reason, your Shih Tzu must obey the 'Sit' command before his meal is placed down. (You may wish to refer to 'Commands', page 112)

2. The leader eats first. Normally, there is at least one time per day that both you and your Shih Tzu eat at the same time (or at least begin eating at the same time!). During these occasions, you must make it clear that you are allowed to begin eating first, because as leader, that is your privilege. You will prepare his meal and leave it on the counter. You will prepare your meal and place it on your table. Next, sit down and make sure that your Shih Tzu sees that you take 2 to 3 bites. He may jump/bark/whine/circle, however ignore this. There is no need to correct the behavior since it only lasts a few moments. Next, during a quiet moment (when the Shih Tzu takes in a breath in between barks or is landing down from a jump), rise and take his bowl into your hand. It is now that you refer to item #1, having your Shih Tzu obey the 'Sit' command before placing down his meal.

3. The leader enters and exits the den first. Any time you and your Shih Tzu are both leaving the house or coming back inside, you will enter/exit first, followed by your Shih Tzu. You will need to practice this, getting down the technique of stretching out your arm to keep him right inside/outside of the doorway.

4. Some things must be earned. While you do not need to do this for every little thing, when giving a new toy or giving a treat, your Shih Tzu needs to obey the 'Sit' command before being given the new item/snack.

Note: Please remember that any time your Shih Tzu is not listening well or is acting up, a huge part of this is improper hierarchy interpretation. You'll want to keep yourself in check to make sure that you (and all humans) follow these steps, every day, at all times. It should be noted that dogs are much more relaxed and content when they have a clear understanding of who the leader(s) is. When leadership is unclear, a dog can feel uneasy and stressed.

Heeling

For this section on heeling, we are going to look to Faye Dunningham, a very popular canine trainer, who has several top selling books on Amazon. This is where part of your 'Book within a Book' comes into play. The author has given us permission to include some condensed sections of her book: The Well Trained Puppy: Housebreaking, Commands to Shape Behavior and All Training Needed for a Happy, Obedient Dog. As she can write like no other can, we give the floor to Faye….

Before we commence, please note that while I do use the word 'puppy' quite often, this type of training can be used for a dog of any age. In addition, there is no dog breed that is exempt from being able to learn any training of any sort.

Moving in Tandem

Heeling is almost like an art form. It is the rhythm of dog and human walking in unison. When heeling, while walking at the same pace, the dog is very aware that the human is in charge. The dog's human controls pace, direction and decides when to stop or reverse course. When your dog is fully trained to heel, your dog will properly follow along whether you are walking, jogging or suddenly stop. A dog that heels always walks beside you and does not run ahead, lag behind or stop for any reason other than if you stop.

There will be plenty of times that you will not mind when your dog takes his time to explore the world. However heeling or not heeling can affect every day of your life; walking can be fun or it can be frustrating.

Some owners skip over this training because they believe that it will be too difficult. It is a shame since just one month of training can be the foundation for a lifetime of enjoyed walks. Another reason why owners do not train their dogs for this is that they expect their dog to naturally walk beside them. A dog has absolutely no idea that he is expected to walk nicely next to you.

Canine instinct does not tell a dog to walk beside a human, taking the owner's cues for speed and direction. This must be taught. When first brought out on a leash, a dog will do as he wishes. He will chase a butterfly, stop to smell flowers, try to run ahead and explore.

It is the owner who must show the dog what is expected. When a dog is trained in the correct way, learning to heel is not that difficult. Hopefully, you will be taking your dog for daily walks, which reinforces the learned behavior. A properly trained dog will always heel and walks can be fun without the stress (and sometimes embarrassment) of having your dog try to take you for a walk.

Heeling is when your dog walks on your left with his head no further ahead than the extension of your left heel. It is done this way because the majority of people are right handed. Having the leash in your left hand allows your dominant hand to be free. While this is the customary positioning, if you are left handed, feel free to train your dog to heel to your right if that is what feels best for you.

At What Age You Can Begin This Training

A puppy should be at least four months old before you begin any training outside of your home's property. Why? Because a puppy should not be brought to outside public places or to indoor public places until he has had all of his puppy shots. Once your puppy is up-to-date on all vaccinations, you may then go ahead and venture outside.

There is a short period of time in which the maternal antibodies that were passed from dam to puppy are too low to continue to provide the puppy with protection against disease, but too high to allow a vaccine to work. This phase lasts from several days to several weeks as it varies from puppy to puppy.

This time is called the window of susceptibility. During this "window", even though a puppy was vaccinated, he could still contract a disease. Because of this risk, any puppy that has not yet had his shots must be kept away from other animals or any places in which other animals could have previously been.

Once your puppy has had all of his puppy shots, you can then allow him to meet other people, go to parks, accompany you to stores, explore the world and importantly, learn to heel while out for daily walks.

If you have an older dog that has never learned to heel, it is never too late to train him. A dog of any age, other than perhaps a senior who is stuck in his own ways and has developed a lifetime of habits, will be able to learn to heel.

Training Your Dog to Heel – Step by Step Instructions

Before Heading Out -To begin, you will want to put a harness on your puppy. Walking an untrained puppy on a leash and collar can be very dangerous. If your puppy lunges forward or if you pull too hard on the leash, the fragile trachea can collapse; this is a very serious injury. In addition, you will find that you have more control over your dog when training him to heel.

You will want to give your dog a few minutes to get used to the harness that you put onto him. Usually, it will be accepted without protest in just a couple of days.

When exiting the home, you should exit first. After the walk is complete, you should enter back into the home first. This is part of training your dog to understand that you are the leader (the Alpha).
Going for walks and having a dog learn to heel works best if walks are done at a certain time each day. Canines have amazing internal clocks, able to sense when things "should" happen. Dogs of all ages do best when they know what to expect. Be sure to choose a time that works for both of you. While you want to opt for a time that fits in well with your schedule and one that you feel comfortable with, also think about your dog's needs as well. You will not want to choose a time when he is normally tired and in need of a nap.

Lastly, choose a special treat that you will give to your dog upon completion of the walk. The treat should be one that is not given normally as a snack. It should be special enough that your puppy learns that it is only given if a session of listening to you, such as this, occurs. Keep the treat hidden in a pocket so that your puppy does not see it or smell it, which would potentially cause him to pester you for the treat and not focus on the heeling lesson.

Heeling Rules and Guidelines - Once you have chosen a good time for walks that works well for both you and your puppy, you have him on a harness, you have a treat in your pocket and you have exited the home first with him following you, you will now begin to walk. Have your dog on your left side.

Any time that your dog tries to walk ahead of you, stand in place and do not move. Using a harness, this will not injure or hurt your dog. Your dog may try several times to keep walking. Do not pull on the leash. Simply remain standing and do not move. While you are remaining standing in one spot, essentially glued into place, any time that your dog comes very close to you, talk to him and pat him. This shows that staying near you means that the leash will not frustrate him.

As soon as your dog stops trying to walk ahead by himself and is remaining near you, give the leash a quick, light tug and continue walking. Hold the leash with two hands. With your dog on your left, you should be holding the leash tightly with your right hand and loosely with your left hand.

Anytime that your dog walks beside you, keep repeating the command word of "Heel" in a happy yet firm tone of voice so that he connects his actions with a command word. Furthermore, offer words of praise as you go along, first in the form of "Good Heel" to reinforce his actions and then with "Good Boy" or "Good Girl".

Change your pace; take turns walking slower and then faster. Do not just walk in a straight line; most dogs stay more focused if the walk is a fun challenge. You can help make this entertaining by winding around telephone poles, taking turns, and more.

You may need to tug and then say "Heel" over and over; however at any time that your dog is heeling, offer great words of praise. Do not stop to pat or hug your dog; but keep saying "Good Boy" or "Good Girl" and "Good Heel" in a very happy tone to show him how proud you are of him.

The first time that you take a turn and your dog does not, he will quickly realize that he must heel to you. You will make that turn and your dog (on harness and short leash) will have no choice but to follow along.

Of course, be very careful, as accidentally stepping on your dog can cause extreme injuries or worse. But, walk confidently and show your dog that you are in control. When this occurs, walk as if you do not notice that he is not exactly following along. The harness will not injure the neck and he will "catch up" to you as long as you do not increase speed.

These training sessions should be done each day, with each session lasting approximately twenty minutes. If you do not give up and you do this each and every day, your dog will learn what he must do to hear your happy "Good Boy" or "Good Girl" remarks.

When the walk is finished and you are still outside of your home, be sure to give your dog tons of pats, praise, attention and finally a tasty treat (the one you previously hid in your pocket). Remember that the treat should be a special one that is not normally given for snacks.

It usually takes about two weeks for a dog to really understand how to heel. Even when it seems that he is well trained, do keep offering the words of praise and the confirmation word of "Heel" as you walk along. Eventually, whenever you say the command word of "Heel" your dog will immediately go over to your left side and stay beside you.

Note: For help with walking with traffic, please refer to the "If Your Dog is Afraid of Traffic' section in the 'Socialization' chapter ahead.

Resistance to Walking

Some dogs are very resistant to walking and in many cases this can be contributed to the surface that they are being asked to walk upon. When a person is wearing shoes, it is very easy to forget that street surfaces can be extremely hot if the weather is warm and sunny. While a dog's paws are sturdy, they are made of skin, albeit thick skin. They have nerves that feel burning sensations, pain and/or injury.

What is the texture and temperature of the surface that you are walking on? Forget that you have shoes on and look at it from your dog's point of view. Are there lots of pebbles or rocks? Is it hot or cold when you touch it with your hand? If so, doggie shoes or paw wax will help. Alternatively, if heat is the reason for resistance, you may opt to walk in the early morning or late afternoon when surfaces have cooled down.

Also, check the weather in regard to how your dog may physically feel when exercising outdoors. If it is very warm to hot, bring lots of water and take rests in the shade if at all possible. Is it cold? Putting a sweater on your dog may be all that is needed to keep away a chill and allow for important exercise.

In addition, your dog may not want to go for walks when you do. Try to learn what time of the day your dog wishes to have exercise. Most will have pent up energy at a certain time of the day and it is then that they would love to release it. Every few days, choose a different time to see if the enthusiasm level of your dog is higher.

Just as some humans like to exercise in the morning, others like to take walks at lunch time and yet others prefer evening workouts... so may your dog. Working together, you should be able to pinpoint the time in the day that your dog most wishes to stretch his legs and accompany you for a journey around the neighborhood. Once he has learned to heel, you can then adjust the time of the daily walk to better fit your needs and schedule, if this is desired.

Some dogs are very sensitive to ground texture and sand can be a big factor. It is so much fun to walk along the shore of the ocean, a lake or another body of water that has a sandy shoreline...But the sand particles can cause a puppy to feel discomfort and this should be looked at if your puppy is resistant to walking on this type of surface.

Sand particles are very tiny. When walking on sand, it is quite possible that some particles can become stuck between paw pads or that the particles are very irritating to his paws (and the sensitive skin between the pads).

If your dog is walking along the sand and suddenly shows signs of discomfort, stop to inspect all four paws. Look for any particles...or any redness, swelling or any sign of irritation. If there are particles stuck into the paw, it is best to rinse them off in the bathtub or kitchen sink and flush the paw...Then pour a bit of hydrogen peroxide on the area. Later that day, or the next day, you can apply some paw wax onto the pads. If there are not any sand particles, but there is any redness, swelling or other signs of irritation, it will be best to bring your dog to the veterinarian. A cut may have gotten infected and an antibiotic medication and/or topical treatment may be needed.

If it is simply a matter of a dog resisting a walk upon sand yet it is not causing any injury, it will help to protect the paws with shoes or doggie booties if you wish to continue to routinely walk there. Trying to force a dog to walk upon these types of textures will not bring success... Your choice will be to either avoid the area or put foot protection on your dog to bring about results that can lead to a relaxing walk along the shore.

If using doggie booties or shoes, it is suggested to first have your dog wear them at home before going out for a walk with them on. When you put them on, cuddle your dog into your lap and slip them on while talking to your dog in order to distract him. For that very first time, leave them on for about an hour and see how he does. The next day, have him wear them for perhaps for two hours. When your dog seems to forget that they are on him, this is a good time to head out for a walk.

Some dogs need a bit of encouragement to join their owner for a walk. The tone of your voice will send a message as to whether your dog should perceive a walk as a fun activity or a dreaded undertaking. Dogs pick up on not just the words that we say, but also in the way that we say them. When getting ready to leave for a walk, it will be helpful to sound very excited. Talk as if you are about to leave on an amazing journey. Act enthusiastic. And do use a very loving but firm voice... It may take a couple of days of like this to send the message, but it should lead to a dog thinking the equivalent of, "If my human is excited about walking, maybe I should be also!"

If a dog truly shows a strong dislike for walking and basically plants his paws down, ready to hold his ground, refusing to move, treats may be needed to use as motivation. If this is the case, when you are out, any time that your dog is walking nicely with you, randomly give him treats. It is suggested to offer truly exceptional treats if a dog needs a lot of incentive. One treat that works very well in this situation is crisp bacon. Bacon is actually not an unhealthy food if it is given in moderation and prepared properly. It is suggested to fry it or microwave it to a very crisp texture. Doing so releases much of the fat. Then, you will want to put the pieces between paper towels and squeeze it all together, so that the paper towels soak up most of the remaining fat. What you are left with are crisp pieces that are 95% meat.

As a last step, crumble the bacon up, so that you have small little pieces. You can put them into a plastic sandwich bag and have that bag in your pocket. Then, as you are walking...every now and then repeat the word "Heel", walk for a few more seconds, say in a happy tone "Good Heel!" and then without pausing much at all, reach into your pocket, grab a pinch of the crumbled up crisp bacon, and put it right in front of your dog's mouth so that he can quickly eat it.

Command Training

Before you Begin -
Command training is recommended for any Shih Tzu that does not yet have the 'basics' down pat. A Shih Tzu of any age, from the little 8 week old pup to the 14 year old senior can learn commands. There's lots of benefits: It makes life easier when you can successfully communicate with your Shih Tzu in this way; you say something, your Shih Tzu responds with an appropriate action. It can also come in quite handy to stop your Shih Tzu from doing something he should not as the command can interrupt his actions. Training

sessions are a great way for you and your Shih Tzu to bond together as you'll be working as a team. And finally, dogs get a huge boost of self-confidence when they learn commands. Canines are smart!... As intelligent as a 2 or 3 year old human, so to allow a dog to use his brain and perform well for you enhances his self-esteem and gives you an overall happier dog.

It should be strongly noted that the actual steps for command training are super easy! It varies very little from trainer to trainer. These steps have been essentially the same for decades. What makes a huge difference is how you prepare yourself for this training (this first section) and how closely you adhere to both this prep advice and the training steps.

Prepare Yourself to be a Great Trainer - Your job as a trainer is to direct your Shih Tzu in a steady and encouraging way. He won't want to stay in 'school' if class isn't fun! Your goal will be to guide your Shih Tzu through the steps of performing a new action, rewarding small steps along the way. It is very important to understand that when you are teaching your Shih Tzu to follow a command, this is not achieved in one day… or even several days. It is a gradual process. Little by little, with your help, your Shih Tzu will learn to master these basic commands. The goal of each training session will be for your Shih Tzu to do just a little bit better than session before; if that happens, things will be going great and you are on your way to having a well-trained dog.

Your 'Trainer Voice' – Even if you're not completely sure of how you will do as a trainer, speak as if you are! Your tone should be friendly, firm and be sure to articulate your words very clearly. When you give praise, make sure you use an exceedingly happy voice.

The Importance of Timing - With command training, a huge aspect to this, is that your Shih Tzu needs to know *exactly* what he did correctly. One mistake that many owners make is rewarding a dog 5 or 10 seconds after an action is done. If you take too long to dig out the treat or you tied up the treats in a baggie with a twist-tie that you need to un-wind, you won't be able to mark the exact moment! By that time, a dog is in a different stance and he'll think that he's being rewarded for something other than his action of following the command.

Choosing the Rewards - Dogs do like to please their owners, but for command training, they need an extra motivation. In regard to training treats, you will want to keep your Shih Tzu motivated when learning by having the treat be something really special. It will not do much good to have it be a snack that you would be giving to him anyway, right? Foods such as small turkey meatballs, slices of organic uncured hotdogs or microwave bacon that is cooked very well (crispy) with the excess grease being dabbed up with paper towels (the bacon can then be crumbled into small pieces that will get your Shih Tzu's mouthwatering).

Treats are only used for a short while - Don't worry about always having to give your Shih Tzu a treat to obey a command, because as you progress, your Shih Tzu will listen due to an automated response. It can take anywhere from 100 to 500 times of repeating an action before it becomes 'automated' for a dog. Though 500 times may seem like a lot, if you do 20'sits', twice per day, your Shih Tzu would be trained in about 2 weeks.

Keeping your Shih Tzu Feeling Good - Try to not let your Shih Tzu be wrong more than 2 or 3 times in a row. If he feels that he is doing badly, he can lose motivation to keep trying. If he's struggling, go back to an easier step in the training, so that he can be 'right' and feel good.

Only Train When You Are Feeling Patient- If you are having a super busy day and are feeling stressed, this can affect how the training goes. Dogs easily pick up on their owner's vibe. While you want to be very consistent and not miss too many days in a row, if you're feeling stressed or otherwise cannot commit to being focused, wait until the next day.

End in a Good Place – As with other things like playing indoor games, a session of command training should end while the Shih Tzu is still having fun and has not yet tired of it. In this way, he'll be much more prone to want to be a student the next day.

The Exact Words You Should Use – Certain words should be used and these are used for two reasons: for consistency and because they are short (canines only pay attention to the first syllable):

"Ah-Oh" – This is said if the Shih Tzu makes an incorrect action. Your instinct will be to say "No", however it's best to never say that word and instead say "Ah-oh" in a fun, amused tone of voice.

"Okay" – This is the word used to release your Shih Tzu from his position. For example, if you are training him to sit, he needs to know how long he is supposed to do so. "Okay" will let him know that he can move out of a 'Sit' or 'Down'.

"Good, *Sit*", "Good, *Come*", etc. Instead of saying, "Good, boy!" or "good" plus your Shih Tzu's name, it is best to say "good" and then the command word/action. This reinforces the training.

Time Involved - With sessions every day, a dog can learn a command in about 2 or 3 weeks. However, commands can be forgotten if you never use them once the training is complete. And while you do not need to keep giving food treats, do this once in a while to show your Shih Tzu that he's being a good dog!

10 Tips to Remember

1. Reward with special treats, not one that your Shih Tzu would receive throughout the day anyway.
2. Reward at the exact moment that your Shih Tzu is in the correct position or has just done the command that you asked for.
3. Don't search in your pockets to look for the treats; have them in your cupped hand, ready to give to him immediately.
4. It is best to train when your Shih Tzu is hungry. Therefore, right after dinner is not a good time. Try to choose a time that you are generally free each day so that your dog gets used to knowing that it is "command training time".
5. The rule should be: Training comes before playtime.
6. Always end each session with your Shih Tzu wanting more…that way he will be much more eager to begin again the next day.

7. Be consistent.
8. Motivate.
9. Be patient. If your Shih Tzu obeys a command in one day, this does not count as mastering the command, it was just good luck.
10. Have fun.

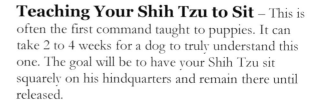

Teaching Your Shih Tzu to Sit – This is often the first command taught to puppies. It can take 2 to 4 weeks for a dog to truly understand this one. The goal will be to have your Shih Tzu sit squarely on his hindquarters and remain there until released.

1. Stand or kneel right in front of your dog, holding a treat in your hand a little higher than your dog's head.

2. Slowly move the treat straight back over your Shih Tzu's head. This should cause his nose to point up and his rear to drop. If his rear does not drop, keep moving the treat straight backward toward his tail. The instant his rear touches the floor, release the treat and mark the behavior by saying, "Good Sit!" in a happy voice.

3. If your dog is not responding to the food lure, use your index finger and thumb to put pressure on either side of his haunches, just forward of his hip bones. Pull up on his leash at the same time to rock him back into a sit. Praise and reward him while he is sitting.

4. Once your Shih Tzu is consistently sitting, wait a few seconds before rewarding. Remember to only reward while your dog is in the correct position of squarely sitting on the floor.

Trouble Shooting – If your Shih Tzu jumps at your hand that is holding the treat, hold the treat lower, so that he can reach it while standing. If your Shih Tzu sits, but then gets up right away, in a gentle but firm manner, keep placing your dog back into a sit. Once he has learned the behavior, he should not break his sit until released. Be sure to not give the treat until he has been in the position for a count of 3.

Tip – Command your dog to sit before each meal. This reinforces your position as pack leader.

Teaching Your Shih Tzu the Down Command - Some dogs learn this one as quickly as 'Sit' but others take a bit longer. With this, the goal will be for your Shih Tzu to rest on both his chest and belly or askew on his hip.

1. With your dog sitting facing you, hold a treat to his nose and lower it slowly to the floor.

2. If you are lucky, your dog will follow the treat with his nose and lie down, at which time you can release the treat and praise him by saying, "Good Down!" Remember to only release the treat while your dog is in the correct position (laying down). Do not give it to him if he gets up; that will be too late and he will think that you are rewarding the action of rising up. If your dog hunches over instead of fully lying down, slide the treat slowly toward him on the floor between his front paws or away from him. Remember to be patient and keep encouraging him; if he can stay focused, he should ultimately lie down.

3. If your dog is not responding to the food, put gentle pressure on his shoulder blades, pushing down and to the side. Give praise & a treat when he drops to the floor. While it's better for a dog to finally listen due to your words instead of you physically moving him, this step may be needed at first to give him the general idea of what you are looking for.

4. Once your dog is consistently lying down, gradually delay the release of the treat. With your Shih Tzu lying down, say, "Wait…wait" and then finally an excited "Good Down!" and release the treat. Varying the time before actually giving the treat will help your Shih Tzu pay close attention. Ideally, he should not move from the down position until you have given your release word of "Good Down".

Trouble Shooting – If your Shih Tzu does not stay down, don't reward him; instead, command another 'Down'. If he can't move passed this step and he will not stay in position, have him on harness & leash and then hold the leash to the floor with your foot to keep him down until you give the release word of "Okay". You will not step so close as to cause his body to move; your foot on the leash will simply keep him in place. With a proper harness, this should not cause injury.

Teaching your Shih Tzu to Stay – It can take anywhere from 3 to 6 weeks for a dog to truly understand this one, since it goes against his instinct to run over to you. The goal will be for your Shih Tzu to hold his current position (whatever that may be and as long as he is within earshot of you) until released.

1. Start with your Shih Tzu sitting or lying down, as he is less likely to move from those positions. Use a leash or harness to guarantee control. Stand directly in front of him and in a serious tone, say "Stay", holding your palm flat, almost touching his nose.

2. Move a short distance away, keeping eye contact with your Shih Tzu, and return to him. Praise him with "Good Stay" and give him a treat. Be sure to give the praise and treat while your dog remains in the sitting and staying position.

3. If your dog moved from his stay before you have released him, gently but firmly put him back in the spot where he was originally told to stay.

4. Gradually increase the time you ask your Shih Tzu to stay, as well as how far you are away from him. You want your Shih Tzu to be successful so if he is breaking his stay, go back to a time and distance he does well with.

Trouble Shooting – If your Shih Tzu keeps breaking his 'Stay' before you say "Okay", do not show him the treat until you give it to him, be what is causing him to move. Vary what you do; sometimes return to him and leave him without rewarding.

Teaching Your Shih Tzu to Come

Teaching Your Shih Tzu to Come – There are two types of owners: those that have zero use for this command because their Shih Tzu comes running to them no matter what and those who are in dire need of it, because getting a stubborn toddler to listen would be an easier task! The goal will be that on your command, your Shih Tzu immediately comes to you regardless of what he is doing. Ideally, the command ends with the dog in a 'Sit'.

Unlike other commands, this one is very 'hands on', due to the fact that you will physically 'force' your Shih Tzu to obey (though, of course, without harming him) in order for him to understand. For dogs that resist this command, it can take a lot of sessions and even then, one should reinforce this, essentially for life by routinely commanding this and if the dog falters, re-doing some sessions to remind him. Do not use this command for something that your Shih Tzu really dislikes; for those sorts of things, it is best to just go over and pick him up.

With this training, reward your Shih Tzu for obeying your 'Come' command, with praise and a treat. Unlike other training, if your Shih Tzu does not listen, you will *not* respond by saying "Ah-Oh". Instead, you will (not too roughly) physically bring your Shih Tzu to the spot from where you originally called him. Since, for this command, you will need to reel your Shih Tzu to you in order for him to understand the command, please ONLY do this with your Shih Tzu wearing a harness and NOT a dog collar. Injury can occur if you pull him to you with only leash and collar. If you do not have a harness, obtain one before you teach this command.

1. With your Shih Tzu on a 6 foot leash (1.8 m) and a harness, command him to 'Come'. Give the command only once. As you firmly say this word, reel him to you, quickly, those 6 feet and immediately reward him with the praise of 'Good, Come' and a treat.
2. Repeat this over and over. Do not yet do anything off leash, even if you do not need to do much 'reeling in'.
3. As your Shih Tzu improves, use a longer leash. You can use a retractable leash to gain a few feet each new session.
4. When you are ready to practice off-leash, do so in a safe fenced-in area. Have the leash attached, but do not hold onto the other end. If he does not obey your command when you say it one time, go to him and firmly lead him back to the spot where you gave the command. Do not give a reward if your Shih Tzu does not perform the command on his own the first time you say it. Put the long leash back on him and require him to do 5 successful 'Comes' before attempting off-leash again.

Trouble Shooting – If your Shih Tzu takes off running the moment you let him off the leash, do not chase after him. Stand your ground and repeat the command. If need be, go back to the beginning steps of training on-leash.

Trick Training

Shake Paw – Both Left and Right

Shake Paw – Both Left and Right – This is a great trick that will put a smile on your face, the faces of anyone watching and can make your Shih Tzu super pleased with himself for gaining so much attention for a simple act. The goal is to have your Shih Tzu raise his paw to chest height (his chest), allowing you to shake 'hands' with him. Ideally, a dog should be able to learn to do this with both left and right paws.

Typical training is that when the command 'Shake' is given, the dog shakes with his right paw. And when the command 'Paw' is given, the dog shakes with his left paw. We'll work on the right paw first:

1.   With your Shih Tzu sitting before you, hide a treat in your left hand, low to the ground.

2.   Encourage your Shih Tzu to paw at it by saying "Get it" and "Shake". Reward him with the treat the moment his right paw comes off the ground and say, "Good, Shake".

3.   Repeat this over and over, gradually raise the height of your hand, until he is lifting his paw to chest height.

4.   Transition to using the hand signal if you wish. The hand signal is to hold your hand in a fist, with your pointer and middle fingers both out straight.

5.   Stand up and hold the treat in your left hand, behind your back and extend your right hand while cueing 'Shake' as mentioned (hand in a fist, pointer & middle fingers out). When your Shih Tzu paws your extended hand, support his paw in the air while you reward him with the treat from behind your back.

6.   Repeat these steps on the opposite side to teach 'Paw', using the words of 'Good, Paw' when he follows along.

Trouble Shooting – If your Shih Tzu tends to 'nose' your hand instead of pawing at it, quickly withdraw your hand and start over. If he does not lift his paw whatsoever, you can gently lift it for him and then reward, gradually using less and less force to move him as he learns to lift it on his own.

Behavioral Training

Socialization Training

For this section on socialization, we are going to look again to Faye Dunningham, a very popular canine trainer, who has several top selling books on Amazon. This is another part of where your 'Book within a Book' comes into play. The author has given us permission to include some condensed sections of her book: The Well Socialized Dog: Step-by-Step Socialization Training for Puppies and Dogs. As she can write like no other can, we give the floor to Faye….

Overview

Before we commence, please note that while I do use the word 'puppy' quite often, this type of training can be used for a dog of any age. There are many adult dogs that would greatly benefit from socialization. In addition, there is no dog breed that is exempt from being able to learn any training of any sort.

While a puppy will naturally come into contact with elements in his day to day living, a puppy will need your guidance when encountering many of them. Socialization is the method of directing that introduction between your puppy and various elements in his world. It not only includes the introduction of things, it also involves teaching your puppy the proper response to the input that he is receiving.

An introduction to a new element (a person, a place, a situation, another animal, etc.) offers a puppy the opportunity of discovery; to see something new, to hear something new. If the introduction is fleeting, the puppy will process and store that limited information. This type of limited and restricted socialization can happen throughout a normal day without any purposeful contribution by you. However, proper socialization will involve teaching your puppy how to go beyond introduction and to actually interact with the element (if there should even be a desired interaction). Additionally, it will involve teaching your puppy how that element should be perceived and how the puppy should react to it. Should he stay away (electrical cord)? Should he have no fear (a family friend)? Should he learn to tolerate it (cars driving by)?

Without your guidance, a puppy can become extremely overwhelmed with his world. It will be your job to properly socialize him to each and every element that is worthy of an emotional and/or physical response. There are many things to socialize your puppy to that are worthy of dictating an emotional or physical response. This includes people (friends, acquaintances and strangers), other dogs (both those known and unknown), and other animals. It will encompass situations such as being at the park, walking down a street next to busy traffic and going to the veterinarian. It will include becoming accustomed to walking on different surfaces such as sand and snow. And it will also include being familiarized with noises such as car alarms, thunder storms and even crying babies.

Without your guidance, a puppy can become very fearful of situations and events. He may be nervous and anxious around people who visit at your home….Or he may bark in response to seeing and hearing cars, other people or small animals. A puppy may have a strong reaction to one element and seem oblivious to another; this often leaves an owner wondering "how" and "why". It may be a matter of a puppy not having received enough positive feedback when first encountering the element… Or it may simply be a matter of a puppy's particular personality and his or her capability to process a situation. Each puppy will need varying levels of training to react and respond appropriately. Some puppies can become accustomed to an element in as little as a week or so…Others may need a much more gradual introduction over the course of several months.

Your Dog's Changing Personality

There is a huge shift in the way that a puppy sees the world between the age of 8 weeks old and 12 to 16 weeks old. This 1 to 2 month window is one of great changes. Many owners do not know that this is normal and is part of the growing process, which can lead an owner to not only become confused, but it can cause them to not follow through with very much needed socialization during this time. Canine instinct dictates that a dog be wary of things, to be on guard for everything to be a possible threat unless proven otherwise. This instinct often does not kick in until the age of 3 to 4 months old. Before this time, a puppy is not able to properly process all of the data in the world around him. His mind picks up only bits and pieces. Those pieces of limited data are then processed with a low level of importance and stored away.

The owner of a new 8 week old puppy may often be happily surprised regarding how their puppy seems to be the friendliest puppy in the world…And that he or she loves everyone! In many cases, this is a temporary display of behavior. As soon as that same puppy has the ability and the capacity to take in all that surrounds him, only then will he react to the entire weight of a situation. And as previously mentioned this change often happens between the ages of 3 to 4 months old.

Home Socialization – How to Build the Perfect Foundation

Owners of new puppies may be eager to bring their new puppy out into the world and it is extremely important to do so. However, one must keep in mind that a young puppy is not fully protected by vaccinations until he or she has had all of their "puppy shots". When nursing from the dam, antibodies of protection are passed down to the pup. Vaccinations begin. There is a window of time in which the antibodies that were passed down from the dam are no longer present (or are at very low inadequate levels), but the vaccination antibodies are not yet abundant enough to offer full protection.

For this reason, owners of new puppies should keep their puppies at home until the full round of puppy shots is complete and

then count out for 2 weeks after that. This is perfectly expected and is actually a good thing. Why? The answer is because the world should not be introduced all at once. For proper socialization skills, a puppy needs the process of experiencing new things to be gradual. It brings to mind the old saying that one must walk before one runs. This is the idea to keep in mind.

A puppy will do much better with a group of dogs when first allowed to become used to playing with one dog. A puppy will behave better when you have a group of friends over to your home if he or she is first allowed to become used to one guest entering into the home. And so it goes on... Most of the following training will be comprised of gradual increments of socialization. It will prevent stress to the puppy and while the process is gradual, it is the fastest route to success. To rush things is counterproductive, and you and your puppy may move backward instead of forward.

Why Socialization Should Begin at Home

A young puppy cannot be thrown into situations that are new, he or she must be allowed to take small steps. If an owner tries to force a puppy into a situation too quickly, before that puppy has gained self-confidence on smaller levels with less intense situations, it can cause a great deal of stress. In worst case situations, it can cause the puppy to have a phobia of the very thing that the owner tried to force the puppy to be socialized to. Your home offers an array of socialization opportunities. There is so much for a puppy to learn about; however it should be done in increments so not to overwhelm a puppy.

The Importance of Touch

It cannot be overstated how important touch is. When a puppy is not handled enough it can cause him to never be able to have tolerance for grooming (bathing, brushing, nail trimming, ear cleaning, dental care, wiping of the eyes). Without handling, he will often not, on his own, be the type of dog that cuddles up to humans. The aloof adult dog that shuns close contact with his humans is the grown-up version of the puppy that was not touched and handled enough. Therefore, touching and handling your puppy is a part of socialization. Most dogs without "touch socialization" are very impatient when their paws are handled....when an owner is attempting to trim nails...when an owner is attempting to locate a sliver and a host of other random reasons to handle the dog over the course of a life time. Dogs also often show great reluctance to having their teeth brushed if they are not routinely desensitized to having their teeth and mouths touched.

An owner should establish a firm precedence that the puppy is to hold still whenever their human is handling them. Your goal is to make it such an ordinary occurrence that should you need to check your dog for an attached tick or you need to grab a non-food possible choking object from his mouth, that he sits still and allows you to do it.

Begin with small steps, simply holding your puppy and patting him. Touch the tail, the ears, and the paws. As we discussed earlier on, a young puppy that is 8 weeks old and up to 16 weeks old can be easily distracted and not fully aware of all that is happening. It is during this age that desensitizing him to being handled works best. As you do this each day, he will be becoming more aware and the 2 elements will blend seamlessly together; giving you a puppy and then adult dog that does not run away from bath time or try to escape a grooming session. Best done at an early age, but able to be done with even a ten year old dog, an owner should gently open the puppy's mouth. Using a finger, all teeth should be touched: front, back and tops.

Your Property – Finding Out What Your Puppy Needs to Be Socialized To

When you bring your puppy outside for his bathroom needs, once he has eliminated you should walk him around your property. Alternatively, you can choose another convenient time of the day. Allow him to stop along the way to investigate what he wishes as long as it is not harmful (chemically treated grass, fire ants, etc.) When young, he may not have yet experienced the scent of a certain flower before…and just that element can bring about the joy of discovery.

If the weather is pleasant, stay outside for a good amount of time. Sit together and allow your puppy to see squirrels and hear the chirping of birds. If you live on a busy street, allow him to have short times of sitting on leash beside you to hear the cars driving by. If it is raining, put on your raincoat and allow your puppy to become accustomed to the feel of the raindrops falling down upon him. If it is snowing, bundle up (and bundle up your puppy – especially if you have a toy or small breed dog – with booties and a sweater) and allow him to become accustomed to seeing the snowflakes falling down and feel how the ground now feels solid as opposed to soft grass.

The key element in all of this, is to take notice of which things your puppy easily accepts as "part of life". With those things, he may act oblivious to the element….Or he may show curiosity, check things out and while you are saying "Good Boy" or "Good Girl" your puppy will then move on to the next element that catches his attention.

For any element that appears to cause nervous, anxious or wary behavior, the element should be "red flagged" as one that your puppy will need to be socialized to. If you socialize your puppy to elements encountered while at home, you will have much

better success when doing so with elements outside of the home and the property.

For example, let's take a look at what to do if your puppy acts frantic in the rain, appearing to have a strong dislike for feeling it falling upon him. Keep the time spent in the rain short: one to three minutes. Do not immediately bring him or her back inside. It will be important to NOT offer soothing words during this short, first initial discovery of an element that bothers your puppy. If you say in a soothing voice, "It's okay, calm down, the rain is not going to hurt you"….It will send a message to your puppy that he is correct in being upset and that you, his leader, agrees since you are now trying to soothe him.

You will want to act in a very casual way. Just speak in a normal tone. You can say just about anything that you want, aside from "NO" or the soothing words of "It's okay", just say it in a matter-of-fact way. The goal is to show your puppy, by your words and your calm actions that the rain is of no bother to you. Each time it does rain, make it a point to bring your puppy outside. Each time you do this increase the time increment by 1 to 2 minutes. Each time, act casual as described above. Ignore any barking, begging, nudging against you or any other attention-seeking behavior. As the session time is ending and you are ready to bring your puppy back inside, if your puppy is acting calm take that moment to offer a special treat and praise before entering back into the home. When you do this on a regular basis, your puppy will learn that since you do not mind the rain (or traffic noises, or birds chirping, or snowfall or any other outside element) that neither should they. You will lead by example and he, ruled by canine instinct, will choose to follow your lead.

Socializing Your Puppy or Dog with Visitors to Your Home

As we discussed earlier, a very young puppy may appear to be oblivious to guests in your home or even show very friendly behavior. As your puppy grows a bit older, he will have then learned that the home and the property is his "territory" and his canine instinct to protect the home will have grown much stronger. On the flip side of protection mode, some puppies will become shy, often nervous when others are around. Puppies that feel this way may constantly nudge at you for attention, shake or try to hide. Fortunately, there is one answer to the many ways that a puppy may negatively behave when guests arrive, since there is only one main trigger: The puppy is not desensitized to the element and socialization training will work to fix that.

For a puppy, when a guest arrives, now has a lot to think about. Not only may he feel an urge to protect, he may also additionally feel as if his territory is being invaded and encroached upon. The thoughts that metaphorically run through a puppy's mind are, "Who is this person?" "Is this a friend or foe?" "Should I go into protection mode?" "Am I in danger and should I hide" "What is their intention?" "Does my human need my guard services?" A dog of any size, from a 4 pound Shih Tzu to a 20 pound Boxer will have a mixture of these same thoughts.

It will be your job to show your puppy, by your words and by your actions that he has no reason to: be afraid, be on guard, be nervous, bark, or show any other behavior other than being relaxed and friendly. If your puppy has been proven to show negative behavior with guests, do plan ahead with your visitors regarding the training that you are going to implement. It is best if they understand what you are doing as opposed to you having to try to explain yourself while also trying to focus on the socialization training.

The most common behaviors of a puppy that is not socialized to guests are: barking, jumping, hiding or nudging you for attention. There are other odd quirks that a puppy can have...Therefore, while your puppy may act out in his own particular way, we will use the word "negative behavior" to encompass whatever he is doing that is causing problems. You may replace this with "nudge you" or "jump around" or "hide in fear", as ultimately the training for this aspect will be the same.

The first reactions that most owners have, when puppies are showing negative behavior, are to say "Shhhhhh", try to reprimand them or remove them from the room. None of those techniques will work.

Saying "Shhhhhh" is the same as offering a soothing message. As we learned in the previous section of "Your Property – Finding Out What Your Puppy Needs to Be Socialized To"....offering any words in a tone that could be interpreted as soothing is the same as confirming that your puppy is behaving correctly. Therefore, when owners say "Shhhhh", they are unknowingly encouraging the behavior.

If you try and reprimand your puppy, it may cause a temporary pause in the negative behavior as you may be able to momentarily avert his attention, but it does not teach proper socialization skills. If you remove your puppy from the room, this absolutely is one of the worst things that you can do. While you may gain the temporary relief of being away from the negative behavior, you are removing any opportunity to implement socialization training. Your puppy will never move forward in his ability to control his actions. It will be become commonplace for him to be removed when a guest comes over and not only will this not stop negative behavior, but it often increases it.

The key is to completely ignore the negative behavior. You may at first think that this is the same as approving it. It is not. Ignoring negative behavior, when done properly, sends out a strong message that the negative behavior does not warrant your attention what-so-ever. As your dog's leader, your puppy will learn (after a few lessons) that if you do not think that the negative behavior is of importance, perhaps he is wrong to display it.

When you couple this with rewarding acceptable behavior, you have a winning combination. When this winning combination is repeated, the message of it becomes instilled in a dog's mind; becoming part of his natural, automatic thinking process...And at that point you have success.

The aspect of ignoring the puppy is crucial. Ignoring is not "mean"...It is actually a kind, gentle and non-reprimanding method to lead by example and show your puppy that all is fine. It will be by these actions (or lack of them, actually) that your puppy will be reassured. Soothing words and attention only serve to reinforce a puppy's perceived fear or intolerance.

All dogs think of their human families as their "packs". Their human is the leader of the pack, known as the "Alpha". When a puppy shows negative behavior, if his leader shows that the behavior is not warranted, the puppy will take note of this message. It will mean a lot to him and when done enough, he will re-think his actions.

If a puppy barks at guests, if the leader's training for this involves ignoring the puppy, the puppy will learn that his barking behavior is so unwarranted that his leader is oblivious to it. If a puppy is afraid, shy or nervous and his leader ignores that behavior, the puppy will learn that since his leader is relaxed and confident, offering no soothing words, that being afraid, nervous or shy is not the correct response.

Therefore, you will speak with your guest and go about your business with them while completely and utterly ignoring whichever negative behavior your puppy is displaying. If he is hiding, do not try to encourage him to come out. If he is nudging at you, put on your best acting hat and behave as if you notice nothing at all. If he is barking, stay calm and pretend that you do not hear one "yap". If he is jumping up and down, imagine that he is invisible.

The only time that you should step in is if your puppy is literally jumping on your guest, causing them discomfort or injury. If your guest can put up with some jumping that can be ignored, have them ignore it. Everyone involved must ignore the puppy during this short time. Only if this intense type of jumping is occurring should you then command your puppy into a "Down". You will wait 2-3 minutes before releasing him from the "Down". If he jumps on your guest again, bring him back to the "Down". If the puppy calms down and refrains from jumping, you will go back to completely ignoring him and then working forward as explained ahead.

Unless you absolutely had to order your dog into a "Down" in order to stop any injury or discomfort to your guest, it will be important to not look at your puppy at all; and most importantly not to make eye contact. Do not use his or her name in the conversation that you are having with your guest.

At some point, out of a combination of exerting worthless energy and realizing that the negative behavior is getting him nowhere, he will pause. It is at the very moment of pausing, that you must take action. Do be sure that the pause is not just done to take a breath. Wait for a count of 5 seconds. If he has stayed calm for a full 5 seconds, immediately give praise. Remember that your tone of voice carries great meaning. Simply saying "Good Dog" with no enthusiasm is not going to mean a lot. When said with a happy, proud tone, it carries much more weight.

Give him a quick, loving pat and go back to speaking with your guest. You have now implanted the thought in your puppy's mind that when he stopped a behavior, he received attention (after being clearly ignored) in the form of praise and a pat.

If he reverts back to negative behavior, repeat the process of ignoring and only giving attention when there is a break of a solid and full 5 seconds.

If your puppy remains behaving nicely for the next 5 minutes, it is now time to further instill in his mind that his good behavior is not only noticed, but rewarded. It is time to give praise as described earlier, give a pat and offer the special treat that you have close at hand. Finish by getting down on your knee, close to your puppy and giving him a loving rub while talking in a calm yet happy voice.

Now, your puppy has learned that behaving nicely for a relatively good amount of time, thus proving himself and showing control equals a treat, praise and extra attention.

As the last step, you will go on to visit with your guest. If your puppy reverts to the negative behavior, you will go back to the step of ignoring and begin again. Remember, that if you give up on your puppy, he or she will never learn to behave appropriately. However, if you invest just a bit of time with this socialization training, you will forever have a well behaved, self-confident dog.

If your puppy remains behaving appropriately, you will have your guest offer a treat to him or her. Since you have gone through a process of teaching your puppy control and he is now calm, it will finish off by teaching him that the guest is not a "foe" as your puppy once wondered, but is a friend who can also produce benefits for your puppy.

If the issue is that your puppy is shy, he will ultimately venture out to say "Hello" or simply to find out why you are ignoring him. At that time you may feel so happy that you want to shower him with attention, kisses and praise. Your guest may also feel very enthusiastic...However, it is best to not overwhelm a shy puppy who found the bravery to interact a bit. For this shy, nervous pup, speak to him in a matter-of-fact voice to show that you approve of his courage. Say, "Good Girl" or "Good Boy" in a happy, even manner while petting him just a bit. Then, go back to your conversation with your guest.

When you do this training for a shy or nervous puppy, there will be a point when he finds the courage to change his behavior. When he sees that by doing so, nothing bad happens and he is actually given praise, most often he will not revert back to hiding or feeling afraid. If your puppy does not go back into hiding after 3 to 4 minutes, offer a treat. When your puppy reaches a point of showing relaxed interest in your guest, it is then that your guest should also offer a treat.

When training to reverse any negative behavior shown toward guests, whether you have just started training and your puppy has not yet stopped his negative behavior or if he has shown progress, the visit should only last for a maximum of 15 minutes.

It can be a longer visit the next time. If your puppy needs more training to find some success, it is best to not overwhelm him with this. Even if he has shown progress, you will want to conclude the visit when you have found success and are able to end things on a good note. If a visit is allowed to be an extended one, your puppy may end up losing control and/or tolerance and it can negate all that was learned.

When this has been done just one time, it is a temporary lesson. If this is done once when a guest comes over, but then is not done the next time a visitor comes by...and the training is not consistent, it will not bring about fully learned lessons, and it will only serve to confuse your puppy. When this is done consistently, each and every time that a guest comes over and if you have the patience to follow through with each step until things end on a good note, your puppy will be successful in regard to his socialization skills with that guest.

The majority of puppies will learn that this lesson applies to all guests that you welcome into the home. In rare cases, a puppy will associate this lesson to that one certain person. It is uncommon, but if that is the case, he or she will need to be trained for each person who regularly comes over to your home.

Strangers, Dogs and Other Triggers – Teaching Your Puppy to be Well Behaved No Matter Where You Go

A puppy cannot be expected to behave in a well-mannered way or to embrace every situation with a cheerful attitude when those things are new to him...Or if he has been forced to experience them for an extended amount of time without having gradual, incremental exposure.

It is best to have involvement in a new activity, exposure to a new environment, or interaction to a new situation be a gradual, incremental experience - even before you learn if it is going to be a problem for your puppy. If you do this, it most likely will never become a problem at all. If you wait and find out that it is a problem, you will then need to invest time to reverse the behavior. Therefore, while the list can be seemingly endless, here are the most common things that your puppy should be slowly exposed to (and we will go into detail ahead):

Encountering Strangers – This can occur in the pet supply store, while taking your daily walk or while out in public in any location.

Other Dogs – Typically, encounters will occur at the dog park or the pet supply store. Your puppy may also need to become used to your neighbor's dog(s).

Traffic – Most often encountered while taking a walk with you on the side of a busy street, but some dogs are also afraid or wary of traffic that passes by the home.

The Process for Meet and Greets with Strangers

For encountering strangers, this will be a matter of showing your puppy how to interact (or avoid) and to correct any actions that are not a part of a well socialized display of behavior. When out in public and encountering strangers, this is one of the most typical times that an owner can feel the heavy weight of trying to deal with a puppy that is not socialized. And for a puppy, without lessons learned, this can be a very overwhelming situation. Therefore, as you work on this, things will gradually become better for both of you. You will not dread the walks and the chaos that may accompany them as much...And your puppy will look forward to the walks, as he gains self-confidence and self-control.

If the route that you take for your daily walk does not often bring you by other people (or does not present an opportunity to engage with others), it is best to choose one place to visit, one time per week that will allow you to socialize your puppy to strangers. The dog park will certainly be such a place, however if you still need to teach your puppy how to behave with other dogs, this may be too much since he or she will need to deal with two new elements: strangers and unknown dogs.

Better would be an outdoor mall, a neighborhood yard sale, a small flea market, an outdoor patio of a coffee shop that permits dogs in their outside seating area, a local baseball game, a hiking trail, the outdoor seating area of a local ice cream shop (weather permitting), or a smaller park that is not an official "dog park" but does allow dogs...There are many such parks that simply require that the dog be leashed.

You will need 3 things to be in order before beginning: Having your puppy on harness, having treats on you and making sure that your puppy follows the "Sit" command. It is recommended, as discussed earlier, to have your puppy on harness as opposed to collar. This is best for all toy and small dog breeds at all times, and best for medium, large and giant breeds as a method to have better control. Be sure to have some treats on you, preferably in your pocket book or pockets, hidden from your puppy, for reward during socialization to people.

In regard to the "Sit" command, when you are ready for your puppy to interact with a stranger, you will command him to sit. You may have seen references elsewhere that claim that an owner should ask the stranger to command the puppy to sit. This is not a good idea! It is a terrible idea to have anyone other than the puppy's direct human leaders to command him. Giving commands shows leadership. A puppy learns to follow the commands of his "pack leaders". This is a part of establishing your authority, and in turn, good behavior. If complete strangers, and a lot of them, are giving commands to your puppy, this rescinds all that you were working for to have your puppy see you as his leader.

When you are out and about with your puppy, the first step is to simply walk among other people. Your dog should be to your left. This is the standard positioning for proper heeling; and it is good for your puppy to always understand that your left side is his "starting" and "ending" point. When out in public and later on when you are exploring the world together, your puppy (soon to be your adult dog) will feel safer and you will have more control if he is to your left as opposed to anywhere that he wishes.

Whether you have a retractable leash or a standard 6 foot leash, you will want to adjust the length so that your puppy cannot go out further than a foot from you. In this manner, walk among other people and talk to your puppy while doing so. Let him take in the new sounds, smells and become familiar with the activity that occurs in groups of people. Undoubtedly there will be people who come up to you to comment on your puppy and ask to pet him. This is your opportunity for one-on-one socialization.

Making a Decision about a Meet and Greet

It is at this point that you must take note if your puppy is ready for one-on-one physical interaction which we will refer to as a Meet and Greet. Not all puppies will be ready on Day One. For some, just being in a crowd of people is enough for the day. For those puppies, just enjoy strolling around people and be proud that your puppy is taking this first step. You can most likely move on to the second step the next time or on the third time.

The way that you will know if your puppy is ready for a Meet and Greet with a stranger is by how your puppy behaves when a stranger approaches. If your puppy is anxious and you force him to interact, it will do more harm than good. Forcing interaction can cause a puppy to become more fearful…And when a dog displays clear signals that he does not want interaction with a stranger, it can even lead to a biting incident if the meeting is forced. Remember, socialization is a gradual process.

If your puppy shows: excessive lip licking, keeps turning his head side to side, tries to back away and/or growls, he or she is not yet ready. The stronger the signs, the more time you need to spend just walking in crowds until he is so accustomed to it (and has learned that nothing bad comes of it) that he will then be ready to Meet and Greet.

Continuing on with the Meet and Greet

If your puppy is calm when someone approaches to comment on him or asks to pet him, do explain to that person that you are in the process of training your puppy to be socialized and then ask that person to please give your puppy a small treat (that you hand over to the person) if your puppy behaves for them. Most people will be more than happy to assist.

Command your puppy to sit. Ask the person to please pet him or her from the same level as the dog. This will mean, depending on the size of your puppy that the person bends over slightly or kneels down. If all strangers interact with your puppy from a standing position it will cause too much of an intimidation factor. Additionally, while your puppy may have not minded being picked up by strangers when younger, as we discussed earlier, as he or she grows and is more aware of the world, the puppy will be choosier about who picks him up. Your puppy needs to trust you that when you both go out in public that it does not equal you allowing strangers to keep handling him.

Once your puppy sits, be sure to offer praise of "Good Sit" (Reinforcing the "sit" command as discussed earlier) and "Good Dog" to show praise for staying in the sit position. Allow that person to pet your dog. You may need to encourage your puppy to remain sitting by saying "Wait…Wait…" as you did while training him to sit. With some puppies, an owner will not need to offer any words.

While a person may want to pet your puppy for quite a while (children could sit there for an hour to pet and play), it is best to keep meetings short until your puppy is used to interacting with all sorts of people. You will then have a better understanding of his tolerance level and his level of interest to either be petted or to play with children. Therefore, while you do not need to officially time it, a Meet and Greet of 30 seconds to 1 minute is best. You can explain to the person that you are keeping initial meetings short for now. Ask that person to end things on a good note and have them offer the small treat (that you had given to them earlier) to your puppy. With the treat being small (just a tad of a taste to show a job well done) within a second or so, you can give the release word of "Okay" and move on to walking among "strangers".

Troubleshooting the Process for Greeting Strangers

Even if your puppy jumps up on a person: Keep the leash short, so that this is not physically possible at first. This is why a harness is strongly recommended; with a dog collar, jumping can cause injury to a dog's neck. Let the person know that part of the training is for jumping and to please turn to the side if the puppy jumps so that the puppy's attempts are in vain and then to ignore the puppy.

If your puppy only jumps on people randomly, still follow all of the training instructions so that your puppy learns that jumping equals a turned shoulder and zero attention and that not jumping equals a friendly pet and a treat as discussed previously. Always end things on a good note; your excursion to the outdoor mall or any other place that you have chosen should come to a finish while your puppy is behaving very well. For a puppy who is new to all of this, 30 minutes to one hour is the maximum time that one should expect him to have tolerance for this, as things may seem overwhelming if in a crowd much longer than that on Day One.

Increase Meet and Greets as your puppy learns to handle them. Normally within 8-10 outings, most puppies will become familiarized enough with this aspect of the world that they will be ready to handle strangers in just about any situation. Once this aspect of meeting strangers is complete, you can move on to meeting dogs, which will then involve a Meet and Greet with both dogs and their owners (and your puppy will already be used to one of those elements). This introduction to other dogs will be discussed in the following section.

The Process for Meet and Greets with Other Dogs

While most dogs do not need to be "friends" with other canines, it is best to socialize your puppy to other dogs. Why? There are many answers! One reason is because if you do so, it greatly decreases the chances that your puppy (and then older dog) will show a life time of barking or disturbance behavior upon hearing, seeing or picking up the scent of another dog. It also cuts down on the chances of your puppy growing up to show aggression toward other dogs. If you ever bring another dog into the home, it will make for a much easier transition.

If you live in a neighborhood with other pet owners, it allows your puppy to learn to be a "good neighbor", which often counts for a lot in a neighborhood of adjacent homes in which you may wish to help contribute toward creating an atmosphere of friendliness and sociability. You will want your puppy (and soon to be adult dog) to be prepared for many things; and meeting other dogs is a fact of life. You will want him to have the confidence to perform the Meet and Greet in the way that canines are meant to and have been doing for thousands of years. Trying to inhibited and repress this instinct is not beneficial.

The "Canine Hello"

Before you take your puppy to commence Meet and Greets with other dogs, let's go over what to expect. One of the most common things that will happen is that the dogs will sniff each other. While some will sniff the other's face or entire body, most

will sniff near the genitals of the other dog. Dogs sniff each other in this way for a very precise reason and while a human may think that it is unnecessary (and possibly unsanitary), an owner should never try to force a dog to suppress this instinct. Sniffing near each other's genitals is not just an arbitrary area that dogs "somehow" got into a habit of doing.

While it may appear that the dogs are sniffing at the genitals, they are actually sniffing the anal area – this is done for a very valid canine reason, as discussed ahead. Dogs interpret others using sight, sound and smell. While humans generally rely mostly on their sight for input regarding another person, a dog will heavily rely on their sense of smell. For a canine, the sense of smell is used as the main method of interpretation an average 55% of the time, much more than humans use it.

You may already be aware that your puppy has anal glands as it is an element of grooming. They are small, often the size of a pea. There are two, with each being located on opposite sides of the rectum opening. Each dog has a distinct and individual smell that emits from these glands. A canine, by sniffing this odor of another dog, will be able to learn vital information about him. Since dogs cannot ask each other about themselves, this way of "finding out" about another dog is important. The scent emitted tells a dog: The gender of the other, the health status of the other and the temperament of the other. Therefore, your puppy, when sniffing another dog, will know within seconds if the dog is female or male....If the dog has any health issues....and if the dog is friendly or is a potential foe. When both dogs have assimilated the information received and both are satisfied that a meeting would be beneficial, the dogs will continue on to Meet and Greet.

First, Meet the Neighbor Dogs and Friend's Dogs

Beginning this training with somewhat "known" dogs is best as you will have more control to help your puppy learn this before attempting socialization with unknown dogs encountered at the park, etc. Keeping in mind the way that dogs instinctually and naturally greet each other, an owner does not need to do much, other than to initiate the Meet and supervise the Greet. With friends or family, arranging a time for this is all that is needed to begin. For neighboring dogs, it is best to plan for this as opposed to having your puppy encounter them while out for a walk. Therefore if you are friendly with any neighbors who are dog owners, you can agree to meet and allow the dogs to get to know each other.

If you do not know a neighbor very well, this is a good opportunity to get to know them. If this is what you wish to do, it is suggested to say hello and introduce yourself without having your puppy with you. Once doing so, you can let them know that you have a new puppy (or dog) and so that everyone gets along well you wish to bring him or her over for a Meet and Greet at a convenient time. Elsewise you can wait until encounters occur while out walking in the neighborhood; however when you plan this out you can be better prepared.

Note: When doing a Meet and Greet with known dogs, if you have an unneutered male and he will be meeting a female, check in advance to make sure that the female is not in heat. If you have an un-spayed female, and she will be meeting an unneutered male, never allow this to occur if she is in heat.

If you have an un-spayed female, when she is in heat it is suggested to limit walks or outings to any place in which there may be male dogs. The mating urge that un-neutered male dogs have can be extremely strong…A male can injure a female if trying to force a "mount"…And of course, you will not want to allow a situation that can result in an unplanned breeding and resulting litter.

In any case, you will never want to drop your puppy from the leash. As talked about earlier, it is highly suggested to have a harness on your puppy as opposed to a collar. This can be especially helpful when encountering another dog. If there is opposition and any jumping occurs, you can safely bring your puppy back to you without putting any undue pressure on the neck (which could possibly lead to injury).

It is best to talk to your puppy in a relaxed, calm voice as the dogs first take note of each other. After that, your puppy probably will not be focusing on your voice very much, if at all. Therefore, take that short window of opportunity to relay that you are calm and relaxed, as your puppy will often read your tone of voice and pick up on the vibes that you are sending. Keeping the leash out long enough to allow freedom of movement, allow your puppy and the other dog to sniff each other as described earlier. They will then decide if they wish to continue on to play, etc.

If the other dog backs off and does not show interest in playing, do not take it personally. There are many reasons why another dog may do this. If he or she is an older dog, they merely may not have the personality that wants to romp around with a puppy. No matter what their ages, the dogs may find out during the exchange of information, that they are not well-suited playmates. It is best to just be happy that your puppy was successful with the "Meet" portion.

If the two dogs appear to be getting along, they may wish to play and this will often occur if both dogs are puppies. This is fine as long as both are on leash. Only after one successful "Greet" is it then suggested to allow two certain puppies to play off leash in a safely enclosed yard. Similar to when your puppy needed to learn that you were the "leader", the "Alpha" of the pack (your family), the 2 dogs often will play a "game" to establish who the "Alpha" is out of the two of them. When dogs are near each other, one will claim the "Alpha" position and the other(s) will accept Beta position(s). This is normal.

The dog that is not Alpha should not be considered the "loser". It is pure canine instinct for one dog to be dominant over the other. Usually, it will be the male if one dog is male and one is female. If one dog is older than the other, then the older one will often show signs of being the Alpha.

The decision about "Who is Alpha?" will often occur without you even knowing. However, if both dogs wish to be the governing one and if each firmly "demands" to be the "Alpha", they may begin to fight. This is most often preceded by warnings. The warnings can include growls, baring teeth, standing off to face each other, tensing into a fighting stance and/or direct staring into each other's eyes. If any of this occurs, immediately separate the two dogs (this is why when first meeting, they must stay on leash even when in an enclosed yard).

With 2 puppies, if they wish to establish which one will be the "leader", it most often happens during play and more specifically, while wrestling. Owners must learn to recognize what is play and what is not. Any warning signs as mentioned earlier are signs of actual aggression and the dogs should immediately be separated. If, while playing, one dog nips the other, the "victim" may let out a "yelp" and ignore the offender for a brief time…If the other dog's body language demonstrates remorse, he will often go back to playing with the understanding that nipping done too roughly will not be tolerated.

If both puppies appear to be tolerating each other but are not playing on their own, you can enter the picture and encourage play. Tossing a ball to them works well and if one certain dog is clearly the faster runner, tossing two balls (one to each dog) should keep both happy.

End the meeting on a good note, when your puppy is behaving. You can offer treats to both dogs (with the permission of the other dog's owner of course) to show that you are proud that your puppy handled things well. When done in this way, your puppy or dog will be less likely to bark at either your neighbor or his dog. Therefore, this is a socialization lesson well worth teaching.

For neighbors that you know well and consider to be friends, you may wish to set up weekly or monthly "play dates", but do be aware that dogs do not "need" friends as most humans do. Being with you and your immediate family, staying active with walks and exercise, enjoying play time with you, being brought along for events like running at the beach or going for a hike and appreciating the moments resting beside you at home on the sofa is enough to keep a dog happy and fulfilled.

While play dates with other dogs that your puppy gets along with is not a bad thing and your dog may enjoy that time, play dates are not "needed" to occur to create a balanced life. This is overstated because some busy owners feel overwhelmed and put pressure on themselves to continually set up play dates for their dog when it crams too much into an already busy day. Teaching your puppy socialization is the focus, so that he or she will be prepared for any meetings, whether planned or not planned.

Encountering Unknown "Stranger" Dogs

At various times your puppy will encounter dogs that are "strangers". This is inevitable since you will be taking your puppy for daily walks and trying to expand his world by bringing him to dog parks and to other locations. Not every dog is going to be a friend. There will always be more aggressive dogs that warrant both you and your puppy staying away. Whenever you head out with your puppy to go somewhere, always bring treats with you. You will want to be able to reward a job well done if an opportunity arises to meet "stranger" dogs, but also for many other good shows of behavior that your puppy may display.

If another dog is not showing signs of aggression (staring intently, baring teeth, growling, taking a firm stance, etc.), then do allow your puppy to follow canine instinct and allow the dogs to sniff each other as discussed earlier.

Whenever your dog behaves well around another dog, after approximately 5 minutes, end the session (so that you end on a high note) and give praise and then reward. After your puppy has built up enough skills to do well with other dogs on a consistent basis, time spent playing and interacting can increase if you wish.

If your dog is not behaving nicely, firmly lead him away and allow him a rest before meeting any other dogs. It may just be a matter of needing to "regroup", especially if your puppy has already said "hello" to several dogs during the excursion; he or she may be feeling a little overwhelmed. While you are taking a rest, keep him beside you on leash. Do not give a treat when the rest is over. Simply allow him an opportunity to enter the situation again and demonstrate better behavior. Any time that he does prove better behavior than before, offer praise and a treat.

If encounters do not go well at all, this means that your puppy needs shorter sessions. Some owners reverse course and back away from Meet and Greets... They believe that since their dog did not do well, that it is best to stop putting their dog into a Meet and Greet situation. But this is not the answer. Avoidance of a trigger of negative behavior will never be beneficial (unless a dog has a *severe* phobia). A puppy will need more exposure, not less. That exposure should, however, be at shorter intervals, allowing a puppy to have a more gradual experience.

As time goes by, your puppy will gain self-confidence when encountering other dogs. You will have allowed him to know that he has the freedom to sniff other dogs to learn about them. You will keep him in control by harness and leash but will have also taught him that you allow freedom for the "Greeting" portion, should it take place and that you also allow freedom for play, should it take place. You will have taught your puppy that dogs come in all sizes, ages and have various temperaments. Your puppy will learn that some dogs are friends, some are foes and some will be "neutral" animals that warrant a "Meet" but you are not forcing a "Greet". By exposing your puppy to all sorts of dogs, he will have a good understanding of the various scenarios that can play out. You will have taught him that behaving nicely brings about good things (praise and reward) and any negative behavior will begin to cease as a canine always learns to choose which action brings about the most benefits.

If Your Dog Barks at Traffic

If your puppy or dog has proven that his response to cars is excessive barking, distraction training will need to be done during socialization training.

You will prepare for a walk in the same way as described earlier, by choosing a route with a small amount of traffic and by having treats on you to give as reward. New to this will be a distraction element. While you can be creative and use a variety of different methods, great success can been found with a simple metal container filled with pennies. Best is a metal container that is small enough to fit in your pocket or in your hand. Action must be done quickly and you will not have time to go searching for it in a bag or backpack. Pennies (or any other objects that will make a rattling noise) should be placed inside; but not too many that they do not have room to move. The goal is to create a "noisemaker".

Walk with confidence and be sure that your voice does not send a message of apprehension that a car will pass by. When a car is approaching, get ready. As the car reaches a distance that your puppy would normally bark, quickly and assertively toss the noisemaker on the ground in the opposite direction of the car, which will cause your puppy to turn around to see what made the noise. While your puppy is looking away in reaction to the noise, the car will pass by. Once this has happened, say "Good Boy" or "Good Girl", offer a pat and a treat. Casually pick up the noisemaker and continue on.

If your puppy was not distracted by the noisemaker, the noisemaker was not loud enough. You will either need to add more pennies, choose a different container, toss it with more force or toss it a closer distance from your puppy (but of course not close enough to scare him... as only "distraction" is the goal). When you learn which created noisemaker (thrown at the right force and distance and at the right timing) causes your puppy to turn and notice it instead of noticing and barking at the car, you have found success and are on your way to final victory.

Your puppy has now learned that the car was not as important as another source of noise/movement. Your puppy has now learned that when his attention was placed elsewhere and he did not bark at the car, it was beneficial to him in the form of praise and a treat. Do remember that one outing such as this does not equal a dog that is socialized to traffic. Lessons must be instilled. Therefore, this should be repeated for at least one week before you move things up a level to walking on a street with a higher degree of traffic. Only move up to a higher level of intensity (more traffic) if your puppy has mastered the current level.

If Your Dog is Afraid of Traffic

Another common reaction that a puppy or dog can have to traffic is that of being fearful. This is understandable since canines have no real sense of what automobiles are. To them, they are large and loud objects moving closer and closer. A fearful dog does not yet have 100% assurance that cars will not physically touch him. Even if he has seen 100 cars pass by, he may still not feel safe that the cars do not present a danger. For a dog that is fearful, he will be afraid of potential danger. While it is done with good intentions, one of the biggest mistakes that owners make is to soothe or comfort their dog when the dog is afraid. They feel that if they offer comfort, it will teach their dog that all is fine. This is not true. In most cases, doing this will actually teach a dog that he is "correct" to be afraid.

It is human instinct to offer comfort when someone is afraid or upset; wanting to do this for your puppy is no exception. However, in order to help your puppy learn that he need not be afraid of something, an owner must train in a way that makes sense to a canine and provide words and actions that translate the intended message as a canine will interpret it. When an owner speaks in a soft, comforting voice and says things such as "It's okay", "Don't be afraid", "It will be alright", etc. this is the same as telling a dog, "You are correct in being afraid, oh yes, this is very frightening, hopefully it will be over soon, don't worry, I will protect you".

If an owner picks up their puppy and cuddles him in an attempt to soothe him, this sends out a strong signal that not only is something "truly scary" but that it is also terrifying enough that the puppy needs physical protection in the form of being lifted from the ground and held. Therefore, by trying to comfort a dog, an owner can instill the notion that cars are terrifying, scary things.

When an owner has established themselves as a dog's leader, this does more than allow that owner to better train and shape the behavior of the dog. It also gives the dog reassurance to follow the lead of that person. Therefore, if an established leader is tense, the dog will become tense. If the leader is happy, the dog will act happy. If the leader is calm, the dog will be become calm. Now that we know what words and actions, however well intended, will make things worse and we know why words and actions can mean so much to a dog, let's look at what is best to say and do.

Quite contrary to offering comfort, when a dog shows fear of traffic, the owner must show by example that there is nothing to be afraid of. You will always be there to protect your dog....Therefore, do not feel that the following method is akin to "leaving your dog on their own"....It is not. What you will be doing is leading by example and giving your puppy an opportunity to gain self-confidence. The best method for socializing a puppy or dog when they are fearful of traffic is to completely ignore any displays of fear. A puppy may try to cling to you, he may cower down, he may whine, he may turn and tuck his tail down and/or shake. It will not matter what your puppy does...Your goal will be to walk with confidence despite any of this, which will ultimately transfer that confidence to your dog.

Your goal will be to begin on a street with very little traffic. This means that for a 15 to 20 minute walk, perhaps 1 to 2 cars pass by. Any more than this will be overwhelming if the dog is very fearful of automobiles. Obviously, you cannot control the movement of the traffic; so you will find that some days bring 1 passing car and another day may bring 3 or 4...And this is alright. Your job will be to find a location to walk that offers the best chances of 1 to 2 cars driving by, on average, during your walk. Be prepared by having your puppy on harness (as talked about earlier for to prevent neck injury and for better control) and have treats with you for reward. Have your puppy on your left side (as we discussed earlier as this is the side for proper heeling) and as you walk, talk! You will want to talk to your puppy in a relaxed and matter-of-fact way, keeping in mind that you do not want to sound comforting or soothing (as described earlier). It does not matter what you talk about...you can tell you puppy about your day at work or you can recap your favorite television show...All that matters is that your puppy becomes aware that you are in a calm mood with no trepidation or fear.

When a car inevitably passes by, do not tense up in anticipation. Continue walking. Your puppy may attempt to plant himself down firmly or try to lie down. This is one reason the harness comes in handy. Keeping the same steady pace, continue walking, as if you are completely and utterly unaware that your puppy is attempting to either stay still or drop down. With the harness displacing pressure across the back, shoulders and chest (and not the neck as a collar would) you will cause no harm to him as long as you do not run.... Just walk at the normal pace that you established as your walk began. If your puppy whines, continue talking about the TV show or your work day or whatever subject you were speaking about. Your goal is to entirely act as if you do not notice any change in your puppy's behavior. You will want to continue on as if the car was no more important than a passing butterfly.

As the car drives by and is then gone from sight, your puppy is going to become confused for a moment. The thoughts that will momentarily pass through his mind are metaphorically going to be: "Oh my Gosh, that was terrifying, why in the world did my owner not notice that horribly scary thing!", "I am shocked that my leader continued to walk as if that scary object did not exist... did my leader not notice that I was trying to blend in with the sidewalk?".... "Wait a moment... things are starting to become a bit clearer...my leader, the person that I depend on for survival, was not afraid of that car at all, in fact he ignored it completely...Could it be?....Perhaps it is.... Yes, perhaps I was wrong to think that the car was scary".... And now you are on your way to success. You have taught your puppy to rethink his reaction. You have taught your puppy to consider the fact that perhaps cars are not scary. This is a turning point; but by no means will the training be done in one lesson. Now that you have taught your puppy to rethink his reaction, it is only by repeating this lesson will you then allow your puppy to not only rethink his reaction, but to strongly consider reacting in the opposite way. By repeating further, you will then allow your puppy to not only consider reacting without fear, but to actually do so.

When you repeat this lesson enough that your puppy handles a passing car without showing signs of fear, it is now time to give praise and reward. Remember, earlier you were using all of your willpower to ignore him; therefore rewards did not come into play. Now, you are at the point that good behavior receives both praise and reward. After one week of handling a certain intensity of traffic in a calm manner, you can then take things up one level, choosing a walking route that is a bit busier. Handle each passing car as described earlier...ignoring the negative behavior and marking good behavior with reward.

Training for Barking Issues

There are 2 main elements to a dog's bark: Understanding what your Shih Tzu is trying to communicate to you and controlling unnecessary barking. With some understanding of why a dog barks, an owner can then take steps to control excessive barking.

Different Noises that a Dog May Make - A dog actually has many noises that he evokes, and not all need to be corrected. The tone of the bark or 'noise' also tells us what a Shih Tzu is trying to communicate. Let's look at the 9 main types of vocalizations your Shih Tzu may make:

Barking in a low tone – This is a dog's way of warning that he perceives a danger or a change in the environment which he feels may be a threat. A bark with a low tone means, "I see something new, it may be a danger". A dog will also bark in a low tone if there is a change to his normal circumstances. Some Shih Tzu are very sensitive and will bark if they hear a flock of birds, wind chimes, a loud car on the street, etc.

Barking with a higher tone – This is an attention-getting bark. A Shih Tzu will bark with a high tone when trying to communicate a need, such as wanting to go outside or wanting to play.

Howling - When a dog howls, this may be the noise of a dog communicating to another dog (dogs can sense other dogs, even if they are not in view). It is also the vocalization that a dog makes to call out *hoping* another dog will hear him. It's akin to calling out to ask, "Is anybody there?"

Growling – This is a warning. This usually follows a low toned bark (that warns of possible danger). The bark will turn into a growl if a person, animal or object (such as a car) comes too close to what your Shih Tzu considers to be his territory. A growl is a distinct type of vocalization, used to warn others to leave or stop their actions. If the dog's body is lowered into a pre-striking position, the growl is then saying. "I may bite you if you do not leave or if I feel you may hurt me". A dog that is growling sometimes combines this with 'tooth snapping' noises. Tooth snapping is the dog's way of saying "I have teeth and I will use them if I feel that I have to!"

Whining - This is a dog's vocalization of being in emotional or physical distress. A Shih Tzu may whine when left alone, missing its owner or when he's confined but wants to be running free. Whining can also indicate that a dog is in pain; this would be in conjunction with wanting to lie alone and not wanting to be touched. In cases of severe pain, a dog may become aggressive, as everything can feel like a threat when a dog is feeling vulnerable.

Whimpering – This is similar to whining. A puppy will usually whimper and an adult Shih Tzu will whine. This means that the pup is in distress: sad, hurting or lonely.

Moaning - While a human may moan if they have an injury, a dog will usually have a low tone moan when he is feeling happy. Shih Tzu will most often moan if they are having their tummy rubbed, having their ears touched or another spot on their body that is ticklish.

Yelping – This is quick, high pitched noise that is a clear fast indication that a Shih Tzu has been injured. A yelp will be a much shorter duration and higher tone than the high pitched, attention-seeking bark. A yelp from a dog is let out the instant that dog feels pain. If your Shih Tzu jumps and hurts his leg or steps on a thorn, you will hear a yelp. Many dogs will yelp and then in just a few seconds, the most intense pain will be gone and the yelping stops. Therefore, yelps are usually loud and short. For example, dogs with luxating patella often yelp when the knee moves and the socket slips out of place and then do not yelp even as they walk around with a kneecap not properly in its place. For this reason, owners should investigate the trigger for any yelp.

Whispering – Dogs can whisper and if your Shih Tzu whispers you know what an interesting and sweet sound this is. Some Shih Tzu are not barkers. They make more of a soft, murmuring noise. Some owners even explain this to sound rather like 'singing' if the dog whispers for a while. This is a dog verbalizing his happiness and communicating in his own way. Consider yourself lucky if your Shih Tzu whispers, you will not have to train him for barking issues.

Training for Barking Issues

Pick Your Battles- The #1 thing to keep in mind is that no amount of training is going to completely stop barking. Humans speak. Dogs bark. A dog is going to be vocal. It is a good idea to choose your battles because you simply can't train a dog to be silent all of the time. You know that adult Shih Tzu that sits by the living room window, and every afternoon at 5PM sees the neighbor come home and lets out a few loud barks? *He's not bothering anyone.* After all, the barking stops after 15 seconds. He *likes* sitting by the window, on guard and letting out a few barks to say, "There's that guy again!" Putting effort and time into forcing this Shih Tzu to remain quiet for that very brief amount of time is not worth it.

What you DO want to train for is unnecessary, nuisance barking that's driving you up a wall. So, look at the war field, choose your battles and ignore the rest.

#1 Most Common Barking Problem - Disturbance Barking - A common example of this is if a dog barks when the doorbell rings. The Shih Tzu may be pacing as well and having a difficult time calming down long after the ringing has stopped. With this, the dog will use either the low toned bark of a warning or the high toned bark of getting your attention. If you think that his barking disturbs you, please remember that in this case a Shih Tzu is barking because he is being highly disturbed himself.

Most dogs will respond well to desensitization training for any disturbance barking such as this. The method behind this type of training is subject your Shih Tzu to the very element that causes him to bark. To discuss how this training works, we will use 'barking at the doorbell' as an example. The goal of this training is to teach your Shih Tzu to understand that barking = zero fun & no attention and that not barking = praise, attention, fun and treats. A dog will quickly catch on.

1. Begin by asking someone to help you out (to pose as the visitor). This can be a friend, neighbor or even a family member (as long as the Shih Tzu cannot see who it is via a window).

2. Prepare by having incredibly special treats for your Shih Tzu. As with most training, small pieces of microwave bacon, cut up turkey meatballs or organic turkey hotdogs work well. It must be something so delicious that your Shih Tzu not only gulps it down but the thought of receiving the treat again is motivating. Place this in your pocket, sealed in a zipped plastic bag so that your Shih Tzu cannot smell the treats before they are ready to be doled out.

3. At a random time, have your helper ring the doorbell, ask them to ring it 1 time, every 15 seconds until you open the door (you will not be opening the door for 10 to 20 minutes, so do let your helper know this).

4. When your Shih Tzu barks, speak in a quiet, calm tone, telling your Shih Tzu, "It's okay", or words to let your dog know that you are relaxed and there is no immediate danger. Only say this 1 time.

5. While your Shih Tzu is barking away, you will 100% utterly and completely ignore him. You will not speak to him nor will you make eye contact. You must act as if you have noise-cancelling earphones on and are completely oblivious to his barking. Flip through a magazine, check your emails, send a text, but whatever you do, as long as your Shih Tzu is barking he essentially does not exist.

6. While it may *seem* that a Shih Tzu literally barks forever or with zero breaks, in actuality there are short breaks or pauses when the dog stops to catch his breath or repositions himself. You must pay close attention for this pause. Your helper is still ringing the bell in 15 second intervals at this time. Whenever your Shih Tzu stops barking for a count of 5, **immediately** give super happy praise and offer a piece of the reward treats that you have in your pocket.

7. Whenever your Shih Tzu begins to bark again (and he most likely will), immediately go back to the 'ignoring' mode. Your goal is to show your Shih Tzu that barking = **zero** attention, no treats, no praise and that life is just not as fun when he barks. In fact, it is downright boring, lonely and socially isolating. A dog will do just about anything to stop this sort of situation.

As the doorbell is ringing every 15 seconds, as soon as your Shih Tzu does not bark **and** calmly sits or lies down (and your dog eventually will), you will then open the door. Prepare for the fact that this may take anywhere from 10 to 20 minutes. Greet your helper in a happy, calm tone. If your Shih Tzu remains calm (and he will most likely be very tuckered out by this time), your helper can give the Shih Tzu a treat as well.

#2 Most Common Barking Problem –
Boredom - Dogs can become bored very easily and once a dog is bored he can become frustrated. Each minute of boredom piles up on the last one; and as the dog bears the weight of it all, frustration mounts. There is an ongoing buildup of energy that needs to be released… But it has nowhere to go… And particularly if the dog is not able to run it off (physically running back and forth across a large yard, etc.) it often manifests with loud, incessant barking.

The best thing that an owner can do, is to not let things get to this level in the first place. One of the obstacles, we suppose, is that many owners do not automatically know what causes boredom and what doesn't. When there is no stimulation or such a small amount that a dog does not register it, a dog will become bored. Puppies usually become bored quickly, adults are moderate and with seniors, it can lean either way. Some older, senior dogs are super happy just sitting back and chilling out; they do not need much stimulation and are perfectly content taking naps and relaxing. But others - not being so physically active anymore - will crave more interaction than when younger and without interaction with his owners and no other stimulation to take its place, the senior dog will become very bored and bark the day away.

To summarize, it's been established that dogs bark due to boredom (2nd most common cause) and they need stimulation to keep boredom away. Let's look at what dogs consider to be stimulation, at least enough that it will distract them and stop them from standing in place, barking to high Heaven.

1) Toys. You simply cannot underestimate toys. But running into a dollar store and grabbing an armful of cheap toys will not do much. Here are some tips:

• Have 2 buckets of toys. This way you can rotate them out. When a dog is a bit tired of bucket #1's offerings (this can take anywhere from 1 to 2 weeks), put those toys away and replace them with bucket #2.

• Throw away toys that are worn out. If squeakers no longer work, if voices have stopped speaking, if pieces are torn off, etc. it is time to replace that toy with a new one. On this same train of thought, if your dog appears to love a particular toy, buy 2 or 3 of them, because when the toy is chewed out - and it will be - your dog might become very upset when it's thrown away. Having several 'copies' of a favorite toy will help both of you.

• Have a good mixture of toys. Some squeakers, some rattles, others should be Kongs filled with peanut butter. A few should be treat-release toys & others should be puzzles. For the puppy or dog that has a hard time being home alone, at least one should be a companion toy. (See also: 'Care Items – Shih Tzu of All Ages', 'Toys', page 36)

2) Interaction Carry-Over Effect. Your Shih Tzu may bark a lot out of boredom if you just expect your dog to 'be there'. Dogs crave human interaction. Give your dog his fill of that when you are home and he'll be much more likely to be calm and keep himself occupied when you are away. When you *are* home, it is important to set aside time to spend with your dog. Your Shih Tzu needs interaction. He wants to play hide n' seek with you. He wants you to chase him around the home. He wants you to take him outside to romp around. Enjoy all of the benefits of having a wonderful pet and your Shih Tzu will reward you by not barking out of boredom. When you do things with your Shih Tzu, you're giving him a gift (release of pent up energy & bonding with you) that will carry over for when the day is a bit dull. Dogs that have: a safe environment, a great toy collection, a daily schedule for grooming, play time, meals and walks, times when they can play with you and a good understanding of command training, will be more willing to metaphorically think, "Oh, okay, this time is for chilling out a bit and staying busy with toys... no problem."

#3 Most Common Barking Problem – Excitement - Another reason why a Shih Tzu may bark is excitement. Dogs can get overly excited when owners arrive home and this can lead to crazy barking and even accidental elimination or urination. Sometimes, barking is worse right as you pull up to your home and get ready to enter through the door. The best fix for this is to expose your dog to the stimulus that excites him; over and over until it no longer has an effect. **Here is what to do:**

1. When you get home, *it will be difficult*, but ignore him for several minutes. Don't even look at him. Check the mail, have a drink, act casual.
2. Then, leave for a couple minutes (don't say a word), come back in, ignore for a bit... Keep doing this until you can see that your dog is not only *unexcited*, but is actually getting quite bored with the whole thing.
3. When your dog has calmed down and is no longer excited when you come in, then very quietly and calmly say. hello. If there are any signs of excitement, casually exit and repeat the coming-and-going routine. Your Shih Tzu will learn that when he calms down this equals hellos and attention from you.

#4 Most Common Barking Problem – Inside, Barking at Outside Element - There are Shih Tzu that will sit near an outside view and bark at every car and person that goes by. The owner will either be home and exasperated, wondering how in the world to stop it... Or it will happen when the owner is not home and he hears about the barking from an aggravated neighbor. Here's the thing: You can't stop the cars and people from going by the house. And if it happens while you are at work, you can't be there to even attempt any sort of training. So, what should you do? The simplest & easiest solution: Do not have your dog sitting by the window. Many owners bypass the obvious, not realizing that the answer is that easy!

We've spoken with owners about this before and sometimes we receive a variance on the reply of "But, it's his favorite spot!" Yes, it may very well be, but it is also the spot that triggers him to bark incessantly and given a good window-less spot elsewhere, with plenty of interactive toys, perhaps a radio or TV playing in the background, some treats, water and a good dog bed, he'll be just fine. Refer back to where we talk about boredom issues and you'll have the problem resolved. Dogs will bark at birds, people, cars, airplanes, squirrels and everything else if they are not busy and distracted with other things.

Also, when you're leaving your dog home alone for the day, don't let the house feel empty. One mistake: It's nice and sunny out when you leave... but then storm clouds roll in half way through the day while you're at lunch... you're about an hour from quitting time at work when the sun is starting to set.... The dog that you left at home in a rather bright environment is now home alone in a darkened, empty house. Not good. Leave on some lights and put on the

TV (find a good talk show channel) or the radio (again, talk shows - but without yelling -are perfect). Give your Shih Tzu a bunch of bright, fun interactive toys as we spoke about, plenty of water and treats (use those treat dispensing toys). Make sure that the thermostat is set to keep things comfortable whether it means the AC kicks in or the heat turns on. Don't forget a good blanket for your dog to lay with, a quality doggie bed and for those that struggle with being alone, a SnugglePet so that they can hear a heartbeat - and it will make a world of difference. (See also: 'Care Items-Shih Tzu of All Ages', 'Toys', page 36)

#5 Most Common Barking Problem - Night Time Barking - This is, perhaps, the most troubling barking of all. And unfortunately, due to stress, many owners handle this incorrectly. When it's handled incorrectly, it actually makes it worse… and a terrible cycle begins… and once that cycle begins, it is hard to break out of it. Some Shih Tzu are great all day and then just as your head hits the pillow, the barking starts. What most owners do, is press their eyes closed and pray. When that doesn't help, there is usually some sort of exasperated "I can't take it anymore!" being mumbled out and the owner rushes over to sooth the dog.

The best way to stop night time barking is to go against all human instinct to run over and soothe your puppy. The key to all of this is: During the first week or so, there will be more barking than normal. It might get so bad, that you secretly search the web for dog adoption agencies… and your boss may question your overtired eyes, asking if you need to book an appointment at a sleep lab. However, if you stick to the following training, after that first week or so, everything will quiet down. Your puppy will sleep through the night. You will never mention a word of those midnight searches for adoption agencies…and your boss will love you again.

What we are about to tell you is simple… in words. The hard part is the self-control that you are going to have to use. But, we know you have it in you, so let's continue on. First, let's make sure that you do the following:

1) Obtain a companion toy. For nighttime barking, we highly recommend a SnugglePet that emits a soothing heartbeat (and if you so choose, also emits a comforting warmth).

2) Choose a designated bedtime. Whatever works best for you, 9 PM, 11 PM, it doesn't matter. Just pick it and stick to it.

3) Feed your puppy 2 to 3 hours before bedtime. No snacks after this time.

4) One hour before bed, turn down lights. Use dimmer switches if you have them. Lower the volume on the TV. Try to create a "relaxing vibe".

5) One hour before bed, encourage your puppy to drink some water.

6) 20 minutes before bed, bring your puppy out to the designated bathroom area. Bring a chair. Bring a flashlight and a book. Or choose this time to check the email on your phone. BUT, stay out there for a good 15 - 20 minutes to give your Shih Tzu every chance to pee or poop if needed.

IMPORTANT: During this time, keep talking to a minimum. Reward for using the designated spot will be PATS only, no snack.

Okay, now you are prepped. Get ready for the self-control part:

1) Place your Shih Tzu in his area. As mentioned earlier, a gated off area with super comfortable bed is good. Another great alternative is a canine playpen. Be sure that the temperature is comfortable, that he is on a quality doggie bed and that he has his companion toy.

2) Your puppy will bark.

3) He will bark some more.

4) He will now bark as if someone is trying to kill him and he will - in his own canine way - scream out to you that you simply MUST go to his rescue.

5) Ignore it… Yes, that sounds simple, but we mean it. Completely and utterly ignore the barking. You can tape a 'sorry' letter to your neighbor's door later.

6) As the barking continues, remind yourself that 1- Your Shih Tzu is not hungry. 2- He is not thirsty 3- He is safe and comfortable 4- He does not need to go to the bathroom (if it is in within 2 hours of when you put him to bed.

7) As you lay awake in your own bed, something will happen. You will think that you are imagining it at first. But, in reality, those barks are quieting down just a bit. And now they are fading out. What's happening? The pup wore himself out barking for attention. When he did not receive it (and he checked and checked, but still did not receive it)… he stopped. Did he learn his lesson? No, he did not. This will repeat for about 1 to 2 weeks. Stay strong. At the 2 week mark, he has now fully learned to self-soothe (with the help of his companion toy and comfortable area)! You doing 'nothing', taught him to do this. Good work!

Exceptions- If more than 2 hours has passed, there is a chance that he is barking because he needs to go to the bathroom. In this case, you will - without any talking at all - bring him out to the designated area. The rules are:

1) No full lighting -using a flashlight is best. Alternatively, use only dimmed light.

2) Zero speaking. Not even 1 word. As if you are in a silent movie, leash and walk your Shih Tzu outside. Stand there as if you are a statue. Give a pat if he pees or poos. Walk back in.

3) Zero playing. Zero interaction. Bring your pup right back to his bed. Give a quick pat. Walk away. Do not look back. You, at this point, may feel as if you are being a bit mean. But, far from it. You are teaching your puppy to be self-reliant and self-soothe. You're a great teacher! Ignoring dogs we love is not always easy, but if done for training methods, it is temporary and will lead to a long life together with peace and happiness.

Multiple Dog Households

- If you have 2 or more puppies or dogs, it is unrealistic to expect zero barking. When 2 or more dogs get together, they *will* bark. This will most commonly be done to communicate to get the attention of the other dog. It may be done to say, "Hey, let's go play" or "Look at this toy!" Therefore, if you are the owner of multiple dogs and they do bark a lot, there will not be a way to completely silence them. However, you can do a couple of things to cut down on the barking a bit.

1) If you have 1 dog that seems to be the one to initiate the barking with the other(s) following along, you can take that dog aside for one-on-one training as described throughout this section. If that main dog is taught to calm down and bark less, the other dog(s) will most likely copy that behavior.

2) Whether you have 1 dog or 10, dogs need daily stimulation both physically and mentally, to remain happy and not be bored. Many owners in multiple dog households assume that the dogs 'have each other' and therefore do not need as much human interaction. However, they need playtime and daily walks to release pent up energy.

Behavioral Issues

Normal vs Abnormal Behavior

Since dogs can act a bit silly or odd at times and this breed has quite an interesting personality, we are often asked about normal vs abnormal behavior. Most of this applies to puppies; though we do have some comments regarding adult dogs. Here we will take a look at some behaviors that owners are most curious about:

Mouthing or chewing –Chewing is normal for a puppy and will be most intense during the teething phase. Though for dogs of all ages, chewing on toys is a way to pass the time and self-entertain.

'Talking' or vocalizing during play - This is actually very cute and you will miss this once he grows older!

Having curiosity - Puppies are super curious and may want to inspect anything and everything in the house; whether or not you personally find it to be interesting. They may attempt to remove objects from cabinets, closets or the trash. It will be important to safeguard your home (please read 'Puppy Proofing' page 19). Most older dogs have learned what should and should not be touched; though those that are very bored or distressed from being home alone may try to get into things that they should not.

Being active and energetic - All puppies should be very active and have tons of energy while awake. They sleep a lot, sometimes 15-20 hours a day depending on the age (this includes both nighttime sleep and naps). Sleep time will lessen as they grow, but while awake, a puppy should be very active and alert. Adolescents and young adults should be active as well; they should be eager to go for daily walks and to interact with you.

Avoiding direct eye contact except briefly- This is normal because direct staring is often a sign of trying to establish dominance. You do not want your puppy to be dominant, as you want to be seen as the 'pack leader' in order for your puppy to listen to you, follow your orders and to learn to behave properly.

Easily distracted, short attention span- This is very normal. *Puppies* have short attention spans. This is one main reason that all training for commands and heeling should be done in short 10-15 minute time frames, several times a day. *Older dogs* should not have an inability to focus. Many issues can cause this, including stroke. So a dog that cannot focus on the easiest of tasks or activity should have a full medical evaluation.

Wants to play with everything and anything- To a puppy everything is a potential toy, even if it seems to you as though it would not be interesting or would not be enjoyable to chew on. You'll need to set the ground rules. You can do this by relocating all objects in the home that a puppy can reach that you don't want chewed on or played with. This includes shoes, pocket books, reading books, the remote, papers, etc. Until your Shih Tzu learns the rules, when you are home yet busy, place your Shih Tzu in his gated off area or playpen. When you have time to keep him by you, use this as an opportunity to teach him the rules; you take away a non-toy object, ask to 'trade' with a fun toy and then give praise.

Pawing, batting at or pouncing on toys or people- This is part of a puppy exploring the world and with great enthusiasm. This is a good sign; you don't want a puppy that is too shy to experience life. It is important to establish right and wrong with this behavior during puppyhood to eliminate any bad habits when a dog is older. Start by training your Shih Tzu the 'Sit' and 'Down' commands.

Barking, whining, mild crying- It is normal for an 8-9 week old to be sad and miss the only home that he has known. A little puppy will miss his mother, his littermates and his original owner. Even an older dog can be sad when moving from a longtime home to a new one. This is temporary. Puppies soon adjust and those that cry at night will learn to self-soothe (see also: 'Barking', page 129). If an older dog is suddenly whining or crying, this is a sign that the dog may be in pain and you'll want to call the veterinarian.

Rolling over on his back to you- This is a sign of submission. It is normal for a puppy or dog to do this for their owner as a sign of respect. It shows that he sees you as the leader and this is vital to having a puppy (and then an adult dog) that listens to you.

Rolling over on his/her back to other dogs - It is also normal for a puppy or dog to roll over when meeting another dog. Many owners worry about this; But, 3 things can happen when dogs encounter each other: **1:** They both stand their own ground with neither dog submitting to the other. This is not a good event, as a 'standoff' can lead to fighting. If so, there are often warning signs that will occur first, including growling and baring the teeth. **2:** One dog tries to be the dominant one. The other dog will respond by submission or will challenge it. Many owners worry if their dog takes action to be the dominant one to all other dogs. But you may not want this because having this attitude can build over time, leading to a dog that tries to challenge you and the hierarchy of the house. If your dog does this a lot, you'll want to work hard to establish yourself as leader. **Or 3:** The puppy or dog submits by rolling over… There is nothing wrong with this at all. It does not mean that your Shih Tzu is being cowardly or anything to that effect. There are 'canine rules'. Males are often dominant over females and older dogs are often dominant over younger ones. If your male submits to older males or your female submits to males, your Shih Tzu is simply following the 'canine rules'. Once that is done, they can be great friends, play together and get along well.

Acting clingy - A Shih Tzu may always want to be near you, follow you or touch you while resting. This is very normal behavior for both puppies and dogs. This breed bonds very closely with his owner and is one of the reasons why so many people love to have Shih Tzu. Overly clingy behavior may develop if a dog is feeling insecure. You can help by speaking to him more often and spending time one-on-one time teaching your Shih Tzu a new command or game.

Twitching during sleep - Most of the time, twitching is a sign of REM, the deep sleep stage in which puppies and dogs are dreaming. Muscle memory causes the twitching and is normal.

Urinating very frequently - It is normal for young puppies to pee after every time they drink, wake up or go outside.

It gets better with age. With an 8 week old puppy, the bowel and bladder muscles need to strengthen. An 8 week old can only hold his needs for about 2 hours maximum. This should increase by 1 hour, each month until a dog can hold on for roughly 8 hours. If a dog normally holds his needs for a good amount of time and then suddenly is urinating a lot, this could point to a bladder or urinary tract infection and that dog should be evaluated by the veterinarian.

Being shy or fearful - An overly fearful puppy or dog may hide in a corner, under furniture or cower in a closet. He may shake and/or whine. In some cases, this is due to lack of socialization. This is why socialization is so very important starting from the age of 8 weeks old. You can read much more about this in the 'Socialization' section, page 118. This can also be due to the environment in that home. Some owners do not realize that their actions and words (to other humans) are having an effect on a puppy or dog. Aggressive tones, shouting, acting upset, etc. will affect dogs. They will react by retreating, acting afraid or even by mimicking an owner's anger by barking and pacing. If you think that this may apply to your Shih Tzu, please reevaluate the atmosphere of your household and make necessary changes.

Eating Feces

Overview Out of all the things your little Shih Tzu can do, there is not much more baffling and frustrating to deal with than if he feces (coprophagia); either his own or that of another animal (most often dogs or cats.) In general, the causes fall into 3 categories: Nutrition, Behavioral and Medical.

Can a Shih Tzu Get Sick from Eating Feces? Depending on whether a dog eats his own or that from another animal, there are many health concerns.

Eating his own poop:

1. Continual coprophagia issues may lead to upset stomach and intestinal distress. Some Shih Tzu may eat feces and then vomit afterward. If the cause is a low quality food, long term malnutrition can lead to a weaker immune system, poor skin and coat, weak bones and teeth and/or gas issues.

2. For any Shih Tzu that is being treated for worms, during the shedding process, eating feces means eating worms and eggs, thus the dog will re-infect himself. It is important to note that most puppies are born with roundworms (and sometimes hookworms). This is because these often lay dormant in the dam's tissue and thus are immune to de-worming meds – the worms are then transmitted to the newborn. This is why all puppies must be de-wormed and those that have coprophagia, may struggle with being free of the parasites. Additionally, a Shih Tzu of any age can contract worms, which often happens from contact with the feces of another dog or from contaminated soil. Dogs can contract tapeworms from fleas. For this reason, all dogs should have twice-per-year screenings for parasites and care must be taken if coprophagia is involved, as this can make the treatment tricky.

Eating Poop from Other Dogs: This is quite risky as well. There are many parasites and disease that can be spread if a Shih Tzu eats another dog's feces. Top concerns include: Worms: Roundworms, whipworms, tapeworms, hookworms. Disease: Campylobacteriosis, corona, cryptosporidiosis, giardiasis, parvo, salmonellosis

Eating cat poop: Many people wonder if a dog can catch worms from a cat. And the answer is yes, many parasites are transferred from animal to animal. If a cat has worms or is shedding worms and eggs, the Shih Tzu can then become infected. Additionally, the 3 diseases that can most commonly be contracted with this sort of coprophagia issues are: Clostridia, Salmonella and Campylobacter.

ISSUES RELATED TO A DOG EATING HIS OWN FECES:

1. A POSSIBLE SIGN OF MALNUTRION
2. POSSIBLE UPSET STOMACH
3. LINGERING FECES SMELL ON DOG
4. EMBARRASSMENT OF OWNERS
5. REINFECTION OF WORMS (IF BEING TREATED)

RISKS OF A DOG EATING THE FECES OF OTHER DOGS:

1 – 4 FROM ABOVE...

PLUS

5. RISK OF CATCHING WORMS: ROUNDWORMS, WHIPWORMS, TAPEWORMS, HOOKWORMS
6. RISK OF DISEASE: CAMPYLOBACTERIOSIS, CORONA, CRYPTOSPORIDIOSIS, GIARDIASIS, PARVO, SALMONELLOSIS

Possible Reasons a Dog Eats Feces

1. Nutritional - The Shih Tzu's diet may be lacking – Please refer to the 'All Meal Feeding Details' section for all info regarding this, page 60.

2. Behavioral Issues - **Boredom.** If a dog is alone without any stimulation, boredom can set in quickly. If you think about it, a dog has very few options when he is home alone. What can he do? Eat, sleep, play with toys, pace, bark and if objects are in reach, rip or chew at things (destructive behavior). If a Shih Tzu is awake and has barked himself out, his toys hold little to no interest and the area is safe (i.e. there is nothing for the dog to rip apart), the only thing left for him to do, is to inspect his feces. This can then lead to ingesting it.

Stress. Many Shih Tzu suffer from separation anxiety, which is an overwhelming feeling of stress when left home alone. The type of behaviors displayed during this time may include: incessant barking, pacing, trying to escape, whining, destructive behavior and for some dogs, coprophagia. A dog can be helped with this, please refer to the 'Separation Anxiety' section, page 170.

Unintentional training. Canines are remarkably smart and pick up on all sorts of verbal and non-verbal cues from their owners. Just from your muttered words and actions, your Shih Tzu has learned all sorts of things. And inevitably, an owner may have mistakenly 'taught' a dog to believe that he should mouth his feces. *How does this happen?* Imagine this scenario: Owner and dog are home alone. The dog is roaming free in the house and has a bowel movement. The owner jumps up, yells out and rushes to grab paper towels. She dashes to the stool, swipes it up and hurries over to the toilet or trash can. She gets rid of the feces and still quite a bit upset, finally sits down to catch her breath. But… what did the dog see? The owner got very excited! Something important just happened! His human stole the feces; it must be something special. Not only did the human take it and run as if it were a treasured toy, she also hid it away! So the next time this happens, the dog takes it upon himself to grab the stool and in some cases, ingest it.

Please note: Though some sources will claim it as factual, there is no proof that a dog will eat feces due to 'hiding' an accident or due to a continuation of puppy behavior.

3. Medical - While there are quite a few illnesses that have coprophagia as a symptom, it is important to note that with most of these, there will be other, much more pronounced symptoms that let you know that a dog is ill. Health conditions in which coprophagia may be present include by are not limited to: Anemia, Diabetes, Inflammatory bowel disease, Intestinal parasites and Thyroid disease.

Exactly How to Stop a Shih Tzu from Eating Feces- There are 3 main things that you'll need to do; with some time and effort, most cases of coprophagia can be reduced or stopped completely.

1. Keep away from cheap, unhealthy foods – As to not repeat text, please refer to the 'All Meal Feeding Details' section, page 60.

2. Limit the Shih Tzu's ability to eat feces - There are several things you can do, both for when you are home with your Shih Tzu and when he's on his own:

In your yard: Even if you have a doggie door and an enclosed yard, it's never a good idea to let a Shih Tzu outside without your supervision. Many things can go wrong: Obviously, this allows a Shih Tzu to eat his own poop if this is a problem for him, but he can also ingest toxic weeds, swallow pebbles, hurt himself or even try to escape under a fence. Do take the time to clean the yard of old feces. Weather permitting, you can use a hose to spray down the feces, however do keep in mind that if it contains worms this can contaminate the soil. Always make sure that your Shih Tzu is on leash (and we recommend a harness as opposed to a collar).

This way, you can direct your puppy or dog away from his stool before he has a chance to eat it. Work on teaching your Shih Tzu the 'leave it' command. This can really come in handy in any situation in which your puppy or dog mouths something that he should not. Training for this is relatively easy…. You start with a toy (not his favorite one), as he approaches the toy, give the command for him to 'Leave it'. He will take pause and look at you simply because you have gained his attention. Reward that immediately with praise and a treat. He may then go for the toy, you will again give the command and reward. As your Shih Tzu catches on, do this with other objects. In time, he'll be listening like a pro.

When home alone: This is when most Shih Tzu eat their own feces, when home by themselves and no one is there to intervene. If your Shih Tzu does not have a bowel movement before you leave the house, you will want to give him more time to do so (adding on 10 to 15 minutes at the designated bathroom area) and/or adjust his dinner time (from the previous night) so that his body is ready to eliminate stools when you take him out in the morning. Each dog has a rhythm, so keeping track of how many hours pass between eating and having a bowel movement, can allow you to adjust meal time so that bowel movements happen when you are there. If your Shih Tzu seems to be under duress when alone, some changes may need to be made to reduce separation anxiety. (you may wish to refer to the 'Separation Anxiety' section, page 170)

3. Use a supplement or additive - It must be noted that while some at-home remedies work, they do not all work for all dogs across the board. One Shih Tzu will respond well to one and another Shih Tzu will have no change, but will respond to another. In addition, a tolerance can be built up. What works great now may lose its effectiveness 6 months later. So, you may need to change methods over time. Therefore, let's go over what to not waste your time with and which ones may be worth trying:

Do not waste your time with: *Hot sauce* – The idea of this is to inconspicuously dribble this over a dog's stools so that as he later comes across it and tries to eat it, the hot sauce will burn his mouth and repel him. There are several things wrong with this: This method does not fix the underlying issue of why a dog eats his feces. It does not help if a Shih Tzu eats his poo when home alone. And finally, the hot sauce can cause burns to the mouth, upset stomach and startle a dog, making this unethical. *Forbid and Deter* - While some deterrent products do work, some not only are ineffective for coprophagia; they contain MSG (Monosodium Glutamate) which can cause minor to severe reactions. Among the troubling adverse reactions seen in both humans and pets include: flushing (feel overly hot), sweating, facial pressure (skin feels tight), numbness (face, neck or any other part of the body), chest pain, increased or abnormal heartbeat, nausea and/or weakness. Both Forbid and Deter contain MSG and for this reason, these are not recommended by us. *Many meat tenderizers* – 90% of meat tenderizers contain MSG because Monosodium Glutamate tenderizes meat. For this reason, most should be avoided. There is one that is recommended (see ahead).

What may work (rated by us in order of effectiveness, 1 – 5 stars; note that there are *no* 5 star methods):

Pineapple- There are lots of fruits that are safe for canine consumption and pineapple is one of them. Pineapple can work in a number of ways. It contains bromelain, which is an enzyme that aids in both the absorption of protein and it helps with digestion. Therefore, with a little boost of protein being better absorbed and with digestion working a bit better, this in itself may stop a Shih Tzu from eating feces. Some claim that pineapple works as a deterrent, as it causes stools to taste foul. It should be noted that this is an assumption and has not been proven to be so. If you try pineapple, you can obtain either the canned chunks or crushed pieces. Puppies can have 2 chunks per meal (or 2 teaspoons) and adults can have 3 (or 3 teaspoons).

 **Pumpkin** – Pumpkin is a great food to keep on hand, since it often helps with intestinal issues, such as when a Shih Tzu has constipation or diarrhea. Since it can help with digestion, it may then in turn help with coprophagia. Do note that it's easy to confuse canned pumpkin with canned pumpkin pie filling and the filling should NOT be given. Only use real pumpkin.

 **Adolph's Meat tenderizer** – This is one of the very few meat tenderizers that does not contain MSG, but does contain papin which can help stop a Shih Tzu from eating poop. What is papin? It is a protein digesting enzyme that comes from the papaya fruit. It aids the body in digesting food which allows more nutrients to be absorbed and therefore, fewer instances of coprophagia. In addition, there is anecdotal evidence that this can cause stools to taste bad, thus acting as a repellant. Note: Be sure to choose the NON-MSG of Adolph's.

 **Potty Mouth** – This is a supplement that tastes just fine, but makes bowel movements taste terrible to about 40% of dogs. Therefore, this may be worth trying if other options have not worked. Serving size is just 1 piece per 10 pounds, so most Shih Tzu only need 1/2 piece and that means that a bag will last for 120 days (4 months). There is no MSG and ingredients are: Brewer's Yeast, Cayenne, Biotin, Vitamin B1, Vitamin B2, Vitamin B6 Niaciamide, Iron and Copper.

Prozyme powder – Prozyme powder is a supplement that is often used to help puppies and dogs that have trouble absorbing nutrients (and may also struggle to maintain weight). It can also help with issues such as loose stools. It has been proven to be effective to treat coprophagia with about 50% of dogs.

NaturVet Coprophagia Deterrent Soft Chews – Out of all chews and supplements, this is one that is effective for about 50% of dogs, making it even with prozyme powder in terms of success. The active ingredients are Yucca Schidigera (a flowering desert plant, used in many holistic remedies), parsley leaf, an enzyme blend and chamomile. There is a variety of NaturVet that also doubles as a breath freshener.

If Your Shih Tzu Eats Feces of Other Dogs (outside) - With this issue, training your Shih Tzu to fully understand and obey the 'Leave it' command will be very helpful, as is of course, keeping a close eye on him. Remember that when your Shih Tzu is on leash and harness, you are in charge. The harness (and not a collar) will allow you to safely pull him away if he goes near the stool of any other dog. Since even the soil around the poop can contain worms, it is recommended to not even let your Shih Tzu sniff at dog poop.

If Your Shih Tzu Eats Cat Feces - Though a cat may be the same size as a Shih Tzu or even larger and this prevents you from doing some of the tricks that can be done with medium or large sized breeds, one thing remains: a feline can climb in a way that a dog never can. Therefore, your best bet is to move the location of the cat litter box to a height that your Shih Tzu cannot reach. Many people find that the top of the washing machine is a good place.

 If you'd like an easy way to see the recommended supplements for coprophagia, look to 'Supplements & Treats' in the Shih Tzu Specialty Shoppe. You can reach the Shih Tzu Specialty Shoppe by entering any page of the AllShihTzu website. Look to the navigation; it is in alphabetical order. Choose 'Shoppe'.

Eating Grass

This is such a common issue that countless information sources touch on this topic; however, there is a problem that is just as large as the issue of eating grass itself: There is actually no scientific data that proves why dogs purposefully munch on and ingest grass. In fact, some studies disprove the most commonly listed reasons.

Why Dogs Ingest Grass - It's Not Really What You May Think- Here's the thing about quite a few topics that you may read about including the issue of dogs eating grass: When something is a bit of a mystery and no one of authority really knows the exact answer, some assumptions and 'best guesses' will be made. As soon as that is done, the next few people who wish to discuss the topic will go off of what they have read (information that is not proven to be true) and will essentially copy it. Now you have double the info that is not based in fact. Jump ahead several years and you then have hundreds of articles that all say the same thing. And in many cases, people will believe what they read regardless of how factual it is as long as enough sources say it to be true. So, you may be surprised to know that if a Shih Tzu is eating grass, this may not be due to the two most commonly listed reasons: trying to induce vomiting and the body needing to ingest 'greens'. This is not to say that these cannot be the reasons, however it is less common than previously thought.

Let's look at the most commonly *listed* reasons for canine grass consumption:

X To induce vomiting - It is a popular thought that dogs will deliberately seek out grass if they want to induce vomiting to clear the stomach of food that is causing them to feel sick. The texture of the grass and edges of the blades are said to cause a dog to throw up. Interestingly, a few studies show that this really isn't true in many instances. In 2008 the University of California, Davis conducted a couple of studies on this. First, they polled 25 veterinary students who were also owners of dogs that ate grass on a regular basis. Only a very small percentage (8%) attested that their dog threw up afterward and none of them reported that they dog appeared to feel ill before eating the grass. Going a step further, 47 dog owners that routinely brought their pets to the university for outpatient vet services were polled. The majority of those people did say that their dogs ate grass or other plant-like elements from the outdoors (79%). However, only 12% of those pets vomited afterward and only 6 % appeared to have some sort of stomach distress beforehand.

The final step in this study was to expand this sort of questioning regarding grass consumption to a large group of pet owners. Out of 1571 dog owners, 68% stated that their dog ate grass at least once a week. Out of that group, the results on this were similar: Just 1/3 of those dogs vomited afterward and just 8% showed any signs of feeling sick beforehand. **So what does this tell us?** From these polls, we can conclude that while a small number of dogs may seek out grass when feeling sick and out of those dogs, a small percentage will actually subsequently vomit; this is not the reason in most cases. It is important for owners to know that while it is possible that a Shih Tzu is eating grass due to his stomach being upset and wanting to vomit, this should not be the accepted reason. If owners believe that the Shih Tzu needs to eat grass for this reason, grass consumption may be allowed and this really isn't a good idea (more ahead on that).

X The body needs 'greens' - This is another commonly listed reason and perhaps true for a small number of Shih Tzu, yet going to grass will not meet those needs. There is a theory that if a dog is not receiving certain nutrients, that he will instinctively seek out those nutrients by eating grass and other outdoor plants. This is a bit of a contradiction of the first theory… how can a Shih Tzu receive nutrients from grass if that grass supposedly will make the dog throw up?

At any rate, it is important to keep in mind that grass does not contain many nutrients. In fact, it is not an easily digested food and the main nutrient that it holds is crude protein. Actual green vegetables including baby peas and green beans (two veggies that are safe and healthy for a Shih Tzu to eat) are packed with elements that grass from the yard is lacking: Vitamin C, Vitamin B-6, Vitamin A, Magnesium and Iron. Green beans also have Vitamin K. If a Shih Tzu is not on a well-balanced diet and is lacking certain nutrients, this goes hand in hand with being hungry which is something that we will dive into next.

Actual Reasons Why Shih Tzu Eat Grass

- As you've read, a very small number of Shih Tzu may eat grass to make themselves vomit, however this is not the most common reason by a long shot. In addition, if the diet is lacking nutrients, grass is not the answer to receiving those. So, let's look at some reasons that hold weight:

Hunger along with nutrient deficiency

Habit/boredom

Curiosity

Hunger along with nutrient deficiency - A Shih Tzu may lick his bowl clean and eat every morsel that you feed him, however if it is not the right type of food, that Shih Tzu may still be hungry. Is he lacking nutrients? Most likely, however it important to note is that since grass holds very little nutritional value and it may upset the stomach due to the blade's texture tickling the stomach and it being hard to digest, it will not help a Shih Tzu in the long run.

One of the most common reasons why a dog may eat several meals per day yet still need more is due to the food having a high level of fillers. Fillers are 'empty' ingredients that bulk up kibble yet pass right through the body. It will appear that a Shih Tzu is eating enough, yet with a high percentage of the 'food' not actually being used to fuel the body, the puppy or dog will technically be malnourished and will not be reaching his daily calorie requirements. That Shih Tzu may then graze and nibble away on grass to supplement his diet and as noted, this will be done in vain.

Habit/boredom - Dogs are funny creatures; if they have nothing to do, they often resort to a habit even if they do not gain much from doing the action. It's not all that uncommon for a Shih Tzu to be brought outside and for the owner to then become distracted… perhaps checking their phone or saying hello to a neighbor…and then they look over and their Shih Tzu is munching away on grass as if he thinks he is a cow in a pasture. In many cases, the Shih Tzu was left to his own devices for a certain amount of time, didn't have anything better to do and metaphorically thought, 'okay, I guess I'll stay busy by nibbling on this grass!' This can be avoided by interacting with your Shih Tzu and keeping him focused on the task at hand, whether this is going outside for bathroom needs or heading out for a walk (more ahead on ways to stop a Shih Tzu from eating grass).

Curiosity - Have you ever gotten down very close to a stretch of grass in the morning and really studied how it sparkles with dew and how the sun reflects off of the shiny blades? Most likely you noticed this to some degree from a standing position. However, we must think about how this looks to a Shih Tzu that is mere inches from the grass. That soft, dew-dropped, sparkling grass that is perhaps swaying in the wind can look awfully tempting to a curious dog. Canines of all ages use their mouths to figure out what things are; and even if a Shih Tzu has no intention of eating grass as if it is a patch of yummy treats spread out before him, if he simply mouths it to figure out 'what is this?' and/or 'is it worth my time to chew on this?' he may discover that the moist blades or interesting texture fits his chewing urges at the time. The next thing you know, he's eating it… and that can quickly turn into a habit as we discussed earlier. Dogs can rapidly transition from an action done out of exploration to a pattern of repeating that action simply because there is no better alternative at that moment.

Why Eating Grass Can Be Detrimental - Many owners wonder if it is safe for a Shih Tzu to eat grass and you may be surprised at the answer. There are quite a few reasons why it is bad for a Shih Tzu to ingest grass and weeds from the yard or park:

Digestive issues - As touched on above, some but not all dogs will vomit after eating grass. This is due to the texture that can irritate the stomach and cause it to come right back out. When a dog throws up something that he ate, not just that element is regurgitated; fluid is often lost as well and this can cause dehydration. Even just a 1% decrease in normal water levels in the body can cause mild dehydration that can disrupt a dog's focus and cause lethargy. In addition to this, since grass is not easily digested it can cause discomfort and other issues as it passes through the intestines. In some cases of very high grass ingestion, intestinal blockage can occur which is considered to be an emergency, often needing surgical treatment.

> **RISKS FROM EATING GRASS:**
> 1. UPSET STOMACH
> 2. VOMITING, POSSIBLY LEADING TO DEHYRATION
> 3. POSSIBLE BLOCKAGE
> 4. BUG BITES
> 5. POISONING DUE TO CHEMICALS

Ingestion of chemicals - Studies have shown that just breathing in lawn care chemicals can lead to troubling health issues, however if a dog ingests them it can be toxic. This applies to both pesticides (used to control weeds) and insecticides (used to control insects). Unless your yard is large and you use no chemicals at all, some elements to consider is that a neighbor may use one or both of these lawn applications that may run off into your yard via rainfall and that parks and other areas that have public grass may be treated with toxic compounds.

Don't assume that a popular park is kept free of chemicals. It is not uncommon for parks used for children's sport games and family picnics to be sprayed to control weeds or to keep grass from growing around trees. Cities will often post warning signs only 24 hours before and after applying chemicals to the grass. However, these toxins can actually remain there for months or in some cases, even years. If a Shih Tzu were to ingest grass that was just treated or were to eat chemical coated grass on a regular basis, this can lead to many health issues including but not limited to: allergy-like symptoms, breathing problems, fever, eye pain, vomiting, abdominal cramping, inflammation, trouble with vision, incontinence, anxiety, irregular heartbeat, dizziness and/or hyperactivity. Long term effects include but are not limited to kidney and/or liver damage, neurological issues, weakened immune system can cancer.

Bug bites - Most common in the summer, the risk of insect bites rises the more that a Shih Tzu noses in the grass or pokes around at the base of bushes and other areas. There is always the risk of red ant bites; however the most common danger is wasps, bees and other flying stinging insects. Many of these actually build nests burrowed into the ground (and not high in trees) and will therefore often hover right above the grass. Many toy sized dogs have terrible allergic reactions when stung and while this can sometimes be treated with OTC antihistamines at home like Benadryl, it can be severe enough to require emergency veterinary treatment.

How to Stop a Shih Tzu From Eating Grass 1) Offer high quality food and snacks. Since low quality dog food can lead to both hunger and nutrient deficiency and of course since a quality diet is vital for a Shih Tzu's overall health, you may want to reassess what your Shih Tzu is eating. Some dogs eat almost as much for snacks as they do for meals, so treats should be evaluated as well. As to not repeat text, please refer to 'All Meal Feeding Details', page 60.

2) Keep your Shih Tzu focused - When you take your Shih Tzu outside for a walk or even just to go to the bathroom, it's best to keep your dog engaged which will keep him focused on other things and far less likely to eat grass. This is always a great opportunity to practice commands ('Sit' when attaching his leash and 'Heel' when walking anywhere, whether or not that distance is short or long). When a dog feels that he has a job to do, this can give him a great sense of purpose and a boost of self-confidence when that task is complete. If you teach your Shih Tzu to heel, your daily walks can be both beneficial for health but also a great method of allowing your Shih Tzu to gain self-esteem and of course will help keep him on track and unable to mouth rocks, grass or other outdoor elements.

3) Implement training -This breed tends to crave his owner's attention and receiving positive or negative feedback can greatly affect a Shih Tzu's behavior. If somehow despite trying to keep a Shih Tzu focused, he starts to eat grass, an owner should give a firm 'No'. This may need to be done with a loud clap to gain the dog's attention. As soon as the puppy or dog is looking at you, offer praise for not eating it anymore and immediately refocus his attention elsewhere. You will want to avoid offering a tasty treat or overly praising your Shih Tzu, since this clever little breed can quickly learn to mouth grass just to then receive a reward when you command him to stop. Therefore, paying close attention to him, keeping him busy with heeling and giving a quick 'No', follow by a 'good dog' and continuing on is best.

4) Do not allow your Shih Tzu to be outside alone- Chances are that you know this rule, of course, but it is worth mentioning. There may be extenuating circumstances… an owner may let their Shih Tzu out into an enclosed yard with full intention of following close behind, but then the doorbell or phone rings and the Shih Tzu is now alone outside. Too many things can go wrong when a Shih Tzu is outside by himself, even in what could be considered a 'safe' enclosed area. He may eat grass, ingest poisonous plants, stick his nose into an ant hill, find a small hole under the fence to squeeze through or even be swooped up by a hawk (this really can happen). Please play it safe and always supervise your Shih Tzu.

Fear of Thunder and Lightning

Thunderstorms bring a lot of disturbance and it is not uncommon for a dog to react to this. Some dogs could have a hurricane blow in around them and they would remain laying down, chewing on their favorite toy. However, the majority of dogs have a heightened sense of awareness during storms. And a percentage of those dogs are absolutely terrified of thunderstorms. Some people talk of this issue as if it is a canine phobia. However, unlike most phobias that are based on an imagined fear, a dog has very good reasons to be afraid of thunder.

What Will a Shih Tzu do When He Can't Tolerate a Thunderstorm? A Shih Tzu may do one or all of the following: Attempt to hide, shake, whine, pace back & forth, drool excessively, bark out of control, chew items that he normally would not and in some cases, the dog may lose all control; some have been known to ram into doors, etc. If your Shih Tzu behaves this way toward thunder, it is time to step in and help him gain control over his actions and reactions.

What Causes This Reaction- Fear/intolerance of thunder and lightning is one of the most common outside-element inducing behavioral problems for dogs. There are **5** main elements that may cause a dog to behave frantically:

1) The flashes of light – This can be quite disturbing to a dog and cause him to lose his feeling of security and control over his normal environment.
2) The noise of the thunder – This is loud for you and I, can you imagine how this sounds to a dog whose hearing is 1000s of times more sensitive than a human's?
3) High winds - Storms sometimes produce high pitched winds that your dog may hear but you do not; and this can cause him to panic.

4) The sound of the rain hitting the roof of your home – With a dog's heightened sense of hearing, the continual pounding of rain can be quite aggravating

5) The air pressure – Surely you know of that feeling you get when a storm is on its way. You can actually sense when a storm is coming; you "feel it in the air". Your dog, with heightened senses, feels this 100 times stronger than you do.

Is This Normal Behavior? Studies are interesting on this subject. Surveys have shown that some dog breeds are more prone to behave negatively to storms than other breeds. While any dog of any breed may dislike thunder, dogs in the Herding, Sporting and Working families are found to be more apt to show this behavior. Why? It is

suggested that these dog breeds have been taught over centuries to be very aware of their immediate environment, but to suppress aggressiveness; thus causing them to have anxiety instead. Rescue puppies and dogs are more likely to be afraid of thunder. It is thought that these dogs have had less socialization to get them used to the world around them. Most have also experienced many unpleasant things before being rescued which may simply make them more skittish in many situations.

How to Help Your Shih Tzu – Not very long ago (relatively speaking), owners were quite helpless for this issue, and many had to resort to desensitization training (we'll touch on that in a bit). However, the invention of 'thunder shirts' (also referred to as thunder vests, stress wraps, anti-anxiety wraps or stress shirts) makes it a lot easier to help a dog. The idea itself of swaddling a dog is not novel, it is similar to how babies are swaddled, however until these structured vests became readily available, owners needed to improvise. The idea of a thunder shirt is to offer a firm fitting, structured 'vest' that is based on the concept of swaddling or compression. Safe and comfortable compression can help anxious dogs to feel more secure. The pressure applied by a thunder shirt has a calming effect that helps approximately 50 to 70% of dogs (depending on which brand is used) with anxiety during times of severe stress.

One of the huge problems that owners encounter is the difficulty in finding a quality vest that fits a Shih Tzu. Also, there are countless brands (even one endorsed by the AKC, that is not highly rated) that are truly subpar. Fortunately, we can tell you that the ThunderShirt Classic Dog Anxiety Jacket is perfect for this breed. There are 3 sizes, xx-small for dogs under 7 lbs., extra small for dogs 8 to 15 lbs. and small for dogs 15 to 25 pounds.

Please be *very* careful if you opt to obtain one: there are MANY that use very similar names and do not work well at all. The one we recommend is a high quality, top rated vest that is adjustable via Velcro straps on the chest. Note that these are also marketed to help with other stressful events such as fireworks, when traveling and even for separation anxiety. While a thunder shirt does help many dogs during lightning storms and fireworks, we do NOT recommend these for separation anxiety. This is not a type of clothing that you would want a puppy or dog to have on them for 7, 8 or 9 hours.

If you'd like a direct link to the exact thunder shirt that we recommend, look to 'Accessories' in the Shih Tzu Specialty Shoppe, it is the 2ⁿᵈ item listed in that category. You can reach the Shih Tzu Specialty Shoppe by entering any page of the AllShihTzu website. Look to the navigation; it is in alphabetical order. Choose 'Shoppe'.

Other Aides – Aside from the thunder shirt/vest, other options include:

1. Supplements. There are many calming supplements on the market. Some work for some dogs. Since these are supplements and not regulated by the FDA, there few real studies to show if these work. Ingredients common to these include a colostrum complex (isolated from colostrum proteins) which is thought to have a calming effect on animals. Also L Theanine (this is found in most teas), said to provide a calming effect and Vitamin B, which is said to help manage stress. If you choose a safe, quality brand (we like Pet Naturals Calming for Small Dogs) you can certainly see if this works for your Shih Tzu. However, do keep in mind that thunderstorms often pass by quickly and by the time this works, the storm may be over. This sort of supplement, may however, help with separation anxiety and calm very nervous dogs.

2. Anti-anxiety medication. Some veterinarians may suggest a mild anxiety medication for a dog. However, we do not recommend this unless you live in an area that receives substantial thunderstorms on a regular basis. Most thunderstorms only last for a very brief period of time and do not happen that often. We don't feel that it is healthy to sedate a dog when the storm will be gone by the time the medication begins to work.

3. Desensitization. Before the popularity of thunder shirts and calming supplements, owners would often employ the dog training technique of desensitization. This can take a LOT of time and just the training alone can be stressful for a Shih Tzu, so we do not really endorse this unless nothing has worked, you are at your wit's end and you live in an area where there are a lot of storms. This is done by obtaining a CD that plays the sound of thunderstorms. You do this on a very low volume, for a short amount of time (5 minutes). As the days and weeks progress, you very gradually increase the volume and the duration.

Other Tips: Sometimes it is not the noise or the wind that scares a dog. It is just the change in air pressure that causes a dog to panic (and therefore something you cannot fix with any sort of training). When a storm does occur, you should remain very calm. Your motions should never be rushed. Some owners will run over to windows to slam them shut or run across the room to close a door. Beware of these actions; your Shih Tzu may interpret them as reinforcing panicked behavior. Also, some dogs just really do best if they are allowed to 'hide'. We, of course, do not recommend that you allow your Shih Tzu to hide from everything that he is scared of! However, in this case, we make an exception. Storms happen so infrequently, it's very hard to train for and a dog can be a 'well-rounded', confident dog even while having a bad reaction to air pressure, winds and loud noise. Not hiding when afraid just adds to the stress. And it's not very ethical to force a dog to endure an act of nature if it can be avoided.

A playpen or doggie bed filled with soft baby blankets and a favorite toy can help to calm your Shih Tzu down and allow him to retreat to 'safety'. This area should not be enclosed. When a dog is scared, he can panic even more if he is confined. Your Shih Tzu should know that he has the option of leaving this area as soon as he wishes to.

Nesting

Nesting is usually something that a pregnant Shih Tzu will do in preparation for the upcoming litter. She will make a makeshift 'den' and gather up items to store there. She may even attempt to 'mother' objects such as stuffed animals. But, did you know that Shih Tzu can display these same nesting behaviors even when not pregnant? Male Shih Tzu *may* also pick up nesting behavior, usually caused by the need for security. This can stem from feeling as if they are not getting enough attention (from the perspective of the Shih Tzu). This is, however, uncommon and is seen far more often with females.

What Can Cause Nesting Behavior in non-Pregnant Dogs- For female dogs, a Shih Tzu may have a false pregnancy. This can happen when the dog's hormones mis-trigger and the dog reacts as if she were carrying pups, when indeed she is not. The medical term for this is called Pseudocyesis and is not uncommon with canines. If this does happen, it will usually occur 6 – 12 weeks after a heat cycle. Pseudocyesis can actually cause a female dog to begin to produce milk. Should this happen, it is best to have a veterinarian perform a complete medical checkup. In some cases, medication will be used to stop the production of milk. It should be noted that it is not recommended to have a female dog spayed if she is in Pseudocyesis; vets recommend waiting until it passes before having the procedure done. And it is certainly recommended to always spay your female dog if you are not planning on breeding her. This greatly reduces the risks of many dog health issues, including ovarian and mammary cancer.

Signs of Nesting - The most obvious sign is when the Shih Tzu becomes very attached to small household items. The items will usually be soft and easily portable via mouthing. These may be toys, however often it is a collection of socks, washcloths and other such items. Once the items are collected, the Shih Tzu will set up a 'nest', as if creating a make-shift litter. The Shih Tzu will then guard over her 'litter' of 'puppies' for quite a while. She may also gather newspapers or blankets to create a warm "home" for her "litter". If a male does this, most often he will choose just one item and will 'protect' his 'puppy' for a while.

What to Do - If your female dog's body is sending off signals of a false pregnancy, she will lose interest in her pretend litter within a matter of weeks. As stated, if milk production has begun, a vet check is needed. However, if your male or female Shih Tzu is showing nesting behavior because of the need for security, there are steps that you can take to help your dog.

1) It is best to not take away the object(s) that a dog is so connected to; this can cause undue stress.
2) Make an attempt to show extra attention to your Shih Tzu. Perhaps add an extra walk into your daily routine, or take an extra 20 or 30 minutes to play with him or her each day; whatever is the Shih Tzu's favorite game or activity. You can also try a playing a puzzle game with your Shih Tzu (meant for owner and dog to work at together), as this can be some great bonding time. Down time is also a time when you can show extra attention, such as when you are resting and watching TV. Have your Shih Tzu sit upon your lap and pat him/her while you watch your favorite show.
3) As you give your Shih Tzu more attention, he/she may stop showing protection over their chosen object. But again, in many cases, it is best to allow a dog to have a favorite object if it helps the dog feel calmer.

Depression

Clinical depression is a real medical condition that can affect canines much in the same way as it can affect humans.

The Symptoms of Depression in a Shih Tzu- Most dogs that are going through an emotional upset will display at least 1 of the following signs:

Loss of Interest– A Shih Tzu will not show excitement to go for walks, play, etc. A dog will no longer be interested in activities that he once enjoyed.
Retreating – The dog may interact with people a lot less, he may retreat to a quiet area to be alone. Some dogs will find a new area (such as a closet) and 'hide'. It should be noted that this is also a sign that a dog is in pain and/or ill.
Weight Loss - A Shih Tzu may now just nibble at his food, when he once used to run over with excitement at the mere smell of it.
Lethargy – The Shih Tzu may simply 'lie around', not wanting to move much or do much of anything.
Sleep Changes – While some dogs will have trouble sleeping, most often this will be a matter of the dog sleeping much more than usual.

What Causes Canine Depression - Studies show us dogs often become depressed due to change, but in addition to that, isolation and boredom can alter a dog's mindset. Triggers for canine depression include:

1) Loss of a pet. There are very few dogs in multiple pet households that will not display any signs of sadness if the other pet passed away. This is a major life event that can severely affect a Shih Tzu's state of mind. To a canine, all members of the household (both human and animal) are his 'pack'. And when a member of the pack is gone, this is very unsettling. Science has long since proven that canines experience a range of emotions including love, affection and distress. The emotional distress that a Shih Tzu may feel can be overwhelming if another dog in the household dies. If your Shih Tzu has experienced the loss of a canine playmate, as to not repeat text, please refer to the 'Having More Than One Dog', 'Loss of a Pet in a Multiple Pet Household' section, page 169.

2) Loss of a human family member. This is undoubtedly one of the most common reasons for moderate to severe depression with canines. The bond between owner and dog is strong and this situation can make a dog feel hopeless, sad, despondent and unable to rise from the sadness without some help.

3) A change to the family. Whether this change is a new human family member or a new animal family member, a dog may take this as a negative experience.

4) Moving to a new home. Moving to a new house can cause a dog to feel out of place and unsure of where he is, why he is there and his place in his new 'den'. In many cases, this is an acute depression that will ebb away as the Shih Tzu acclimates to the new environment. It can help to try and keep some of his important things in the same spot as the old house. For example, his playpen in the left corner of the living room, his food and water bowls in the kitchen near the slider and his toys in a bin to the side of the sofa, etc. In addition, moving can be stressful and a dog may be picking up the hectic vibe from his owners. Taking time to stroll through the new neighborhood and playing some light-hearted fetch in the yard can help both you and your dog take a relaxed break from this often busy event.

5) Longer time periods alone. Many dogs already need to work through some separation anxiety issues when their owners are gone for the day, so if there are circumstances that lead to a Shih Tzu being alone for even longer periods of time than normal, this can have an effect on the dog's mood. As to not repeat text, please also refer to 'Separation Anxiety', page 170.

6) Illness or Injury.
Anytime that a dog is experiencing pain or he is suffering from an injury or health condition, the dog may act depressed. During the beginning stages of many diseases, health issues and injuries

there may not be any other symptoms aside from acting withdrawn, therefore it will be important to bring your Shih Tzu to the vet for a complete physical. A dog may appear depressed when suffering from a vast array of issues including heartworms, infectious disease, UTI, thyroid issues, canine diabetes and many more canine health concerns.

7) After surgery. It is not uncommon for a dog to have depression after surgery and spaying and neutering are the two most common surgical procedures that are done to pets. There are a few different reasons for this.

1. The anesthesia used for the surgery may cause short term depression-like feelings due to chemical changes in the brain for some pets. This is much more common with more invasive surgeries in which the dog was under for longer periods of time. In these rare cases, depression often resolves after 1 to 2 months.
2. The anesthesia can take up to 24 hours to fully wear off and during this time a Shih Tzu may be exceptionally tired and/or groggy. As the medication slowly leaves the body, this can also affect a dog's appetite; many will need to eat bland foods for a couple of days. These elements can appear to be depression, however are just the effects of the general anesthetic.

3. Both neutering and spaying do cause some short term discomfort and when a dog is feeling discomfort this will affect his mood.

4. The pain medications given to dogs after these procedures can cause lethargy and sleepiness which may be mistaken for depression. If pain medication is causing other issues such as lack of appetite, discussing this with the veterinarian may be warranted, as alternative medications may be used.

5. Owners may feel concerned and overly worried as their Shih Tzu recovers and those emotions can easily be picked up and mimicked by puppies and dogs. It's best for an owner to have trust in the vet and try to display positive thinking while their dog is recovering while of course keeping an eye out for any signs of post-operative issues. Do remember that recovery can take 1 to 2 weeks; puppies often recover much faster than older dogs and females need a bit longer than males. Within this short amount of time, your Shih Tzu should be back to feeling just fine.

8) During the winter. Some dogs can develop Seasonal Affective Disorder (SAD) during the winter. This can happen due to fewer hours of sunlight for the long duration of the winter months. Like humans, some dogs are sensitive to changes in melatonin production that occurs during this time. Since very cold or stormy weather can impede your ability to bring your Shih Tzu outside during the winter, a dog often gets less exercise and this can increase depression as well.

It is suggested to bundle your Shih Tzu up in appropriate clothing (lined vest, parka, thick hoodie or sweater), use protection for the paws (quality paw wax or dog booties), protect the nose from chapping with a quality nose butter , *importantly* to dress warm yourself (if you are shivering and uncomfortable, you will be less inclined to stay outdoors) and bring your Shih Tzu for two walks per day in the winter unless the weather is so severe that doing so would be dangerous. Even taking one walk per day and having a good 20 minutes of playing in the snow with you can stave off depression. Every moment spent outside will have an effect on your dog's mood.

In severe cases, owners can speak to the veterinarian to discuss the use of light boxes; which can simulate sunlight. Lux is the standard measurement of light flow. A typical living room light sends out 100 Lux and outdoor sunlight is 10,000 to 20,000 lux. Seasonal depression in canines may be relieved by setting up a light box near your Shih Tzu's resting area that emits at least 10,000 lux. Clinical trials show that the most effective models are those that stand high and send light downward.

9) After giving birth. Due to huge hormonal swings, a female dog may experience some post-partum depression after giving birth. This does not happen to all dams and the severity of the depression can range from mild or severe. In many cases, it is just a matter of giving the body some time to adjust to the hormones leveling out. Another element to keep in mind is that pain can mask as depression so post-delivery checkups are vital in maintaining both physical and mental health with canines.

Prevention - **If you know that a change is coming,** as soon as possible, work with your dog to allow him or her to become accustomed to the new element. If you will be moving, try to take your Shih Tzu with you to the new home as many times as possible, before you officially move in. Spend at least an hour each time. Bring his favorite toys. Walk him around both the entire inside and outside of the home. Doing this repeatedly will show a dog what the boundaries of his new house will be. Take time to play in the yard with your Shih Tzu. Take him for a short walk on what will become his new walking route. When it is time to make the move permanently, try to set up all of the dog's favorite items in the same places as before. For example, the food dish in the right corner of the kitchen, the toys in a toy basket in the left corner of the living room.

If a there will be an addition to the family, do not push your dog to become immediate and best friends. This takes time. Allow your Shih Tzu to become used to the new smells of a baby or the new aspects of having another pet in the home. Offer the same amount of attention, if not more. It is easy to get caught up in the excitement of your new change, but making sure to give your Shih Tzu an overdose of attention will make this so much easier on your dog.

At-Home Treatment - Ruling out any possible health issues, if a Shih Tzu is depressed due to an event (loss of a family member, moving, too much time alone, etc.) there are some things that you can do at home to help bring your dog out of his funk.

1) Introduce a New Element - It is very common for a depressed dog to have no interest in normal activities. He may be completely unenthusiastic to go for a walk or play with his toys. However, introducing a new activity can be just the trick. One of the most effective methods is to choose an activity away from the house. Just the new sights and sounds of someplace new can help make a depressed dog more alert and allow him to focus on something other than the element that was causing the depression. Some ideas include exploring a new 'easy' hiking path (be sure to bring along water and a few treat so that you can have a picnic along the way) or an outing to a beach or other shoreline (pond, lake, etc.). If you notice some improvement in how your Shih Tzu is feeling, try to bring him to this new location and enjoy spending time together there 1 to 3 times per week. As to not repeat text, please also refer to the 'Care Items – Shih Tzu of All Ages', 'Toys' section, page 36.

2) Keep up with Exercise- Unless there is a health issue that is causing a dog to feel down, regular exercise is an important part of an overall treatment plan. While most depressed dogs will not be rearing to go when it's time for a walk, it's important to try to stick with your Shih Tzu's normal exercise routine or even bring things up a notch by adding another short walk to the day. Exercise can release a 'feel good' chemical called endorphins and coupled with exposure to light can help ease depression.

3) Limit Changes for Some Elements- If one of your dogs has passed away and your Shih Tzu is sad and missing his best friend, do not rush into getting a new dog. The loss of one family member and the stress of getting used to a new one can often be too overwhelming. Dogs, just like humans, need time to mourn. It can take several months for a dog to work through his grief. In addition, this would be a bad time to rearrange furniture or make any other noticeable changes in the home. As time slowly heals wounds and the sharp sadness of missing someone gradually fades, a dog will then be much more open to a possible new puppy or changes in the house.

Medications and Veterinary Treatments - In cases of chronic depression where the at-home treatment methods do not work, there are some medications that have been shown to be effective with canines. The good news is that while with humans, these anti-depressants often need to be taken for long periods of time, it is quite different with dogs. With Paxil, Zoloft and Prozac, most dogs respond very well in as little as 1 week and can usually be taken off after 6 months with the depression cured. Another option is Clomicalm (Clomipramine Hydrochloride), which is an FDA approved medication for separation anxiety. It is a non-tranquilizing calming medication that has also been found to work effectively for depression.

Begging

Does your Shih Tzu know how to get what he wants? Do you routinely give in, later wishing you hadn't? Or perhaps you sometimes give your Shih Tzu a certain food knowing that it wasn't the best choice, but darn it your dog has begging down to an art form. If your Shih Tzu begs for things on a regular basis, some changes should be made. Not only will it make life easier for you, it will also help make your Shih Tzu a calmer, happier dog. Why? All that begging is stressful. A dog is put on alert and he a sense of urgency and unrest until you finely give in. However, if a Shih Tzu learns to stop begging, he can then go about his day on a more even keel.

In addition, if a dog begs for food that isn't part of a healthy diet and wins out more often than not, this will affect him over time. What a dog eats and his activity level are major influencers of his health.

Why Dogs Beg - In order to stop a particular behavior that a dog displays, it is important to understand why it is done in the first place. A Shih Tzu will beg for one of two reasons:

1. He is unsure of the outcome. He desperately wants something (most often a certain food). It has not been established if he is allowed to have this, so he will make every attempt to obtain it.

2. He knows the outcome is favorable. He knows if he begs hard enough and long enough, he will receive the object (or action) that he desires. Dogs don't have the slew of material objects that we humans have. Their toys and food are highlights of their day. Those things mean a lot to them. What would mean a lot to you? Imagine that you knew that if you begged long enough (several hours or even on and off all day) that it would end with you receiving a new car. You'd probably do it, right?

The Physiological Factor - While your Shih Tzu begs to satisfy a want, you comply to gain something as well. When you hand over that piece of food you feel as if you are showing love. After all, when we love somebody (or something), we want to make them happy, even if it is temporary and even if it may not be the wisest choice in the long run. Begging is not easy to watch or to hear, and surrendering to it not only immediately calms your Shih Tzu down, it makes you feel that you are a good owner by keeping him happy. It's only later that you realize things are getting out of hand. In some cases, a Shih Tzu may work so hard to get something, (barking, whining, jumping) and makes such a commotion, that conceding to the dog appears to be the only way to make him quiet down.

How to Stop Begging Behavior - Knowing that the two reasons a Shih Tzu will beg is that he either is not sure of the outcome or he knows he will eventually win you over, the training to stop this is rather straight forward: You must train your Shih Tzu to learn that begging will not bring desired results. Of course, this is easier said than done. It takes a tremendous amount of willpower and it also takes a bit of time. Here are the steps to follow:

1. Decide which foods your Shih Tzu is allowed and not allowed to eat. While main meals are important, snacks and treats play a huge role in health as well. In fact, for some dogs that constantly beg for treats or their owner's food, they may be given so much that they eat less at meal time, essentially taking in more calories due to snacks than meals.

Reassess your Shih Tzu's snacks. Keep what he really loves (or obtain better ones). Have special ones reserved for rewarding good behavior (following commands, housetraining, etc.) and others as fillers between mealtimes.

If there are certain foods that your Shih Tzu begs for that you feel are okay for him to eat, it is best to work these into his meals. For example, if he always begs for a piece of a banana any time you peel one or barks to be given some tuna fish, add a bit of that food into his kibble. Just be sure it is a food that is safe for canine consumption and is relatively healthy and low in calories. This way, you can stay strong while training to stop begging, since you'll know that he's receiving the food in his bowl.

2. Everyone in the house must be in agreement. All people in the household must be on the same page that training to stop begging is about to begin. Dogs are very clever and if there is a weak link in the chain, your Shih Tzu will find it. If you and three others stick to the plan, but that forth person can't stand it and slips the Shih Tzu food, the entire training effort will be done in vain.

3. Do not give in. Dogs are marvelous at being able to wear down owners. When they beg, they seemingly have endless energy. They'll go and go, seeming to never stop! However, dogs *will* stop. The key is to outlast them. There are methods to make this stage go faster (see ahead) however the basis of the training must remain: No matter what, no matter how much barking, whining or jumping is done, no matter how cute your Shih Tzu looks or how bad you feel for him, he will not be given what he's begging for. All behavior must be 100% completely ignored.

One of the biggest hurdles here is feeling that you are a bad owner for making your Shih Tzu sad. They are wonderful with facial expressions and you're not the only owner to see actual sadness and hurt reflected in those awesomely pretty eyes. However, if you take excellent care of your Shih Tzu, offer good meals, groom him well, play with him and overall offer him a wonderful life, don't feel bad for ignoring his begging.

4. Distract. You can distract with toys or an activity, however this can be a bit tricky. You do not want to inadvertently train a Shih Tzu that if he barks enough, he may not get a certain food, but he may get pats or be taken for a walk or some other form of reward. Keeping this in mind, have a few select toys at the ready. When your Shih Tzu starts to beg, completely ignore him.

When there is a break in the barking or whining (even if it is just for your dog to catch his breath) use that opportunity to hand him an interesting toy. Do time this right so that he does not think he is being rewarded. This may throw him off track… or he may ignore it, however it's worth a try. As you transition from one thing (eating, preparing your food, etc.) into the next thing, you can encourage your Shih Tzu to pay attention to the new element. Most begging stops once the object of longing is out of view.

5. Reward good behavior. As time goes by, periods of a break from barking and whining will become longer. For example, a Shih Tzu may bark like mad when you're at the dinner table, re-think his actions by laying down for a bit and then come back with full force to beg some more. During that window of good behavior, reward it. Use words of praise, pats of affection and reward via one of the toys (if it has not already been offered). With an enthusiastic tone of voice, let your Shih Tzu learn that his behavior is excellent. Dogs aim to please, so by teaching your Shih Tzu that he's doing great, he will be more apt to repeat whatever action brought him attention and approval.

BEFORE YOU BEGIN
- DECIDE WHAT WILL & WILL NOT BE GIVEN
- EVERYONE IN THE HOUSE MUST BE IN AGREEMENT

WHILE TRAINING
- DO NOT GIVE IN
- USE DISTRACTION
- REWARD FOR GOOD BEHAVIOR
- HAVE PATIENCE

ADDITIONAL
- OFFER ATTENTION IN OTHER WAYS

6. Have patience. This training phase can last anywhere from 1 week to 1 month. However, it does have an end. You just need to be strong enough to reach it. When a dog learns that his efforts do not bring about any changes, he will not put energy into that effort any longer. Canines are great like this; they will follow the path of least resistance and take actions only if favorable. The key is to stick with the training long enough for the Shih Tzu to figure it out: Begging = nothing; Not begging = praise and reward.

7. Step things up a notch in other areas. Since it will be typical for an owner to feel bad for ignoring a Shih Tzu, it can help to offer fun and happiness in other ways. Take your Shih Tzu out to explore a new route, bring him along to a pet supply store to pick out a new toy, carve out some time to teach a new command or play a game of fetch. When you feel that you're doing an outstanding job as a caring owner, it will be easier to stay strong when your dog begs.

Note: Once your Shih Tzu has learned to stop begging, you'll notice that he's happier. The pressure and stress of working so hard to be given something will be gone. Dogs often do best when rules are established and clear lines are drawn.

Sleep

How Much Sleep is Normal for Shih Tzu

Newborns - Newborn Shih Tzu puppies - from 1 day old to 3 weeks - sleep just about all of the time, up to 22 hours per day. They will mainly only be awake to eat; after that it's right back to bed, warm and safe next to the dam and littermates. The age of 3 weeks old is a huge turning point; at this time both hearing and vision are working well and with this comes a new found curiosity. A heightened interest in exploring his little world and for playing with siblings will cause the pup to stay awake a bit longer now. From 3 weeks to 8 weeks, a puppy will sleep anywhere from 20 to 21 hours per day.

Puppies - Owners of new puppies often worry about the pup being overtired and perhaps sleeping too much and missing out on things. The first few months - age 2 months to 5 months - a Shih Tzu puppy will sleep from 18 to 20 hours per day. This includes both nighttime sleep and naps taken all throughout the day. This is a really funny stage, because often a Shih Tzu puppy will be so interested in his world that he struggles to stay awake. It's not uncommon for a Shih Tzu to zonk out in the middle of playing or even eating, resting his head on the rim of the bowl because he just couldn't make it to his bed. Each month that the Shih Tzu matures, he will sleep a bit less and stay awake for longer periods. By 6 months old, many Shih Tzu are on the sleeping schedule of adults.

Adults - Adult Shih Tzu sleep roughly 12-14 hours per day. There are some reasons for sleeping less or more (discussed ahead). This may seem like a lot - especially when compared to how much we get- however most of this will be done at night. When you subtract 8 or 9 hours of nighttime snoozing from 13 average hours of sleep, this leaves 4 to 5 hours of on-and-off again naps. The amount of naps will depend on how much the Shih Tzu sleeps at night and most will shadow what their owners do. Since canines - like us- need a good amount of deep REM sleep, if they do follow their owner's sleep schedule of 8 hours a night, this leaves a good 5 hours or so that will be napped away during the day. And if an owner is only sneaking in 6 or 7 with the Shih Tzu following suit, this makes for a lot more napping of up to 6 or 7 hours during the day. So, how much you actually see your Shih Tzu sleeping will depend a lot on your own schedule and whether or not you are home with your dog or are away at work or school.

Seniors - As a dog ages, there are many changes: decreased metabolism, a slowing down that reduces activity, etc. and often an extra hour or so of sleep time is needed for the older, senior Shih Tzu. These are gradual changes, so you may not notice that your Shih Tzu sleeps an extra 20 minutes or so; but as the years pass, this adds up to falling asleep an hour earlier than usual and it is then that it really becomes apparent.

When a Shih Tzu Has Trouble Sleeping

- With puppies, it can take a while for them to accept their schedule; many may seem downright nocturnal, making you wonder if somehow an owl was crossed in the Shih Tzu's bloodline. It takes a couple of months for a pup to understand the cues of a day winding down and feeling isolated can cause a puppy to stay awake whining or barking at night. For those of any age, this breed will show appreciation for many of the care elements you provide and often won't be shy at all to announce when things are not right. Here are the top reasons why a Shih Tzu may not be sleeping as good as usual:

Quality of the bed - Even quality beds don't last more than 4 years or so; cushions will lose buoyancy and won't be as supportive as they once were. A puppy may be outgrowing his smaller bed and seniors may need an orthopedic mattress that offers better support for aching joints.

Location - This breed does not like to feel isolated and it can even cause dangerous levels of stress. While it is a good idea to give your Shih Tzu his own space - especially if you want him to get used to that area for when home alone - it should be in a quiet corner of an active room. Shih Tzu need a good place to rest but still like to be close to the 'action' so that if they happen to prefer it, they can join in.

Drafts - What may have been a good sleeping area in the summer may not be good in the winter and vice versa. Drafts from cold weather or cold spots due to AC's may cause temperature discomfort that keeps a Shih Tzu up or causes him to have interrupted sleep.

Reasons a Shih Tzu may Sleep Too Much

- Dogs will vary the amount of time that they sleep by an hour or so, just like humans. However, whenever there is a marked increase in how much a Shih Tzu is sleeping this is reason to take note. Possible reasons include:

Mimicking- Even if you don't sleep much, if you spend a lot of time watching TV or zoning out with video games, etc. your Shih Tzu may take that as a sign that it's time to stop all activity and rest. After all, very few Shih Tzu will run around and stay super active if the owner is plopped on the sofa, aside from young puppies that may have high energy levels.

Lack of Stimulation - If a dog has nothing better to do, he'll often do one of two things: bark or sleep. This breed often chooses the latter and you really can't blame him. Dogs need interaction, challenges, sights to see and scents to smell! It's best for a Shih Tzu to have a fun session of command training after dinner, be taken for a late evening walk and have some interactional playtime as opposed to just lazing around.

A dog's world is as small or as large as you allow it to be. If a Shih Tzu is kept at home without much going on, he's going to sleep more. If he's taken to different places, goes on new walking routes, is challenged by learning new commands, etc. he's going to have a more stimulating existence and therefore sleep only as much as he needs to and no more.

Illness or Injury - Any time that a dog suddenly sleeps much more than normal, this is a red flag that there may be a medical condition. For puppies that appear to be suddenly weak and dizzy, this is a possible sign of hypoglycemia, most often seen in those 2 to 4 months old. With adults, any condition that causes the body to fight off disease or caused discomfort will make a dog sleep more. If you notice that your Shih Tzu is sleeping much more than usual, you cannot attribute it to any of the issues mentioned and it lasts for longer than 3 days, this is your signal that it's time for a vet visit, even if there are no other symptoms.

Common Sleep Related Issues & Questions - Do dogs really dream? Yes, absolutely! In 2001, MIT researchers published a paper, stating that our pets *do* dream. They have eye twitching, lip movements and even vocalizations that point to REM sleep. REM sleep is the phase of deep sleep when dreams occur. There report even talks about how animals have complex dreams full of memories of actual events. So that's pretty neat; our Shih Tzu are most likely having dreams about us!

Should my Shih Tzu sleep in my bed? If a Shih Tzu is normally left home alone during the day (3 or more days a week), sleeping in an owner's bed is NOT recommended. This can prevent him from becoming accustomed to his area (playpen or gated off area) and can make separation anxiety much worse! If an owner *is* typically home with their Shih Tzu, while you'll want to hold off until your Shih Tzu is housebroken, there's nothing inherently wrong with a Shih Tzu sleeping in his owner's bed. There are some cons, however. A Shih Tzu is small and there is always a chance that he could be rolled over on or fall off of the bed. You will want to create a safe haven by having your Shih Tzu near the wall (if your bed is against one wall) and make 'boundaries' with pillows. Also know that once your Shih Tzu is allowed to sleep in your bed, that spot is claimed. For life. For this reason, if an owner is currently single, some thought should go into the future when someone else may want the other side of the bed. Other reasons why we would discourage sleeping in an owner's bed is if the dog has trouble with listening and is in need of training to learn hierarchy (Alpha leader, Beta follower) or if a senior Shih Tzu is in need of a quality orthopedic bed.

* See also: 'How to React to Whining and Crying', page 25.

Digging

Some Shih Tzu love to dig! This not only can make your yard look like a gopher's field and cause your Shih Tzu to get dirty, it can be dangerous if your Shih Tzu digs under a fence and sneaks away if you do not have him on a leash. A Shih Tzu that loves to dig will do so in the yard, the sandbox, the park or just about anywhere that the dog has access to sand, dirt or gravel. A Shih Tzu may enjoy making many small holes in the ground or work each day on a larger one. Another element is 'digging' indoors, when a puppy or dog does this to carpeting or other flooring.

How to Stop Unwanted Digging - To help a Shih Tzu control digging behavior, there are 4 things that can be done:

* Control access to the area that he may dig
* Distraction techniques
* Offer a specific area
* Reward for good behavior

Controlling Digging Access - A Shih Tzu will not dig holes in a yard if he is supervised and not allowed to dig holes. Dogs that are bored and alone will begin to do things to keep themselves occupied. Always supervise your Shih Tzu. Even if you have a fenced in yard, if left by himself, a dog may dig under the fence and then be gone! (Not to mention the dangers of hawk attack, coyote attack and possible poisoning by ingesting toxic weeds and grasses).

Distraction Techniques - If a Shih Tzu begins to dig and then is offered the choice of: digging or a fun, new dog toy, the dog will usually choose the toy. You do not need to buy new toys (if you already have enough good ones), because if you keep 2 separate toy bins (as we recommend), one bin will always have 'new' toys. If the dog begins to dig, he can be easily distracted with a toy from a group that is not in use that week. Finding the toy of interest, the dog will usually stop digging to investigate the 'new' toy. Toys that require a dog to interact in order to achieve a result work wonders. Treat release or interaction toys work best.

Distraction may also be done by enticing the dog into play. A quick distraction of 5 to 10 minutes of play time can make the Shih Tzu forget why he was digging in the first place. Whether distracting with toys or play time, a dog should be rewarded each time he stops digging and does something else in its place.

Offering a Specific Area - If you enjoy digging yourself (if you like to garden) and spend a lot of time doing this, you may wish to then allow your Shih Tzu to have his own spot to dig while you are digging. You may wish to obtain a sandbox just for your Shih Tzu. In this way; you can both be outside, enjoying the day and digging away. You can encourage your Shih Tzu to use the designated spot by burying some treats and goodies that he can find. Often, if a dog is given his own area to release a specific urge, he will be far less likely to go elsewhere.

Reward - Nothing teaches a dog faster than a reward for good behavior. Dogs that are scolded for unaccepted behavior struggle to learn new concepts. Dogs that are given praise for good behavior quickly learn what is expected and love to please their owners. If your Shih Tzu is digging and you command an authoritative and firm "No" and he stops digging, offer great praise, hugs, kisses, pats and a small treat. Then be sure to offer a toy (as described) as an alternative to the digging fun.

Indoor Digging - While your Shih Tzu may not be digging a hole to China in your living room, it is not unusual for a puppy or dog to dig at carpeting or other flooring. Why do they do this? It is that same canine instinct to dig and bury even if it is not physically possible. Other Shih Tzu may softly dig at blankets and other elements to hide toys or to create an area to rest and/or sleep… and as long as this does not involve the destruction of any bedding or other objects, there is no reason to deter this behavior.

To ward off this behavior and stop the destruction of carpeting and flooring, using an apple bitter spray on areas that a puppy or dog tends to dig at can be very helpful in addition to distraction techniques. If this is a moderate to severe issue, it may be necessary to gate off certain areas of the house. For puppies, digging and chewing at carpeting can stem from teething issues, which can be very intense for some pups. You may also wish to refer to the 'Teething' section, page 71.

Licking and/or Chewing at Paws

While dogs will lick to taste and it is also done as a form of communication, when a Shih Tzu concentrates on one specific area such as the paws, this can cause quite a few problems. It is not uncommon for owners to fail to identify the root cause or only see partial improvement; and meanwhile the effects of continual licking focused to one area compounds each day.

Clinical Signs of Excessive Paw Licking and Chewing - When a Shih Tzu focuses actions such as licking and/or chewing to the paw region, the continual friction from licking and/or persistent gnawing from using the teeth can lead to the following problems:

• **Sores** - The friction will begin as a tiny sore - undetectable at first. As the Shih Tzu continues to lick or chew at the area, the sore will widen and deepen.
• **Bleeding** - When licking or chewing continues, the sore(s) will crack open. Unlike a cut, this is often a cracking to the affected area that upon close inspection may resemble shattered glass. The skin will be dry and spots of blood will ease through. This often only serves to cause a Shih Tzu to lick more due to 'wound licking' which is an instinctive response to lick an injury or irritation.

- **Infection** - Once the skin has been broken, it is vulnerable to infection. The paw(s) may appear red, swollen in an area, may have discharge and will be sore.
- **Hair Loss** - Near constant moisture on the skin coupled with a pulling that weakens hair follicles often results in hair loss on the paws that are being compulsively licked or chewed. Minor trauma to the skin over a long period of time can be just as harmful as acute trauma.

Behavioral Signs of Paw Licking and Chewing - Shih Tzu with this affliction often will:

Target Certain Paws - Licking and/or chewing may be focused on one particular paw, most often for Shih Tzu that do this due to stress. When this is due to itching problems a Shih Tzu may focus on the front paws but will also try and reach hind paws when lying in certain positions. As we move forward, you will see that identifying whether a Shih Tzu only chews or licks at one front paw or tries to reach all of them can greatly help in determining why this is being done.

Appear Restless - This is often a common symptom regardless of the trigger. Shih Tzu that are stressed as well as those that are suffering from allergies and those that have a compulsive disorder are all uncomfortable to a certain degree. A Shih Tzu may have trouble sleeping well, resting and relaxing since only short amounts of time lapse before the urge to lick and/or chew at the paws comes back into play.

Reasons for Paw Licking and/or Chewing - There are several reasons why dogs do this:

1) Allergies - While with some allergies, a Shih Tzu will have other signs and symptoms other than just licking his paws, consisting of a wide range of issues including: itchy eyes, eye and/or nasal discharge, itching over the entire body, hair loss over other areas of the body, vomiting, changes to the stool including diarrhea, sneezing, and/or coughing and wheezing, with others it *may* be just the paws. *When limited to his paws*, this is an indication that if it is indeed an allergy, it may be due to a contact trigger. If so, it is easier to treat and once the paws have healed & the allergen is removed from the dog's environment, licking and chewing should stop.

How to Treat This at Home - If this is due to *simple contact allergies, that are causing an acute issue*, you can try to fix this at home as long as there are no other signs of concern. If your Shih Tzu does have other symptoms or if the skin has broken open to the point of bleeding, you will want to have a veterinarian examine the paws. There may be an infection and also a need for prescribed medications and testing to determine an allergy. For acute issues, if the paws have minimal sores and there is minimal to moderate hair loss, and you suspect a contact allergy it can help to remove the trigger.

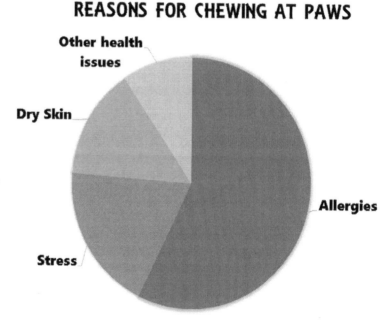

REASONS FOR CHEWING AT PAWS

In the spring, summer and fall, it is not uncommon for a Shih Tzu to lick at his paws or chew at his feet after being outside. Irritants in the grass and on the ground surfaces can attach to the paws and be tracked back into the home. In addition, if you have recently obtained new carpeting or have started to use a new carpet deodorizer or floor cleaner, it may be causing a reaction. In the winter, ice melt chemicals can cause intense itching and chemical burns to a dog's paws. Even if you do not use these at your home, they are often used in other areas and cars can easily track them into your own neighborhood.

It can help to:
- Thoroughly rinse off the paws before entering back into the house. For Shih Tzu with paw issues that are related to outdoor contaminants, wiping with a canine wipe or wet rag is not sufficient. Rinse the paws under running water.
- All people in the household should remove shoes before entering into the living areas.
- Floors should be vacuumed using a HEPA certified vacuum cleaner. These remove 99.97% of particles as small as 0.3 micrometers - these are the irritants that you cannot see but may be the source of intense itching and subsequent licking or chewing for your Shih Tzu.
- Use products to offer relief and healing; please refer to the 'Health-Body Specific', 'Paws' section, page 191.

* *If these steps do not help, it will be time to seek professional veterinary treatment* - The two most important things that a vet will do is to test to determine the exact trigger and offer prescribed medications that may include antihistamines, anti-inflammatories and possibly antibiotics if the paws have developed an infection. You may also wish to refer to the 'Allergies' section, page 215.

2) Boredom or Stress - While boredom can certainly be factor in licking the paws until they are raw or chewing at the feet until there is hair loss, for this breed a stress related issue causing Acral Lick Granuloma is not uncommon. The skin of the paws can become severely damaged. Skin may be licked raw, causing tiny pockets of bacteria and broken hair follicles. This sort of severe condition will be deep enough to affect oil glands and capillaries. What can make a Shih Tzu so stressed out that he licks at his paws until they are bleeding and crusted with sores? Each dog has his own ''line in the sand' of how much stress will cause a tipping point of manifesting outward with self-destructive behavior. The most common reasons include:

- *Separation Anxiety* - While some puppies and dogs will whine or bark, others will chew at themselves as a way of dealing with the stress of being alone. The longer a dog is left alone, the more likely he is to have trouble coping. To treat separation anxiety, look to the 'Separation Anxiety' section, page 170.
- *Change in Environment* - This includes the loss or the addition of a human family member or pet. Moving to a new home may also cause distress. You may wish to refer to the 'Depression' section, page 148, to help a Shih Tzu that is struggling with change.

3) Dry Skin - While dry skin can affect any part of a dog's body, the paws are also exposed to the abrasions received by walking and are therefore more vulnerable to drying. Winter is the most typical season of dry skin issues due to the air being much more arid and the effects of cold winds. When a Shih Tzu licks his paws to relieve minor itching of dry skin, the moisture deposited on them only serves to exasperate the problem. If the paws are deeply cracked, are bleeding or you suspect infection this is your sign to have the veterinarian examine them. Otherwise, for general dryness that is affecting the paws, you may wish to follow a two-step process of combating the dry air and offering relief to paws.

1- Humidifiers are the best option to add moisture to the home; though some methods such as adding houseplants and/or leaving doors open while showering will help to a small degree.

2- The use of quality paw wax along with proper moisturizing shampoos and conditioners can heal dry paws.

4) Other Less Common Reasons- Sudden chewing at the paws/ constant licking may be due to less common triggers: Hormonal imbalances, pain from a sliver or pebble stuck in the paw, parasites (fleas, ticks, mites) or yeast infection (between toes). Very rarely a neck injury may trigger nerve pain that radiates to the paws & in some rare instances hip pain - including hip dysplasia- may cause discomfort that shoots down the leg into the paw(s).

Treatment and Remedies to Treat Damaged Paws- Not all issues can be treated at home. Red flags that warrant the attention of a veterinarian include: Prolonged bleeding, deep sores that expose inner tissue, pain that causes limping or interferes with normal activities, pus or extreme redness, any other signs of infection, any signs of physical or emotional distress. For additional details on how to keep paws healthy and how to heal damaged paws, as to not repeat text, please refer to the 'Health-Body Specific', 'Paws' section, page 191.

Aggression

Most Shih Tzu are loving, friendly and get along very well with everyone. However, just like any other dog breed, some Shih Tzu can have aggression issues. When a person expects to have a friendly loving companion and finds themselves with an aggressive dog, this can be very overwhelming. However, with proper training, in most cases you can get your Shih Tzu under control.

Aggression Toward People- Overview- There are several reasons why a dog may be aggressive toward people, including:

- **Fear -** A dog may be afraid of strangers and the unknown. This can make a dog protective and this manifests with growling, nipping and even trying to bite people.
- **Improper Status -** When a dog is aggressive towards human family members, this is often a sign that the dog is confused about his place in the family.
- **Health Issues -** When any dog that is normally well behaved suddenly becomes aggressive, this can be because the dog is suffering from some type of health issue. When a dog is in pain, he may nip, snarl, growl and even bite those who love them. This is because a dog can feel very vulnerable when ill; he may lash out at his humans who are suddenly perceived as threats to him.

If your dog becomes aggressive when his normal behavior is calm and happy, you must take your Shih Tzu for a full and complete medical checkup at the veterinarian. Even if your last appointment was 3 weeks ago, something may have happened from then to now. Please do not try any of the following training methods until you are 100% sure that your Shih Tzu is completely healthy.

Training for Aggression Toward Strangers – First and foremost, be sure that your Shih Tzu sees you as leader. Refer to the 'Teaching Proper Hierarchy' section, page 108.

Your Shih Tzu needs to learn that as long as he is with you, strangers are a normal part of life and he must behave around them. It is natural for a dog to be aggressive toward true strangers, those who may come to your home to sell you something, for example. Having your Shih Tzu bark and show *some* (non-touching) aggression toward these types of strangers is not a bad thing. In the case of a break-in, your dog's barking may just scare off the intruder. As long as your Shih Tzu calms down once that person has left the property, all should be fine. If you approve of your little Shih Tzu protecting the home as a "watch dog" you can say "good dog", give a pat and then show your dog that all is well with reassuring words and calm actions.

However, when you are walking your dog or in a social situation, you will want your Shih Tzu to behave. This must begin by slowing teaching your dog what is expected of him and what is not acceptable. You will need helpers for this. Try to round up friends, neighbors and family members that your dog is not used to. Explain to them that you will be starting a training program for your dog and see if they will agree to take turns in helping you with this. Once you begin training, it should be done every day until your Shih Tzu behaves acceptably and the training is complete.

The goal of this training is to reward your dog with good behavior and to socially isolate your dog for bad behavior. **When your Shih Tzu interacts well,** even for just a minute, you must behave as if your dog just did the most wonderful thing in the world. Give treats, pats, happy words and praise. ***Any time that your Shih Tzu shows aggression***, place him inside his gated area or in his playpen. You will then implement social isolation for 5 minutes. This means that you must ignore your dog completely. Do not say "bad dog", do not say his name, do not talk to him or even make eye contact. Simply continue your conversation with your visitor (more ahead) and allow him to see that life is certainly not fun when he does not behave. After the 5 minutes, attempt to have your dog interact with your helper again. Each action, good or bad must be acted upon with either praise or isolation.

This will begin by having someone arrive at your home. Whoever arrives should have dog treats in their pocket. When you know that your helper is to enter, have your Shih Tzu sitting down beside you, with his leash and harness on. Open the door and reassure your dog that all is fine. This is done with calm (not soothing) words and slow actions.

Have your Shih Tzu see that you greet your visitors without any tension.

Any time that your Shih Tzu shows aggression, follow the previous steps. Have the 1st visit last for about 15 minutes. Have different helpers come to visit on different days. Increase the visits by 5 minutes per day until the maximum time of 30 minutes. By following this training method exactly, your dog should be very used to 'strangers' and much better behaved within 2 weeks or so.

Training for Aggression Toward Human Family Members - If your Shih Tzu is completely healthy and is aggressive with human family members, the most probable explanation is improper hierarchy interpretation. As to not repeat text, please refer to the 'Teaching Proper Hierarchy' section, page 108.

In addition to the steps listed there, other more serious hierarchy steps may be needed, including:

1. The dog does not sleep on any human's bed. Even if the Shih Tzu is aggressive towards one person and not another, he must not sleep on ANY human's bed. He will need to be given a quality dog bed.

2. The dog is always kept at a lower physical level than the owners. Do not sit on the floor with your Shih Tzu and do not allow your Shih Tzu to sit up on the sofa with you.

3. If your dog is *not* biting at you (we'll discuss severe aggression ahead), randomly place him on his back, with his tummy facing you. Gently yet firmly hold him in place. Your hand will be stretched with your thumb under one armpit and your ring and pointer finger under the other armpit. Your palm will rest on his chest to keep him in place without putting too much pressure that would impede breathing or crush him in any way. He will wiggle a lot. It may last for a couple of minutes. If you speak to him while you do this, do not sound angry, taunting or mean. Be very matter-of-fact. You may look at him, but also do not stare into his eyes. He will wiggle and wiggle… and then he will remain still. This is him submitting to you. You just sent a very clear message that you are the leader.

4. Any bad behavior immediately means that the dog is 100% ignored. As if he is invisible. No looking, no speaking, no eye contact, nothing. If need be, place him in his gated area or playpen for 15 minutes. Let him back out to try and prove he can behave. If not, he is ignored once again. If he does behave, he is then spoken to and allowed 'back into the family'.

Rules #1 and #4 should become part of 'normal' life, essentially continued forever. You may also find the 'Nipping' section, page 74, to be of help.

Severe Aggression - When a dog is completely out of control - which includes actual biting that breaks the skin - stricter actions must be taken. Please note that we recommend hiring a personal canine behavioral specialist for cases in which the dog is biting and breaking skin. This is a serious matter and training for this at home may not be suitable. The health and safety of your human family members must come first. If you go forward with this training, if things do not improve or if at any time you fear for your safety, immediately sequester the dog and call a personal canine trainer for assistance.

This said, social isolation training to prove hierarchy can work in many of these cases. You will take extreme steps to show your dog that you (and all humans) are leader. It only has a chance of working if it is followed precisely. Before beginning, hold a family meeting. Explain to everyone that intense training will begin and that it will require the help of everyone in the house. Four days will be dedicated to this, therefore all family members should make every effort to have 4 uninterrupted days that they can stay home as much as possible. If this training works, a dog will revert back into a loving pet and the 4 days will be worth it all.

Day 1 and 2: Full and Absolute Social Isolation- While in his normal living area (do not crate/pen/gate the dog if this is not normally done – If the dog is actively biting, sequester the dog and call a personal canine trainer for assistance), the dog must be completely and utterly ignored by everyone (not just those he is being aggressive toward). He will be unconditionally ignored except for placing his food on the floor for him and allowing him to go to the bathroom… zero talking to him, never saying his name, not acknowledging him at all. This also means giving zero interest to negative behavior. If the dog barks, no one must say "no". The dog must be ignored to such a level that he is invisible. If your dog pushes against someone for attention, they must act as if the dog does not exist and so forth. It is essential that your dog sees all regular family members and is in the home with everyone... but is being ignored completely.

A great sign that this training is working, is if your Shih Tzu sleeps a lot more than ordinary on day 2. When a dog starts to think that maybe he is not the leader and it is his human(s), he may start to unwind. The stress of having to be the leader ebbs away and that dog may sleep a lot more than average.

Day 3 - Start the day the same as the first 2 days. However, each member of the family is going to take a turn calling the Shih Tzu to them. This should be done every hour, for the first 5 hours. The person should call out to the dog to using the command word of 'Come'. If the Shih Tzu responds, he should be given a quick pat, but no interaction. The human then leaves the room, making it clear that it is the human who is choosing to break interaction. If the Shih Tzu follows that person, the dog should be ignored. Once those first 5 hours have passed, now this can happen at random times. And the human's actions will be different. Once the Shih Tzu comes over, the human will interact via pats, praise and some play for approximately 5 minutes. When those 5 minutes are up, the human must then exit the room, making it clear that it is the human who is choosing to break interaction.

The Last Day (And Possibly Forever) - The final day will be one that sets the standard for all days in the future. If a dog was severely aggressive, attention should only be given when a human initiates it. And it should end when that person wishes for it to end. A dog can be loved, played with, taken fun places, watch TV with you, etc. However, for dogs that were very aggressive, it must be the humans who begin and end any and all interaction. When the dog tries to get attention, he should be ignored for a minute and then the human may interact if is he/she so wishes.

If this training does not work, it is highly suggested to take your dog to a personal canine trainer. A personal canine trainer will be able to see the dog one-on-one and determine any deeply hidden reasons for severe aggression.

Shaking

The Clinical Signs of Shaking and What it Means - Many owners wonder if shaking is the muscles or the nerves. The answer is that technically, shaking is involuntary, rapid movements of the muscles called oscillations. However, in some cases when nerves are stimulated in a certain way or damaged, they may cause the muscle fibers to react in this way. Terms such as tremors and shivering apply to certain types of shaking. When a Shih Tzu shakes, it may involve the entire body from the withers to the base of the tail, the legs from the thigh to the paws and sometimes just the head will have tremors.

Top 3 Reasons for Shaking without Other Symptoms

1) Being cold. This may sound too simple, however it is one of the most common reasons for when a Shih Tzu starts to shake uncontrollably and is particularly common with puppies. Adult Shih Tzu may shiver due to feeling cold as well and is most often seen in older, senior dogs.

How to Help – There are 4 things you can do to help a Shih Tzu stay warm.

1- When indoors during cold weather, check your Shih Tzu's normal resting areas for any drafts. During the summer, check to see that your Shih Tzu is not normally positioned where cool AC air will be focused directly onto him.
2- It is recommended to keep the house at a minimum of between 68 and 72 F (20 and 22 C); however, this may not solve the problem completely.
3- If your Shih Tzu is shaking without any other signs such as not eating, vomiting, heavy panting, etc. most likely he or she will benefit from added layered blankets in his resting/sleeping area and having a warm sweater/hoodie/vest/shirt placed on him during the day can help a lot.
4- During the winter, you'll want to protect your Shih Tzu when you take him outside. A waterproof coat or parka should be placed onto him if there is any precipitation including freezing rain, slush, sleet or wet snow since this,

coupled with chilly temps, can cause a deep uncontrollable shivering that can take a long time to recover from. If it is below the freezing mark, a sweater, vest or cotton covering will help keep the Shih Tzu's main body insulated.

2) Stress. Feeling anxious, nervous or stressed can cause a Shih Tzu to shake. There are some common triggers such as being in a new home, dealing with a sudden onslaught of new people or being put into a new situation or event that the dog is not socialized to. With this said, sometimes events that we would not consider to be stressful are taxing to a dog. This can include overexcitement of greeting a favorite person (especially if the Shih Tzu has been home alone), anticipating a meal (particularly if meal time is running late) or even in anticipation of being brought outside (often seen with Shih Tzu that have a lot of pent-up energy that they have been holding in).

How to Help 1- If a Shih Tzu puppy is shaking due to the stress of a new house, this should resolve on its own as the pup gets acclimated to his new environment. Be sure to have a comfortable area for the pup that includes a quality bed, enticing toys and 'cuddle items' such as stuffed dogs and a properly sized blanket. New puppies often need to be reminded where food and water is located.

2- If a Shih Tzu shakes due to nervousness in regard to other people, other animals or new situations, this can often be resolved over time by removing the dog from the trigger and then offering a slow, gradual socialization. You may also wish to refer to the 'Socialization' section, page 118.

3- If the shaking continues, you will want to have your Shih Tzu evaluated for other possible causes.

3) Low Blood Sugar. This will most typically develop with Shih Tzu between the ages of 8 and 16 weeks; though it can happen to older dogs if due to diabetes or other medical issues. Often referred to as hypoglycemia, this rapid drop in blood sugar levels can come on quickly. While many pups will only have visible shivering, some will shake and whine persistently. As to not repeat text, please refer to 'Puppy Care', 'Hypoglycemia', page 30.

Possible reasons for shaking in order of most likely to least likely:

Being cold

Stress

Low blood sugar

Fear

Illness

Seizures

Generalized Tremor Syndrome

fleas

Other Less Common Reasons for Shaking - If shaking continues and the listed treatments do not resolve the issue, there are other less common medical issues to consider:

Being afraid – If a dog is experiencing fear, he may shake. Essentially, a dog may be afraid of just about anything: cars, strangers, lawn mowers, other dogs, etc. In many cases, socializing the dog to his world can make him feel much more confident and take away his fear. For specific help with these issues, you may wish to refer to the 'Socialization' section, page 118.

Illness - A range of diseases from distemper to liver disease can cause shaking. It should be noted that there will be a wide array of other symptoms including: changes in weight, changes in appetite, coughing, wheezing, weakness, fever, eye or nasal discharge, excessive sleeping, restlessness and many more. Chronic shaking that is not resolved by the remedies of keeping the Shih Tzu warm, treating for possible low blood sugar and limiting stress OR that is accompanied by any signs that may point to a health problem, disease or illness should be treated by a reputable veterinarian ASAP.

Seizures - While shaking is sometimes a symptom of seizures, there are very specific signs, depending on the severity of the seizure. The most common cause of seizures in dogs is idiopathic epilepsy. This usually has 3 distinct phases:

1- Pre-ictal phase. This first phase lasts from mere seconds to several hours. There will be some odd behavior that may include whining, shaking, restlessness and/or drooling.

2- Ictal phase. This second phase lasts from mere seconds to 5 minutes. In rare cases of lasting longer than 5 minutes, this would be referred to as 'status epilepticus' and is an emergency situation. If the seizure is mild, the dog may only have a change in mental awareness (staring out at nothing, snapping in the air, etc.). If it is severe (grand mal) all of the dog's muscles will spastically and erratically contract. A dog will often drop to the ground, head drawn backward and legs seemingly unable to move.

3- Post-ictal phase. The third phase - once the main episode is over - lasts anywhere from a few hours to several days.

A dog will have symptoms including confusion, excessive drooling, pacing, restlessness and/or vision problems. Diagnosis includes ruling out poisoning, head trauma, liver disease, kidney disease and heart issues including heartworms. Spinal fluid may be checked and CAT scans or MRI performed. This is treated with anticonvulsant medications including phenobarbital and potassium bromide.

Generalized Tremor Syndrome - This is also called white shaker dog syndrome, since at one time it was only seen in pure white dogs. This is now seen in dogs of all coat colors. With this condition, the entire body shakes but without any other symptoms and for this reason it can be mistaken for other issues such as hypoglycemia or being chilled, as mentioned. While a dog of any age can develop this, it most often strikes those between 9 months old and 2 years old. While the cause is unknown, it responds very well to prednisone treatment with improvement often seen within one week.

Head Shaking - It can be very concerning if a Shih Tzu is having head tremors; in other words, shaking that is limited to just the head. This may involve a fast rhythmic back and forth movement (as if the dog is nodding a 'no' repeatedly) or shivering that appears to tremor down and around the head. For others, this may be a purposeful, quick shaking of the head as if to flick off an irritation.

1) The same reasons for full body shivering - Owners should first look to the 3 most common reasons for shaking which include being cold, having low blood sugar and feeling stressed.

2) Ear issues including fleas, mites, ear infection and inflammation of the ear canal - In this case, a dog may voluntarily shake his head as if agitated. He may also rub his head against surfaces such as the wall or carpeting. Additionally, there may be pawing at the ears.

3) Idiopathic head tremors - With this, there will be clear head bobbing in a vertical 'yes' motion or a horizontal 'no' motion. Episodes come on without warning (meaning no other worrying signs), typically last 3 to 4 minutes and the dog is seemingly perfectly fine afterward.

While a dog of any age may be affected by this, it most commonly strikes dogs that are 3 to 7 years old and is seen in both genders at the same rate. The cause of this type of head shaking is unknown and is only diagnosed by ruling out other medical conditions. Many dogs can be 'snapped' out of an episode with a high sugar treat such as peanut butter or honey. Veterinarians find it helpful if owners can take a video of this happening to a dog as it is a very specific type of rhythmic movement. There is no current treatment, however so far studies show that this has no ill effects to dogs and distraction often works to stop an occurrence.

Red flag Signs of Emergency Situations - It's really important to go with your gut instinct any time that your Shih Tzu begins to shake uncontrollably. Simple instances of shivering from the cold can easily be fixed and trembling due to excitement will resolve on its own. However, since there are so many possible serious medical conditions that owners should not hesitate to seek in-person treatment at the veterinarian clinic or animal hospital. Signs that call for a professional evaluation include, but are not limited to: heavy panting, vomiting, diarrhea, panicked behavior, swollen abdomen, trouble breathing, weakness, altered behavior, persistent crying, changes in appetite, pawing at the ears, restlessness and/or fever.

Situational Issues

Afraid of Other Dogs

The Shih Tzu breed - in general - gets along well with other canines. Some owners have multiple Shih Tzu and they travel around the house like a little pack. There are also lots of Shih Tzu living with a much larger dog and the two couldn't be closer friends; they will even sleep together. With this said, each Shih Tzu has a mind of his own. Some will be wary of strangers, some will be scared of loud noises and some Shih Tzu may be afraid of other dogs. The fear may be fact based if a Shih Tzu has been attacked by another dog and was injured; he may always have a fear of strange dogs and this is understandably so. Other times, since the Shih Tzu a toy breed dog, the chances are good that your dog will be smaller than *many* others that he encounters and it is natural for the smaller dog to be wary of the larger one. Shih Tzu in multi-dog households tend to be better with unknown dogs, it is usually the one-pet Shih Tzu that will show nervousness, anxiety and fear when a strange dog approaches.

Behavior When Seeing Another Dog - Some Shih Tzu may be a bit more secure and brave when in their own territory (house and surrounding yard) and more fearful when out in public, at a park or while taking a daily walk. Though, the sight of a neighbor's dog can cause a Shih Tzu to shake and show other signs of fear. The most common signs that a Shih Tzu is scared of other dogs include:

• Cowering - If you are on a walk, the puppy or dog may hug your leg or motion for you to pick him up.
• Lowering of the tail - Not only can this indicate fear, it is also a sign of stress.
• Shaking - This breed shakes and trembles for several different reasons; being afraid is certainly one of them.
• Whining - The Shih Tzu may whimper and whine.
• Avoidance - A Shih Tzu may tug on the leash or take other action to move away from a dog that is coming toward him.

How This Affects You - When a Shih Tzu is fearful of other dogs, it affects owners as well. Just bringing the dog out for a walk can be an overwhelming event. Owners may try to time the route as to not encounter other dogs; however there is always a feeling of being on guard… Is another owner about to turn the corner with his dog and set off my Shih Tzu? It can limit trips to the park and other places that help a dog become socialized to other people and situations. It is not uncommon for an owner to pick up their Shih Tzu when another dog approaches. It is human instinct to protect our pets and when you have a Shih Tzu puppy acting afraid of a dog that is perhaps 4 times larger or more, scooping up the Shih Tzu and holding him is a common reaction. Unless the other dog is a true threat, this is not the right approach, but it is certainly understandable.

Tips to Help - While there is some training that you can do to help a Shih Tzu feel more confident and brave there are a few things to keep in mind:

1) While there are methods of improving a dog's confidence to greet other dogs, a Shih Tzu may always have a fear of certain types of dogs. Each dog has his threshold. A Shih Tzu may learn to do well with other toy breeds and even medium breeds, but his limit may be large breeds. With other Shih Tzu, the dog may learn that if the other dog is sending friendly signals, it is okay to interact; however the Shih Tzu may not even attempt to do this with dogs that are not outwardly friendly. Not only is this alright, it is the safest thing to do! Therefore, do not expect friendly interaction each and every time; in some instances a Shih Tzu's fear of another dog may be very well justified.

2) Throughout training and beyond, never push your Shih Tzu to do anything. Dogs do best when training is done very slowly and gradually. The dog needs to believe that it is his idea to become a bit braver. It must be his decision to learn to meet and greet. No one (dog or human) can truly learn to have courage if forced into a situation to 'deal with it'. When the decision to do something is voluntary, there is already a much better foundation of determination and intent.

3) Never act upset at your Shih Tzu. Fear is an uncontrollable and powerful emotion whether or not is makes sense to you and regardless of whether you feel it is valid or unjustified. Any sort of punishment or even a 'bad' vibe from you can make your Shih Tzu feel worse.

Training to Help a Shih Tzu Overcome His Fear of Other Dogs

1) Establish Leadership - Any training you do, whether it is housebreaking, command training or this sort of socialization training - can only work well if a dog views his owner as his leader. As to not repeat text, please refer to the 'Teaching Proper Hierarchy' section, page 108.

2) A slow and gradual introduction to other dogs is best. In other words, you'll want your Shih Tzu to dip his paw into a puddle, not jump into the ocean. So, this is best done if you have a friend or family member who owns another dog. And of course, you will want that dog to have a history of being friendly with others. During this time, try to avoid walking your Shih Tzu down routes and paths that a lot of other dogs may be on; you'll want to concentrate on planned, supervised interactions at first.

Since most Shih Tzu feel safe and secure at home, this should be done outside your home in your yard. Inside the home often does not work, because a Shih Tzu may feel that the other dog is invading into his space and territory. This can just make things worse. Therefore, it is best to plan for a friend, neighbor or family member to visit with his dog outside your home in the front or back yard. If you do not know anyone with another dog that is known to get along well with other dogs, your other option is to choose a quiet dog park that has separate sections based on the

size of the dog. When you visit a park in which there are just a handful of other pets, you can initiate a meet and greet with the dog of your choosing. Let another owner know that you are working with your Shih Tzu on tolerance and bravery and most will be happy to oblige.

3) The Meet - Once you have established that you are the leader, when the dog is brought over (or you bring your Shih Tzu to the park to meet another dog), act and speak in a matter-of-fact manner. You will want to send a signal to your Shih Tzu that you do not view the approach of others as a fearful event. Have your Shih Tzu on a 6 foot leash (and harness - not collar). You will want to keep the leash short; otherwise, your dog may just decide to run its length and cower down as far away as he can.

After greeting the other person, crouch down for a moment to the other dog's level to pat him and say hello. This will show your Shih Tzu that you are accepting the other dog and that you do not see him as a threat. Do not put all of your focus on your dog. Your goal will be to interact with the other person. You will be ignoring your Shih Tzu while secretly keeping an eye on him. Chat away in a friendly manner, ignoring any whining, cowering, shaking or tail tucking. If a few minutes pass and your Shih Tzu shows no signs of calming down, it is best to remove him from the area (lead him away, do not carry him).

He may need quite a few quick meets like this before he is ready to engage with the other dog. However, just allowing the approach and as leader, ignoring his signs of fear, you are working towards establishing a 'rule' that if you say it is okay, it is okay. At some point - whether after 2 tries or 20, a Shih Tzu will find a touch of courage to interact.

In order for there to be an interaction between 2 dogs, both must agree on the exchange. If they do, the dogs will sniff each other. It is important to allow this to happen. When they do this, they are smelling each other's anal glands (those two tiny glands on your Shih Tzu that need to be expressed sometimes at the groomer's). The scent released by each dog tells the other: Their gender, their basic health, their age and also if they are receptive to interacting.

If the other dog does not seem interested in playing, do not try and force an interaction and do not take it personally. Some dogs will not be interested in romping around with another dog that is much younger, older, etc. In time, greeting other dogs like this may lead to the two romping around a bit. Always keep a close eye on things; if another dog nips or behaves in a threatening manner, separate them at once.

Remember that not all Shih Tzu can be taught to stop fearing other dogs and if they do tolerate training, it is a gradual process. In time, with enough positive interactions, a Shih Tzu may come out of his shell and no longer be afraid. You may also wish to refer to 'Socialization', 'The Process for Meet and Greets with Other Dogs', page 124.

Having More than One Dog

When you have a Shih Tzu and wish to bring another dog into the home, you may imagine that you will simply have double the fun! You may picture both dogs being best friends and playing together like little brothers and sisters. While this all sounds great, it can take a while for both dogs to settle into the new arrangements and become accustomed to each other. When a new dog enters into the family, this can cause a hierarchy issue based upon the natural instinct of a dog needing to know his or her place in the pack and the addition of a new dog can disrupt this.

Establishing Proper Hierarchy Among the Dogs - Though you have read about teaching proper hierarchy, which establishes that you are your Shih Tzu's leader (Alpha), there is also the matter of the sub-group of animals, who need a leader themselves (the Beta leader). Though we are trying our best to not repeat any text in this book in an effort to keep page number reasonable, we will repeat a small section about this (modified, but as found in the 'Marking' section, page 51):

In a house with proper hierarchy, the humans are the leaders (Alphas) and the dog is the Beta. However, in multiple dog homes, within the group of the Betas, there is *also* a leader: the Beta Leader. In other words, there is always a 'top dog'. If it is not clear (in the Shih Tzu's mind) who the Beta Leader is, there may be unrest.

You can help by establishing which dog is the Alpha Dog, so that the dogs do not have to figure it out or fight for the position. It is *usually* the older dog. However, you can take notice when the dogs are playing. Is one of them more outgoing? Is one dog more 'pushy' when it comes to choosing toys? Which dog runs to their food first? Noticing this, will help you know who is trying harder to be the Alpha Dog.

Once you know, you can then help both dogs. Remember that the dog that is *not* the Alpha Dog is just as important and loved as the other dog. Not being the Alpha Dog is not a negative thing. Both dogs will be less stressed and happy, knowing their place in the 'pack'.

Essentially, you will do everything for the Alpha Dog first. When it is time to feed your dogs dinner, give the Alpha Dog his food first. When handing out treats, the Alpha Dog gets his first. When it is time to take the dogs outside for a walk, put the leash or harness on the Alpha Dog first. These small gestures help the dogs feel secure that you- the main leader- are showing them that you understand the 'pack'.

A note on interaction: It is completely natural for an older dog to discipline a younger dog. It is not acceptable if strong aggression is shown and the younger dog is injured. However, for the home to run smoothly, you should allow the older dog to "put the younger dog in his place" as long as there is no nipping or actions that scares the younger one. For example, an older dog may nose the younger dog away if he gets too close to his toys.

Boundaries - For your Shih Tzu to get along with another dog, clear boundaries must be shown and both dogs must be trained to understand how you expect them to behave. Most likely you have been following the guidelines for your 1st dog in giving your Shih Tzu his own designated area to sleep/play (his gated area or playpen) when home alone. Your Shih Tzu should also have a designated area to eat. This should be in a quiet corner of a room where no one will bother him and your Shih Tzu should always know where he can expect to find water and food. When you have two dogs, these guidelines should be followed for each dog separately. While it is envisioned as cute to have both dogs eating side by side or sleeping right next to each other, unless 2 dogs decide that they are comfortable with that, they must have their own areas. This does not mean that your dogs will not interact or play with each other. This simply allows each of them to have their own boundaries for what is most important to them.

Eating areas- Both dogs can eat in the same room, however each dog has their own invisible boundary that they will not want crossed as they eat and drink. If the food and water is placed too close together, the dogs will have a tendency to fight for what they consider to be their territory. If you see any aggressive behavior during feeding time, this means that you should place their bowls further apart.

Resting/Sleeping areas - Each dog should have their own bed and resting area. This is especially important if you have an older dog and a younger dog in the house together. Your older dog will want his own private area to retreat to when the younger dog is wearing him out. Again, this can be in the same room, but in separate corners of that room. When you have dogs with a large age difference, it may be best to choose separate rooms.

Toys - While it is a bit harder to keep toys separate, each dog may have a few favorites. Therefore, it can help for each dog to have a toy bin kept near that dog's bed/resting area that holds a few 'prized possessions'. The dogs may fight to claim a certain dog toy; however this will be discussed ahead.

If There is Fighting Between Dogs - Once it is established which dog is the 'Beta leader', this does not give that dog a right to fight with or act aggressive toward your other dog. Normally adjusted dogs are very happy with 2 dogs in the home or 10 dogs in the home. If your Shih Tzu growls or bites your other dog or if your Shih Tzu is the one getting bit, this must be acted upon immediately. You may attempt to reprimand the aggressive dog. However, social isolation works best. A strong and firm "NO!" followed by isolating the offending dog for at least 30 minutes is suggested. During that time, the offending dog should be completely ignored. No eye contact, no petting, no words spoken. Complete 'banishment' from the pack for 10 to 15 minutes.

When Dogs Ignore Each Other - It can be upsetting to see two dogs ignoring each other when the whole goal was to bring in a 2nd dog to be friends with the first. Often, this is just a temporary transitional phase. It can take an established dog several weeks to become accustomed to a new puppy that is brought into the household. It is a huge adjustment when a dog suddenly is not the only animal in the home. Dogs like routine; they like knowing when things are going to happen and exactly what is going to happen and when a new puppy comes into the picture, everything is turned upside-down for a while. Ignoring another dog is a much better sign than aggression. This is because ignoring does mean that the dog is tolerating the other; he is just not quite ready to be friends.

Mood Changes with the Introduction of a 2nd Dog - When a new dog is brought in the established dog may become moody. This is often just a reaction to a change in the household. A Shih Tzu may seem withdrawn and distance himself from you. It's hard to not take it personally, however it will get better with time. The best thing that you can do is to not ignore him back. At the same time, you do not want to overdo things either. If you overdo your affection, your dog may believe that he is being rewarded for his distant behavior. Therefore, give a few extra hugs… offer extended play time or additional play time and take some extra time each day just to spend one-on-one time together.

If an Older Shih Tzu is Bothered by a Puppy - An established dog may struggle with the hyper nature of a new puppy. Be sure that feeding areas are well spaced apart. In addition, it is very important that an older Shih Tzu is able to get away from a puppy whenever he wants to. Young adult, adult and senior dogs can have a very low tolerance for 'puppy play'. Puppies are usually very hyper, very silly, very active and they may nip when playing, etc. An established older Shih Tzu needs to be able to retreat from this when he feels that he needs a break. Be sure to never gate them both into a room together, etc. It is best if you allow them the option of playing in the same room and leave it up to them. Most likely, the puppy will try to play and after a while the older dog will want to retreat to find some quiet time. After some time, both dogs will learn to get along and older dogs - given time - will often start to 'mother' a younger pup.

The Need to Spay/ Neuter in Multiple-Dog Households - If all dogs in a multiple-dog household are not fixed, this will often cause the dogs to mark, have territorial issues and of course, you don't want them humping each other. If both are fixed, they will be able to relate to each other simply as equals and be friends.

Loss of a Pet in a Multiple Pet Household - When two pets live together, they become part of each other's lives. When one passes, this can be a very disturbing, very sad time for the remaining pet. It is such a sad time for everyone involved, since owners are feeling an incredible sadness… and a Shih Tzu will often display signs of mourning as well… With the whole family feeling sad and feeling emotional pain, how is one to cope? Studies have shown that the majority of dogs in multiple pet households, in which one pet passes away, show signs of emotional distress. The most common sign of this is a change in eating patterns. A Shih Tzu may not show interest in treats and may not finish meals as normal. Other signs are moping around, not wanting to engage in playing as normal, retreating to be alone and/or sitting by the door as if expecting their friend to come into the house. It can be just heart-wrenching.

As sad as it may seem, the best way to help a Shih Tzu cope with this is *before* another pet passes. If a pet is ill or very old and you know that he or she is going to pass away relatively soon, studies show that having more 1-on-1 time with the pet that will be remaining can help. Getting him used to going for walks without the other dog, playing outside with just the owner and going to the dog park without the other dog, are steps that can prepare a dog for the upcoming loss. It is sad to just think about doing this…. Instinct tells us to let them spend as much time together as possible. However, we must remember that canines are different than humans…. And it does help to do this, if you know in advance that a pet is going to pass away.

If there is no warning and some terrible event suddenly takes away a pet, this can be quite a shocking time for everyone and of course, there is no way to prepare. However, there are some things that you can do to help your Shih Tzu. It is recommended to allow a couple of weeks to pass to just allow the situation to sink in. Everyone will be feeling sad and an owner may just not feel up to taking on new things. However, do cuddle with your Shih Tzu as much as you can. Offer extra hugs, extra pats and extra attention. Do not take it personally if your Shih Tzu wants to retreat. It is a form of mourning and part of the process that canines go through.

After a week or so, it can help to encourage your Shih Tzu to join you in doing something new. When a Shih Tzu is in mourning, often he does not have much enthusiasm to play the same games. However, finding a new activity that you both have not done before can take focus off the sadness and offer a break in which both of you can have some fun. Teach an agility activity (weaving in-between poles or cones, running through a tunnel, etc.) or if the weather is very nice, set up a kiddie pool for your Shih Tzu….anything new to take his mind off things for a bit and have fun for a while. Don't rush into getting a new pet… Give things time.

Separation Anxiety

One of the biggest concerns that owners have is leaving their Shih Tzu home alone and how the puppy or dog responds to that. While there are few dogs that enjoy being by themselves for long periods of time, when a Shih Tzu has separation anxiety, this goes way beyond simply missing his owner. This can be a serious condition that causes both mental stress and is physically wearing on the body. Fortunately, there are some things that you can do to make the situation better and to ease your dog's stress level.

Signs of Separation Anxiety

Before you leave
- Pacing
- Trembling
- Clingy

While you are gone
- Barking
- Frantic behavior
- Destructive chewing
- 'Accidents'
- Depression
- Excessive Licking

When you get back
- Trembling
- Hyper
- Emotionally exhausted
- Clingy
- Continuation of depression

Signs and symptoms of Separation Anxiety - Signs of separation anxiety can begin long before an owner even leaves the house; as soon as a Shih Tzu hears the car keys jingle or even sees that an owner is preparing to leave, his nerves can begin to get rattled. Many of the signs will begin after the owner leaves, and is not there to see it however it can often be heard from outside of the house… or neighbors may relay the disturbance.

Before You Leave: Signs of nervousness such as pacing as you prepare to leave, trembling and/or becoming clingy.

While you are Gone:

• **Excessive barking** - This can often be super intense. A dog may bark until he wears himself out; he'll rest and then start up again. Whether a puppy or adult, a Shih Tzu can literally bark for hours until he is hoarse.

• **Panicked, frantic behavior** - The thing about separation anxiety is that the stress that a dog feels builds and builds as the time ticks by. While a dog may have slight anxiety at first, as the day goes by he can get worked up into a frenzy. This can make a Shih Tzu literally bounce off the walls. A Shih Tzu may repeatedly bang his body into walls, claw at the gates and try to escape his confines. Toys may be flung about, water & food spilled and scattered, scratches on the wall, etc. This can lead to self-injury and/or damage to the house.

• **Destructive chewing** - This sort of behavior has nothing to do with chewing due to boredom; this will be uncontrolled chewing of anything that the dog can mouth. Items are often ripped apart and nothing is off limits; essentially anything that is within reach may be chomped to pieces.

• **Urination and defecating** - Despite the level of house training that a dog has, when overwhelming feelings of panic and stress develop when home alone, the Shih Tzu may urinate and defecate with seemingly no control. In addition to this, it can go a step further where the dog then eats his feces (coprophagia) which has several causes, but separation anxiety is one of them.

• **Depression** – The ongoing stress of this day after day can really take a toll on a dog. He may spend his days curled up, not wanting to play or do anything other than wait until you arrive back home.

• **Excessive licking** - This is a nervous behavior and as with chewing, a dog may do this as a self-calming method. This can be very detrimental, as excessive self-licking can lead to hot spots in which the coat thins or the skin becomes completely bald. The skin can also then become infected.

When You Arrive Back: Trembling, trouble remaining calm, obvious emotional exhaustion, excitement, a rapid release of pent up energy and emotions (jumping, circling you, etc.), excessively clingy. Some dogs are unable to snap out of their depression and will continue to behave moody and withdrawn even after you are back home.

Time VS Level of Distress - Each dog is different. Some Shih Tzu can enter a state of severe separation anxiety just minutes after being left home alone. For others, they will do fine with shorter periods (1 or 2 hours) but they will have a certain line, that when crossed, panic and fear steps in. In either case, the training to help a Shih Tzu will be the same.

What Causes Separation Anxiety - This happens to both genders at the same rate and is not related to how a puppy or dog is treated when with his owners; i.e. paying a lot of attention to a dog or 'spoiling' him will not cause him to be unable to cope when home alone. The age that a dog can develop separation anxiety is broad reaching; it can begin at any age at all, even if the environment or duration of time left alone is unchanged. In some cases, a Shih Tzu puppy will do just fine but then grow into this. The reason for this is typically because a puppy lives in the moment and his mind often jumps from one thought to the next; cognitive recognition is not fully developed when at a young age. As he matures, he becomes much more aware of time and is better able to realize when he is by himself.

Older senior dogs can develop separation anxiety as well. This is often due to health issues that cause the Shih Tzu to feel vulnerable and is coupled by the fact that an older dog often depends more on his owners for care than his younger counterparts. Another factor is that vision and hearing loss, which is common with senior dogs, can make a Shih Tzu feel antsy; being alone only amplifies those feelings. It should be noted that a higher percentage of adopted shelter dogs experience separation anxiety. This may be due to what the dog experienced during his puppy years. Even older dogs can be helped to handle separation issues and will benefit from training.

If a dog suddenly has Separation Anxiety issues, it is often due to a change. This includes:

• **Moving to a new house** - A Shih Tzu may not yet feel "safe" and it will take time for a puppy or dog to know that the new home is indeed "their home"

• **A change of ownership** - A seemingly confident and well behaved dog may develop separation anxiety when new owners take over, no matter what the age of the dog.

• **A change in schedule** - If a dog was normally left home alone during night time hours and now it has turned to day time hours… Or if an owner was usually home on weekends, but now is not, this can cause separation anxiety to develop. Dogs have amazing internal clocks and know when to expect things. Therefore, if a change happens and a dog is not prepared, he may panic since he "knows" that it is not the time that his owner should be leaving.

• **Loss of a family member -** Dogs experience many of the emotions that humans do. If a human or if a canine family member no longer resides in the home, a dog can become distressed. This is especially relevant if a human family member who was a main caregiver to the dog is now gone… Or if a Shih Tzu had an animal playmate (another dog or even sometimes a strong attachment to a cat) and that pet is now gone.

Possible Medical Problems – Looking at the list of signs and symptoms of separation anxiety, incontinence is the one that may be due to other causes. The #1 medical reason that causes a dog's bladder to leak is bladder infections. Other possible causes are urinary tract infection, bladder stones, kidney disease and Cushing's disease. Older, senior dogs may have a loss of bladder control. In many cases, a dog with these medical issues will have urination accidents when home alone and when the owner is away. If you suspect any of these or any other medical issues, do please have your Shih Tzu checked by the veterinarian before you begin any of the training for separation anxiety. There are some medications that can cause a dog to lose control of bladder and/or bowels. If your Shih Tzu is taking a prescribed medication, please first check with your vet to find out if incontinence can be one of the side effects.

Other Issues- With house soiling problems, do be sure that this is not a matter of housetraining. Remember that a puppy can only hold his needs for a few hours. A good guideline is that a 3 month old can hold his needs for only about 3 hours, a 4 month old for about 4 hours and so on. The maximum amount of time that an adult dog should be expected to hold his needs is 8 hours. Therefore, expecting a dog - that is home alone for 10 or 11 hours - to hold his bathroom needs the entire time is unrealistic. If you are in the process of housebreaking your Shih Tzu or if you need to brush up on housebreaking, you may wish to refer to the 'Housebreaking' section, page 43.

Training and Help for Separation Anxiety

Fixing this issue is a combination of several elements: New departure methods, making sure your Shih Tzu's environment is perfectly set up and timed practice runs. It may also involve some extra help such as separation anxiety aides. Each element involves many sub-elements. Offering just a couple will do very little to help a Shih Tzu. If your Shih Tzu is suffering from separation anxiety, do please make a commitment to follow as many as humanly possible.

A Plan for Pre-Departure -

Whether your Shih Tzu makes it clear that he understands that you are about to leave, or if he is calm when you walk out the door, just about all dogs do sense that their owner is preparing to leave the house. Therefore, let's talk about how things should change in regard to what happens before you even leave. Think about what sounds or actions happen as you prepare to leave. This usually includes (but is not limited to):

Practice with short, timed sessions

Make sure your little one has the highest quality items

An excellent supply of both chew & boredom toys

A companion toy that is soft & emits a soothing heartbeat

A piece of your clothing that has your scent

- Putting on your shoes and coat
- Handling your car keys
- Opening the door to inspect the weather
- Pouring a cup of coffee into a "to-go" cup

The 1st step in the training will be to show your Shih Tzu that doing these things does not necessarily mean that you are leaving for a long period of time, or leaving at all. On days that you will not be leaving, perform one (or some) of these actions, randomly throughout the day and then simply go on with your day. For example, if you are planning on reading a book, simply pick up your keys, jingle them and then sit down to read as if nothing were out of place. Open the door to inspect the weather but then go back to watching TV.

This should be done many times throughout the days that you are not planning on leaving and it should continue to be done essentially forever, as it will be part of desensitization and this should be reinforced so that your Shih Tzu never again learns to read these "cues". Once your Shih Tzu no longer becomes nervous when you do these things, each day that you are home, take the time to do just one….Handle the keys, or look out of the door, etc.

On days that you DO leave, here are departure guidelines:

1) Do not place your Shih Tzu in his designated area (a playpen or an enclosed indoor area with doggie gates works well) right before you leave. Your dog should be able to enjoy his area without making an association that being there leads to something "bad". At times that you are home, leave the entrance to this open and encourage your dog to go there to find treats and fun toys. When you are going to leave, place your Shih Tzu in his area a good 20 minutes before you actually leave.

2) Take your Shih Tzu outside for bathroom needs before you leave, even if you do not think that he/she needs to go.

3) If time permits, set aside 15 to 20 minutes (or even 5 if that's all you have) for some outdoor playtime. Running around in the yard or going for a morning walk can allow a dog to release energy (making him more prone to rest or nap later) and helps thwart the feeling of having the canine equivalent of cabin fever.

4) Do not shower your Shih Tzu with hugs and kisses and promises that you will return. While it is human instinct to want to say goodbye in this way, it sends a signal to a dog that their owner is leaving for a good amount of time. You can give this sort of attention well before you leave (20 to 30 minutes). When you are ready to depart, do this in a matter-of-fact way. If your Shih Tzu seems to get nervous as you are closing the front door, do not reenter to soothe him. The training steps ahead will work to build up independence skills and reentering to offer soothing words or hugs will counteract this.

5) Never scold your Shih Tzu for bad behavior that stems from separation anxiety. This is uncontrolled behavior and scolding only adds stress to an already stressed dog.

Setting up the Proper Area: If someone placed you in a small room without anything to keep yourself occupied, you might experience separation anxiety as well! Here are some tips to make sure that your Shih Tzu remains safe and has enough needed items and objects to be able to self sooth and keep busy.
• Have your Shih Tzu in a safe, canine playpen or a secure gated area. This area should be large enough for the Shih Tzu to move around. There should be a section for resting/sleep, for eating and for playing. If a Shih Tzu feels confined, this often triples his feelings of panic.
• The area should be in a warm comfortable room (A/C in the summer, well heated in the winter)
• Learn what your particular dog likes. Some love to be able to look out of a window…for others, this can bring distress.

Have the following in the area:

Toys - It cannot be overstated how the correct toys are vital to a Shih Tzu being able to handle being alone. Some Shih Tzu can become so attached to favorite toys - only accessible when home alone- that they begin to look forward to this time that they will have access to them. You'll want to provide:
• Treat release toys
• Interactional toys for boredom
• Chew toys
• Companion toys * Without a doubt, the right companion toy is the #1 element to help Shih Tzu with separation anxiety. As to not repeat text, you may wish to refer to 'Care Items - Shih Tzu of All Ages', 'Toys', page 36.

Water and Food – You may wish to have water in a dispenser versus a bowl if your Shih Tzu is prone to disturbing the water bowl. It can be really helpful to leave treat-release toys with food. A mix of kibble and a bit of peanut butter (smooth) can work well. If you will be gone during one of your Shih Tzu's scheduled meal times, leave enough food in the treat release toy to equal both a meal & a snack. If you will only be gone long enough for him to miss snack time, leave the equivalent of a snack sized portion. When your Shih Tzu gets hungry, he will work for the food which can help pass the time.

Doggie Bed - Have a well-cushioned, quality, soft and clean dog bed in this area, so that your Shih Tzu has a 'safe' area to rest and sleep. If the bed is subpar and a dog is uncomfortable all day, this is going to have an effect.

Pee-pads – No matter how well a Shih Tzu is housebroken, if you will be gone longer than he can realistically hold his needs, you'll want to have pee pads down. Even if you don't think he will need to go to the bathroom, it's always a good idea to place down a few, just in case.

An article of your clothing that holds your scent – This can be a shirt or socks or other small piece of clothing, that is not overly dirty yet is not laundered before you give it to your Shih Tzu. It should be something you have recently worn against your skin.

Just as Important – How to Set up the Home Environment

Lights – If you think about an empty yet well-lit house VS an empty, dark house, the well-lit house is going to offer a better environment. This is particularly applicable if you will be arriving home as the sun is setting or afterward - of if the forecast is for a cloudy or stormy day; however we recommend it for all Shih Tzu, in all cases.

Leave on lights to make the house bright & 'sunny'

Leave on the TV with a pleasant show on...

... Or leave on some easy-listening music

Try a calming collar or calming supplement

See your vet if all of these things do not work

Soothing Noise/Sights - It can help to have a TV or radio playing in the background. Some dogs like this, since it can simulate normal noises present when owners are home. But for other dogs, it can cause more distress if they do not know where the sounds are originating from. If you can set up a TV that a Shih Tzu can see, this is best. It has been proven that canines can and do watch TV and recognize images on them. Best is a family themed or 'old school' TV channel, that airs shows like I Love Lucy and the Dick Van Dyke show. Be careful to avoid channels that would have loud, upset voices such as those that air talk shows that showcase family arguments, etc.

Do Some 'Practice Runs' - For Shih Tzu with severe separation anxiety, it can be very helpful to train in small steps. Using the listed guidelines for 'A Plan for Pre-Departure' and for 'Environment' you can then begin training your Shih Tzu to be alone in the following way:

Step 1 - Not Actually Leaving On days that you are home - following the Departure and Environment guidelines- do not leave the house, but DO remove yourself from the room. Your Shih Tzu will be in his designated area with all needed items. Go to any room that your dog does not have a direct line of sight to you...but can hear you. No matter how much he whines, cries, jumps, paces or does otherwise, stay out of sight for 5 minutes and then very matter-of-factly, reenter the room. Wait 3 to 5 minutes and then allow your Shih Tzu to leave the pen or gated area.

When your Shih Tzu learns to be fine with 5 minutes, increase this to 10...then 15, then 20 and so on. When your Shih Tzu shows no signs of separation anxiety at the 20 minute mark, you will now be ready for Step 2.

Step 2 - Actually Leaving for Timed Periods On days that you are home - following the Departure and Environment guidelines- Leave the house for 10 minutes and 10 minutes only. Dogs are very intelligent, so it is best if you actually drive away. Do this randomly for about 1 week. On week 2, increase this time to 15 minutes. On week 3, increase to 20 minutes. On week 4, increase this to 30 minutes.

Follow these times as closely as you can. The goal will be to show your Shih Tzu that he IS capable of being alone - and not being panicked- for 10 minutes. When he gains the self-confidence that he did okay for 10 minutes (which will be greatly helped along by following pre-departure guidelines and setting up the right environment), he will learn that he can do just fine for 15 and so on.

Tip- Each dog is unique and you will need to read your Shih Tzu's behavior to see if it is time to increase these sessions. For some dogs, an increase will be able to be done every few days...For others it may be every couple of weeks. The important element to keep in mind is that while this type of training can take a while, the end result will be a confident dog that can handle being home alone, will be able to self soothe (with the help of the types of toys & methods mentioned earlier) and will no longer have separation anxiety.

Also note that while you are in the mist of training, we expect there will be lots of days that your Shih Tzu will be home alone for those 7, 8 or 9 hours. You cannot do anything about that if you work out of the home or are in school, so keep training in this way. Once done, these short training sessions will start to have an effect on how he feels on those long days.

How to Handle Things When You Arrive Back Home - When you finally come home after a long day at work, it is natural to want to greet your dog and give him big hugs, kisses and tons of attention. However, when a dog suffers from separation anxiety, making a big deal out of arriving back home can be counterproductive. If an owner rushes inside and then rushes to their dog to really pour it on thick, this can be the same as sending a direct message that says "I can't believe I made it back home! Oh, this is a miracle, let's celebrate!" And this tells a dog that they were correct to be worried.

So, what should you do? When you enter the home, do not greet your Shih Tzu. This will be a bit difficult until you get used to the routine. However, it is best to casually enter, quietly walk to the kitchen to have a drink of water, thumb through the mail... and then after 1 to 3 minutes, calmly approach your dog and in a matter-of-fact manner, say "hello". After this, bring your puppy or dog outside for bathroom needs. Once that business is taken care of, it will be time to hug, kiss and play! If the weather permits, spend some time outside to run around with your Shih Tzu, allowing him to release pent-up energy and enjoy time with you. Remember, training for separation anxiety does not mean withholding affection from your Shih Tzu all of the time, it means holding it back at the exact moments when it does more harm than good.

Additional Help for Separation Anxiety - If you will be gone for extended periods of time, it can be very helpful to offer your Shih Tzu a break in his day. If possible, go home during lunch time. Even a 10 minute session of play and a bathroom break for your Shih Tzu can be very helpful. If this is not possible, you may wish to see if a friend or family member (or a neighbor) would like to visit your Shih Tzu one time per day. Sometimes older, retired friends, family or neighbors welcome this request. They have the pleasure of spending time 'doggie sitting' and will be more than happy to help out. If you choose to do this, be sure that they follow the guidelines for when they leave and that they make sure that the designated area holds all of the needed items.

Another option - if you are normally gone for long periods - is to hire a dog walker. Older neighborhood children may be thrilled to be asked to do this job. Alternatively, you may want to check with your local high school's guidance counselor for a list of recommended students who may appreciate this part-time job. If you do choose someone, have them come over when you are home (3 or 4 times on various days) so that your Shih Tzu can become used to them. Be sure that they know to follow all of the rules and that they have your emergency contact number. Just 30 minutes to 1 hour per day of someone coming to your house to bring your Shih Tzu outside for a bathroom break and to play with him can make a huge difference. Many owners who have Shih Tzu with separation anxiety ask if a Doggie Day Care would help. And the answer is, it all depends on your particular puppy or dog. Some dogs love the company of other dogs and will enjoy that time. Others are not yet socialized to other dogs enough to enjoy play time and/or the stress of being away from home overpowers the stress of being home alone.

Supplements & Aids - While they do not work for every dog and the degree to which they work does vary, some dogs respond very well to calming collars and/or calming supplements. Our recommended calming collar slowly releases a lavender/chamomile fragrance that naturally relaxes some dogs. In regard to supplements, those that contain L-theanine and colostrum work very well for some dogs and importantly, are safe. L-theanine is an amino acid that has relaxing effects; it does not cause drowsiness; however, it works to increase dopamine which is an organic chemical released in the brain to regulate mood and relaxation. Colostrum has relaxing properties that reduce stress.

If All Else Fails 1) There are some dogs that will not be able to handle being alone, no matter what the method or techniques used to train him. For these dogs, medication may be prescribed. In many cases, the side effects are not worth the benefits in all but the most severe cases. This is something that should be discussed with the veterinarian. The two types of medication most often used are: *Benzodiazepines (tranquilizers)* - These have some negative side effects including sleepiness, increased appetite and the possibility of increased anxiety. Studies have found that these can interfere with memory and the ability to learn. *Monoamine oxidase inhibitors* (anti-depressant)- Some MAOIs can have dangerous side effects in dogs that have recently ingested cheese products. One that is tolerated well is Clomicalm.

2) Not available in all areas, a Certified Applied Animal Behaviorist (CAAB) or a board-certified veterinary behaviorist may be able to help a dog via one-on-one desensitization and conditioning training. This tends to be expensive but has worked with some dogs.

Should You Get Another Dog? In most cases, when a Shih Tzu has another dog with him, this does eliminate the issue of separation anxiety. However, it should be noted that in some cases, both dogs will be unable to cope and/or the dogs may have a period of adjustment in which they are not getting along with each other well enough yet to offer companionship and comfort. We would never advise someone to take on the huge responsibility of having a second dog for this reason alone. However, if you've wanted another dog and have given careful thought to the cost and time involved with having multiple pets, this does often help.

For all recommended separation anxiety aides including companion toys, playpens & calming supplements, look to "Separation Anxiety' in the Shih Tzu Specialty Shoppe. You can reach the Shih Tzu Specialty Shoppe by entering any page of the AllShihTzu website. Look to the navigation; it is in alphabetical order. Choose 'Shoppe'.

Your Shih Tzu & Your Baby

If your Shih Tzu is used to being the 'baby' in the home and if you are expecting a human baby, this will be a big adjustment for everyone. However, by implementing training both before and after your new arrival, everything can run very smoothly. Those who have issues with their dog and baby are usually those who did not plan ahead of time.

Preparation- As soon as you learn that you will be expecting a baby, training should begin for your Shih Tzu; this will ensure that your Shih Tzu has plenty of time to become accustomed to changes. Some of the changes will be:

* The layout of the home
* Those wonderful new scents of a baby
* Your Shih Tzu's schedule, as you may need to rearrange daily activities around the new baby.

Basic Commands- Things will run much smoother if your Shih Tzu understands and always listens to basic commands. You will want your Shih Tzu to immediately: Sit, Stay and Heel on command. If your Shih Tzu has not yet mastered these commands, begin training right away. You may wish to refer to 'Commands', page 112.

Before Baby Arrives - There is much to help your Shih Tzu become accustomed to, so it is best to begin right away. You can help your dog become used to the scents of your new baby by taking some baby powder and rubbing it into the carpet, a soft wash cloth etc. and allowing your Shih Tzu to become very familiar with the scent. If you have a baby mobile or other baby toys that make noise, it will help to sit down with your Shih Tzu and have your dog hear these noises. With months of hearing twinkling baby songs, this will not be surprising one bit when your baby arrives.

If you believe that you will be changing the layout of your home, do this as soon as possible. Dogs love consistency. If a baby highchair is going to be in the spot where a Shih Tzu's food bowl once was and his bowl is going to be moved to another corner in the kitchen, make this change now. If your Shih Tzu balks at the idea of having his food and water moved and you absolutely must change the location of his dishes, you can try to do this slowly. Each day you can move the food dish and water bowl a few inches. After a while, you will reach your goal!

Some owners have found that playing recordings of a crying baby was extremely helpful in helping shy or nervous Shih Tzu that they feared may be afraid of the loud crying noises a baby can make. You can do this by "borrowing" a friend's, neighbor's or family member's baby noises. Just ask permission to record the baby for a while. Most babies will let out some cries during a recording session. You can then play this recording for your Shih Tzu. At first, do this on a very quiet setting, talking to your Shih Tzu in a matter-of-fact, calm voice and patting your dog while he hears the crying. As your Shih Tzu becomes used to the noise, you can then play it louder each week. You will reach the point of being able to play the recording at the natural volume and your Shih Tzu should become accustomed to it. Before bringing your baby home from the hospital, send home a blanket or gown that the baby has been wrapped in. This will help your dog get used to your baby's particular scent.

Toys - Your Shih Tzu will have no idea of the difference between his toys and the baby's toys unless you explain this. It is best to choose a designated area for your Shih Tzu's toys and if possible, a designated area for your baby's toys (and where you expect the soon-to-be toddler's toy bin will be). Spend months showing your Shih Tzu which toys he is allowed to play with and which he is not allowed to touch. This is very important; as you would not want your Shih Tzu thinking the baby is playing with "his" toy and mouthing it from the baby's hands. Each time your Shih Tzu goes over to the baby's toys, clap your hands loudly and then immediately give your Shih Tzu one of his own toys. Done in this way, you are not reprimanding your dog for being curious, but you are distracting your Shih Tzu and then showing him what is appropriate to play with. Be sure to end this by patting your Shih Tzu and giving words of praise to show that you are proud of him. If a Shih Tzu needs extra motivation, reward with small treats as well.

Managing Time Limitations - Even the best parents in the world (of both babies and Shih Tzu) cannot be in two places at once. With the arrival of a baby, there will be times when your Shih Tzu cannot receive the same amount of attention that he was once used to. It is best to make this change before the arrival of the baby and not afterward when your Shih Tzu may become jealous. If the main caretaker of the Shih Tzu will be the main caretaker of the baby, try to have another household member begin taking your Shih Tzu for walks, feeding him, grooming him, etc. Done in slow, steady steps, this will allow a Shih Tzu plenty of time to become used to receiving care from another human family member.

After the Baby Arrives -Associate the baby's presence with positive things. Give your Shih Tzu treats and lavish praise for desired behavior around the baby. Do not place the baby on the floor with your Shih Tzu without supervision and never yell at your Shih Tzu for approaching your baby incorrectly. Gently show the dog what you wish for him to do and offer a reward for responding. Due to the fact that a baby's immune system is not strong, ensure that your dog is healthy and is up to date with de-wormings before the baby arrives. Humans cannot catch such disease as heartworms, parvovirus or distemper; however the Campylobacter jejuni bacteria (symptoms in dogs is runny diarrhea, lethargy and/or fever) can be passed to humans, as can ringworm.

Jealousy- Even with very careful planning, months in advance, some Shih Tzu may be a bit jealous or become clingy to you once the baby is home. It is best to continue on with your planned schedule and follow the guidelines listed. If your Shih Tzu is extremely clingy, do acknowledge him by giving a quick pat and then do what you must to care for your baby. If you are sitting on the sofa feeding your baby, you can also have your Shih Tzu lying close to you to cuddle. When you take the baby for a walk in the stroller, you can take your Shih Tzu along as well. In time, your Shih Tzu will become used to having a little brother or sister.

Seasonal Care

Summer Care

If you live in an area that experiences seasonally hot temperatures or perhaps you even live where there's hot weather year round, you'll want to know about some important care elements that should be in place in the summer.

Your Shih Tzu's Indoor Area - Since many owners are working to keep their house cool via AC and fans in the summer, many don't think that any changes need to be made to a Shih Tzu's inside area where he plays, rests and sleeps, however there are some elements to reassess.

Your Shih Tzu's Playpen or gated off area - Check to evaluate the amount of sunshine that is coming through windows. In the summer, the sun's rays hit the Earth at a different angle and of course, it shines for almost twice as long as cold, dark winter months. There may be some days of particularly cloudless skies that sun streams strong directly into a Shih Tzu's area. When owners are not home during the work week and with the family often active on weekends, this may not be noticed. Take a moment on a day that you're home to see if there are blocks of time that the sun is shining right into your dog's area intensely enough that it would make him uncomfortable. If so, you can either move his area to a better location or keep certain shades or curtains closed.

The other element is to take note of strong AC currents. While you'll want to keep the house cool, this toy breed does not do well with cold air pouring directly on him. Gated areas or playpens should be situated where they will benefit from cooling systems but are not in direct line of the cold air being cycled out.

Keeping Your Shih Tzu Cool and Safe in the Summer Heat

Inside: **A cooling mat** – If you do not have AC or to plan in case your AC cuts out, cooling mats for canines can work incredibly well to keep a dog comfortable. These are also great for cooling a dog down after he has been outside. A quality cooling mat will be a pressure active gel pad; it will not have any electrical cords or power sources. The gel inside absorbs heat from a dog's body and is a safe way to keep a Shih Tzu cooler in the summer. These are portable and can even be used outdoors if needed.

Outdoors: 1) Exercise with care

One of the tricky things about summer care is that you'll want to keep up with your Shih Tzu's normal exercise schedule since cutting back can cause behavioral issues due to pent up energy not being released however you'll need to take steps to prevent overheating and damage to the paws via hot surfaces. This breed does best with two walks per day and if a Shih Tzu is taken outside early in the morning and then again later in the evening when the day is cooling down, this alone can help you avoid the searing summer heat and sun. Depending on the weather conditions it may be advantageous to change the routine somewhat; you may find that a longer walk in the cool morning and a shorter one in the evening works better in the summer than a 50/50 split.

2) Take care when in the yard - You may enjoy spending time outside in your yard in the summer and may be wondering if it's okay to keep your Shih Tzu with you. You may spend hours gardening, barbequing or even swimming. You'll want to provide an area of shade, a way to cool off via water or both. Many dogs love to splash around in a small plastic children's pool and this is a great method to helping a Shih Tzu stay cool in the summer. Another option that many dogs enjoy is an oscillating sprinkler which can keep a puppy or dog occupied for quite some time while the water keeps his body cool.

3) Protect his paws. Asphalt surfaces can reach up to 80 degrees Fahrenheit higher than the air temperature on hot summer days and pavement made of concrete can be up to 30 degrees hotter. While a dog's paws are made of thick skin, they are not invincible and can suffer from first degree burns within 5 seconds. This will cause a drying and peeling effect that will then be exasperated as the Shih Tzu moves about. This can be avoided by applying a quality paw wax. A good brand will be absorbed quickly (within 10 seconds or so) and will provide a layer of protection between the paws and any hot roads or sidewalks. This is normally applied 2 to 3 times per week. Another option is to place doggie shoes on your Shih Tzu; some actually enjoy wearing these and some are less tolerable.

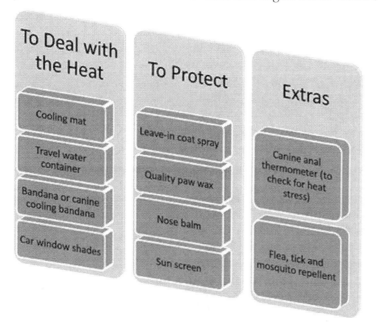

4) Bring water. No matter how far you are walking or where your destination is, it's always smart to bring along water for your Shih Tzu anytime you venture out in the summer. Not only do dogs drink much more during hot months and offering water more often can help keep a dog from becoming dehydrated, but also taking a break every 20 minutes to offer cool water can prevent summer heat stress. Portable canine water containers with an opening large enough to place ice cubes inside and those that have a lid that serves as the bowl are a good choice.

5) Protect the nose - The nose is especially vulnerable to sunburn just like with humans. Once the top layer is damaged by the sun, it can begin to peel. If steps are not taken to help that heal, it can lead to cracking and more serious issues. Dabbing a snout butter or balm on the nose 15 minutes before heading out can help keep the leather protected and healthy.

6) Protect the belly - Breeds that stand close to the ground, like the Shih Tzu, are prone to sunburn on the belly. This is because the stomach can get sunburned from the reflected light from ground surfaces and the skin in this area is usually very sensitive. It's always a good idea to rub a bit of canine sunblock on the stomach and groin area if you'll be outside for more than 30 minutes in the summer. If you'll be taking your Shih Tzu to the beach, lake or other outdoor area with hot sand and/or water which can reflect UV rays, paws, nose and belly protection is a must.

7) Prevent skin and coat dryness - While winter weather can really dry out a dog's skin and coat, summertime can cause issues as well. The sun can gradually have a burning affect, which can actually cause the hair to change color. If a Shih Tzu is outside a lot, dark hair such as brown or black can eventually develop a red tinge. Also, during the summer skin can dry out, causing itching and peeling. The best method to avoid these problems is to use a quality leave-in coat conditioning spritz. These are light sprays that will prevent sun damage. An added bonus is that the right product will also work as a deodorizer and make a dog smell fresh and clean. There is no need to use a lot; it's recommended to spray and then brush downward to distribute the product.

8) Use a cooling bandana - Canine cooling bandanas can be a great way to keep a Shih Tzu puppy or dog feeling comfortable on hot days. These can be used both indoor and when outside. Be sure to use one that is sized for toy breeds so that there is not too much weight placed on the neck. An alternative is to simply soak a 'regular' bandana in cool water and secure it to the Shih Tzu, taking care that it fits as a collar should, with two fingers able to be slipped between that and the neck.

Driving Your Shih Tzu in the Summer - With a few safety rules, you can easily bring your Shih Tzu with you in the car despite summertime heat.

1) Any time you are going to enter into your car with your Shih Tzu, turn it on and run the AC to first cool it off since cars can become overwhelmingly hot when parked, It is best to open the windows for several minutes to allow the hot air to escape and then close them to allow the colder air to circulate.
2) Check your Shih Tzu's car seat to make sure it's not hot (similar to how a steering wheel can become super-hot to the touch in the summer).
3) While it feels good to have cold air blowing on you on a hot summer day, when you have your Shih Tzu in the car, take care that the vent is not blowing directly on him. This breed is very sensitive to temperature changes.
4) Shih Tzu that tend to suffer from motion sickness may need to have a window partially opened in conjunction with the AC running.
5) Depending on the height of your puppy or dog's car seat, you may find that using car shades is very helpful in keeping the sunlight out of his eyes which can cause a dog to be quite uncomfortable and also increase motion sickness.

Shih Tzu and Swimming Pools - If you want your Shih Tzu to swim in a large pool, keep in mind that Shih Tzu can swim, however it is a myth that dogs are automatically excellent swimmers. It can take time for a dog to understand how to keep himself afloat. Here are some pool safety steps:

1) Never throw a dog into a pool or other large body of water. A dog that is thrown in will 'doggie paddle' to the best of his ability to reach land out of survival instinct, however this is certainly not a method that will teach him that swimming can be fun.
2) Even if he seems to be enjoying himself, supervise him while he's swimming. A dog may swim out too far and find himself in trouble. Just like humans, dogs can tire out and struggle to get back.
3) Most pools have high levels of chlorine to keep the water clean. This can be an eye irritant, so routinely check your Shih Tzu's eyes for signs of redness. A canine saline rinse can help clear up bloodshot eyes. Also, if it is left on the coat, chlorine can severely dry out both the skin and hair. Once done, you'll want to thoroughly rinse your Shih Tzu off.

Heat Stress or Stroke - No matter how many precautions an owner takes, you can never be completely sure how a dog is going to react to summer heat. And once heat stress occurs, steps must be immediately taken to cool the dog off; if not this can lead to heat stroke which can be fatal. For these reasons, you should know the signs and symptoms of heat stroke with Shih Tzu and what to do if you think it is happening. Heat stress (Hyperthermia) is when a dog's internal body temperature is 103 degrees Fahrenheit. Heat stroke is a step above that, with body temperature being 106 or higher. It is very dangerous and can lead to multiple organ failure. As to not repeat text, please refer to the 'Exercise', 'Heat Stroke' section, page 106.

Summer Insects - Be sure to always protect your Shih Tzu from ticks and fleas. You'll also want to use a safe mosquito repellent for any times that you have your dog out after dusk when these pesky bugs are in full force. Look for a NO chemical, safe spray with natural ingredients to fend off bugs. There are some great products that work for fleas, ticks, mosquitoes and flies all at the same time.

Another element to keep in mind is the issue of hornets, wasps, bees and other stinging insects. Dogs are prone to get bit since they tend to stick their noses into areas where these insects may be, such as in bushes and such. Dogs are often stung on the face and while this is painful enough, some may also then suffer an allergic reaction which can be dangerous. If your Shih Tzu is stung by a bee or other stinging bug, keep an eye on him for signs of an allergic reaction; this includes swelling around the face, breathing difficulty and/or signs of weakness. If a Shih Tzu is stung 3 or more times, he should be taken to the vet regardless of how he seems, since toy sized dogs can have severe reactions and it can take up to 45 minutes for these to develop. You will want to check your dog to see if the stinger is present. Do not try to remove it with a tweezers, since this can release more venom. It's best to use your license or a credit card to scrape it out. A mixture of water and baking powder made into a paste can be applied to help with swelling and pain. You may also wish to refer to the 'First Aide', 'Stung by a Bee, Wasp or Other Stinging Insect' section, page 285.

Winter Care

For those of you who live in an area that endures cold weather, it is important to know how to winterize your Shih Tzu. For many of us, winter means cold temperatures, wet participation in the form of freezing rain and/or snow and drier air as well. These elements can affect a Shih Tzu's coat, skin, paws, ability to control body temperature and more.

Grooming and Protection of the Coat - Taking care of a Shih Tzu in the winter time will focus quite a bit on proper care of both the skin and the coat. The main reason for this is that

whether or not it is snowing out, the air in the winter is much drier than in the spring, summer or autumn. Moisture that remains in the air is called the humidity factor. When it is cold out, the air is not able to hold onto very much moisture. And don't think you're safe by staying indoors! When that arid air meets the warm temperatures of a heated house, it dries out even more. For this reason, your Shih Tzu simply will not be able to escape the damage that winter air can do to his coat and skin without some help from you, since the humidity factor is very low in the winter.

2 main things can occur without proper winterization:

1) Skin can become dry and chapped. When this happens, hot spots (red, irritated skin), and itchiness will occur (sometimes severe). Once this happens, thinning of the coat is not far away.

2) The coat can become full of static and this causes split ends. Split ends (if not trimmed back) will run up toward the root. Hairs will then break off and the hair will thin out.

So, you will want to use a good product at the right times - While all owners should be using a quality leave-in conditioner, it is important in the winter more than ever. Spraying on a good amount will coat the hairs and create a shield that protects the hair from the harmful effects of a cold, dry winter season. Remember that your house will hold less humidity than normal as well, so even if you take your Shih Tzu outside less during cold weather, this is still an important grooming step.

Here are the steps:

1. Keep up with your brushing routine to keep the coat free of dead hairs and tangles, so that the product can work properly.

2. It is best to apply the leave-in product in the morning to start the day and then a lighter coat right before bedtime.

3. To apply, a small pin brush works best; you'll want to choose one that is textured in the right way to distribute the product but not too rough as to irritate the skin. Work in sections, spraying the leave-in conditioner near -but not on- the roots. As you go, stroke down to the roots. Once you have gone over every area, spray some into your hands, rub them together and then scrunch at the ends of the coat to really coat the tips.

4. Don't go overboard; too much will weigh the coat down, make the hair oily and block healthy air circulation to the skin pores. As you go, think 'lightly mist'. The application done in the evening will be a light touchup for any that has rubbed off during the day. It will be to continue the protection as your Shih Tzu sleeps (hair rubbing against fabric during the winter can cause static).

Timing of Baths - You should be sure to keep up on your schedule of a bath every 3 weeks. The goal will be to use a moisturizing shampoo to clean off all residue - be sure to scrub down through the coat very well and rinse super well since any dry soap particles will be more irritating to a Shih Tzu's skin in the winter. This is followed by using a moisturizing conditioner to protect. If skin is flaky and peeling use a specialized shampoo for dry skin. With flaky skin, you may need to shampoo more often for the product to do its job (usually once per week).

If your Shih Tzu has very dry winter skin, allow your Shih Tzu to air dry and refrain from using a blow dryer. Plan baths well in advance so that your Shih Tzu does not need to be taken outside with damp hair (this could prove dangerous in the winter).

Protecting the Paws and Nose- Skin can go from healthy to dry in the blink of an eye, so part of caring for a Shih Tzu in the winter will be to protect the skin but also to inspect it on a daily basis in order to find any potential issues very early. **Here are important skin care tips for winter:**

1) Protect the paws with a quality paw balm and if your Shih Tzu shows intolerance for the winter ground surfaces or tends to slip, see if he likes booties. We must remember that paws are made of skin and when subjected to harsh weather can dry out as much - if not more - than skin on the body. One HUGE issue is salt and ice melt chemicals that is placed down in the winter. Even if you do not use these products, city municipal services often do; they will be trekked into your neighborhood via cars. These can be damaging to paws, causing chemical burns and/or problems with the nail beds.

Even if you use booties when outside, rubbing in some good paw wax once a week can keep the paws protected and moisturized and prevent cracking. If paws are already dry and cracked, a high quality paw wax may heal these issues, keeping you from having to make a vet appointment. If the paws are so sore that it impedes walking, if there is any deeply cracked skin, bleeding or other concerns, do make an appointment with the vet, as there may be an infection.

In regard to shoes/boots, you'll want to choose a pair that is rugged, easy for a Shih Tzu to actually walk in and are weather-resistant. Those with Velcro closures at the ankles work good for this breed.

2) Protect your Shih Tzu's nose. The harsh cold winds of winter can do quite a bit of damage to a Shih Tzu's little nose. And before you even notice that it is dry, there can be cracking and crusting issues. Since a puppy or dog licks their nose quite a bit, even a few minutes outside in the winter can cause chapping. Winterizing the nose is really fast and easy. Using a good paw/nose balm or some nose chap sticks, just 3 or 4 small dabs will place a protective layer on the nose and keep the leather safe from the winter air.

Control the Humidity in the House - Keeping the humidity level in the house at a moderate level will help

with dry skin and coat. It can also help with a dog that develops a dry cough due to arid air. If you choose to purchase a humidifier do keep in mind its capacity. Most units will only work for one or two rooms. If the dry air in the house is really affecting your Shih Tzu, place a humidifier near his sleeping area. Also, please remember that humidifiers must be regularly cleaned to keep them free of bacteria. There are some home remedies to create moisture, including:

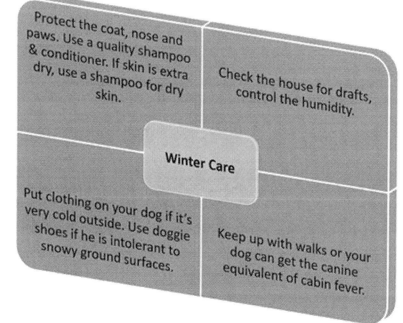

Protect the coat, nose and paws. Use a quality shampoo & conditioner. If skin is extra dry, use a shampoo for dry skin.

Check the house for drafts, control the humidity.

Winter Care

Put clothing on your dog if it's very cold outside. Use doggie shoes if he is intolerant to snowy ground surfaces.

Keep up with walks or your dog can get the canine equivalent of cabin fever.

1- Placing metal bowls of water on top of heat registers or heaters
2- Leaving the door to the bathroom open during and after showering
3- Taking a large Ziploc bag and punching roughly 20 holes in it, placing a large wet sponge inside and then placing that on counters and other areas. You may need 5 to 10 of these spread over the house.
4- Obtaining houseplants, since they release moisture after they are watered.

Taking a Shih Tzu Outside in the Winter - Not only will you need to take your Shih Tzu outdoors for

bathroom needs (unless he is pee pad trained) it will be important to maintain normal activity levels as much as possible. It is quite common for dogs to eat a bit less in the summer and a bit more in the winter. If you combine this with a decrease in exercise, you have the recipe for declined health. Exercise - and walking in particular - keeps both the heart and muscles healthy. Also, dogs can become exceedingly frustrated and moody if they do not receive regular exercise. Unless there is a blizzard or sub-freezing temperatures, it is best to properly clothe your Shih Tzu (and yourself) and head out for his once-a-day or twice-a-day walk. Toy breed dogs struggle to maintain core body temperature much more than their larger counterparts. Therefore making sure that your puppy or dog is warm is an important part of winter care for the Shih Tzu. Any time that the temperature is below 32F (0 C) (factoring in the wind chill), be sure to place a nice sweater or soft hoodie on your Shih Tzu. If it is snowing, put a water-proof parka on your Shih Tzu.

Playing in the Snow - Some Shih Tzu dread the snow and will expect their walking path to be perfectly shoveled

and will bring you their booties to put on them before even going close to the door. However, some love the snow as if it was the best creation on Earth. It's fine to allow your Shih Tzu to have fun playing in the snow if he is supervised and if you keep the time to about 20 minutes or so. Even with full clothing on, more than 20 minutes playing in moderate snow during below-freezing temperatures is risky in regard to possible hypothermia. Some Shih Tzu get so excited that the body warms up due to moving around so fast and then there is a sudden drop-off point of the cold settling in. And we must stress again, that this must be supervised. Once back inside, be sure to use a soft, absorbent towel to dry your Shih Tzu (pat, do not rub). It can help to put a t-shirt on him as his body works to warm back up.

Changes to Expect in the Winter - Part of providing good winter care for a Shih Tzu and getting your dog ready for winter is knowing what is normal and what is a sign that something is wrong. Here are some things to expect:

1) It is normal for there to be a slight increase in food consumption and a slight decrease in exercise during the winter season. Even if you normally bring your Shih Tzu out, for many owners there will be certain days of weather that is so bad it is just not feasible to venture out. For these reasons, there may be a small increase in weight. 1/4 to 1/2 pound is considered normal. If you notice any gain larger than this (or a weight loss) that would be reason to bring the concern to the veterinarian.

2) Behavior may become a bit more restless. Dogs can experience cabin fever in the winter just as some humans can and they may not always follow the lead of their owner. You may have an owner that is just fine with staying indoors with a roaring fire and a cup of cocoa but her dog may become frustrated that he can't burn off pent-up energy. For some Shih Tzu, even going from 2 walks per day to 1 can be hard to handle.

You can help your Shih Tzu by doing some fun things in the house. Winter is a great time to work on commands or tricks! Also, even simple things like encouraging your Shih Tzu to follow you around the home to pick things up (you carry the basket, your Shih Tzu picks up the items) can be fun if you use an excited tone of voice and offer praise as you go along. Playing a game of hide n' seek, allowing your Shih Tzu to chase you or even letting a Shih Tzu play with a frozen ice cube on a slippery floor (always great for teething puppies) can be enough to cheer up a dog that feels more confined in the winter. In addition, some dogs can feel as if their schedule is thrown off when days are shorter and sunlight is limited. A Shih Tzu may want to go to sleep much earlier than normal, etc. It can help to perform a grooming task right after the sun sets such as brushing the teeth. This sends a message that even though it got dark out, the day is not quite over yet.

3) Senior Shih Tzu may have aches and pains due to arthritis flaring up. Reevaluate his bed to see if it is time for a better orthopedic one and if there seems to be a significant amount of increased discomfort, do not hesitate to bring this to the attention of the vet.

Health – Body Part Specific

Anal Glands

All dogs (both male and female) have a pair of anal glands, also referred to as scent glands. There is one on each side of the anal opening. These hold an oily substance that is released in tiny amounts when one dog meets another. This is why dogs sniff at each other's rear ends. Smelling this scent allows the dogs to communicate important information. It lets each dog know the other's gender, health status and even his mood. In addition to tiny amounts being released when dogs encounter each other, minuscule amounts are also often released when a dog pushes out a bowel movement. Because over the course of days and weeks the oil is being released and replenished, there is usually not a problem.

However, if a Shih Tzu rarely encounters another dog and/or if his stools are soft, his glands may not release any oil at all. In these cases, the glands may become engorged. When engorged, they will swell with excess oil. This stretches the skin on this sensitive area. For this reason, the main sign of engorged anal glands is when the dog scoots his bottom across the ground. It may appear that the dog is 'wiping his bum' but he is, in fact, trying his best to scratch an itch.

At this point, due to friction when the dog scoots, the gland(s) may break open. If they burst in this way, all of the oil will spill out at once. Some owners of female dogs mistake this for blood related to the heat cycle. With anal gland fluid however, the smell is exceedingly strong. Some compare this to a skunk.

If the skin does indeed burst open, releasing a gush of fluid, the skin will then be broken and vulnerable to infection. You can give your Shih Tzu a bath, however do not rub the area; instead gently pour water over it. You can then dab some antibiotic ointment on it, to help prevent infection. Keep an eye on this area for several weeks. If it is swollen, becomes red, has any pus or shows any other signs of infection, you will need to bring your Shih Tzu to the vet. He will flush the area, possibly close any open skin with stitches, and prescribe medications.

If you see that the glands are swollen, you will want your groomer or veterinarian to express the glands. This means that they will essentially be popped; similar in a way to popping a pimple, however much more difficult due to the location and much messier due to the oil and the smell. For this reason, it is best left to the professionals. The average fee for this is $15 to $20.

Another issue that can happen, is if the glands become engorged, but do not break open. In these cases, if an owner does not notice (therefore they are not expressed), the oil can harden. It can morph into a thick paste-like substance that has a consistency of peanut butter. This is referred to as impacted anal glands. At this point, it will be too late to have them expressed. Dogs with impacted anal glands may still do the scooting motion, will be more prone to licking the area, may hold the tail funny and/or may show signs of pain when sitting.

In these instances, a veterinarian will need to perform a minor surgical procedure. Dogs are first given a sedative. A small incision is made on each sac and a catheter will be put into the duct of the gland. The vet will then slowly inject water into the gland until the thickened substance is removed. They are then flushed out with water and fluids to prevent infection. Most veterinarians will then inject an antibiotic ointment into the glands to protect against any possible bacterial infection. A prescribed oral antibiotic may be given for 7 to 10 days afterward.

Because these things can happen, it is suggested to inspect your Shih Tzu's anal glands to get a good idea of their normal size. You may even wish to snap a few photos. In this way, if you suspect that they are swollen, you will know when you compare a 'before' and 'after'. Please do not hesitate to have them expressed, should they need this, as the consequences of not doing so can cause a lot of discomfort to your Shih Tzu (and will hurt your pocket or wallet, should they transition from engorged to impacted).

Ears

Ear Care

Inspecting the ears – You will want to inspect the ears at least every 2 weeks. When you lift the Shih Tzu's ears to look at the underneath of the flap and to see the entrance of the canal, the correct color of the skin is pink. You

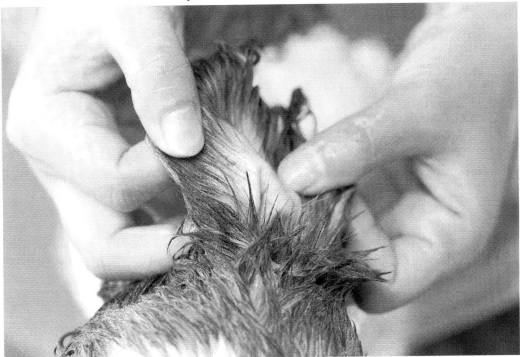

should look for any signs of infection (red, rash, or sores), excess wax (you will visibly see wax) and signs of long hairs (hairs that grow out from the ear canal enough to be visible). You will also want to sniff each ear to see if there is a bad odor. If there is excess wax, you will want to clean the ears even if this means doing it before it was scheduled. If you see long hairs, these should be plucked out, as they can work along with the wax to harbor bacteria. And if there is a bad smell, this points to infection (more ahead).

Cleaning – To keep the ears healthy and to help prevent infection, we recommend cleaning the ears every 6 to 8 weeks, unless otherwise directed by your Shih Tzu's veterinarian. The last thing you want to do, is to clean them too often; wax is naturally occurring and helps to trap dust and tiny debris, so that it does not enter deeper into the ear canal. But when there is buildup and a good amount of debris caught in the wax, cleaning the ears out can help to prevent ear infections.

Cleaning supplies – The list is quite small. The #1 thing you need is a quality ear cleaning solution. Please do not try at-home remedies. Such fluids as vinegar, alcohol, and hydrogen peroxide can irritate the delicate skin of the inner ear, so do choose an appropriate canine ear cleanser. We really like the Zymox line of products. You will also want sterilize gauze pads (size small) or sterilize cotton pads.

Instructions – You will want to do one ear at a time. Once the first ear is completely done, do the second.

1. Hold the ear flap and using your other hand, gently dribble the solution into the ear canal. Do NOT attempt to go deep. You will see the solution, so only place enough so that it does not overflow. The solution will slowly make its way down, however you do not need to watch and wait. It will be time for Step #2 as soon as you have dribbled the solution into the canal.

2. Massage the base of the ear for 15 seconds. This is done by having your thumb on one side of the Shih Tzu's ear and your forefinger on the other side. Gently press your fingers toward each other and move them around in a gentle circular motion. During this time, you may hear the solution squish around as you massage solution down further.

3. Use the cotton to swipe out the ear. You will place your finger in the middle of the rolled cotton in order to keep it firm. Do NOT attempt to clean out the inner ear. Just swipe as far as you easily can. Rotate the cotton pad several times and then remove it. Do not be surprised at what you see after removing the cotton pad. The solution that you just massaged in helped to loosen compacted wax and dirt. The color of the debris that you clean up may be anywhere from a yellow to a dark brown.

Note: Cleaning the ears should not be painful for a dog. If your Shih Tzu shows signs that he is in pain when you do this, this is a sign of infection or other issue that needs to be seen by the vet. Unless told differently by the veterinarian (if your Shih Tzu's ears are infected or other), you will want to clean the ears 1 time per month. Doing it too often (every 1 or 2 weeks) can be counter effective.

Plucking hairs – Normally, there are fine hairs in the ears. However, sometimes, one or two strands will grow long and stick out from the ear. In these cases, you may use an ear powder (to make it easier to grab the hair(s) and either use your fingers (make sure your hands are very dry) or a small forceps tool that latches onto the hair allowing you to quickly pluck it out. Do not over-pluck. Only remove those long hairs that you clearly see.

Infections - The medical term for an ear infection is otitis externa. This is the #1 health issue that brings puppies and dogs to the veterinarian. The cost to have it treated ranges from $100 to $125 USD and this does not factor in the cost of medications and cleaning products that are part of the treatment. Ear infections can happen to a Shih Tzu of any age and this condition is usually very painful. Most Shih Tzu will have at least one round with this during their lifetime. For most dogs, it will be acute (occurring once and clearing up with treatment). Some Shih Tzu, unfortunately, are plagued with chronic infections, which reoccur over and over even with proper care.

Types of Ear infections and The Causes of Them - There are 2 main types of infections that affect dogs:

1) Bacterial - This is the most common type of infection. Of this, there are two subcategories:

• *Nonpathogenic:* This is the most common type of bacterial ear infection. The dog's body overproduces staph bacteria. Many things can cause this, including: a foreign body that is stuck in the canal, allergies and parasites. Less common but still possible are autoimmune skin issues and glandular disorders.

• *Pathogenic:* With pathogenic forms, an outside source of bacteria reaches the dog's ear and settles in. This can happen in countless ways; however, some examples are a puppy or dog lapping water from a contaminated source such as a dirty puddle.

2) Yeast (fungal) - This can be in the outer or inner ear. The most common reason for this is water in the ear. Even just a bit of moisture can become trapped in the canal which makes for a perfect breeding ground for bacteria; it is moist and dark. Another issue that can contribute to this is excess long hairs which help to hold in water.

Symptoms of Ear Infections - Whether it is due to yeast or caused by bacteria, the signs and symptoms of ear infections are the same:

• The itchiness and pain will cause a Shih Tzu to rub his head against a surface such as the wall or carpeting, paw at the ears and/or shake the head
• Red, inflamed looking tissue on the ear flap and/or in outer canal
• Discharge - Drainage is often thick and may be a yellow color. Though, if dirt and debris is mixed in with the discharge, you may see specks of brown or black or the debris may cause the discharge to be a yellow-brown color. In some cases, it may look like a cloudy pus. While the Shih Tzu sleeps, discharge may crust over.
• There may also be a bad odor emanating from one or both ears. This is more common with yeast infections but may also be present with bacterial issues.

If treated and allowed to progress, it can cause dizziness and difficultly keeping balance. This is because the ear drum can rupture, which allows the infection to spread to the middle ear. This throws off a dog's equilibrium.

If still left untreated, it can cause hearing loss. Inflammation and discharge may cause temporary hearing loss. However, if a Shih Tzu puppy or dog does not receive proper treatment and the infection is allowed to ravage the ear, it will often spread to the middle ear. Without appropriate care, there can be permanent damage to the inner structures that result in permanent hearing loss.

Home Remedies that May Work in Some Cases - Everyone finds themselves in a bind once in a while when paying for a vet visit is really going to strain the budget. Since this is the #1 reason why dogs are brought to the vet, all owners are encouraged to budget money for this issue, as it is sure to strike at one time or another. There are many types of ear infections and we do highly recommend taking your Shih Tzu to the vet to have him diagnosed. He will determine if the issue is yeast, bacterial or even mites. He will determine the extent of the infection and then decide on the proper dosing and duration of treatment.

This said, in some cases of infection, the vet will prescribe a medication that you can obtain over-the-counter. It will be an enzymatic ear solution, often with 0.5-Percent hydrocortisone. If this is prescribed, you may wish to purchase this yourself. In many cases, this can save you money. The prescribed solution may run about $40 and the OTC one can be half that amount, a bit less than $20. Again, we prefer the Zymox line of products and the one to treat bacterial, fungal, and yeast infections is Zymox Enzymatic Ear Solution with 0.5-Percent Hydrocortisone.

We do not endorse using hydrogen peroxide, vinegar or rubbing alcohol. There are also herbal remedies (many use a fluid extracted by the Mullein flower), however at this time we do not recommend this either.

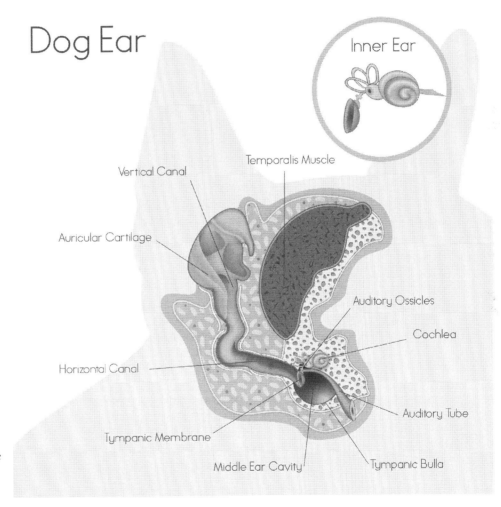

Prescribed Treatment for Ear Infections - While you can use the OTC product and it may clear up minor issues, when a Shih Tzu has a full-fledged, raging infection you will want to seek the care of a reputable, experienced veterinarian. The vet will perform an examination to look for signs of swelling, redness, discharge and irritation. The inner canal should be inspected for a foreign body such as grass seeds, tiny blades of grass, a sand pebble and other elements that may have fallen down into the ear during playtime outside. The veterinarian should take a sample swipe of the outer canal to look for bacteria, yeast or parasites (mites). For Shih Tzu that have chronic ear infections, other tests should be run as well such as looking for thyroid issues or allergies.

A professional cleaning should be performed at the office. Once done, this will be followed by prescribing medications to be given at home. This may include both oral medicine and cleaning solution (ask about the Zymox). You will probably be instructed to perform a daily cleansing in order to keep them clean enough to absorb the medication. Be sure to follow through will all doses, even if your Shih Tzu appears better. Just a trace of bacteria left in the ear can grow into a widespread infection.

Chronic Ear Infections - It can be so frustrating to work to clear up an infection, only to have it come back again and again. Each time that the ear is assaulted in this way, it can cause small amounts of damage. In time, this will add up and can lead to permanent damage including loss of hearing. Owners will need to work together with a trusted veterinarian to ensure proper treatment both at home and with prescribed medications. When the problem keeps coming back, the vet should look for an underlying cause. One of the most common reasons for reoccurring problems is an allergy. If so, aside from ear infections there may also be other signs of allergies such as watery eyes, wheezing, coughing and/or skin and coat problems.

While prescribed medications are given, owners must work to keep the ears both clean and dry. Cotton balls should be gently placed in the ears before baths are given and the outer flaps and outer canal should be wiped dry afterward. Dogs with chronic ear infections should not be allowed to swim until the condition is under control. Hygiene is vital, so be sure to remove excess wax and pluck any long hairs as these may contribute to the issue.

When a dog does not respond to antibiotics and is nearing the point of permanent damage, surgery may be recommended as a last course of action. There can be bone degeneration that can be seen via x-rays. It may seem drastic; however, with stubborn infections it is actually quite successful. The surgery is called Total Ear Canal Ablation (though other less evasive operations may be done; they do not have the high success rate in eradicating ear infections as this does). During the procedure, the diseased ear canal is removed; though the hearing organ remains. This involves pre-surgical dosing of antibiotics for 10 to 14 days. After the surgery, the dog is given medication to control pain along with another course of antibiotics. The success rate for resolving chronic ear infections is quite high with this surgery and many owners report that their Shih Tzu had a happier and easier going personality once he no longer had to endure ongoing pain.

Mites – Technically, this is not an infection, it is an infestation. And mites can happen to any dog, of any breed. This is not limited to unclean dogs and even owners who take great care of hygiene problems can find that their Shih Tzu has gotten mites. Mites are *very* contagious. When present, they live in abundance in the ear, but also can travel to other areas on the dog, such as the neck, chest, back and so on. And this is often how dogs catch them from one another. When on the body, they can be transferred when 2 dogs simply rub against another while walking past, playing with each other, etc. They also have the capability to jump short distances, therefore they can pass from a dog to your Shih Tzu by jumping onto the coat when in close proximity.

The signs of mites are:
- A dark discoloration of the inner ear flap and/or entrance to the canal
- A strong smelling odor coming from the ears
- Discharge
- Itchiness – This usually manifests by the dog shaking his head in an attempt to relieve the discomfort
- You may see a crusty substance when looking in the canal

Treatment - This cannot properly be treated at home. Your Shih Tzu ears will need a prescribed insecticidal medication. It is important to apply it as long as directed; even if things seem to be clearing up. In most cases, it will need to be applied for 3 weeks to ensure that all mature mites and larvae are eradicated. A specialized flea powder should be sprinkled onto the coat of the dog to kill any mites that have traveled outside of the Shih Tzu's ears.

Prevention of All Types of Ear Infections - There are some things that you can do to stop a Shih Tzu from getting ear infections. Here are some tips:

1) Keep the ears dry. Even though this breed only needs a full bath about once every 3 weeks, any water that enters the ears can remain there. This creates a moist and dark environment that is the ideal breeding ground for bacteria and yeast. Always place cotton in your Shih Tzu's ears during baths. Even with this protection, be sure to wipe the flap and the outer canal as soon as you remove him from the tub or sink.

2) Routinely inspect the ears. Look for discoloration, excess wax, long hairs and any odor. Catching problems early offers the best chance at a speedy recovery.

3) Do routine cleanings. Even if there is no problem; this can catch things before they even begin. When you clean the ears, it removes excess wax, dirt, debris and may pull out yeast or bacteria in the very beginning stages. Use a quality cleaning solution. Making a set schedule can help you stay on track. Though we recommend doing this once every 4 weeks, many owners find it easy to do this task after baths, which means every 3 weeks and that is just fine as well.

4) Do not allow your Shih Tzu to drink from any potential contaminated water source. This includes lapping at puddles and ponds.

5) If your Shih Tzu is going to swim do be sure to dry the ears well right afterward.

6) If an allergy is suspected to be the cause of chronic infections (and this can cause other issues such as dry skin, coat thinning, etc.) do take steps to resolve the allergy issues. Allergy information can be found in the 'Allergies' section, page 215.

Paws

Most dog owners think of dog paws as being tough, strong and in a way, like shoes for the dog. However, there is much more to consider. The paw pad is made mostly of keratin, which is an exceptionally thick protein. This is a type of skin - albeit a thick one - and therefore vulnerable to many of the issues that 'normal' skin is vulnerable to. The thickness of a dog's paw is directly related to how often he walks outside and the roughness of those outdoor surfaces. Puppies will have much softer (and more sensitive) paws than older dogs. Older Shih Tzu that are routinely taken for walks outside on a variety of surfaces (sand, cement, grass, etc.) will have thicker, more resilient paws than dogs that are kept inside more often. So in general, as your Shih Tzu matures, his paws will become thicker and more durable; however all dogs - of any age - will need protection during certain circumstances.

Such elements as walking on hot surfaces, cold surfaces and surfaces containing pebbles can cause damage. Ice melt and salt in the winter can cause damage as well. Because the paw pads are made of skin, they are susceptible to dry skin issues. Dry skin on the paws can cause a dog to lick/chew at them (though this also may be due to an underlying issue of allergies).

Dogs can also suffer from broken skin,

infection and other paw issues; these will be discussed here.

Why Paw Wax is So Important – A good, quality paw wax will keep the paw skin healthy. It will also add a breathable layer of protection that prevents damage from hot surfaces in the summer, cold surfaces in the winter, irritation from small bits of sand and pebbles and lock in moisture to help prevent drying. Another great element is that wax helps a dog with traction (sled dogs always have on paw wax) and finally, if your Shih Tzu does have some skin damage there (dryness, peeling, irritation), a good canine paw wax will aid in allowing those things to heal.

Signs of Paw Issues

- Any swelling – this can be the entire paw or a portion of the paw
- Bleeding
- Secretions coming from the splits in the pads or between toes
- Blisters
- Limping
- Chewing on the paw
- Licking the paw
- Odor
- Peeling
- Cracking

When to Treat at Home VS Going to the Vet

• **For peeling or minor to moderate cracking**, you can often heal this at home by applying a quality paw wax. If cracks are deep, you'll want the vet to have a look to rule out any possible infection or to offer antibiotics to prevent infection. It will be important to use a quality product that will heal the paws as quickly as possible, since this is such a difficult area to treat on a dog. A thick effective healing butter should be applied each night at bed time, with a sock slipped on so that the Shih Tzu won't lick the substance off. Even though quality products will be safe for canine consumption, the sock helps make sure that it seeps into the cracks and remains there overnight. And be sure to keep applying it regularly to prevent the issue from reoccurring. As to not repeat text, you may also wish to refer to 'Seasonal Care', 'Summer Care' page 179 and 'Seasonal Care', 'Winter Care', page 182.

• **For moderate to severe swelling, deep cracking, redness, moderate to severe bleeding, secretions or pus, deep sores, pain that causes limping or strong odor,** these are issues that must be diagnosed and treated by the veterinarian.

• For *small superficial cuts* you can clean the cut with warm, soapy water and then pat it dry. Inspect the area for any possible slivers. If possible, keep your Shih Tzu inside until the paw has healed. Keep an eye on the area for any redness, swelling or worsening condition.

Moderate cuts should also be cleaned, dried and inspected in the same way. If the cut is not actively bleeding, once cleaned you can dab some topical antibiotic ointment on the cut and then cover the paw with a sock. You may have a hard time finding one that is small enough. The RC Pet Products Sport Pawks Dog Socks is perfect for the Shih Tzu, it comes in both XXS and XS. If possible, keep your Shih Tzu inside until the paw has healed. Keep an eye on the area for any redness, swelling or worsening condition.

Severe cuts or cuts that do not stop bleeding must be looked at by the veterinarian. Deep cuts such as this may need to be flushed and stitched. The vet may prescribe oral antibiotics as well as topical treatment. The paw will need to be protected to allow it to heal and healing can take some time.

Any time issues do not respond to treatment- If you do not see any results with the at-home treatments after 3 to 5 days or if symptoms worsen, do not hesitate to bring your Shih Tzu to the vet.

Paw Issues

For licking/chewing at the paws or **for sores due to licking/chewing**, please refer to the 'Behavioral Issues', 'Licking and/or Chewing at the Paws' section, page 157.

Yeast Infections on the Paws- The symptoms of this are a greasy like substance on the paw(s) and/or a wax like substance on the paw(s) and a bad odor (most often compared to a musty smell). This can be diagnosed with a smear from the paw that the vet will then examine. This can be treated with prescription anti-fungal medication provided by the vet.

Zinc Deficiency – If your Shih Tzu is lacking zinc in his diet, this can affect the dog's paws. Symptoms of this are cracking and sometimes an odor. For this reason, if at-home treatments for cracked paws is not working, you'll want the vet to check your dog for this or any other possible, more serious issues. Your Shih Tzu's veterinarian can diagnose this with a skin biopsy and by careful examination of your Shih Tzu's diet, age and medical history. Canine zinc supplements will correct this.

Rare Issues Nasodigital hyperkeratosis - This is a health issue that can affect a dog's paws, nose or both. When it affects the paws, it causes the pads of the paw to grow exceptionally large. A biopsy of the skin on the paw will determine if this disease is present. An experienced veterinarian will then be able to trim off excess skin. It is then very important to take care of the paws while they heal. Preventive treatment is then done to stop the pads from growing back to abnormal size; this is usually done by soaking the dog's paws in a propylene-glycol solution.

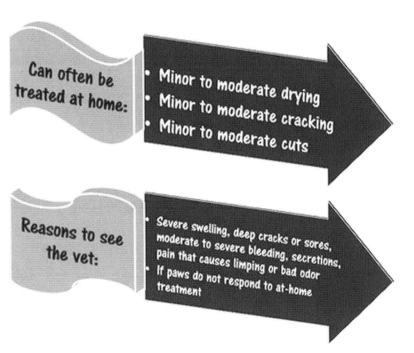

Can often be treated at home:
• Minor to moderate drying
• Minor to moderate cracking
• Minor to moderate cuts

Reasons to see the vet:
Severe swelling, deep cracks or sores, moderate to severe bleeding, secretions, pain that causes limping or bad odor. If paws do not respond to at-home treatment

Auto-immune disease of the skin – This is a somewhat serious canine disease in which a dog's immune system goes out of control. The dog's system will mistake healthy skin cells for unhealthy ones and begins to attack them.

Symptoms are: Sores (usually with a pus-like substance in them), crusty sores (which happens after the pus-like sores break open) and sometimes but not always, sores such as this on the dog's nose and/or ears. This is diagnosed with a test sample of the skin of the paw. Treatment is dosing with immune suppressing medication.

General Protection of Your Shih Tzu's Paws - There are many things that you can do to protect your Shih Tzu's paws. Of course, this only works if done on a regular basis.

• If your Shih Tzu gets any mud or dirt on the paws, wash this off as soon as possible.

• Outdoor elements (pollen and such) can attach to the paws and not only cause issues with drying skin but also the paws will bring those allergens into the home. While canine wipes can remove some of this, ideally you will want to rinse the paws off in the kitchen sink (which is not all that hard to do with this toy breed).

• After taking your Shih Tzu for a walk, take a moment to check the paws for any small pebbles, cracks, sores, blisters or bleeding.

• When hiking or walking on rough terrain, stop every now and then to check your Shih Tzu's paws. You'll want to look for cuts, cracks or any other signs of injury. Dogs will usually only begin limping once an injury is severe and they can't hold the pain in any longer.

• Trim any long hairs that grow out from between the paw pads, as these can pull at the skin on the paws, causing discomfort.
• Paws that stay wet for long periods of time can cause problems. After baths, time outside in rain or puddles or after swimming, dry off the paws and make sure to get the area in between the toes.

• If your Shih Tzu is stung by a bee or wasp on the paw, be sure to remove the stinger. Never use a tweezers. Use a credit card to scrape the stinger out.

Seasonal Prevention & Care - For full details regarding seasonal protection, please refer to the 'Seasonal Care', 'Summer Care' section, page 179 & the 'Seasonal Care', 'Winter Care' section, page 182.

 For recommended paw protection and healing butter balms, look to 'Grooming' in the Shih Tzu Specialty Shoppe. You can reach the Shih Tzu Specialty Shoppe by entering any page of the AllShihTzu website. Look to the navigation; it is in alphabetical order. Choose 'Shoppe'.

Nose

There are a number of issues that are related to a Shih Tzu's nose that you should be aware of. Issues can pop up quickly. Though some concerns are more common depending on the time of year, each season brings about a new element that can affect the nose of a dog of any age.

Wet or Dry, Cold or Warm: Your Shih Tzu's Nose - Many people take note of both the tactile temperature of a Shih Tzu's nose and its level of perceived moisture to determine if the dog is healthy. No doubt, countless owners have heard that the nose should be wet and cold. However, there is a lot more to it than this.

Wet or Dry - In many cases, both a wet and a dry nose are considered normal, to a certain degree. In just one day, a Shih Tzu's nose can change from one to the other. However a big swing on either end of the spectrum may point to a problem. For example, an overly wet nose may be a sign of a soon-to-come runny nose and a consistently overly dry nose can lead to cracking and peeling. If your Shih Tzu's nose fluctuates from moderately moist to slightly dry, without any other issues, this would be considered normal. Some elements that can cause temporary dryness or are a precursor to more severe drying issues include:

• Too much sun exposure (even if indoors and the dog is under a window, etc.)
• Chapping from winter weather or excessively licking the nose
• Being situated close to a heat source (heating vent, radiator, etc.) this is due to both the heat and the dry air.
• When just waking up - One of the leading causes of a nose feeling wet is that the puppy or dog licks it throughout the day; since this doesn't happen when a Shih Tzu sleeps, it may be dry when he first wakes up.

If your Shih Tzu's nose is regularly dry without any other red flag issues (peeling, cracking), it's recommended to:
• Move the dog's resting area away from heat sources, if applicable.
• Use a humidifier if the air in the house is very dry; this is most common in the wintertime.
• Protect the nose with balm or butter (more ahead) to guard against outdoor elements; this is for both hot sunny days and cold winter days.

Cold or Warm - With this element, there can also be a range of what is considered to be normal. If a Shih Tzu has a dry nose, it may automatically feel warmer to the touch than if it were moist. In general, it is common for a dogs' nose to fluctuate between feeling cold and warm. There are some things that can temporarily make a dog's nose quite warm:

• Sun exposure - The nose leather naturally does not have any protection from the sun and if a Shih Tzu is outside for 30 minutes or more on a hot, sunny day the leather can absorb the heat, making it feel warm.
• Slight dehydration - A loss of between 1 to 5% of body fluids constitutes slight dehydration and can cause the nose to feel warm and dry, along with possible trouble in focusing, irritability and/or headache (the dog may rub his forehead against surfaces)

If your Shih Tzu's nose is regularly warm without any other troubling signs (fever, lethargy, cracking, and/or feeling hot, etc.), it is a good idea to:

• Protect the nose from too much sun exposure (more ahead)
• Make sure that your Shih Tzu is drinking enough water. Dogs that are not hydrating enough can often be encouraged to drink more when a canine water fountain is used.

Dry, Cracked and/or Peeling Noses - The nose is comprised of skin; however it is very sensitive as it has only 3 layers of skin as opposed to the 5 layers that cover the body. This is one reason why a dry nose can quickly escalate into a peeling or cracking issue. The outer layer, called the stratum corneum; has grooves that give it texture. Being very thin, any problem that causes this layer to peel away or develop cracks will expose the pink layer underneath. These sorts of issues can be very painful for dogs, so it is important to treat this as soon as possible and to take steps to prevent issues from developing in the future. The most common causes of cracked and peeling noses are the same ones as chronic dryness, that have not been resolved, thus leading to a more severe problem:

• **Sun exposure** - Without protection, a sensitive nose can not only become dried out, over time there can be sun damage and in some cases, an actually sun burn to the nasal skin. Ahead we will discuss treatment.
• **Dry air** - This is particularly common during the colder months when the house is heated. The air may be very dry, which can cause dry skin problems over the entire body, but may be much more noticeable on the nose. While using humidifiers will help, you will want to address the cracking and peeling to bring the nose back to its healthy state.
• **Dehydration** - A Shih Tzu may be slightly to moderately dehydrated without any other signs other than dryness; though issues such as irritation, decreased ability to focus and lethargy may not be immediately picked up on by some owners. Using a canine water fountain can work well to encourage a Shih Tzu to drink more. Additionally, adding water-rich foods to his meals or offering them as snacks can count toward the dog's daily water intake… Watermelon, raspberries and/or blueberries are good choices as they are safe for canines to eat in moderation and high in water (92, 87 and 85% respectively).
• **Chapping** - The skin on a Shih Tzu's nose can become chapped and this is very common in the winter when weather can be harsh, with cold air and whipping winds.

At Home Treatment of Cracking and Peeling - Treatment for chapping, peeling and minor crusting issues will involve using a quality healing nose balm or butter. This will soothe the sensitive skin and add a layer of relief to nourish, heal and moisturize. Here are some tips:

• We recommend a product that does not contain chemicals and is organic, if possible, since a puppy or dog will tend to keep licking at the nose.
• Look for one that is scent-free, as a scented product may cause a Shih Tzu to resist having it applied.
• Apply this liberally each evening right before your Shih Tzu goes to sleep for the night.
• Also apply this to the nose every 4 to 5 hours. Near meal times, apply this after the Shih Tzu eats.
• Once the nose has healed, dab a small amount on 2 to 3 times per day so that the nose is shielded from future damage.

With the right product, expect to see improvement within 5 to 7 days and complete healing within 2 to 3 weeks. Do be sure to also address any issues of water intake and dry air in the house.

Many cases of cracking and peeling can be treated at home; however you will want to check with the vet, especially if there is:

- Bleeding - If cracks are deep enough that they are bleeding; this often means that the issue involves all 3 layers of skin. Infection can set in.
- A sign of infection - A severely cracked nose leaves the skin open and vulnerable to bacteria and infection. If there is any pus oozing from the cracks, if the nose appears to have areas that are swollen, if your Shih Tzu is showing signs of pain, if there is a fever, etc. these are red flags that the vet should perform an examination as antibiotics and other prescribed medications may be needed.
- The nose is not healing - If there seems to be no improvement after 7 days with the home remedy.

Nose Crusting and Sores - Small crusty flakes can be a sign of healing; if there were small cracks or pieces of skin that flaked off, those areas can scab over. Crusty scabs on the nose are

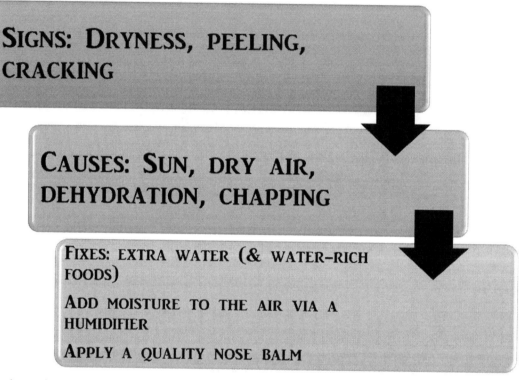

SIGNS: DRYNESS, PEELING, CRACKING

CAUSES: SUN, DRY AIR, DEHYDRATION, CHAPPING

FIXES: EXTRA WATER (& WATER-RICH FOODS)

ADD MOISTURE TO THE AIR VIA A HUMIDIFIER

APPLY A QUALITY NOSE BALM

often red or brown and can simply be the body's method of protecting the sensitive skin from germs while the skin cells rejuvenate. **There are some medical conditions which can cause rather severe sores that crust over on the nose. This includes:**

•**Discoid Lupus Erythematosus** - This is a type of skin disease that also affects the lips, ears and eye lids. In some cases, there will be open sores on the genitals. With this disease, there can be discoloration to the dog's nose as well. Treatment involves both corticosteroids and immunosuppressive medications. Since sunlight exposure can worsen the condition, owners are often instructed to apply sunscreen to the dog's nose for any outdoor activities.

•**Pemphigus Foliaceous** - This is an autoimmune skin condition. Symptoms include crusty skin lesions along with boils that most often develop along the bridge of a dog's nose. These often grow into somewhat rather large pustules that easily rupture and then turn into dried crusty scabs. With some dogs, this can travel up to include the entire muzzle and even up to the ears. In rare cases, it will develop on the paw pads. Minor cases are treated with topical hydrocortisone. Moderate to severe cases are treated with Prednisone. It should be noted that as a dog is tapered from this, the disease may flare up again.

•**Distemper** – This is rare and is typically only seen in puppies that have not been vaccinated. Changes to the paws is a more common symptom; however with some pups there will be crusting and a hardening to the nose. Other signs include sneezing, coughing, discharge from the eyes & nose, fever, lethargy, vomiting and/or diarrhea.

At home Treatment for Crusty Nose Issues - If a Shih Tzu has a minor case of crusting that can be attributed to an earlier bout of dryness or slight cracking due to weather, a lack of humidity, chapping or slight dehydration, this can be often treated at home using a quality balm or butter as with dry, cracked noses. If you do not see improvement within 7 days or if there are any other symptoms, including but not limited to change in appetite, fever, vomiting, diarrhea, weakness and/or lethargy, the puppy or dog should be examined by the veterinarian.

Runny Noses - Many dogs naturally have a small degree of a very thin, clear nasal discharge, however this is often not noticed due to the dog licking the nose before owners take notice. If discharge is runny enough that fluid leaks out soon after wiping the nose with a dry cloth, if the discharge has any color to it (yellow, gray, green, brown, etc.) or if the discharge is thick, this points to a health issue that will need veterinary treatment. Possible reasons include:

•**Allergies** - This is by far the most common reason why a Shih Tzu will have a runny nose. And this can take some owners by surprise since allergies can develop in a Shih Tzu of any age, at any time. This includes seasonal allergies (pollen, weeds, grasses), food allergies (the most common cause is not whole foods, but the chemical preservatives, coloring and flavoring that can be found in commercial brands) and contact allergies (carpeting, laundry detergent, material such as wool, etc.) Of these three, seasonal allergies are the most likely culprit of a runny nose without any other signs such as itchy skin (though this can occur as well).

Treatment can range from OTC Benadryl for acute episodes to prescribed antihistamines for moderate to severe cases. Keeping the house as free from allergens as possible is an important part of treatment. HEPA certified filters should be used in both AC's and in vacuum cleaners. Bedding and other washables should be washed and dried using hypoallergenic detergent. More frequent baths may be needed to wash pollen and other airborne chemicals off of the Shih Tzu's coat.

• **A blockage** - If you have a curious Shih Tzu, you'll understand how common this is. A wide range of tiny items can be sucked up into the nose when the dog is sniffing around. This includes blades of grass, seeds… even such random things such as pencil erasers and a small artificial nail has been recovered from the nose of toy breeds that inadvertently snorted these objects. In some cases, you may be able to spot the culprit and if it is visible, you may be able to remove it with a tweezers. If you are unsure, wait for the vet to do it. In some cases, it will be lodged further up the nasal canal, where it causes quite a bit of discomfort. Signs are odd breathing, snorting, pawing at the nose and/or slight bleeding, along with discharge that may be leaking out of just one nostril. The veterinarian will be able to remove the obstruction; though this sometimes needs to be done with the dog under sedation.

• **Tooth infection** - The roots of the upper teeth are located very close to nasal passages and for this reason, a dental infection can cause a runny nose. Even if you routinely clean your Shih Tzu's teeth, offer healthy dental treats and have his teeth examined by the vet, infection can still occur. Many Shih Tzu will eat less, due to discomfort and/or may seem anxious or distressed (tooth pain can be quite severe). This is treated on a case by case basis, with possible extraction and with antibiotics to clear up the infection.

Less common causes - There are a wide range of diseases and conditions that can trigger a runny nose. Rare, yet possible include but are not limited to cryptococcosis (a fungal disease), nasal growth (polyps, tumors), distemper and pneumonia.

Bloody Noses - Seeing your Shih Tzu have a bloody nose (Epistaxis), is understandably worrisome. Let's look at some possible causes:

Trauma - Even if you did not see it occur, it only takes a split second for a dog to bonk his nose against something hard enough to cause an acute bloody nose. **Let's go over what to do if your Shih Tzu gets a nosebleed:**

1) Try to remain calm, since your dog will pick up cues from you (both your tone of voice and your actions), which can cause him to become stressed as well and this can increase the rate of blood loss.
2) Gently apply a soft ice pack (wrapped in a washcloth) to the bridge of the nose, while you are seated and have your Shih Tzu cradled in your arms. Apply a light, steady pressure more so to the nostril that is bleeding.
3) If the bleeding does not stop after 15 minutes, it will be time to take the dog to the vet.

Remember that if you do not know what caused the trauma to the nose, it may also involve other parts of the body… for example, if a Shih Tzu fell from the sofa and landed wrong, there may be injury to the hips, back, neck, etc.

Always look for any signs of distress (limping, whining, resting in an odd position, etc.) and bring your dog to the vet clinic if you suspect that there are any injuries.

Other less common reasons - The list of what can cause an acute bloody nose or a chronic nose bleeding issue is very wide ranging. This includes seemingly random events such as snake bite (we do know of one toy dog that was sitting by a river with her owner, was bitten by a snake and sadly passed away from the toxin)… to cancer, nasal polyps, or even Rocky Mountain spotted fever. It is never normal for a dog to have nosebleeds and unless it was caused by a minor trauma that quickly responded to at-home treatment, always bring your Shih Tzu to the vet to have this symptom diagnosed.

Nose Color Changes – Common Triggers Many owners ask if it is normal for their Shih Tzu's nose to change color. The answer is yes, this *can* happen, although some of this is preventable. The nose of your Shih Tzu may change color because of:

1) Eating or drinking from a plastic dog dish. There can be a reaction that happens with many types of plastics that - among other things - can cause a color change on a dog's nose. In some cases, this reaction will also cause the dog's lips to become swollen. There are additional issues with plastic bowls including the fact that they scratch easily and those tiny crevices can harbor bacteria. We always recommend stainless steel or ceramic bowls for both food and water.

2) Prolonged exposure to sunlight, common in the summer. While dogs need some sun on their noses (a lack can cause color loss), too much is just as bad. On hot, sunny days or when you plan for your Tzu to be outside for long periods of time, apply a bit of nose balm on your Shih Tzu's nose. A lot of sun can dry the nose out, cause peeling that exposes the pink layer of skin under the top layer and can fade the nose.

3) Lack of sunlight, common in the winter. This is commonly referred to as 'winter nose' or' 'snow nose'. During a long winter season, lack of enough sunlight can cause a fading or in some cases, spots of pink. This is almost always temporary. Do reassess if you are taking your Shih Tzu outside enough; color change can be your sign that you are not. Either way, this most often resolves itself once you are well into spring and most certainly by summer.

Pink spots - The most typical reason for a pink spot to appear on a Shih Tzu's nose is a peeling of the top layer (or two) of skin, that then exposed the inner layer. In these cases, it will be important to protect this delicate area with a quality nose butter or balm to allow it to heal. For some dogs that have this sort of deep peeling, there may permanently be a lighter color where the damage occurred. As mentioned, this can also be due to 'winter nose'.

Nasal depigmentation (Dudley nose/ vitiligo) - While uncommon with this breed, this is a condition in which the nose fades, sometimes quite dramatically. It can go from black to brown to pink and even white. No treatment is given, as this is seen as a cosmetic issue only.

Protecting Your Shih Tzu's Nose - There are a few things that you can do to keep your Shih Tzu's nose in good health:

1) Nose balm. This is a must-have grooming item. In the summer, it protects a dog's nose from the sun, which can cause everything from dryness to burns. In the winter, it prevents chapping, drying and cracking. If a Shih Tzu has an issue with peeling, cracking, chapping or dryness, it can heal these issues. Look for organic, scent free balms of high quality (they will be thick enough to stay on despite some licking) and will have natural ingredients to moisturize, nourish and restore skin.

2) Add humidity. Arid air, most typically a problem during the cold winter months, can wreak havoc on a Shih Tzu. It can affect the skin on the entire body (causing dryness and itching), the eyes (dry eye) and the nose (drying that leads to peeling and cracking). Running a humidifier near the area that your dog sleeps and rests can help quite a bit. Other home remedies include adding houseplants to your rooms, setting up open water containers out on radiators and leaving the bathroom door open when showering.

3) Hydration. Don't assume that your dog will automatically drink his required amount of water for the day. Dogs can become distracted and/or may not drink stale water. Wash the bowl each day, offer water that has been filtered and bring along some H20 when you take your Shih Tzu outside for walks and exercise.

4) Supervise outdoor sniffing. Oh, the trouble our dogs can get into when they are allowed to use their nose to explore when outside… From red ant bites, to bee stings to snorting up a pebble… a wide range of problems can occur if a dog sticks his nose under bushes, in tall grasses or other areas. While dogs do need to sniff around (after all, it satisfies a natural canine instinct), do be careful about where your Shih Tzu does this.

 For recommended nose protection and healing butters, look to 'Grooming' in the Shih Tzu Specialty Shoppe. You can reach the Shih Tzu Specialty Shoppe by entering any page of the AllShihTzu website. Look to the navigation; it is in alphabetical order. Choose 'Shoppe'.

Eyes- Including Tear Staining

Cherry Eye - This happens when a dog's third eyelid slips out of place and bulges out. The inside corner of the eye will have a rather large pink or red bump that takes over the normal sclera (the white part of the eye). It is thought that this develops due to a weakening of connective tissues. It very rarely happens to both eyes at the same time, however once it happens to one eye, it is common for it to happen to a Shih Tzu's other eye within a few months. It is important to have it treated as soon as possible, since the longer the gland remains out of place, the more swelling will occur, potentially leading to other, more serious problems in the future. This does not often resolve itself and will need to be treated with a relatively simple surgery in which a small piece of the gland is removed. The remaining tissue will be sutured back into its proper place. Recovery is often fast and most Shih Tzu will not have this issue again with the eye that was treated. Since it does so frequently affect the 2nd eye in the relative future, some veterinarians will recommend performing this procedure on both eyes at the same time as a preventive measure.

Inflammation - It's not uncommon for a Shih Tzu's eyes to become inflamed. It can happen due to elements that go into the eye (most common reason) or disease (not common, but possible). **The symptoms are:**

*   Excessive blinking/ squinting
*   Excessive water discharge/ tearing
*   Sensitivity to bright lights
*   The eye color may begin to appear dull or even bluish in color
*   Redness may occur
*   The eye may become swollen, either upper, lower or both

Diagnosis and Treatment- The veterinarian will examine the Shih Tzu's eye with an instrument that allows him to see the interior of the eyeball. Blood tests may need to be perform if the cause is not apparent. Anti-inflammatory medication will be given if the eye is swollen. Antibiotics will be given is there is an infection or reason to believe an infection may develop. Eye drops may be given to help with pain. If a disease such as Lyme disease, brucellosis or other is deemed the cause, treatment will vary according to the health issue.

Dry Eye - Known officially as Keratoconjunctivitis sicca, this affects the natural film that protects the eyes. If that clear film gets a tear or rip in it, the cornea of the dog's eye will no longer be protected. This film can also slowly degrade due to undernourishment. This health issue with a casual name can actually be very painful. The eye will become so dry that it stings terribly and if not treated will interfere with eyesight. This is also sometimes referred to as 'brown eye', as the eye may develop a brown tinted film. Scar tissue may appear on the dog's eye. Blood vessels may grow rapidly throughout the dog's eye, spiraling out and becoming so thick that you cannot see any white (the sclera).

Causes of this include:

- An injury to the eye that tears the film
- Not receiving enough nourishment

Other less common reasons:

- Hypothyroidism
- Infections
- Side effect from medication

The treatment for dry eye is a 3 part process. The dog will be given eye drops for extra lubrication to the eye, medicine will be given for swelling and infection and medication will be given to stimulate natural tears. In rare cases, surgery must be done to fix the tear duct if damaged.

Entropion – This is a genetic condition in which either the upper or lower eye lid rolls inward. It may also be referred to as an inverted or folded in lid. There is a high incidence rate of this with the Shih Tzu breed, as it is commonly seen with short-nosed breeds (due to more tension in the ligaments of the inner eye) and it also occurs more commonly with two breed sizes: toys and giants. While the inverted lid itself will irritate the eye, the real issue is that if the lid is rolled inward, tiny eyelashes can scratch the surface of the eye. This in turn can lead to corneal ulcers (upcoming section). Another secondary issue that may develop is scar tissue developing and this can lead to vision problems and even vision loss in some cases. In most cases, if a Shih Tzu is to develop entropion, it will occur within his first year.

Symptoms: Signs of this will vary depending on the breed of the dog; it is different for toys than it is for giants. With toy breeds, there are often only 2 symptoms:

- Excess tears
- Inflammation

Because of this, we highly encourage owners to rule this out if a Shih Tzu has tearing.

Diagnosis and Treatment – Diagnosis is fairly straightforward, as the veterinarian should be able to clearly see the issue upon examination. Treatment is a bit trickier. Two things need to be done: Treatment should be given to clear up any other issues that are caused by the entropion (drops for dry eyes, ulcerated corneas are treated with antibiotic drops or ointment). The next step is to correct the positioning of the lid and this is done via a minor surgery. The lid is repositioned and sutured in place.

Prevention – Since this is a genetic issue, the key to reducing incidences is for breeders to thoroughly screen dogs and bar Shih Tzu who have had entropion from any breeding program.

Distichiasis & Ectopic Cilia – Both of these issues are very common with the Shih Tzu breed. This is a condition in which the eyelashes grow abnormally. This is not to be confused with the above Entropion (the lid is inverted). Rather just 1 or 2 eyelashes grown in the wrong direction. With distichiasis, a lash will grow in an odd place on the lid itself. With ectopic cilia, the lash(es) will grow through the inside of the eyelid, inward toward the eye. This, as you can imagine, is very painful for the dog. Ectopic cilia, particularly, often leads to corneal ulcers (next section).

Symptoms, Distichiasis: Eye pain, twitching of the eyelid, excessive tearing, bloodshot eyes, change in iris pigmentation.
Symptoms, Ectopic Cilia: Severe eye pain, severe abnormal twitching of the eyelid, excessive tearing.

Diagnosis and Treatment – Diagnosis is fairly straightforward, as the veterinarian should be able to clearly see the issue upon examination. With distichiasis, often the eye lash(es) can just be plucked out. However, it is very important to note that they can and most often will grow back again. Within 4 to 5 weeks, they will then need to be removed again. A minor surgery can be performed to remove both the eyelash and the follicle to prevent it from growing back again.

Corneal Ulcers - The cornea is the clear, shiny membrane, which makes up the surface of the eyeball. The cornea is made of 3 layers: The epithelium, the stroma, and the deepest layer is called the Descemet's membrane. When these layers wear down, this is called a corneal ulcer or a corneal abrasion. A corneal ulcer is erosion through the whole epithelium and into the stroma. If the erosion goes through the epithelium and stroma to the level of Descemet's membrane (the very deepest layer), it is termed: descemetocele. If the Descemet's membrane ruptures, the liquid that is normally inside of the eyeball leaks out and the eye actually collapses.

There are several causes for corneal ulcers in dogs. For the Shih Tzu breed, the most common is trauma. An ulcer may result from an injury, for example if a Shih Tzu rubs his eye too harshly on something or a foreign object scratches the eye. The second most common cause is due to entropion (see Entropion, above) and the third most common cause is chemical burn to the dog's cornea. This may happen when irritating shampoo gets into the Shih Tzu's eyes. For this reason, it is strongly suggested to only use a quality canine shampoo (never use human shampoo) and to be as careful as possible that any shampoo or conditioner does not enter into the Shih Tzu's eyes while you are bathing him. Other, rarer, reasons are bacterial infections, viral infections, and other diseases. These may begin in the dog's eye or develop elsewhere and then affect the eye.

Some diseases that may have a link to this include Keratoconjunctivitis Sicca (a drying of the cornea that happens when there is an abnormal tear formation), and diseases of the endocrine system (diabetes mellitus, hyperadrenocorticism, and hypothyroidism).

Symptoms:

• A corneal ulcer can cause a Shih Tzu to be in a lot of pain. In reaction to pain, most dogs rub the affected eye with their paw or will try to rub it against surfaces, such as their blanket or the carpeting in an effort to find relief.
• A dog may try to protect his eye, by keeping his eyes closed.
• In some cases, there will be a discharge that puddles in the corner of the dog's eye. It may stay there for a while and then eventually run down the dog's face.
• To protect the eye, a dog may keep the lids tightly closed. Occasionally, there will be a discharge that collects in the corner of the eye or runs down the face.

Diagnosis and Treatment - Mild, superficial corneal abrasions are usually not visible to the human eye. However, a veterinarian will be able to spot this using a luorescein stain. The vet usually numbs the dog's eye first and then puts a drop of this stain on the dog's cornea. The dye will stick to an area of ulceration and then it is easily seen using a special black light called a Wood's light. This is the most basic test performed and may be the only test needed if the ulcer is mild and is acute (meaning it will heal on its own). If the ulcerated area is severe or chronic (meaning it is continual and does not heal on its own), a biopsy is usually taken before applying the stain or any other medication. Treatment depends on whether there is a corneal abrasion, corneal ulcer, or descemetocele.

Corneal abrasions generally heal on their own in 3-5 days. Medication is used to prevent bacterial infections. This medication will be antibiotic ophthalmic drops or ointment. To help a dog with the pain, a pain reliving medication such as atropine ophthalmic drops or ointment will be given. Antibiotic drops must be applied 5 to 6 times per day. The ointment requires application every few hours. Atropine, the medication for the pain, is usually given 2 times per day. This medication can make a dog very sensitive to bright lights. It is suggested to keep lights dim and to not go outside into the bright sunlight while being treated. If a Shih Tzu has a corneal ulcer or descemetocele, steps are taken to protect the eye and to help with the healing. In these severe cases, surgery is performed to close the eyelids and cover the ulcer or descemetocele. This ensures that the eye will be properly protected. If both eyes are affected, one eye may be closed in this way for several days, and then the other eye will be done, so that the dog may see from at least 1 eye at a time.

When an ulcer is not healing as it should, there can be a buildup of dead cells on the rim of the ulcer. These dead cells stop normal cells from the corneal surface from moving over the ulcer's edge and filling in the tear. If this happens, the dead cells are removed from the edges of the ulcer before the eyelids are surgically closed. In some cases, removing the dead cells may be all that is needed to start the healing process, so surgical closing of the eyelids may not need to be done. A checkup should be done about 7 days after this treatment, with the stain test, to see if the dog's corneal ulcer has healed.

Abrasion VS Corneal Ulcer- Sometimes, a dog will be diagnosed with a simple abrasion that is in fact, an ulcer. After 2-3 days of treatment, your dog should be reexamined to be sure that healing is progressing as it should. If not, this may mean that the dog has a more serious ulcer and treatment should begin for that.

Care and Proper Cleaning- A huge part of taking care of your Shih Tzu will be to guard the eyes against irritants and to keep them clean.

Removing Something from the Eye - While you can't do much about sand and other particles getting into the eyes, you can check them each time you enter back into the house. If you see a piece of debris in your Shih Tzu's eye, you'll want to remove it.

Here's how:
1) Use a sterile canine eye cleaning solution.
2) Use your fingers to open the eye, gently pushing both upper and lower lids open wider.
3) Squeeze 4 to 5 drops into the cup of the lower lid.
4) Let go of your Shih Tzu and allow him to blink. As he does, a combination of the solution and tears will spill out from his eye. Be sure to swipe this up with a clean piece of gauze.

Daily Care - Here are some tips to provide daily care for your Shih Tzu's eyes:

1) It is during grooming that debris can often inadvertently end up in a Shih Tzu's eye. When cleaning the ears, take care so that ear cleaning solution does not splash in your Shih Tzu's eyes. When brushing, take care that hairs do not float into the eyes; a shedding Shih Tzu can create hundreds if not thousands of dead hairs per day and the brush can make these airborne. Take breaks often to free the brush of hairs.

2) Several times per day the entire area should be wiped. You should use quality canine eye wipes OR for Shih Tzu that tend to develop tear staining, tear stain prevention wipes (more ahead). For daily wiping, we highly recommend Earthbath All Natural Specialty Eye Wipes. These will gently & effectively clean the eye area and also prevent tear stains. You'll want to do this in the morning if your Shih Tzu tends to accumulate 'eye gook'. After feeding meals, wipe the area to remove any small food particles. Use one wipe per eye, throwing away a sullied piece and using a new, clean one for each eye.

3) Take note of any excessive discharge, irritation or other signs of problems and have the veterinarian have a look since most problems can be more easily treated during the beginning stages before swelling and other secondary problems develop.

Tear Stains- This is a common and troubling issue in which the hairs around the dog's eyes turn a red or brown color. This may be around one or both eyes or just underneath the eyes and the hairs may feel brittle, hard or "crusted"

What Causes Tear Staining – Common Reasons – No Need to Go to the Vet:

• **Genetics** – Some Shih Tzu are prone to developing tear stains. You must be hyper-diligent in preventing moisture from causing stains.
• **Water** – If a Shih Tzu is drinking water with a high mineral content it can cause tear stains. Already a strong suggestion based on the horrible chemicals found in tap water, only give your Shih Tzu filtered or bottled water.
• **Dog food** - Artificial coloring in manufactured dog food can cause discoloration on hairs. It is not the fact that the dog ingests the coloring (though this is not good for him), it is the possibility that the hairs touch down into the food when the dog is eating.
• **Teething** – When a puppy is teething, he is much more prone to tear staining. Keep up with cleaning the area and treating for it; things will get better once he is done teething.
• **Irritation of the Eyes** - Anything from food particles to sand from outside and cause irritation, which leads to watery eyes…which leads to staining.

Other Reasons – Bring Your Shih Tzu to the Vet to Rule Out:

• **Blocked Tear Ducts** - This is the cause in about 10% of all cases. This can be a partial or full blockage. Signs are excessive tearing. If a Shih Tzu has a near constant watery discharge, this is not normal! This needs to be corrected with surgery.
• **Inverted or ingrown eye lash(es)** – A tiny eyelash may grow awkwardly, pointing into the eye. This is easily fixed by a vet.
• **Inverted eye lids** - Known as entropion, this is a condition in which the eye lid partially folds or rolls inward. It can be very painful. If left untreated, it can cause decrease in vision or in some cases, complete loss of eyesight.
• **Ear Infection** - Just about everything on a dog's face is interconnected and therefore, an ear infection can trigger tearing and in turn, stains.
• **Other Infections or Disease** - It is rare, but there are some diseases that one would never think could cause tear staining. One such case is a dog that actually had a herpes infection in the eye. Therefore, if tear staining remedies do not quickly take care of the issue, your dog should be brought to the vet ASAP.

Treatment – There is a LOT of false information floating around out there regarding treatment for tear staining. While researching tear stains in dogs, you may have come across many home remedies. Some of them are very dangerous. We have seen concoctions ranging from bleach (which can cause permanent blindness) to lemon blends that can severely irritate the eyes and cause more issues. Before an owner attempts to remove the tear staining from a dog's face it is most important to have eliminated the source of the staining. Otherwise it will just come back and many times it will be worse than before. After making sure that all of the things mentioned earlier have been checked, you can begin to think about removing the tear staining.

At-Home Treatment - What does NOT Work and 'Maybe's'

X **Boric acid mixed with corn starch. DO NOT USE THIS.** It can be dangerous to use this around the eye area.
X **Adding vinegar to drinking water.** We have found in our experience that most Shih Tzu puppies and dogs do not like the taste and will be reluctant to drink their water. There is little proof this works.
X **Cornstarch powder. DO NOT USE THIS.** This can cause irritation to the dog's eyes, thus causing more tears, which causes wet hairs, which causes bacterial infection… and the cycle begins all over again.
X **Tums.** Too many Tums (or Tums like products) can equal too much calcium. There are options that work better.

X Milk of Magnesia, corn starch and peroxide. DO NOT USE THIS. This can cause irritation or damage to the dog's eyes

X Buttermilk in powder form is a treatment touted by some sources. The dosing is 1/4 of a teaspoon per day. This is a 'maybe' at best.

Removing Tear Stains – What Actually Works

We do **not** recommend the most commonly used one: Angel Eyes. It's been around for a long time and perhaps due to marketing or the catchy name, it's the one that many owners rely on. It is a decent product. However, it is not our recommended choice. When it comes to keeping a Shih Tzu tear stain free, this is no time to be half in the game. Use the most effective product that can produce quick results so you can clear up the problem and prevent them from returning. The best product will be one that works in 6 ways:

1- It will be an easy topical solution that is easy to apply.
2- It will have a gentle yet effective cleanser.
3- It will have a gentle yet effective astringent.
4- It will have an herbal antibacterial agent
5- It will be formulated to be safe for dogs of all ages - from young puppies to the senior dog and every age in between.
6- It will not contain bleach, peroxide, or harsh chemicals.

We love Eye Envy (#1 choice), Betta Bridges and TropiClean (both are very close 2nd's). When you use the right product, you'll be shocked at the amazing results. Do keep in mind that if your Shih Tzu has an underlying health issue as discussed, that would need to be resolved first. Once the stains are gone, you must wipe the eyes daily with the right eye wipe or the stains may come back. *If you would like to see our list of recommendations, along with reviews, look to 'Grooming' in the Shih Tzu Specialty Shoppe. You can reach the Shih Tzu Specialty Shoppe by entering any page of the AllShihTzu website. Look to the navigation; it is in alphabetical order. Choose 'Shoppe'.*

Prescribed Medications – In some severe cases, prescription medications may be given. We do not recommend this unless your vet has strongly suggested this. The most commonly prescribed ones include:

• **Tetracycline** - There has been success in eliminating tear staining by having a dog on a ten day course of low dose chlortetracycline or tetracycline. Occasionally this may need to be repeated. However, this should not be given to puppies that have not yet cut all of their adult teeth; this is because Tetracycline has been shown to cause teeth which have not erupted, to be permanently stained yellow.
• **Lincocin** - Dogs not responding to tetracycline may respond well to Lincocin. The typical dose of this for a toy breed dog is 50 mg twice a day.
• **Delta AlbaPlex** - An antibiotic of the tetracycline class, Delta AlbaPlex also contains a low level of steroid. This can work for tear staining as the steroid will help eliminate inflammation that goes along with excessive tearing, thus allowing the antibiotic a chance to work.
• **Flagyl** – This is an anti-diarrhea medicine commonly used in dogs to treat yeast or Giardia infections causing irritable or inflammatory bowel syndrome. This can be effective in the treatment of tear stains, particularly when the staining is the result of red yeast. This is given for 2 weeks.
• **AK-TROL** – This is a human prescription eye drop containing neomycin, polymyxin B and dexamethasone. AK-TROL is also available in an ointment form. This can cause permanent staining of the teeth.

Tail

Hold and Set – The Shih Tzu is one of many breeds that naturally holds his tail curved over his back. It is a 'natural' tail, meaning that it is never docked. In fact, the AKC standard tells us exactly that with '… tail curved over the back.' There is no one 'perfect' length and the AKC standard refers to this as well, stating: 'Although there has always been considerable size variation…'. The tail should also be '…compact, solid, carrying good weight and substance', meaning that you will rarely see a Shih Tzu with an overly thin tail.

This all said, there will be many times that a Shih Tzu does not hold his tail up over his back. Most Tzu let the tail fall down when sleeping, at rest and even due to some emotional responses such as when sad, depressed or anxious. When in action, a Tzu may hold his tail straight up. And at other times, he may extend it back like a spear! This is all normal and there is usually nothing to worry about unless you see your puppy or dog holding it in a very odd way that implies some sort of injury or other health concern.

If a Shih Tzu Holds His Tail in an Odd Way - There are 4 conditions that may cause a Shih Tzu to hold his tail oddly:

1. Engorged anal glands. These small glands (one located on each side of the anus), hold oils (commonly referred to a scent oils). Miniscule amounts are released when one dog encounters another and some is also released when the dog has a bowel movement.

Sometimes, the oil will build up, causing the glands to become enlarged. This can cause somewhat intense itching (the dog may scoot his bottom along the ground in an attempt to relieve the itching) and the dog may hold his tail in a funny way. You may also wish to refer to the 'Health-Specific Body Parts', 'Anal Glands' section, page 186.

2. Back problems – Since the tail is a continuation of the spine, issues in the back can radiate down into the tail. This includes pain due to a ruptured disk and other back pain issues.

3. Age related posture – As a dog ages, he loses some muscle and tendons may weaken. In addition, arthritis comes into play as well. All of these issues may cause an older, senior Shih Tzu to have what appears to be a weakened tail hold. As with all holding and movement issues, you will want to make sure that the tail has not been injured and that it is just a matter of the dog choosing to hold it in an odd way as opposed to not being able to move it or hold it as he normally does.

4. Tail injury – The list of accidents that can happen that may injure a dog's tail is endless. Owners accidently step their dog's tails, the tail can be caught in a car door, a house door or even can become injured when if the dog is playing too rough with another dog.

Diagnosis and Treatment – The vet will examine the tail, check the spine and take x-rays. Since the tail consists of bone, either a bruise, sprain or break will be determined. Anti-inflammatory medication may be given, which also helps with pain. In most cases, rest ranging from 2 to 6 weeks will allow the tail to heal. Often even breaks will heal on their own without a need to set the tail; however, if the fracture is at the base, surgery may be needed to prevent nerve damage.

Health- Stomach, Intestinal

Vomiting

Vomiting may be acute or chronic and may present by itself or with other troubling symptoms such as diarrhea. In many cases, this can be treated at home, however we will discuss times that you must call the vet.

Sudden, Acute Vomiting or Vomiting - This is when a Shih Tzu – unexpectedly, without previous issues - suddenly throws up. It usually passes quickly however during the time that the Shih Tzu is ill, it can be rather intense. There are several reasons why this may happen and owners should keep in mind that what appears to be an acute case of vomiting may turn into an ongoing issue if it occurs again within 72 hours. The 2 most common reason for this are:

1) Ingestion of a food or non-food element that causes non-toxic irritation. With an acute case of vomiting that passes quickly without other symptoms, this is usually due to the Shih Tzu ingesting grass, weeds, other outside plants or a food (usually taken out of the trash) that irritates the stomach and causes the dog to quickly expel it. A dog may also have diarrhea with this.

If your Shih Tzu just ate grass or something from the trash that he shouldn't have, there's a good chance that he'll vomit one or two times and then be fine. However, if you suspect that your puppy or dog may have ingested something toxic, even if you are not sure what it was, call the vet ASAP. If you know what your Shih Tzu ate and are not sure if it is toxic to dogs, you can call your vet. The most common toxins to dogs include (but are not limited to): Any food sweetened with Xylitol (most often found in sugarless candy & chewing gum), chocolate, coffee (both the grounds and the beans), grapes, raisins, the core of most fruits, any beverage with caffeine, macadamia nuts, onions, garlic (only in large quantities), certain moldy walnuts and raw potatoes.

2) Eating or drinking water too fast. Some Shih Tzu will vomit - and be fine afterward - if they gulp down a large amount of water too fast or swallow a meal too swiftly. *Water* - If a Shih Tzu has been outside running around, he may come back in and drink his water too fast, gulping down too much air, which can cause him to vomit the fluid right back up. It's always a good idea to give super-thirsty dogs smaller amounts. For example, fill the bowl 1/3, when he's done fill it 1/3 again and then one more time. *Food-* Food that is upchucked due to eating too fast will not be digested; chunks of food may be thrown up anywhere from immediately to 15 minutes after eating. If your Shih Tzu eats too fast, use a slow-feeder stainless steel bowl or place a portion pacer into his bowl.

What it Means if a Shih Tzu has Vomiting and Diarrhea - When diarrhea occurs along with vomiting, this points to a more serious issue. It is not just a quick stomach irritation since the digestive system and intestinal tract is now involved. There are several reasons for this including:

1) Eating a new food. This can be a food someone gave him that was too greasy, etc. If this is the case, both symptoms of vomiting and diarrhea will pass rather quickly; usually within 2 to 12 hours. You can treat this at home to help a Shih Tzu's stomach rest and if this continues or if other signs develop, you'll want to seek treatment (more ahead on both topics). This can also be due to a sudden food change. If you just changed main meals, follow treatment instructions and then go back to the Shih Tzu's 'old' food to start over and make a slower, more gradual change.

2) Parasites - Mostly due to ingesting contaminated soil or the feces of other dogs and sometimes from spoiled food, a Shih Tzu can catch a parasite. Many cause diarrhea and some cause both diarrhea and vomiting. This includes: Coccidia, giardia, hookworms, whipworms, roundworms, tritrichomonas, cryptosporidium, and tapeworms. Bacteria that cause diarrhea include Clostridium, Campylobacter, E. coli, and Salmonella. Signs to watch out for: Some worms will be able to be visibly seen in a dog's feces; though not always. You'll want to look for fever, dehydration, weakness, vomiting and/or diarrhea that does not clear up after 12 hours, abnormal behavior, signs of distress or any other clinical sign that seems out of the ordinary.

3) Viral causes - Even dogs that have been vaccinated can get one of several viral infections including corona virus, parvovirus, and calicivirus. How does this happen? There are a couple of reasons.

• *Puppies* - There are windows of vulnerability in which the protective antibodies passed from the dam to the pup have weaned down and the full protection of the vaccine has not yet kicked in.
Adolescents and adults - If booster shots are delayed there may also be a time when the dog is not fully protected.
• *Dogs of all ages* - With some viral infections such as coronavirus, this is considered a non-core vaccine. Only dogs considered at risk will receive this and it is not included in the normal vaccination schedule.

You'll want to monitor your Shih Tzu for other signs including abnormally dark feces, fever, weakness, reluctance to drink or excess thirst and/or vomiting and/or diarrhea that is ongoing.

What it Means if a Shih Tzu is Vomiting Yellow Foam or Mucus - It should be noted that yellow vs white liquid and foam or mucus are very different. When a Shih Tzu vomits yellow foam, this is indicative of stomach bile. It will vary from watery to thick. It may be interlaced with foam or the foamy substance may form around the edges of the puddle. Bile is a substance that works to neutralize acids in the stomach before it works its way to the dog's small intestines. In addition, it also works to counteract microbes that may be in any digested food.

Reasons for vomiting yellow foam include:

1) The Shih Tzu's stomach is too empty. This is the most common reason that a Shih Tzu will vomit up yellow stomach bile with or without foam and mucus. If so, it typically occurs with dogs that are only fed one meal per day. The easy at-home treatment is to change your Shih Tzu's feeding schedule to include smaller, more frequent meals. Most Shih Tzu do best with two meals per day: morning and evening. If you already feed two, change to three. Some owners tend to avoid this if a morning meal means a bowel movement afterward when the owner has either already left for the day or is preparing to do so. In this instance, you may want to feed your Shih Tzu as soon as the day begins. This can leave time a bit later - 20 to 30 minutes - for a visit outside to the designated bathroom area before you need to leave the house.

In addition, filling a Kong or other toy with treats that the Shih Tzu can slowly release and then eat during the day can be a good way to offer a snack that will prevent the stomach from becoming so empty that there is an excessive buildup of bile that may be vomited out.

2) Gastritis- While having an empty stomach is by far the most common reason; there is also a small chance that this is due to a more serious issue of gastritis (inflammation of the stomach). With gastritis, the vomiting of yellow foam will be ongoing - it may come and go however if it lasts for more than 1 week, the veterinarian will run tests for this disease. Other signs of this include black tarry stools, a green color in the vomit (which indicated bile that is produced from the Shih Tzu's gallbladder), flecks of blood and/or bits of undigested food mixed throughout the yellow foam. The stomach can become chronically inflamed due to repetitive ingestion of inappropriate foods, infection (often a parasite), metabolic/endocrine disease or adverse reaction to medication. The veterinarian will narrow down the causes by doing a complete physical examination, blood work, a chemical profile, abdominal X-rays, ultrasound and a fecal floatation.

What it Means if a Shih Tzu is Vomiting Clear or White Foam, Mucus or Liquid - White foam may be an issue of an empty stomach as with the yellow foam or it can be a random, acute case that does not lead to anything. However it can also point to one of several very serious and sometimes fatal issues.

Serious Reasons for vomiting clear or white foam or liquid include:

1) Blockage - When a dog swallows a non-food item or a chunk of food that is too large to safely pass, this can cause a partial or full blockage of the stomach and/or intestines. In some cases, the dog's first symptom may be vomiting of clear or white fluid - this can happen hours before any other clinical signs. This brings to mind a dog that swallowed a chunk of medical tape - unbeknown to the owners- that was tucked into a lower bathroom cabinet. Hours afterward, he vomited a puddle of clear fluid and seemed fine afterward. It was not until about 7 hours later that he showed other signs of distress. Once taken to the vet, he needed emergency surgery to remove the tape, which had wound its way through the dog's intestines. It came very close to being a fatal situation.

Shih Tzu have a high level of curiosity and are capable of mouthing and then swallowing all sorts of dangerous items. This includes Popsicle sticks, keys, rolls of floss, jewelry, shoe laces, pen caps, paper clips… If it can fit in his mouth, it can be swallowed. For this reason, if your Shih Tzu vomits white or clear liquid with or without foam or mucus, you'll want to:

1- Search over the areas of the house that he had access to, looking for anything that was disturbed as a possible clue that he may have gotten into something that he should not have.
2- Closely watch him/her for any other developing signs or to see if he vomits a second time. Other red flags are: straining to eliminate a bowel movement, restlessness, acting panicked, whining, non-interest in eating or drinking, retreating, any signs of discomfort. In these cases, this warrants an immediate vet visit and this is considered an emergency.

2) Bloat - This exceedingly serious condition involves the stomach rotating or twisting in response to eating and exercising too closely together or eating too fast. However, if you see the warning signs of bloat, always seek help even if you do not believe that your Shih Tzu did either of those two things. Other symptoms include: Bloated abdomen, heavy panting, dry heaving, restlessness, pacing, not able to sit or lie comfortably, retreating, anxiousness and/or hunched over positioning. This is considered an extreme emergency and a dog with bloat needs to be treated ASAP.

3) Other possible causes - There are many other possible causes that vary greatly. This includes kennel cough, diabetes, kidney disease, infection of the digestive tract, food allergy, hepatitis and even rabies.

What to do if Your Shih Tzu Vomited White Foam – See 'At Home Treatment' ahead.

What it Means if a Shih Tzu is Vomiting with Blood
- While some cases of vomiting can be treated from home with close supervision, if a Shih Tzu is vomiting blood or if there are specks of blood in the vomit, this is a clear sign of an emergency. You should take your puppy or dog to the vet or closest animal hospital immediately. Reasons for blood in vomit can include: Ingestion of a foreign body, damage to the intestinal tract, trauma, serious bacterial or viral infection, serious parasitic infection, tumors of the stomach or esophagus, ingestion of poison, ulcers, liver disease, kidney disease. Blood may be present in the Shih Tzu's vomit, stools or both. There may or may not be diarrhea. The most important fact is that throwing up blood almost always points to a serious medical emergency that requires prompt medical intervention.

What it Means if a Shih Tzu Vomits Right After Eating
- If your Shih Tzu expels his food immediately after swallowing it, this is technically regurgitation, which means that the food is expelled before it begins to digest. Fortunately, the most common reason for this can easily be resolved at home. It typically happens if a dog eats too fast or too much. You'll want to:

1) Serve smaller but more frequent meals. If you normally give your Shih Tzu one meal per day, switch to two. Those who already eat twice may do better with 3 smaller feedings.
2) Use a slow-feeder bowl or place a stainless steel portion pacer in the existing dish. This should be done at any rate to help prevent bloat and can help when a Shih Tzu retches due to eating too fast.
3) Shih Tzu can tend to eat with too much enthusiasm if food is presented while the dog is in a state of excitement. Avoid giving your Shih Tzu a meal when he is revved up. If he is very hyper and dinner is overdue, it can help to offer a small snack and work to calm him down before his full meal is offered.

What it Means if a Shih Tzu Vomits During or Immediately Following Exercise
- This will typically happen if a Shih Tzu is allowed to run around or is taken for a brisk walk right after eating, before the food has had a chance to digest. Canines have a much more sensitive gag reflex than humans, therefore allowing a good 20

minutes to pass before heading out for a walk or taking your dog out for a game of fetch can often prevent this sort of vomiting event from happening.

Treatment of Vomiting at Home - Many cases will be acute instances in which a Shih Tzu throws up and then simply needs some time for his stomach to rest. Here is what you can do from home, as long as there are no red flag symptoms that call for a visit to the vet:

1) **Withhold the next meal** unless your Shih Tzu has appeared to bounce back to his normal self and is eager to eat. Be sure to offer plenty of cool, clean water.

2) **Feed your Shih Tzu light meals for up to 24 hours.** This would be home cooked food of plain oatmeal, small banana slices and sweet potato. If he does well with that, you can also offer white breast chicken meat without skin and without any seasoning, mixed with plain sweet potato or plain white rice. These are easily digestible foods that can offer sustenance while allowing the stomach and digestive system to rest.

3) **Prevent dehydration.** If your Shih Tzu has vomited a lot or has had both vomiting and diarrhea, you'll want to take steps to restore hydration. Mixing plain, unflavored Pedialyte with water (a 50/50 ratio) can help restore a dog's electrolyte balance and help a weakened dog recover from loss of fluids.

4) **Limit exercise and walks.** While some dogs are able to shake off an episode of vomiting and bounce back to normal within just minutes, many will need a good 24 hours to fully recover.

5) **Pepto Bismal** - There is some debate over this treatment, even among veterinarians. Some say that it is best to allow a dog to vomit and have diarrhea so that the bacteria or other triggers can be flushed from the system. If OTC medicine is given to prevent this expulsion, it may prolong the condition. However, for others, giving a dog Pepto is normal protocol for minor episodes of acute vomiting and vomiting along with diarrhea. The main ingredient in Pepto is bismuth subsalicylate, which coats the stomach and intestines to help combat nausea, diarrhea, heartburn, indigestion and upset stomach. It is considered to be safe for canines, when correct dosing instructions are followed. This can be part of an at-home treatment plan for acute cases. It is best to call your veterinarian's office first; in most cases he/she will give you the 'okay'. The correct dosing is based on the Shih Tzu's weight. Unless otherwise directed by the vet, you will want to give your Shih Tzu 1 teaspoons for each 5 lbs. (.45 kg) of body weight. It is given every 5 to 6 hours. If there is no improvement after 4 doses (20 to 24 hours), this is your signal to bring your Shih Tzu for an examination.

When to Take Your Shih Tzu to the Veterinarian - Since the reasons for a Shih Tzu vomiting can range from nibbling on a fallen bird to drinking too fast to parasites and even the dangerous condition of blockage, you will want to get immediate help if any of the following is present:

• Violent, projectile vomiting - This is much more than a dog leaning down and throwing up. In this case, vomit will be flung from the mouth and often the nasal passages with extreme force.
• Blood - Seen in the throw up and/or stools
• Severe weakness
• Intolerance for food (even with easy foods listed above)
• Intolerance for water
• Bloated stomach
• Excessive drooling
• Any signs of distress - pacing, restlessness, panicked behavior, retreat from the family
• If vomiting episodes continue for more than 24 hours - Since reasons can range from a food allergy to parasites to bacterial infection, you'll want your Shih Tzu to have veterinary care.
• If you suspect any form of poisoning

Diarrhea

With diarrhea, many of the same triggers that cause vomiting will cause this. So do please refer to the previous section. In addition to those causes listed, diarrhea may also be due to:

1) **A food intolerance** - Milk based products is at the top of this list. Some dairy foods such as cottage cheese

and whole white yogurt are tolerated well (and can actually be helpful for some stomach and digestive issues) however many other types of milk products such as ice cream, milk (whole, 2%, 1% and skim) and cheese (such as deli cheese, etc.) can cause diarrhea. It should be noted that large quantities of cheese can have the opposite effect and cause constipation. If an owner gives a Shih Tzu table scraps of certain foods, such as very fatty meats or foods with high oil/fat content, this can cause diarrhea as well. The best way to resolve this sort of issue is to have all family members agree to only feed the Shih Tzu his planned meals and snacks consisting of foods that the Shih Tzu tolerates well.

2) Food allergy - When people talk about a dog having a food allergy, many times this actually pertains to a dog suffering an allergic reaction to a chemical found in manufactured food; artificial coloring, flavors or preservatives. However, some Shih Tzu can have trouble with certain 'real' foods. And it should be noted that dogs can grow into allergies. Only about 10% of dogs with allergies will be allergic to one or more of these foods: beef, chicken, lamb, pork, rabbit meat, fish, egg, soy, wheat and/or dairy products.

Aside from diarrhea, other signs may include skin issues (itching, red hot spots, thinning hair), moderate to severe itching around the anus and/or chronic ear infections. With diarrhea caused from food allergies, once steps have been taken to treat a Shih Tzu for diarrhea, he will recover but almost immediately have troubles again once his normal food is introduced back into his diet. Trial and error is the most common method to resolve this. The Shih Tzu is taken off all foods, put on a bland diet and then one food is introduced every 2 weeks to identify which one is causing intestinal distress. If a Shih Tzu is having a reaction to the chemicals in manufactured food, a change to a higher quality brand or even a switch to home cooking may be in order. You may also wish to refer to 'Allergies', page 215.

3) Infection - There are 3 different types of infection that can cause a Shih Tzu puppy or dog to have diarrhea:

1. *Parasitic*. This includes roundworms, hookworms, whipworms, coccidia, and giardia. All puppies should be properly de-wormed by the vet and even so, most veterinarians suggest a fecal test once per year to check for intestinal parasites. Most of these parasitic infections are treated with multiple treatments of the appropriate de-wormer medication, along with owners sanitizing both the indoor and outdoor areas of living space. Both coccidia and giardia are treated with antibiotics and also a cleaning of both environment and the dog, since these can shed onto the coat.

2. *Bacterial*. This includes Salmonella and E. coli. Less common, but possible is Clostridia and Campylobacter. Salmonella poisoning can happen due to eating tainted food or is transmitted from another dog or even a person. It can pass back and forth from animals to humans. Once infected, a dog (or person) can spread this through feces or saliva (another reason why it is important to never let your Shih Tzu eat the feces of another dog). With E. coli, dogs naturally have some of this in their system; however, it is kept in check and does not make them ill unless the immune system is compromised. For this reason, a young Shih Tzu puppy or an older, senior Shih Tzu may come down with E. coli and subsequent diarrhea. Other causes are if a Shih Tzu were to ingest a food that had E. coli on it, which includes some raw meats or drinks from a puddle of water that is infected with this. Diarrhea due to bacterial infection is often treated with fluid replacement and antibiotics.

3. *Viral*. This includes Parvovirus and Distemper, which most often occurs with puppies that have not received their full vaccinations. Coronavirus is another possibility though this happens most frequently in large kennels.

4) Stress - Reasons why a Shih Tzu may become stressed to the point of having diarrhea include severe cases of separation anxiety, long periods of boredom, a high energy or negative environment (too much loud noises, yelling, domestic upset, etc.). Other times, a certain situation may cause a Shih Tzu to have trouble coping and he will, in turn, have a bout of diarrhea. Some examples are moving to a new home, the introduction of a new pet or being transported or traveling when not accustomed to it (car or airplane). As to not repeat text, you may wish to refer to 'Bringing Your Shih Tzu Puppy Home', page 17, 'Separation Anxiety' page 170 or 'Traveling with Your Shih Tzu' page 278.

5) Inflammatory bowel disease - This is a catch-all term that is given if a dog has ongoing, chronic diarrhea due to one of several conditions including Colitis. Signs of this include persistent diarrhea, low grade fever, weight loss, lethargy and/or vomiting. This is more typically seen in dogs that are 5 years and older, though it can happen to younger Shih Tzu as well. Blood panels, a urinalysis, fecal testing and other tests may be done to diagnose this. Antibiotics and medications to protect lining of the intestine may be given. In many cases, a change to a different food will help. Your Shih Tzu's vet may recommend canned food, since these are cooked to 150 to 170 degrees Fahrenheit, which allows helpful digestive enzymes in the food to remain intact whereas dry kibble does not.

6) Other less common reasons for diarrhea include: Kidney disease, liver disease, cancer, pancreatitis, lymphangiectasia and hemorrhagic gastroenteritis.

Acute VS Chronic VS Intermittent Diarrhea - Acute diarrhea will be a short episode, typically lasting 2 to 5 days that responds to at-home treatment and does not reoccur again within the next 3 months. Chronic diarrhea is when a Shih Tzu suffers from this for more than 5 days. It may appear to get better once the dog is treated at home, but resurfaces soon afterward. For this, diagnosis and treatment at the vet's is needed. Intermittent diarrhea is when a Shih Tzu has bouts of this often throughout the year. It comes and goes. It may be a week or a month between occurrences. For this, diagnosis and treatment at the vet's is needed.

How to Treat Acute Diarrhea - There are several things that you can do to help a Shih Tzu if he is having diarrhea.

1) Assess. The first thing that you should do if your Shih Tzu is having diarrhea is to assess the situation. While you don't want to overreact, it is also important to know if the dog's health condition warrants an immediate trip to the vet, a phone call or can be treated at home. Signs in addition to diarrhea that may point to a Shih Tzu needing to be seen by the vet right away include:

• High fever - The normal body temperature of canines is 101 to 102.5 degrees Fahrenheit (38.3 to 39.2 degrees Celsius). You'll want to monitor this at least twice per day.
• Vomiting - Diarrhea alone is very draining on a dog and can lead to dangerous dehydration. If you add vomiting to that, his health status can become compromised quickly.
• Trouble breathing - If there is heavy panting or other respiratory issues along with the diarrhea, this is a red flag.
• Extreme lethargy - It is normal for a Shih Tzu to feel tired and weak when he is having diarrhea, however if you notice very marked drowsiness, if your Shih Tzu is not responding to his name, etc. this is also a sign that veterinary intervention is needed.
• Dehydration - It is important to help a dog replace lost fluids (more ahead) however if a Shih Tzu has explosive diarrhea or a severe case of this with expulsion more than once per hour, the body can become so dehydrated that it is impossible to play 'catch-up'. Symptoms of this include marked weakness, pale gums, slow gum capillary refill time (If you press your finger against a spot on your Shih Tzu's gums that area should lighten, but once you remove your finger, if it does not return to normal color within a count of 3, this is a sign of dehydration), sunken in eyes and/or distressed breathing.
• Bloody diarrhea - If a dog has bloody diarrhea, this is a serious medical condition that requires immediate, emergency treatment. Please note that 'normal' diarrhea can turn into bloody diarrhea, so if a Shih Tzu starts to get sick, an owner must pay attention to the color of the stools. Sudden, bloody and watery diarrhea is a sign that there is a sloughing of the lining of the intestines and this can quickly lead to life-threatening shock.
• If you suspect poisoning - Have a look around all areas that the Shih Tzu has had access to, taking note of any open cabinets, bottles or other items that the dog may have gotten into, etc. If you suspect that your Shih Tzu is having diarrhea due to eating something toxic, do not hesitate to call the vet. In most cases, time is of the essence.
• No improvement/ worsening conditions - If your Shih Tzu has diarrhea that lasts for more than 5 days, is not eating after 24 hours, is not drinking or has any of the listed symptoms, shows any other signs of distress and/or is not showing any signs of improvement each day, these are reasons to bring him to the vet ASAP.

2) At-home treatment will be the same as with vomiting. If you deemed your Shih Tzu well enough to be treated at home, as to not repeat text, please refer to the previous section, 'Health- Stomach, Intestinal', 'Vomiting', 'Treatment of Vomiting at Home', page 210.

3) Additional Treatment - Treat the anus area - With repeated bouts of diarrhea, a dog's anal opening can quickly become sore, red and irritated. Diarrhea can burn as it is expelled due to its often high level of acidity. This can lead to pain and/or itching. Here is what you can do:
1. Keep it clean - It is best to gently wipe the anus after each episode of diarrhea with a doggie tushie wipe, which is

specially formulated to clean the sensitive skin of this area. If you do not have any on hand, a non-scented baby wipe or a canine body wipe can be used.

2. *Apply a barrier cream or gel* - You will want to dab an ointment, cream or gel onto the Shih Tzu's anus area that will work to create a barrier so that the hot, stinging diarrhea does not touch the skin as it is expelled. Be careful regarding what you use; some human facial creams or creams for dry skin can actually cause more burning. Petroleum jelly is one of the best choices (owners should always have this on hand since it is needed to take a dog's temperature rectally). If you do not have this, Vitamin D ointment can be used as a substitution.

3. *Check for skin damage/infection* - If the sensitive skin of a dog's anus is repeatedly subjected to hot, burning diarrhea, the skin may break open and then be vulnerable to infection. Keep an eye on this area to look for signs of skin cuts. If you notice any or if the skin does not heal once the diarrhea is gone, this is a reason to contact the vet as a topical antibiotic may be needed.

Constipation

When a dog is constipated he or she will have trouble pushing out a bowel movement, will not have a bowel movement at all, or may have very small, infrequent movements or stool will be very hard like small rock-like pebbles.

Causes of Constipation

#1 The most common reason is dehydration. Did you know that poop is 75% water? It is! So, if your Shih Tzu is not drinking enough water, not enough water will make it down into the intestines and this can cause hard stools that is difficult for a Shih Tzu to push out.

#2 Ingestion of a foreign substance - Please remember to routinely 'puppy proof' your house. Even if your Shih Tzu is an adult! Curious (or bored) Shih Tzu can very easily gobble up small items such as paper clips, paper, a coin! Also, watch your Shih Tzu when you bring him outside. When a dog ingests grass, he may also swallow a small pebble…or who knows what.

#3 Medication Side Effects –All sort of medications can cause constipation. Most commonly it will be antihistamines. Iron supplements can cause problems with the stool as well.

#4 The fourth most common reason for Shih Tzu constipation is, surprisingly, habit. This can happen if a puppy or dog is left home alone for long periods of time and holds back the urge to go to the bathroom. A dog can also hold back bathroom needs when in a new place… like a boarding kennel or while traveling on an airplane or for a long car trip.

#5 For older, senior dogs, a diet of only dry food can cause constipation.

Prevention - Let's look at the steps that you can take to prevent your Shih Tzu from suffering with constipation.

1) Give lots of water - Some dogs are picky with their water, they will not lap at old, stale, warm water. So, be sure to keep that water bowl fresh. Use filtered tap water (unfiltered tap water can contain also sorts of 'nasty's' that can cause allergies, stomach upset and coat issues). Be sure to keep it refilled throughout the day with cool/cold water. Also, have 2 bowls (or even more), so that you can easily throw one in the dishwasher or set aside in the sink and offer water in a nice clean one. Food particles from food are easily transferred to the water dish; therefore, the need to clean bowls often is something that owners must be aware of. On hot days or on days when your Shih Tzu exercises a bit more than normal, be sure to offer more water. The amount of water that a dog needs changes with the weather and with his activity levels. So, to avoid constipation and for healthy bowel movements, enough water is a must.

2) Puppy proof your house even if your Shih Tzu is an adult. A curious or a bored dog can very easily sniff around and then mouth small objects. Shih Tzu have been known to swallow paper clips, small tuffs of paper, even hair pins!

3) Do not let your Shih Tzu eat grass. As to not repeat text, you may wish to refer to the 'Behavioral Issues', 'Eating Grass' section, page 142.

4) Offer a well-balanced, healthy diet. In general, you will want to offer a high quality commercial food or home cook. Even if you go the way of manufactured, snacks can be wholesome 'real' food… green beans and peas are 2 great ingredients that can be mixed into meals to offer more greens. And for snacks, try giving your Shih Tzu little baby carrots.

5) If your Shih Tzu is constipated and is also taking medication for allergies, check with the veterinarian. If the constipation is very bad, switching to a new medication or lowering the dose may be needed. He may also suggest adding a new medicine to treat your Shih Tzu's constipation.

6) If your Shih Tzu is home alone for most of the day, be sure to offer a happy, comfortable environment so that he or she can feel more comfortable with having a bowel movement. If confined to a very small area, your dog may hold back the urge. As to not repeat text, you may wish to refer to the 'Housebreaking' section, page 43 or the 'Separation Anxiety' section, page 170.

7) For an older, senior Shih Tzu, be aware that a dry diet that can cause constipation. If you feed kibble, allow it to soak in water before feeding or add low-salt chicken broth and warm it up. If you home cook his meals, great!... the food will already be moist.

8) If your Shih Tzu gets constipated while traveling for a long distance in the car, be sure to pull over every couple of hours. Keep your dog on leash. Allow your Shih Tzu to stretch his legs, have a drink and a snack and take a bathroom break.

Treatment - All of these Prevention Steps should help to treat minor to severe constipation problems. In addition, some pumpkin may help. Be sure to obtain REAL canned pumpkin and not the pie filling. Just a spoon or two, once or twice per day can help. Some sources suggest milk and this is 'iffy', it can help or it can cause additional stomach upset. If the constipation lasts for 3 or more days OR if your Shih Tzu shows any signs of pain, it will be time to bring your Shih Tzu to the veterinarian. A mild laxative may be prescribed.

NOTE: NEVER, ever try to give a dog a laxative meant for humans - this can be fatal! Laxatives prescribed by a vet that contain lactulose are very safe and effective. If you are concerned that your Shih Tzu has some sort of obstruction that is not allowing the stool to come out, this is an emergency situation. Bring your Shih Tzu to the vet ASAP.

Health – Other

Allergies

Some owners are concerned about their Shih Tzu having allergies, but will not follow through with the steps to prevent and treat for them. We must remember that having a dog means that you have made a commitment to taking care of another soul and therefore, budgeting away money for such things as vet visits and associated testing should be done. It's still amazes us how many owners bounce back-and-forth, desperate to try anything… anything but bring their Shih Tzu to the vet. So, please do not be one of those owners. If you try all of the following and you cannot

pinpoint what is causing your Shih Tzu's allergies OR if his symptoms are severe and do not respond to at-home treatment, please do not hesitate to bring your Shih Tzu to the veterinarian.

This said, even if the veterinarian cannot pinpoint the exact triggers, if you follow the steps listed here, you can – most likely- improve things drastically. And by this we do mean *all* of the steps that are applicable to you. For example, if you dust your home and make sure that everyone takes off their shoes, but you do not use specialized filters in your AC, you mind as well not have even bothered with the first two steps. Allergies are not an easy thing to deal with and what a dog may be allergic to is often smaller than the human eye can even detect. So, moving forward, do please note that each suggestion is listed for a reason and we highly recommend making every effort humanly possible to adhere to them all.

Allergies can be classified into 3 different categories:

• **Contact allergies** - The dog is allergic to an external element that he is coming into contact with.
• **Environmental allergies** - This is often seasonal issues such as pollen, but can also include such things as cigarette smoke or even dust mites.
• **Food allergies** - A certain food or dog food additive (preservatives, coloring, etc.) will cause a reaction.

All 3 types have similar symptoms. And some dogs can have more than 1 allergy. Therefore, it is common for owners to have no idea which type(s) a dog has until testing has been done. We strongly encourage owners to have testing completed by an experienced veterinarian (more ahead). First, let's discuss each type, common triggers and what you can do while you are waiting for the appointment/test results.

Contact Allergies

Contact allergies will be something in the environment that is causing an allergic reaction.

The most common signs include:

• **Itching** – While fleas, mites or dry skin can cause some itching, moderate to severe itching is typically due to some type of allergy. Some dogs may scratch open their skin, thus leading to potential skin infections. A dog may obsessively lick or chew parts of his body; often the paws since they are the most accessible.
• **Coat loss** – A dog that is constantly exposed to a trigger may have patches of coat loss or areas in which the hair is dry and thinning.
• **Nasal Discharge** – While this can also be a sign of an inhaled trigger, this can happen due to contact allergies as well.

Actions to Take Regarding Triggers for Contact Allergies – Action should be taken to

remove/change to all possible elements that can be causing the Shih Tzu to have the allergic reaction.

• **The carpeting in your home** – A dog may be allergic to the carpet itself or to allergens trapped in the carpet. Aside from changing your home from carpeting to hardwood floors (we do not expect owners to be able to have this done), you can help your Shih Tzu by laying down blankets for him or her to sit, lie and play upon. *Also*, using a vacuum cleaner with a certified HEPA filter can help tremendously. Vacuum the entire house (even rooms the Shih Tzu does not enter) at least once every 3 days. Certified HEPA vacuums will not only suck up allergens from the flooring, they also clean the air that is being sucked in as well.
• **The carpet cleaner that is used** –If you use one, use a cleaner that is hypoallergenic and odor free.
• **Laundry detergent** - This can leave remnants of triggers on clothing, sheets and more. Use a hypoallergenic laundry detergent for everything that you wash.
• **Canine shampoo**- Typically cheap canine shampoos will be abrasive and contain inexpensive ingredients that can cause reactions and irritation. Change bathing products. If your Shih Tzu's skin is red, irritated or itchy, use a quality medicated shampoo first. Once his skin is healed, use a quality shampoo, conditioner and leave-in product.
• **Smoke** – Not only can a dog be allergic to 2nd hand smoke, a dog just as a human can develop cancer because of it. It is recommended to have any smokers do so outside or in a room that is completely separate from where your Shih Tzu wanders such as the garage.
• **Fleas**- While fleas cause itching, dogs can be allergic to the saliva of the fleas. For this reason, it is very important to always use year-round flea protection for your Shih Tzu. If you can actually see fleas, you will want to clean all sheets, blankets, dog beds and such in hot water and dry them on a hot cycle. The house must be treated for fleas with a fogger. Your Shih Tzu must be cleansed with a flea shampoo. You may also wish to refer to 'Fleas', page 231.
• **Grass/yard chemicals** - Lawn care products can cause rashes, itching and other signs of allergies. This will include any grass at all that your Shih Tzu comes into contact with. This may be areas that you have no control over such as grass along your walking route and/or at the park. Many towns and cities spray for bugs, weeds and other such things. While signs are often posted for a while, those chemicals can remain for months. Sometimes as much as 6 months and therefore long after those signs have been taken down. In your own yard, limit what you use. Use none at all if possible. Please note that pesticides and weed killers labeled 'organic' or as 'safe for pets' may not be at all! Some companies that offer these varieties have been sued for fictitious claims. You'll want to avoid any grass that you know has been treated. Everyone in the household should take off their shoes as soon as they enter (guests, household members, *everyone*).

Home Treatment for Contact Allergies

1) Always rinse off your Shih Tzu's paws when entering back into the home. This is best done by rinsing his paws under the tap of the kitchen sink. If possible, carry him there so that his paws do not leave any allergens on the flooring.
2) Use a quality medicated oatmeal anti-itch shampoo. Shih Tzu with severely dried skin may benefit from 1 time per week baths with the right products.
3) Continue to use your quality conditioner and leave-in coat spray.
4) For 'hot spots', which are tender, sore areas, use a 'rescue lotion'. We recommend DERMagic Hot Spot Salve.

5) Giving your Shih Tzu an Omega 3 or Omega 3, 6, 9 fatty acid canine supplement can speed up the healing process.
6) Watch for skin irritations that have developed into sores and/or open leaking scabs. This will be a sign that an infection has developed. A veterinarian must treat this with antibiotics. Ahead we will discuss prescribed treatments for allergies.

Environmental Allergies

Many dogs have summertime seasonal allergies (pollen, weeds) or winter seasonal allergies (dust mites when houses are closed up without healthy fresh air being circulated); though some are allergic to both triggers, in which case the dog will suffer year-round.

The most common signs include:

• Coughing – This is often a dry cough
• Sneezing
• A shortness of breath
• Wheezing noises
• Snoring
• A discharge of mucus from the mouth or nose
• Eye discharge – May be any consistency; watery or thick
• Scabbed skin
• Red eyes
• Reoccurring ear infections

Actions to Take Regarding Triggers for Environmental Allergies
Action should be taken to remove/change to all possible elements that can be causing the Shih Tzu to have the allergic reaction.

• Keep your Shih Tzu inside when the lawn is mowed.
• Keep your dog inside during days of high pollen counts, this information is often displayed alongside weather reports.
• Always rinse off your Shih Tzu's paws when entering back into the home. This is best done by rinsing his paws under the tap of the kitchen sink. If possible, carry him there so that his paws do not leave any allergens on the flooring.
• Always 'wet wipe' the coat after your Shih Tzu enters back into the home. Use quality, unscented canine wipes to do this.
• During the summer, if you have an AC, use a high quality HEPA filter. A true HEPA filter is rated to remove 99.97% of all particles that are 0.3 microns in size or larger (a micron, also known as a micrometer is one millionth of a meter). Change these as needed (often every 3 months).
• Do not keep your windows open.
• Any time that you are not running your AC (spring, fall, winter), run a quality asthma/mold/allergy air purifier that runs with a HEPA filter. You can find these online or at your local home supply store. These will filter out dust & mold (two elements that a dog can be very allergic to).
• Vacuum with a HEPA certified vacuum cleaner on a regular basis. It will remove triggers that have embedded into carpeting and also filter the air.
• Wash all bedding (yours and your Shih Tzu's) with hot water and hypo-allergenic detergent. Wash curtains, tablecloths, stuffed toys and any other household items that can be washed in a machine.
•'Wet dust' the house well on a regular basis. Using a dry cloth only moves particles around. Using a damp cloth or a cloth along with a dusting spray will pick up dust, dust mites, pollens and more, so they can be disposed of.

Home Treatment for Environmental Allergies

1) Prescribed allergy medications that your vet gives to you will work best. However, if you are waiting for the appointment, speak to your veterinarian about giving Benadryl to your Shih Tzu. This is considered safe for dogs. Dosing is 1 mg per pound of body weight, given 2 to 3 times per day.

2) All other treatments are identical to 'Home Treatment for Contact Allergies' (previous section)

Food Allergies

Dogs can have either food intolerances or food allergies; though it should be noted that in many cases a dog will not actually be allergic to a 'real' food, but will instead be allergic to an ingredient that is added to commercial foods. This includes artificial coloring, preservatives and other 'non-food' elements such as fillers. With this said, there is a small chance of a dog being allergic to just about any food including fish, lamb or wheat. Food allergies are not as common as some may think. Food allergies only account for 10% of all canine allergies and of that 10% less than 3% are allergic to a 'real' food.

The most common signs include:

• **Skin reactions –** This includes itching, rash, hives, paw biting, irritation around the anus area and/or obsessive licking
• **Digestive/intestinal reactions –** This includes nausea, vomiting and/or diarrhea.

Actions to Take Regarding Food Allergies – Action should be taken to change all food that the dog is ingesting.
• All main meals and all snacks will need to be changed to newer, more wholesome brands that have much less of a chance of causing a reaction. You may switch to high-quality manufactured brands that do not include chemicals or you may decide to home cook.

Home Treatment for Food Allergies

1) Immediately switch to a very basic, home cooked diet. This eliminates all possible chemicals and can offer relatively quick relief. Always offer the chicken for protein and you may mix & match 1 or 2 other ingredients to your Shih Tzu's preferred taste:
• Chicken (whole white chicken meat, no skin, no seasonings, baked, broiled or boiled)
• White rice (plain, no butter, no seasonings)- Please note that white rice is wheat free
• Sweet potato ((no butter, no seasonings)
• Oatmeal (plain)
2) Dogs need time for their bodies to stop reacting. You will want to speak to your vet, however we recommend at least 2 weeks on this bland diet.
3) Once signs of allergies are gone, you may introduce one new food every 2 weeks. It is important to wait the full 2 weeks. As to not repeat text, please refer to the 'Food and Nutrition', 'All Meal Feeding Details' section for foods you can start to introduce back into the Shih Tzu's diet, page 60.
4) At this point, you will need to decide if you wish to change to a higher quality food (you may wish to opt for a grain-free one) or to home cook. Both options have their pro's and con's. You may look to the 'Food and Nutrition', 'All Meal Feeding Details' section, page 60, for more information.

Testing for Allergies- If you cannot pinpoint the trigger that is causing allergies with your Shih Tzu, a veterinarian can perform allergy testing. There are 2 types of testing that vets often do:

1) ELISA (enzyme-linked immunosorbent assay) blood tests. A blood sample is taken and tested for reactions to allergens including pollens, dust and molds. * ***This is not recommended,*** since there can be a lot of false-positives. If the vet only uses this sort of testing, we recommend locating a different vet.
2) An intradermal skin test. * ***Recommended***. This is much more accurate than the previously mentioned ELISA testing. For this test, a dog is sedated and an area on his side is shaved down to the skin. Within this shaved area, a small amount of antigen is injected into the dog's skin for each possible trigger. There will be a small reaction for those that the dog is allergic to. It should be noted that for accurate results, a dog should not be given any steroids or antihistamines for 3 weeks prior to testing.

Prescribed Treatment for Allergies

1) Antihistamines may be prescribed. These include Benadryl, clemastine, chlorpheniramine, and hydroxyzine. This type of medication is known to work in about 30% of all cases and often works much better when used together with an Omega 3 fatty acid supplement and the elimination of the element which is triggering the allergy.

2) A mild topical steroid cream such as hydrocortisone may be prescribed for localized itching.

3) Topical antibiotics will be given for any areas that look to be infected.

4) Immunotherapy is used in cases in which the avoidance of the allergy trigger is impossible, if the dog has shown symptoms for approximately 5 months and if other treatments of Omega 3 and antihistamines do not work. The dog then will be given skin tests to check for hypersensitivity. Once a trigger is identified, the dog will be injected with altered antigens on a slow and steady basis. These are given either weeks or months apart, depending on the type. This helps the dog become desensitized to the allergic cause and works quite well. Up to 80% of dogs show marked improvement.

5) In more severe cases, steroids including cortisone or prednisone may be given. This is given to the dog via injections or by oral form. Injections are usually given to a Shih Tzu with anywhere from a 1 week to a 6 month wait between shots. Oral steroids are sometimes preferred because if side effects appear, the oral dose can be discontinued and the dog will stop having side effects rather quickly; once an injection is done, it cannot be reversed. Oral steroids for Shih Tzu suffering from allergies are usually given for 3 to 5 days in a row and then evened out, usually every other day. *Please note* that steroid treatment for dogs with allergies is reserved for very severe cases, in which all other efforts have failed because it can have very bad side effects. Each dog will react differently; however the most common side effects are weight gain, excessive drinking, increased urination, hyperactivity, panting, diarrhea and/or depression. Long term effects can be a drastic change to the Shih Tzu's coat, resulting in a very dry coarse texture. The dog may develop skin issues and liver problems.

Arthritis

With the most common form of arthritis (osteoarthritis also known as degenerative joint disease) a dog's joints become inflamed and painful. It is caused by smooth cartilage breaking down and no longer properly protecting bones. There are 4 types of arthritis with canines:

• Osteoarthritis – this is the most common form, if your Shih Tzu has arthritis, most likely it is Osteoarthritis
• Immune-mediated
• Infective
• Idiopathic (where the cause is unknown)

Causes of Arthritis in Dogs

1) An injury - Most commonly to a ligament. Shih Tzu that have had luxating patella or hip dysplasia are very prone to develop arthritis in those areas (knees or hips).

2) Obesity – The Shih Tzu breed is not prone to being overweight; however some older adults and seniors may carry a few too many pounds, especially if they have become sedentary. The more weight that's on a joint, the more stressed the joint becomes, and the more likely it will wear down and be damaged.

3) Genetics - The joints may be genetically weakened or unsteady as a dog grows. It also may be caused by improper bone development.

The Symptoms

• Steady onset of weakness in one or more limb.
• Signs of fatigue - A dog will not want to go for walks, etc.
• Stiffness – A dog will show signs of difficultly in rising from a down position, walking stairs, etc. This is usually worse in the morning and may improve as the day goes.
• Joints may be swollen.
• Pain –Many dog owners will not be able to know that their dog is in pain from arthritis until it has progressed. When a dog is in pain or not feeling well, there will be behavioral changes – the dog may often retreat to be alone or have

less of a 'zesty' personality.

Prevention - For those who have Shih Tzu with former injuries to the knee(s), hips or other areas, owners should be on high alert as the Shih Tzu grows older. In some cases, arthritis due to former injury can start to set in as soon as 1 or 2 years afterward. Those with senior Shih Tzu (8 years and up) should also be on high alert. While you cannot completely control if your Shih Tzu develops arthritis, there are some things that you can do to try and prevent this:

• **Keep your Shih Tzu at a healthy weight** – It's not uncommon for owners to be so used to seeing their dog each day that they do not notice weight gains, especially when a Shih Tzu transitions from adult to senior. This breed is small, but older Shih Tzu may have an extra pound or two in the stomach area. Keep yearly vet checkups and additionally you can weigh your Shih Tzu at home by stepping on the scale yourself and then while holding your dog and subtracting the difference.

• **Keep your Shih Tzu on a daily routine of exercise** – This is so important not only for arthritis issues but for overall health. The goal will be to provide daily exercise via walking at what is considered a brisk pace for your Shih Tzu. One walk per day is good and two are great. You'll want to have your Shih Tzu walk energetically but without overdoing it, as you don't want to stress the body. Remember to follow hot weather and cold weather guidelines.

• **Limit actions that can cause injury** - Certain actions such as jumping from too high of a height can cause injury. If your Shih Tzu has a habit of leaping off the sofa, your bed or another favorite spot, it is suggested to place canine steps or a ramp so that the body is not jarred when jumping down. Another thing to try to prevent is tripping down the stairs (we can't even count the number of owners who have fallen down a staircase - often along with a Shih Tzu - because the dog was sitting up at the top and both slid down). Use gates for certain 'accident prone' areas if it makes sense to do so. *Photo courtesy of Twa-Nas Pe-Kae Shih Tzu*

• **Supplements** - There are several supplements that can help to keep a dog's joints healthy. While no amount of any supplement can correct structural damage to a dog's joints, Glucosamine and Omega 3 can decrease inflammation, improve the body's ability to repair and strengthen tissues and increase mobility.

How This is Diagnosed

• X-rays are currently the best method to access the severity of arthritis in dogs

• Joint fluid may be collected and analyzed

Treatment

• **Anti-inflammatory and pain medications** - NSAIDs and steroids are often given and can help to control pain and swelling. These will be prescribed by your dog's veterinarian. For long-term use, dosing is often low to prevent negative side effects and for that reason, other treatment options shown ahead are often incorporated into a treatment plan.
• **Supplements** - As mentioned earlier under 'Prevention', Glucosamine and Omega 3 can decrease inflammation, improve the body's ability to repair and strengthen tissues and increase mobility.
• **Acupuncture** - This may help with pain management and is catching on as an alternative treatment for many canine health issues. Most canine acupuncturists will use lavender oils and soft lighting to help a dog relax. Then tiny needles are inserted just barely below the skin into key points of the dog's body; most dogs tolerate this well. A session can last from 5 to 20 minutes. Many owners report that this does help their dogs.
• **Alternative medicine for canines** –Prolotherapy is one of the newest nonsurgical trends in veterinary medicine. It is a nonsurgical treatment which stimulates healing. This involves regular injections of dextrose and other substances, such as lidocaine and vitamin B12, to stimulate cell growth and strengthen joint tissue.
• **Steps and ramps** - Climbing up on and then coming down from beds, sofas, chairs and other furniture can be hard for a dog with arthritis. Steps or ramps for dogs can be a great help.
• **A proper orthopedic dog bed**- Just lying down on the floor can cause discomfort for a dog that has arthritis. A quality orthopedic bed should be placed in areas where a dog usually rests or sleeps - you may need two; one for his normal sleeping area and one in the family room or living room.
• **Exercise**- When a dog is feeling stiff from arthritis, the worse thing for him is to stay house-bound; it only exasperates the problem. With your vet's 'okay' one or two 'easy' walks per day will help a Shih Tzu loosen up and feel better.

Bad Breath

There's nothing like that feeling once you have your Shih Tzu groomed perfectly… the coat looks great, tear stains are cleared away… and your puppy or dog comes bouncing over to you… And then you're knocked over by a whiff of bad breath that is so overpowering, you're wondering if your Shih Tzu just ate straight from the garbage. If this has ever happened to you, you're not alone. Whether there are random acute episodes of your Shih Tzu having stinky breath or if your dog has a stubborn, chronic issue that is not going away, halitosis is not uncommon with canines.

Most people associate good smelling breath with minty scents. Many toothpastes, mouth washes, breath mints (hence the worth minty) and gum that is marketed to improve breath use either spearmint or peppermint. Since it is hard (but not impossible) for our dogs to have breath that smells like mint, owners do expect that the breath be neutral in order to classify as non-smelly. While this can be achieved, it should be noted that it is normal for a Shih Tzu's breath to smell like the food that he just ate. This is particularly true of dry kibble and is caused by tiny particles of the food to remain in the grooved ridges on the tongue, in the oral tissue (most often the inside of the cheeks) and between teeth. It is not normal for a dog to have breath that smells like feces, urine, a very sour smell or any other odor that is considered foul and powerful enough to notice when the dog breathes on you.

Reasons for Bad Breath

1) Teeth - This may even seem obvious to some owners yet this is still overlooked due to some Shih Tzu dogs not showing any signs of issues and the teeth themselves looking quite good. However, there are several elements that can be happening in, under and around the teeth that can cause very stinky breath. Plaque, tartar and dental infection are the main leading causes of both bad breath and undiagnosed dental issues. A long time ago, it was thought that dogs cleaned their own teeth by chewing on toys and treats. This has long been proven false yet is still believed by some owners. Without brushing (with proper canine dental products) there will be a gradual buildup of film. Plaque is always present in the mouth; it is a sticky substance that will buildup and become thick around the teeth and at or even under the gum line if not brushed away. As this sits on the teeth, it slowly eats away at the enamel. Tartar, also known as calculus, is what happens when the plaque is not cleaned away. It is colored either yellow or brown and further damages the teeth.

Tooth infection is not uncommon for toy breed dogs in general and the Shih Tzu is not an exception. It is an issue that will NOT resolve itself. Eventually, tooth infection will lead to quite a bit of discomfort which often manifests as a reluctance to eat and the tooth can either crack or loosen. With canines, infection can travel from the tooth into the bloodstream, where it can then spread throughout the body to vital organs, including the heart and brain. Therefore, ruling this out as a cause of bad breath is important.

What to do:

1. If you suspect that bad breath may be stemming from unclean or infected teeth - and this is especially a possibility if the Shih Tzu has not had regular brushing at home and/or his teeth have not been recently examined by the vet, the dog should be brought to the veterinarian for a full dental. This involves a complete examination to look for infection and then under anesthesia, x-rays, a full cleaning which will involve scraping both under the gum line and on all teeth and finally a rinse. If an abscess is found, treatment is necessary to prevent the infection from spreading and causing further health issues. Often, the two choices are a root canal or an extraction of the tooth.
2. Whether you have a brand new Shih Tzu puppy or a senior dog, now is the time to start brushing your Shih Tzu's teeth. It only takes a few minutes per day and will have a huge impact on your dog's dental health. Not only is this the best remedy for bad breath, it will help your dog hold onto his pearly whites for his lifetime. It's important to use the right toothbrush and paste. As to not repeat text, please look to the 'Dental Care' section for more details, page 88.

2) Teething - In regard to Shih Tzu puppies that have bad breath, this can often be attributed to teething issues. It is not uncommon for the breath to have a sort of sweet-sour smell. Some owners describe this as a sour milk smell. This sort of bad breath is due to mild bleeding that occurs in the mouth that mixes with saliva and bacteria that is normally present.

What to do: While this will resolve itself once the teething phase is done, brushing the teeth now will help in several ways:
1. It will help prevent future infection since infection in the gums now can affect the adult teeth that are going to emerge
2. It will help keep gums strong which is the foundation needed for a healthy bite set
3. It will help temporarily relieve the itch; most Shih Tzu puppies love to have a nice scrubbing since the bristles feel great on those scratchy gums
4. It establishes good habits for a lifetime; puppies that become used to this now will grow up to be adult dogs that sit nice for this grooming task.

3) Dog Food Breath – It's common for a dog to smell like the food that he just ate. This is what many refer to when they speak of 'dog breath' and it can linger for hours after a Shih Tzu eats a meal. In most cases, this happens with very dry kibble due to the chalky consistency of the fine particles. As this mixes with saliva, it can form a sort of paste that is difficult for the dog to swallow. It can end up packed up around the teeth, causing the smell of the food to remain in the mouth for quite a while. Each time the Shih Tzu exhales, that odor will be released.

What to do: Any food that has gone stale will be more apt to chalk up and then produce bad smells, so if you tend to buy large bags of food that takes too long for your dog to eat, you may want to downsize to smaller containers that are finished off quicker. It can also help to encourage your Shih Tzu to drink right after eating. Water fountains are a great choice for boosting water consumption since dogs are attracted to the flowing water though even offering an ice cube after a meal can do the trick.

4) Bad Breath from Eating Poop - If your Shih Tzu's breath smells like feces, he very well may have eaten feces, either his own or that of another dog. This is known as coprophagia. For this issue, as to not repeat text, please refer to the 'Behavioral Issues', 'Eating Feces' section, page 138.

5) Foreign Object - There are many things that a Shih Tzu can mouth that can get stuck between the teeth or even pierce the inside of the cheek or tongue. If this happens, there will be localized inflammation and possibly infection that can cause a noxious mouth odor. What can get stuck in the mouth is only limited to what a Shih Tzu has had access to. A chuck of food may be wedged between the teeth, though small strings and wooden splinters are two of the most common culprits.

What to do - In some cases, you can remove a piece of food with your dog's toothbrush. In the case of a splinter in the mouth, this is something that the vet should handle to make sure that the entire object has been removed and to prescribe antibiotic medication if needed.

6) Health Issues - There are a wide range of health issues that have bad breath as a symptom:

Diabetes can cause a dog's breath to smell very fruity and sweet. While this is more common with senior dogs, juvenile diabetes can strike younger dogs. Other signs include changes in appetite, weight loss or gain, weakness, changes in urination and/or increased UTI's.

Kidney issues can cause breath to smell like urine. Other symptoms include vomiting, diarrhea, constipation, weight loss, increased thirst and/or lethargy.

Liver or lung disease - With both liver and lung disease, there may be strong chronic bad breath.

Digestive issues - If there is excess gas in the stomach, this can cause a dog to burp quite a bit, which in turn can cause bad breath as the smell of stomach odors and digesting food are expelled from the mouth. It should be noted that burping may also be caused by eating too quickly and can often be remedied by offering meals in a slow-feeder bowl which displaces the food to encourage slower ingestion.

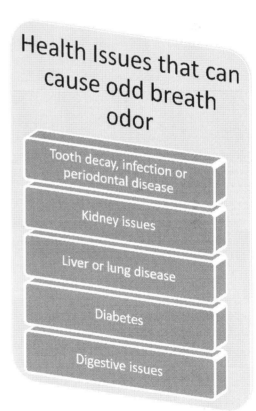

How to Keep Your Shih Tzu's Breath Smelling Nice - If you have had all possible health issues ruled out and you are looking for at-home remedies to make a puppy or dog's breath smell fresh, fortunately there are several effective methods.

1) Once-per-day brushing. This is by far the most important prevention and treatment not only for halitosis but to prevent tooth decay and infection. With a quality toothbrush and effective paste, you only need to brush for 3 to 4 minutes, once per day. Some Shih Tzu may resist at first, however will settle down and get accustomed to this within just a week or so. Using a flavored paste that dogs are receptive to, such as chicken or beef flavor, will often help.

Since canines are incredible time keepers, it's suggested to set aside a certain time each day that this is done such as after dinner.

2) Dental dog chews - If you are going to give your Shih Tzu a snack, why not have it be one that wipes away bad breath and promotes good oral hygiene? Dental treats will be textured to help remove plaque and will contain antiseptics that fight against bacteria. Look for treats that have no added by-products, or artificial colors. Treats that contain real ingredients and not artificial flavors are the ones that will actually work. Look for ones made with dill, parsley and mint.

3) Canine mouth wash - Luckily, you don't have to teach your Shih Tzu to swish and spit. There are canine mouth washes that are actually added to a dog's water and are meant to be ingested. These work by killing bad bacteria in the mouth and also in the bowl and can be a great method to help with this. Look for a flavorless canine mouthwash that does not affect the taste of the water (and cheap ones can make things worse due to a drying effect). With quality brands, you only need to add 1 teaspoon for each full cup of water.

4) Encourage the use of chew toys - While chewing on toys alone without any other methods involved will not be sufficient enough to for clean teeth and fresh breath, they do have their place. Every Shih Tzu needs a great toy collection. Toys are self-soothing instruments, combat boredom, give a dog a way to release energy and direct curiosity. At the same time, chewing will trigger the production of saliva that keeps the mouth moist which then in turn washes away odor and cavity causing bacteria.

 Recommended toothbrushes, toothpaste, canine mouthwash & dental treats are in the Shih Tzu Specialty Shoppe. You can reach the Shih Tzu Specialty Shoppe by entering any page of the AllShihTzu website. Look to the navigation; it is in alphabetical order. Choose 'Shoppe'.

If your Shih Tzu does not respond to any at-home remedies, it will be time for a full checkup with the veterinarian to rule out possible health conditions.

Breathing Problems

Brachycephalic breeds such as the Shih Tzu are prone to breathing issues. A lot of this has to do with the structure of the head. With flat-faced breeds, internal passages are compacted. Though this is not uncommon with the breed, moderate to severe breathing issues are not something that should be assumed to be normal. In some cases, veterinary intervention may be needed.

Brachycephalic Airway Syndrome

This is the term given to brachycephalic such as the Shih Tzu that have breathing issues related to their body structure. It is a general term that includes at least one of the 4 issues of stenotic nares, elongated soft palate, collapsed larynx (voice box) and trachea issues (abnormally small or collapsed trachea). The 3 most common issues seen with the Shih Tzu are collapsed trachea, elongated palate and stenotic nares. With 50% of Shih Tzu that do have airway syndrome, *both* elongated palate and stenotic nares are present.

The most common symptoms seen with Brachycephalic Airway Syndrome include:

- Trouble breathing – This includes trying to catch his breath, struggling to take in enough air, etc.
- Panting
- Trouble eating – The dog may gag or even regurgitate food
- Snoring – The degree of snoring may vary depending on the humidity level in the house and the position in which the Shih Tzu is sleeping.
- Noisy breathing – There may be gasping, rattling or wheezing noises
- Coughing – During an attack, the dog may inhale in such a way that sounds like coughing or the Shih Tzu

may have an actual cough; sometimes sounding like honking noises.
- Exercise intolerance – Not only may breathing become difficult when the dog is active, it may force him to stop, as he gasps for breath.
- Collapse – In very severe cases, the dog may collapse.

Now, we will look at the 3 most common conditions that fall under the category of Brachycephalic Airway Syndrome and then touch on breathing spasms due to reverse sneezing and steps you can take to help your Shih Tzu breathe better.

Collapsed Trachea

The windpipe is surrounded by rings of cartilage. If these collapse inward (due to either an inherited 'weak' trachea or due to injury, such as pressure from being on leash and collar), it is referred to as collapse trachea (or Tracheal Collapse). Though young Shih Tzu puppies may show signs of this, it typically develops in dogs around the age of 6 years old.

The Symptoms

- Coughing – The majority of dogs with this will have a distinctive cough that is often referred to as a honking noise.
Noisy breathing
- Gagging
- Trouble breathing
- These symptoms may be more apparent right after the dog has exercised or when a dog is excited
- In severe cases, the gums of a dog may turn blue (due to a loss of air) and the dog may faint

How This is Diagnosed - Experienced vets will know right away by the particular cough that is present. X-rays are then taken to confirm. In some cases, x-rays will not show a tracheal collapse, however a dog may still be treated for it. If you do desire proof and x-rays are inconclusive, some universities and referral centers perform a test called Fluoroscopy. Fluoroscopy allows visualization of the trachea as the dog inhales and exhales; it is essentially an imaging machine that offers real-time 'moving images' of a dog's internal body structures.

Treatment- Non-Surgical - Studies, though ongoing, have shown that approximately 70% of dogs respond well to non-surgical treatment. Treatment will involve a combination of many elements:

• **Eliminating a collar** - Immediately, a collar should never be worn and a harness will be used whenever the dog is on leash (this is recommended to prevent this issue). You may wish to refer to the 'Care Items - Shih Tzu of All Ages', 'Collars, & Harnesses' section, page 34.
• **Avoidance of cold** - Breathing in very cold air can cause a breathing spasm, therefore you may be instructed to limit your Shih Tzu's exposure to the outdoors during cold weather.
• **Avoidance of exercise during hot weather**- With this breed, moderate to heavy activity in hot (and especially hot and humid) weather can make breathing difficult so with those that suffer from collapsed trachea, exercise should be restricted during the hottest part of the day. You may still be able to walk your Shih Tzu early in the morning and then later again in the evening as things cool down.
• **Weight loss** - Though this is not a problem that is typical with this breed, if your Shih Tzu is overweight, weight loss is recommended as it will put less stress on the body.
• **Non-Steroid Medication** - Most veterinarians will prescribe a non-steroidal anti-inflammatories/pain medications. These are NSAIDs and the most common ones prescribed for dogs are Deramaxx, Etogesic, Previcox, Metacam, Zubrin or Rimadyl.
• **Cough suppressants**- Common cough medications include hydrocodone, butorphanol, or tramadol.
• **Corticosteroids** - The most commonly one prescribed is prednisone and this is used on a short-term basis only due to the potential for side-effects with long-term use. This is often given via an inhaler.

• **Antibiotics** - Dogs with collapsed trachea are prone to develop lower respiratory tract infections. Therefore, antibiotics will be prescribed as needed.

Surgery - If non-surgical treatment does not produce any relief and if a dog is having moderate to severe breathing difficulties and/or is in a lot of pain, surgery is often recommended. Most will involve placing prosthetic polypropylene rings to the outside of the trachea. The success rate of this surgery is 75%. It should be noted that it is most often successful with dogs under the age of 6 years old. Since this most commonly develops by this age, there is a small window to both diagnose this and have the highest surgical success rate; you'll want to bring your Shih Tzu to the vet ASAP if this condition is suspected.

Elongated Soft Palate

The soft palate is the flap of skin at the back of the throat. If the palate is too long it can partially block the entrance to the trachea, or windpipe. This increases airway resistance which can lead to breathing problems. Just about 100% of Shih Tzu have elongated soft palate, again due to the facial structure of the breed. It can range from very slight which causes no symptoms at all, moderate which will cause some problems to be noticed and severe which interferes with the dog's quality of life. Shih Tzu with breathing problems as puppies should be examined for this issue, as it can worsen over time.

The Symptoms

* Newborn puppies may dribble milk from the nose when feeding
* Excessive panting
* Unable to calm down quickly when excited
* Choking on food
* Spitting up whole pieces of food
* Loud, raspy breathing when overheated
* Snoring
* Excessive saliva
* Fainting from lack of air (in extreme cases)

How This is Diagnosed - In minor cases, when it is deemed safe, the vet will examine the mouth when a dog is awake. However, if a judgment call is made that the examination will cause a dog to become overly excited and this in turn will cause dangerous breathing problems, the dog will be sedated. The veterinary surgeon may perform:
* Pre-anesthetic complete blood count and biochemistry
* Blood gases – to check blood pH and CO_2 concentration
* X-rays – The vet will also be looking for a narrowed trachea and any heart abnormalities

Treatment - In minor cases, some changes can be made to help a Shih Tzu breathe better. This includes limiting the dog's activity during hot weather, trying to avoid over-excitement and encouraging different sleeping positions via canines beds and pillows. However, in most cases in which the obstruction is causing breathing distress that interferes with the dog's quality of life, surgery is recommended. And it is important to reiterate that this issue often worsens as a dog grows older; in time ligaments in the lynx may stretch, and often to the point of collapse.

Surgery involves shortening the palate. Many vets prefer to do this after a Shih Tzu has reached the age of 1-year-old. This is because the palate may still grow when a pup is maturing, and if done too early, another procedure may be required at a later date. Sometimes a dog may need to have his tonsils removed also, and the vet should do this during the palate clip if required. Laser surgery is now the most common way to shorten the palate. It cauterizes as it cuts, which decreases bleeding and swelling, and shortens recovery time.

During post-op recovery, only soft food should be given to allow the throat time to heal. This can include rice with minced pieces of chicken, eggs, oatmeal and sweet potato. Dog food can also be softened with warm water, warmed gravy or warmed low-salt chicken broth. Healing time varies, but the typical healing time is between 2-3 weeks.

Stenotic Nares

Stenotic Nares is the medical term for pinched nostrils. This is caused by inherited malformation of the cartilage in the nose. Essentially, the nostrils are too small (too narrow). These narrowed breathing passages will cause a dog to have trouble taking in air. About 50% of Shih Tzu have stenotic nares to some degree and with those that do, 50% also have the previously mentioned elongated palate. Although stenotic nares are present at birth, the symptoms of respiratory difficulty may not begin until a dog is several years old. Surgery is the treatment in moderate to severe cases.

The Symptoms

- Noisy breathing (especially when the Shih Tzu breathes in)
- Exercise intolerance
- Cyanosis (blue appearance of the gums, due to lack of oxygen)
- Fainting (in severe cases)

How this is Diagnosed - Stenotic nares are relatively simple for the veterinarian to diagnose by simply looking at the size of the opening of the nostril. However, there may be other issues that go along with this such as a soft palate or a collapsed larynx or trachea that are less obvious and typically require light, general anesthesia for diagnosis. Diagnostic tests are also necessary to determine the general health of a dog. In addition to obtaining a medical history and performing a physical examination, other diagnostic tests may be necessary, including listening to the dog's chest with a stethoscope, in order to help rule out other causes of respiratory difficulty and x-rays to check that the heart and lungs appear normal.

Treatment - Treatment is divided into medical management and surgery.

Medical Management - If your Shih Tzu has only mild signs & does not have any other breathing related conditions, this may be able to be managed with non-surgical treatment. This includes:

• **Weight loss** - As with many health issues, losing excess weight and maintaining a healthy weight can help a great deal. While the Shih Tzu breed is not typically one to be overweight, it is more common with senior Shih Tzu and even just a loss of 1 lb. can help.
• **Avoid stressful situations** - Dogs that become stressed or over-excited will have more trouble breathing. Also, you'll want to avoid the strain of exercising during hot, humid weather.
• **The use of a harness** – Though we always recommend this for all Shih Tzu to prevent issues, using a harness any time the Shih Tzu is on leash is part of the treatment program. You may wish to refer to the 'Care Items - Shih Tzu of All Ages', 'Collars & Harnesses' section, page 34.

Note: Mild cases can turn severe, so carefully watching your Shih Tzu is very important.

Surgery - The surgical procedure for this condition involves widening of the opening through the nostrils, by removing a small piece of the wall of each nostril. This can be done with a scalpel or a surgical laser.

• **Argument for Delaying Surgery** - It is important to note that a Shih Tzu may have more pronounced pinched nostrils (stenotic nares) during the teething phase. As the puppy matures, the nose may open, allowing the breathing problems to decrease or completely resolve. Veterinarians who are not breed specific will often want to surgically fix this as soon as it is diagnosed. However, this may resolve on its own as the Shih Tzu matures. Therefore, with minor cases, you may want to talk to your vet about waiting until the teething stage is complete.

• **Argument for Having Surgery Performed ASAP** - A dog with stenotic nares needs to use extra pressure to forcefully inhale. This can cause a dog's larynx to become weak. With moderate to severe cases, eventually, the larynx may collapse, causing the dog to be unable to move a sufficient amount of air into the lungs. Affected dogs often appear blue (cyanotic) and this can be fatal.

Note: If a Shih Tzu has both elongated palate and stenotic nares, both severe enough to cause difficulty breathing, surgery is almost always the answer.

Breathing Spasms- Reverse Sneezing

Though the conditions mentioned should be ruled out, fortunately, one of the most common causes of random breathing spasms is something that does not cause any ill effects to the dog: reverse sneezing. This is common with both brachycephalic breeds and with toy breed dogs, and therefore very typical for the Shih Tzu. When a dog has a 'normal' sneeze, air rushes out of the nose; and with this, air rushes in. Since many Shih Tzu already have stenotic nares to some degree, this can make these spasms even more pronounced.

The Symptoms - There will be sudden and random attacks of loud, funny breathing. While it can be mistaken for the honking noise of collapsed trachea, with reverse sneezing there will be consecutive snorting sounds. Often, the dog will take a stance of extending his neck and spreading his elbows apart. In some ways, it may appear as if the dog is choking on something or trying to cough up a hair ball. The episode will generally be very short, lasting only seconds to perhaps 2 minutes at the most. As soon as it is done, the dog will breathe just fine and behave as if nothing is wrong.

While it may happen out of the blue, there are some things that can trigger this: breathing in very cold air, having a rush of excitement, during moderate exercise, wearing a collar that is too tight and/or breathing in an irritant such as air freshener spray or perfume.

Treatment - It is very important to rule out the issues involved with Brachycephalic Airway Syndrome that reverse sneezing can mimic. If your Shih Tzu does have these sorts of breathing spasms, it can be very helpful to take a video of this to show to the vet. If it is indeed reverse sneezing, though not harmful to the dog, there are some things you can do to limit these attacks:

- Gently cup your hand over your Shih Tzu's mouth and nose area (allowing room for breathing!). This often can help because during an episode too much carbon dioxide is released from the dog's body. With your hand gently cupped in front of the mouth and nose, it allows a dog to inhale carbon dioxide, restoring it to a balanced level.
- Place a very small dab of peanut butter onto the dog's nose. It will prompt the dog to stick his tongue out, which can relax the throat and help to restore breathing back to normal.
- Gently massaging the throat area with soft downward strokes can sometimes help, as it also works to relax the area.
- Encourage your Shih Tzu to drink or offer a small snack.

Breathe Better Tips for All Shih Tzu Dogs

Even if all serious conditions have been ruled out, a Shih Tzu may still have some minor breathing problems. And this, of course, can be frustrating and worrisome for owners who are being told that everything is normal, but they still see their puppy or dog having breathing difficulties.

There are some steps that you can take to help a Shih Tzu breath better:

1) Taking action to avoid overheating is key. Limit exercise during very hot weather. Since daily exercise is very important for good, overall health, in the summer take walks early in the morning and then again about 1 hour before the sun sets, as these are the coolest parts of the day. Be sure to bring along water any time you are out and about with your dog and take frequent breaks in the shade.

2) Keep moisture in the air. For some Shih Tzu, breathing in very dry air can make breathing more difficult. The use of humidifiers can help with this. If you cannot set them up over the entire house, one placed near the dog's sleeping area can be helpful for nighttime breathing problems.

3) The position in which your Shih Tzu rests and sleeps can cause issues, and this is particularly evident with snoring. The dog should have a quality, supportive bed in which his body does not sink into the mattress. In addition, placing a small pillow under his head to elongate the neck can help him breathe better at night.

4) If your Shih Tzu seems to have problems when excited, try to intervene before it reaches a point of affecting his breathing. This can include taking short breaks from play, making interval introductions to a new place or when meeting new people and distraction if a Shih Tzu is responding to a trigger.

5) A collar can cause breathing problems in two ways. If too small, it can constrict the neck and breathing passages; a collar should be loose enough for you to easily slip two fingers under it. If a leash is connected to the collar, this puts stress on the neck, which not only can interfere with breathing, but can also lead to tracheal injury, particularly with a Shih Tzu that is already prone to this congenital condition. Always use a harness instead.

Coughs and Other Noises

There are different types of coughs that a Shih Tzu may have: A Shih Tzu may appear to have trouble breathing or be making sounds that make it seem as if the dog cannot catch his breath, it may be a hacking, the Shih Tzu may appear to be gagging and/or seem to be in discomfort. With coughs, there may or may not be a discharge. And finally, the cough may come and go (acute) or it may an ongoing problem (chronic). Sometimes a cough can be a minor issue, yet for some dogs it can be a sign of a serious medical condition.

Not Quite a Cough - There are some minor conditions that can cause a Shih Tzu to make some odd noises, but it will not technically be a cough.

Reverse Sneezing - This is called reverse sneezing because a dog will have spasms that cause him to quickly draw air into his nose as opposed to a sneeze in which air is quickly blown out. When a dog has a reverse sneeze, he will make a sort of snorting noise and extend his neck… and this can appear to be a cough, although it is not. For more details on this, please refer to 'Breathing Issues', 'Breathing Spasms-Reverse Sneezing', page 228.

Hiccups - Just like us humans, dogs can have hiccups and some Shih Tzu owners can mistake this for coughing. These can occur out of the blue or a Shih Tzu may hiccup after eating too fast or after exercising. Just like reverse sneezing, anything that causes a change to the dog's breathing pattern can help to make hiccups go away; please refer to previous paragraph on reverse sneezing.

A Goose-like Honking Noise- If your Shih Tzu is making noises that can be described as a honking sound, this can point to Collapsed Trachea. This is a somewhat serious condition that many toy breed dogs are susceptible to. The windpipe of a dog is made up of rings of cartilage. If one or more of those rings are damaged, they can collapse inward and cause an obstruction in the windpipe. This causes a Shih Tzu to have difficulty breathing at which time the puppy or dog will make coughing noises that sound similar to a honking. For more details on this, please refer to 'Breathing Issues', 'Collapsed Trachea', page 225.

A Deep, Dry, Hacking Cough - This can be a sign of Kennel Cough. Don't let the name fool you… dogs that have never been near a kennel can contract this. It is a highly contagious respiratory disease in which the upper respiratory system is infected. It affects a dog's windpipe and voice box. This usually causes a very deep, dry cough, but some dogs will have a honking cough, similar to the one described previously that is a symptom of Collapsed Trachea.

Other signs and symptoms include: A dry, deep, ongoing cough, vomiting or dry heaving. The coughing may become so bad that there is a watery nasal discharge. And with all dogs that have Kennel Cough there may or may not be fever, loss of appetite and/or weakness.

Diagnosis and Treatment - This is diagnosed by the veterinarian examining the Shih Tzu and also by running blood tests. With mild to moderate cases, it may be left to run its course, similar to how humans have to wait for a cold to end. If a Shih Tzu is having moderate to severe trouble breathing and the cough is severe, anti-inflammatory medication may be given, along with cough suppressants. Only if a dog has a fever is antibiotics given, since this can morph into pneumonia.

A Wet, Mucus Cough- This may point to Pneumonia, which can be caused by many things: Viruses, fungi, bacteria or parasites. Most healthy, adult Shih Tzu dogs do not catch Pneumonia, it only tends to strike very young puppies or much older, senior dogs. It should be noted that if a Shih Tzu has suffered from Collapsed Trachea (details previous), this leaves him vulnerable to catching Pneumonia.

Signs and Symptoms- A very wet cough. In many cases, when the Shih Tzu coughs, a wet spray of thin mucus is noticeable. The dog may also have a fever, rapid breathing and/or rapid pulse. When a Shih Tzu has had Pneumonia for a while without treatment, the coughing may become extremely severe and the dog may sit with his head held out and his elbows turned out which is done by instinct to try and be able to better breathe.

Diagnosis and Treatment - This is diagnosed with x-rays and with blood tests. This is a very serious condition and any Shih Tzu that is showing signs of this type of cough should be taken to the veterinarian or closest animal hospital right away. Antibiotics will be given and the puppy or dog will need to have a follow-up visit to make sure that the lungs have cleared out.

Prolonged Coughing only at Night or While Laying on the Chest - This sort of cough can point to heart disease (also referred to as congestive heart failure). The heart is not able to properly meet the needs of the dog's body and becomes weakened. This affects many other areas of the body as well, including the kidneys, liver and lungs (which will cause the dog to have a troubling cough). In early stages, the coughing will be erratic. In later stages, a dog may be coughing all of the time. Owners may not be aware that there is a problem until the Shih Tzu has been ill for quite some time. It is often only when the heart is so weak that other areas of the body are infected, that owners will know that something is wrong. This is why regular, yearly checkups are so important.

Diagnosis and treatment - A veterinarian will diagnose this via x-rays and an ECG. Underlying conditions, including Heartworms, will be treated. Heart medications will be prescribed, along with lifestyle changes that include a low salt diet and a lower level of exercise.

Coughing due to Allergies — Normally, if a dog is suffering from allergies, there are other signs that you will notice first and rarely is a cough the only symptom. Normally allergies present as issues with the skin (itching, peeling, dryness); though the dog may also have eye irritation and in some cases, coughing. If you suspect allergies, please refer to the 'Allergies' section, page 215.

Other Conditions - Other canine health conditions that can produce a cough are: Chronic bronchitis, Fungal infections, parasites (Heartworms or Roundworms), Influenza, Distemper or Ingestion of a foreign body

Please note: A random, light cough is no reason for concern. Additionally, if you think that your Shih Tzu is coughing, it may just be a reverse sneeze or hiccups. When in doubt about ANY coughing issue, please take your Shih Tzu to the veterinarian. Collapsed Trachea is VERY common with the Shih Tzu breed…And this is sad since it CAN be avoided by NEVER connecting a leash to your dog's collar - Use a harness instead.

Fleas

Most dogs will contend with fleas at least once in their lifetime. Even if an owner cannot fathom how fleas may have attached themselves to their dog; it should be considered as a possible reason for intense scratching. All it takes for a Shih Tzu to have fleas is a visit to a vet, pet store, doggie park, etc. since a flea can jump from 1 dog to another from up to 6 feet away.

The Symptoms

• **Scratching** - While fleas are extremely tiny, their bites can cause intense itching. Some dogs are allergic to the flea saliva that comes into contact with the skin as the insect nibbles to feast on a dog's blood, which exasperates itching even more. Shih Tzu may scratch their ears or any other part of the body. This may be done with the paws, but for areas that are hard to reach a Shih Tzu may rub a body part onto a surface such as flooring or bedding. He may also chew at itchy areas - usually the paws.

• **Irritated skin and/or coat loss** - Since fleas reproduce so quickly, a dog can rapidly have a huge infestation and for those that are allergic to the insect's saliva just one bite can cause such deep itching that there is hair loss as the Shih Tzu gnaws at his body - most often the paws since these are easily accessible.

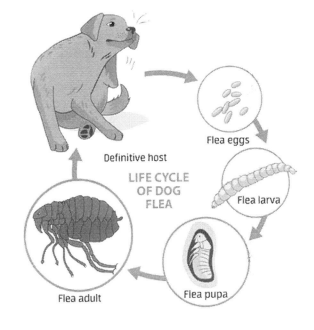

• **Very tiny dark specks** - Fleas do jump but they are wingless and therefore cannot fly. For this reason, you will not see a swarm of fleas circling a dog. If you take a close look, particularly on areas of your Shih Tzu that he hasn't been able to scratch, such as the tail and back, you'll typically see tiny black dots that are about the size of specks of finely ground pepper. These may be brown or black. If you swipe some off with a damp white paper towel, fold it over and squeeze, you may see tiny red specks of blood.

Why Fleas are So Hard to Kill - Fleas are resilient and almost inexhaustible. They like a temperate, moist climate best, but they can go into a dormant state for as much as a year, waiting until conditions for survival and reproduction are more favorable. They live (or lie dormant) both indoors and out in carpets, furniture, bedding, floor and wall joints, indoor plants, gardens, and yards.

They'll infest the car too, if your Shih Tzu has been in it while fleas were attached to him. Depending on how long your Shih Tzu has been infested, there can be several hundred to several thousand fleas on the coat. A typical full-out flea infestation on a dog will consist of roughly 4000 fleas. These insects are so tiny, with 4 different life cycles that essentially a dog with fleas will be the host of a bustling and active civilization of insects; most of which is not seen by owners.

There will always be 4 things on a Shih Tzu with fleas:

1- The adult fleas - These feed off of the blood of the puppy or dog and are what causes the majority of the itching.
2- Eggs - Just one female adult flea can lay 50 eggs per day. Most will fall off the dog and settle into bedding, carpeting and more.
3- Larvae - When the eggs hatch, larvae emerge. After 5 to 20 days, they spin tiny cocoons.
4- Pupae - While inside the cocoons, the fleas are referred to as pupae. They spend anywhere from 3 days to 1 year inside, emerging as adult fleas when conditions are ripe.

Know that for every flea you see, there are - statistically speaking - 100 others in various stages of reproduction.

Your 3 Point Plan of Attack to Get Rid of Fleas on a Shih Tzu:

1) Remove all of the fleas, eggs, larvae and pupae on your dog and any other pets that live with you
2) Thoroughly eradicate all four stages of fleas in your home
3) Attack the fleas in all stages in the yard, garden, and car

The advertising literature for some flea control products makes it sound as though your problem will be solved by using just one method of flea control. One method alone usually will not work. Use this three-part plan of attack; it's the best way to achieve good results.

1. Treat Fleas on Your Shih Tzu. You'll want to use 2 products for this:

1- A flea comb - both before and after the flea baths
2- Flea shampoo - this will serve to treat the entire body and reach deep into the Shih Tzu's coat

The Comb - You'll want to choose a quality comb with a sturdy double row design that can handle the dense coat of the Shih Tzu. Going over the coat multiple times using a flea comb will help remove both fleas, any eggs, larvae and pupae. Eggs are super tiny and larvae are almost transparent; so when you use the comb (and shampoo) you will usually only visibly see the adult fleas which will look like black specks. **How to use a flea comb on a Shih Tzu:**

1. Go slowly over every area of the coat
2. Comb in the direction of the hair growth
3. After each stroke, dip the comb in a container of a soapy water (you can use your Shih Tzu's normal shampoo to make this mixture)
4. Take your time to carefully go over all areas of the head since it will not be possible to shampoo these spots

The shampoo - While the comb will get some of the fleas, you'll need to bathe your Shih Tzu in a quality flea shampoo that is also gentle to the skin and coat. Be careful about what you use since any harsh products will irritate already sensitive skin that has been ravaged by the bites. Look for flea shampoos that are oatmeal based and also free of dyes, alcohol and parabens (these are preservatives put into many shampoos and products that a Shih Tzu can have a negative reaction to). **How to bathe a Shih Tzu in flea shampoo:**

1. Fill the tub with lukewarm water.
2. Soak the Shih Tzu's neck area first.
3. Lather the shampoo all the way around the entire neck and scrub well. The goal is to form a barrier so that fleas from the rest of the body do not scurry up to the Shih Tzu's face.
4. Now work your way down the rest of your Shih Tzu's body, using lots of shampoo, enough water to keep it sudsy and massaging deeply to reach down into the dense coat. Be sure to get all areas including the genital area, tail and belly.
5. You will not shampoo/scrub the face because you do not want the soap to get into your Shih Tzu's eyes, nostrils and/or mouth. Since fleas love to live on ear flaps, use pieces of gauze dipped into the shampoo to wipe the inner ears - not going too deep.
6. Rinse your Shih Tzu extremely well - you should see dead fleas in the water. When you think you've rinsed enough, do it one more time.
7. Pat (not rub) your Shih Tzu dry and go over the coat again with the comb - particularly on the face since you did not shampoo that area.

2. Treat the House - Using both a proper flea comb and a good flea shampoo will only work if you eradicate the fleas and all stages of those fleas that are in the house. Most fleas spend most of their time off your Shih Tzu, jumping on just long enough for a meal. The rest of the time they live somewhere in the environment. They will be in the crevices of furniture, on sheets and bedding, in the rugs and carpeting and in every room of the house that your Shih Tzu has been in.

1. Wash everything that is washable (cushions, sheets, blankets, pillow coverings, clothes, etc.) in hot water if possible and dry on a hot setting.

2. Vacuum everything you can - carpets, floors, chairs, sofas, beds, curtains, etc. This will be much more effective if you use a quality non-toxic flea powder that is first sprinkled down.

3. Spray the house down, preferably with a chemical free product. Those with peppermint oil and clove extract can effectively kill fleas and eggs without exposing your Shih Tzu to harsh toxins.

4. It may be necessary to bomb the house - this will send a light mist into crevices that typical cleaning cannot reach. It's best to choose a product that lasts for at least 6 months after using as well as one that dries quickly (30 minutes to 1 hour).

Note: If you use a traditional exterminator, ask about the chemicals they employ and how they affect pets. Be sure to check out the credentials and ratings of the company you are thinking about using.

3. Attack Fleas in the Yard, Garden, and Car - There are many choices if you wish to do this yourself or you can consider hiring a professional to do your house and/or your yard. There are some non-toxic alternatives to use in your yard that are safer than typical pesticides. Diatomaceous Earth is a drying agent that creates an inhospitable environment for fleas. It is actually food grade, which means that while it is helping to kill fleas (and even some types of parasitic worms) it is technically safe for human or animal consumption - this means that after applying this, you don't have to worry about your Shih Tzu being outside.

Protect Your Shih Tzu with Flea Control - Even with flea prevention, a dog can still get fleas. Please choose your Shih Tzu's flea protection wisely. Many dogs can have adverse reactions to flea prevention products. We highly recommend opting for all-natural flea protection such as Natural Chemistry's Natural Flea & Tick Spray for Dogs that contains sodium lauryl sulfate (a surfactant found in many personal care products), cinnamon, cedar wood, clove oil, water and vanillin or Sergeant's Green Flea and Tick Drops for Dogs, which uses peppermint oil, cinnamon oil, lemon grass oil, clove oil & thyme oil.

Hyperventilating

Hyperventilating describes what happens when someone is breathing faster or deeper than normal. With humans, it is not uncommon for it to occur if someone is stressed or is having anxiety. However, with dogs, this happens for different reasons. As an owner, you are understandably concerned if you have seen your Shih Tzu hyperventilating and do not know for sure why it is happening. This section will discuss the various reasons why this happens to a dog. We will also talk about what mimics this, what to do and when it is serious enough to bring your puppy or dog to the veterinarian.

Reason 1: Many owners mistake reverse sneezing for hyperventilation. It is easy to confuse these 2 things, since both involve breathing noises and both issues can be quite startling. Reverse sneezing is an odd occurrence that is sometimes described as a type of unusual hiccup, although it involves a spasm of the soft palate and throat as opposed to the diaphragm. When this happens, the Shih Tzu inhales through his nose quickly and repeatedly. With most, there is a sort of gagging or snorting noise that occurs. In many cases, the dog will extend his neck and the chest may expand out as well. So, as you can imagine, instead of having a sneezing episode of repeated exhalations, a Shih Tzu can have an episode of quick inhalations. Please refer to the 'Reverse Sneezing' section, page 228.

Reason 2: Issues with the trachea can cause a Shih Tzu to hyperventilate. In many cases it will be a case of a Collapsed Trachea. This describes what happens when the rings of cartilage that are formed around the windpipe are injured. Sometimes they are damaged and sometimes they collapse inward due to a weakening. For more details on this, please refer to 'Collapsed Trachea', page 225.

Reason 3: Less common is polyps. With this condition, abnormal growths in the throat or windpipe interferes with normal breathing. While this can cause a Shih Tzu to hyperventilate, more commonly a dog will make snoring type noises when breathing. If your vet suspects polyps, he will do a thorough examination and if they are found, these are often surgically removed.

Reason 4: Over-stimulation. Though rare, if a Shih Tzu is extremely stressed or exceedingly excited, he may hyperventilate and struggle to catch his breath. Obviously, you will want to calm the Shih Tzu down by re-directing and offering calm words.

Reason 5: Nasal mites. This last possible reason is actually quite common among canines, but for many dogs it goes undiagnosed because sometimes there are no symptoms. For this reason, many owners have never even heard of nasal mites. However, for some dogs that have this, it causes problems. An infestation of mites in the nasal cavities can cause a dog to shake his head repeatedly, have coughing fits AND have reverse sneezing, which as discussed above can be easily confused with hyperventilation. This is diagnosed with a nasal swab (quick and painless) and treated with prescription medication.

Helpful Tip: Many owners become frustrated because their Shih Tzu appears to hyperventilate when at home, but feels and acts just fine at the veterinarians. If this is happening, it is recommended to take a video of your Shih Tzu during an episode. While the vet should perform medical tests to rule out the possible health issues discussed, being able to see exactly what happens to your Shih Tzu can be very helpful.

Lethargy

The Shih Tzu breed is known for being alert, active and lively. So, it's easy to notice when a Shih Tzu suddenly begins to act overly tired and is certainly a reason to take note. While there are some very common reasons that may cause a dog to seem fatigued, there are also some health issues that can cause this as well.

Energy Levels to Expect - The Shih Tzu is an active dog. Despite his small size, he has quite a bit of energy. He also closely bonds with is owner, and many Shih Tzu will push themselves to keep up until they reach the point of exhaustion. For example, let's say that an owner is busy cleaning the house… a Shih Tzu will often stay by his owner's side and follow her from room to room as she goes about her tasks. The Shih Tzu may feel very sleepy and ready for a nap, however the urge to remain close and have his human's companionship often outweighs his urge to rest. After a while, the Shih Tzu may get so tired that when he's finally brought to his resting area, he conks right out.

With little legs carrying a little body, it takes more out of a Shih Tzu to keep up than his larger counterparts. Scampering around the house may not seem like exercise, however over the course of a day if a Shih Tzu is moving around quite a bit, he can tire out just from that.

Puppies are special little creatures and oh-so cute. It is very typical for a Shih Tzu puppy to be supercharged with energy, romping all round, rolling over like a silly-head and bopping from here to there, only to tire out in a matter of seconds and fall asleep right where he is. The energy level of puppies is like a roller coaster; so it is normal for a puppy to have intermittent time of being active, tiring and then napping. As he matures, this will level out. When the Shih Tzu reaches his one year mark, he will nap a lot less and sleep better through the night.

Shih Tzu of any age up to about 10 years old should have good amount of energy, be alert to their surroundings, be ready to play, walk and accompany owners outside of the house. An adult may take an afternoon nap and will need some windows of relaxation, however he/she should not be overly tired during the day and if this is noticed it can point to an issue as we will discuss ahead.

Senior Shih Tzu can tire much easier than their adult counterparts, and in many cases this is a natural part of the aging process. However, marked tiredness that suddenly comes on can point to any number of health problems, which we will go over next.

Reasons Why a Shih Tzu Puppy May Act Tired
- As we touched on, it is normal for a Shih Tzu puppy to have a lot of energy and when you couple that with a high level of curiosity, you have a pup that is full with vigor and intentions, but simply cannot handle staying up for all he wants to do and all he wants to see. Young puppies can sleep up to 18 hours per day, so this means that it is normal for them to tire out and take several naps during the day.

With this said, there are some health conditions to be aware of. The most common one is hypoglycemia which refers to a rapid drop in blood sugar levels. Some cases do not have any specific cause other than age, however in some instances this can quickly develop due to either not eating often enough or due to stress (which can include feelings of being overwhelmed in a new house, etc.). As to not repeat text, you may wish to refer to 'Puppy Care' page 27.

Why a Shih Tzu of Any Age May Seem Overly Tired
- Whenever a dog acts out of character and is simply not himself, acting lethargic, mopey or otherwise showing signs of being drained out, it is important for owners not to pass this off. While a dog can just be having an 'off' day, if a Shih Tzu is overly tired for more than 24 hours and sleeping does not seem to resolve things, this often points to an environment factor, a health issue or an issue with the atmosphere of the household.

• **Health issues**: If a dog is feeling ill or is in pain, he often will either retreat and want to rest or he may act overly clingy. Some will go back and forth, and this can confuse owners even more. The majority of health issues have fatigue or lethargy as a symptom. Since weakness can be the initial symptom to manifest at the beginning stage of many illnesses and diseases, this is often noticed first before any other indications. Additionally, if a Shih Tzu is ill there may be a fever present that is not noticed by owners. If a Shih Tzu is acting lethargic and has trouble rising from a down position this can point to hip problems or nerve damage. Added signs of decreased appetite and changes in stool are other common signs of illness that may be developing as well.

Just a few of the possible issues that may cause lethargy include: Diabetes, heart problems, heartworms, hookworms, hypothyroidism, infection (including distemper, parvo and leptospirosis), leukemia, liver disease & poisoning.

Even if there are no other symptoms and even if your Shih Tzu has just had an exam, it is important to bring the dog in for a full physical. The veterinarian should perform a CBC (complete blood count), urinalysis, and do a full body exam. Dogs will have a better prognosis and more successful treatment the earlier that issues are diagnosed; therefore owners are encouraged to not delay a vet visit if lethargy without obvious emotional or environmental causes lasts for more than 24 hours or if sudden and severe weakness that interferes with walking and normal daily activities occurs for any length of time.

• **Environmental factors:** When a Shih Tzu acts tired and down in the dumps and all health issues have been ruled out, it may be due to a change in the environment. This can be anything that has disrupted the Shih Tzu's normal routine and what he considers to be his 'life'. Examples are if a family member (human or animal) is no longer in the home, if a new family member has started living in the house or even if a favorite playmate such as a neighbor's dog is no longer available to interact with. Dogs are emotional creatures and the Shih Tzu breed can become very attached to others. Therefore, if someone or something is no longer there, a Shih Tzu may be depressed and missing the relationship. If this is the case, it is important to note that things do often get better with some time. Losing another dog or a main caretaker can be exceedingly rough on a dog and there is often a period of mourning. A Shih Tzu may whine, have no interest in activities, have a decreased appetite and want to sleep all day. (See also, 'Depression', page 148).

Time does heal and as days pass by memories will fade somewhat and most dogs eventually return to normal behavior. One thing that can help an unmotivated, lethargic and depressed dog is to introduce a new activity that has never been done before. Whether this is a walk along a river bank, playing in a children's pool outside on a summer's day or a trip to the local pet supply store to choose some new toys, an experience of something novel can perk up a Shih Tzu's mood and help him focus on something other than the thing that is making him sad.

• **Home Atmosphere** - While the most common reasons for a Shih Tzu acting tired are related to some sort of health problem or a change in the house such as the departure of a family member, there are some instances when a Shih Tzu mimics the general mood of his owner or the general vibe of the household. And owners do not need to be outwardly depressed or feeling down. Dogs have an incredible sense of their human's moods and can pick up vibes without any words spoken at all. If there are stressors, health problems or other issues that are causing an owner to feel under the weather, this can eventually cause a dog to react to that with altered behavior. Another possibility is if the household is having problems such as lots of arguing or yelling. This can be very upsetting to a dog and the response may be retreating and curling up. In these cases, it can appear to be an issue of being lethargic when in fact the Shih Tzu is responding to the turmoil.

Lethargy with Senior Shih Tzu

- Older Shih Tzu will have a gradual slowing down and because this happens progressively owners may not notice until there is a striking difference in resting and sleeping needs compared to the dog's younger self. Due to a lowered metabolism, senior dogs need fewer calories to fuel the body so there is often a lower food intake as well. Aches & pains may cause the senior dog to have trouble sleeping, which causes him to nap more during the day. With this said, sudden weakness is not a normal part of the aging process. There are many health issues common with older dogs that will cause the dog to be tired. This includes diabetes, arthritis and tooth infection. Far too many seniors are silently suffering and not receiving proper veterinary care because owners pass off lethargy as normal behavior once a dog reaches a certain age. Any noticeable changes in behavior, eating, exercise tolerance and/or activity levels should be reported to the veterinarian.

Severe Depression and Listlessness

- Some dogs can experience a funk that goes beyond acting tired. This will include changes in behavior such as cowering under a bed & other serious symptoms including a marked decrease in appetite that may even lead to weight loss. If a dog is acting this way it is always vital to rule out health issues and look to the household environment to see if any changes can be made. In very rare cases, canines can be diagnosed with clinical depression. When it is so severe that it interferes with a dog's quality of life, medication intervention may be recommended. Some common medicines that are used to treat this include Paxil, Prozac or Zoloft. Most dogs respond quickly & can be weaned off medication after 6 - 9 months. (See also, 'Depression', page 148).

Remember, just like humans, dogs have times of being tired and needing to rest. However, a wide range of health issues can cause weakness or lethargy long before other symptoms manifest. In most cases, when a dog is acting so out of character that an owner questions if something is wrong, it usually is. Owners are encouraged to not delay bringing their Shih Tzu in for a full checkup if the puppy or dog is acting overly tired.

Limping

Sometimes limping is a simple matter that can be dealt with at home, though sometimes it is a huge red flag to seek professional medical help. Let's try to sort this out.

Reason 1: The limp may be stemming from the paw(s). There are 3 issues that are not uncommon with the paws that can cause a Shih Tzu to favor one over the other or to walk with a faltering step.

Burns. Burns can happen so quickly and it is an element that many owners don't think about. The most common reason for burns to the paws is when the dog walks on hot pavement. And since owners have shoes on, they often to not realize just how hot it is. While it is highly recommended to always use a paw wax to keep paws protected, you will especially want to do this during the summer. It can also help to try and stay in shaded areas or at least take frequent breaks in the shade.

Embedded objects. Tiny pebbles are the main culprit. When outside on the grass or when walking on the sidewalk, tiny rocks can become stuck in between the paw pads, causing quite a bit of pain and then limping. This is also a common problem for those that walk along the beach (any areas that has sandy shores). The very best thing that you can do to protect your Shih Tzu from hot tarred roads and tiny pebbles getting stuck in the paws is to use a quality paw wax or slip doggie shoes on him.

Long hairs that grow out between the pads. It is one area that many owners don't think about when grooming their Shih Tzu. However, sometimes long hairs will grow there, pulling on the skin and causing pain when the dog walks…and this can cause a Shih Tzu to limp or favor one leg. This can be easily fixed with some simple grooming… You will want to clip hairs to be EVEN with the bottom of the pads… Do NOT try and snip hair that is between the pads! Only trim what is growing PASSED. If the skin looks very irritated, it should be looked at by a veterinarian, as the pull of the hair may have caused a breakage of the skin and there is a chance that it has become infected.

Reason 2: Injury to knee or hip. The Shih Tzu breed is prone to luxating patella. Hip dysplasia is always a *possibility*, however the Shih Tzu only makes up 3% of the dogs affected by this. While a Shih Tzu can be predisposed to luxating patella, just the wrong movement or too much impact when jumping can cause it to happen. To read more about this issue, please refer to the next section, 'Luxating Patella'.

Reason 3: Other medical reasons - This can range from a simple pulled muscle to a severe kidney infection. Because the reason for limping can actually be very serious, we highly encourage you to seek treatment at the vet's.

Luxating Patella

The patella (kneecap) is held together by tendons and tissue. When a dog has luxating patella (also known as subluxation of the patella, floating patella, floating kneecap or patellar luxation), the kneecap slips loose of the normally strong hold. The kneecap of the puppy may slip out and back in again or remain out. If not fixed, this can cause a dog to have chronic limping & pain. In severe cases, the dog may become lame with very limited or zero motor functions of the legs.

What Causes This- Occasionally it's caused by an injury, but in the absence of such proof, the weak tendons and/or shallow kneecap groove of luxating patella is considered hereditary, meaning this is passed down from dam or sire to puppy. A puppy may not show signs of this and only when he matures will it develop. This is much more common with toy breed dogs than larger dogs. Research shows that females are 5 times more likely to have this than males.

The Symptoms - A Shih Tzu may show just one or all of the symptoms of this. Also, symptoms may come and go. Many puppies let out a loud yelp when the kneecap slips out and then actually continue to walk and play without problems - at first - even though the kneecap is out of place. Later, when swelling and inflammation sets in, a dog will then have pain and mobility issues. Aside from the loud yelp of pain when the kneecap slips out of place, you may also notice: • Limping • An odd skipping walk • Avoidance of bending the hind leg • Suddenly stopping in the middle of running/playing. Often a dog will sit and then will hold his leg in an odd position or straighten it out.

How This is Diagnosed - Your dog's veterinarian should take a full round of x-rays and/or perform an ultrasound. It's important to know to what degree the kneecap has slipped. There are four degrees (grades) of luxation:

Grade 1: The knee only slips out when the vet moves it.
Grade 2: knee luxates occasionally when the Shih Tzu is walking or running. He may not seem to mind much or he may yelp, but it usually slides back by itself as the dog continues moving. Or it can be slipped back manually (the veterinarian may do this or may show you how to do this, if you wish).
Grade 3: The knee luxates frequently and causes chronic limping. Even when it is put back into place, it soon slips back out.
Grade 4: The knee moves out of place, stays that way & it cannot slide back into its socket. This grade is very rare but does happen sometimes.

Treatment

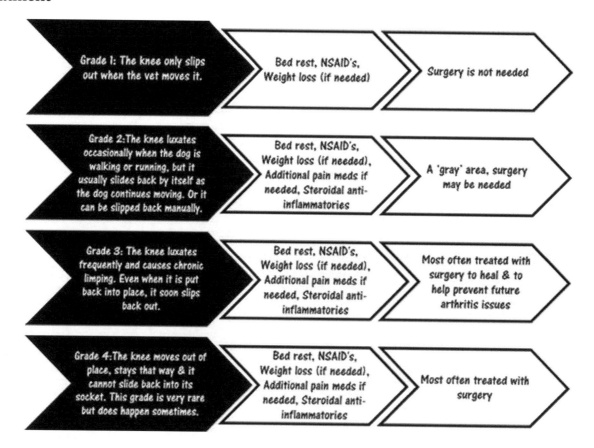

Rest- The first step in treatment is 'bed rest'. Whether the kneecap slipped back into place or if the vet was able to manipulate it back, it is important that the leg not move so that the tendons, ligaments and connective tissue around the area has time to heal. Therefore, a dog must be kept in a small, confined area where he cannot stand, walk or attempt to jump for about two weeks. A crate may be needed, however best is if you have gates that can be repositioned or you can obtain a very small canine playpen. The space must be small enough that the Shih Tzu cannot pace or walk around. It is understandable that owners find this difficult; after all, no dog likes to be confined to bed rest. However, we cannot overstate the importance of following this treatment step.

It's really sad how many owners tell us that they're very worried about their Shih Tzu not recovering, yet they come up with excuses of not following this step. The length of time that bed rest will be needed with depend on the severity of the issue. It can range from one week to six.

Non-Steroid Medication - Most veterinarians will prescribe a non-steroidal anti-inflammatories/pain medication. These are NSAIDs and the most common ones prescribed for dogs are Deramaxx, Etogesic, Previcox, Metacam, Zubrin or Rimadyl. Once a Shih Tzu is healed, many vets will suggest giving one dose an hour before exercise.

Weight Loss - While the Shih Tzu is not typically a breed that easily becomes overweight, the goal for a dog of any breed is weight loss (if at all possible) since even a pound lost is less strain on the body. IF your vet suggests this, for weight loss, we suggest feeding the same amount of food, but choosing foods that will add up to less calories. This can be accomplished by adding fresh fruits and vegetables to meals, to take the place of higher calorie ingredients.

Additional Pain Medication - Often the listed medication will be sufficient to bring discomfort to a tolerable level for Grade 1's. However, if a dog is suffering, most vets will give a stronger pain medication.

Steroidal anti-inflammatories - These can be damaging to the immune system, and have some side effects. Therefore, this is not always used on a toy breed dog. If it is, it is for short term only and at a low dose.

Surgery - Surgery is performed if a dog is in constant pain. Most often, surgery is not done for a grade 1. Grade 2 is a 'grey zone', where some vets will suggest it and others suggest waiting to see if bed rest and anti-inflammatories will work. For grade 3 (and 4), surgery is most often the best answer. If one waits too long and delays surgery for these severe cases, arthritis can set in, causing more pain and complications. Recovery is about 8 weeks and this can seem like a long time; however prognosis is good and most dogs fully recover, able to walk, play and be as active as ever once they heal. We strongly suggest choosing a Board Certified surgeon.

Medications to help prevent arthritis - The knees are prone to arthritis and if a knee has slipped, it is even more prone to this. For this reason, some vets will suggest a monthly shot of Adequan (or a similar medication). Adequan is an injectable solution used to control the signs of degenerative joint disease and traumatic arthritis. It promotes healthy cartilage in the joints and can improve range of motion

Ongoing Treatment Once a Shih Tzu Has Healed – It is important to do follow-up care.

Exercise - If a knee heals and the surrounding tissue is deemed strong, it will be time to gradually get a Shih Tzu back to walking and exercising as normal to strengthen the area. With the vet's approval, start walking your Tzu on a slight incline as opposed to level surfaces when taking him for a walk. This will help strengthen the muscles that surround the patella.

Omega 3 - Omega 3 supplements help control inflammation and also block enzymes that break down cartilage.

Prevention & How to Keep this at Bay

1) Only purchase a puppy whose parents and grandparents have been cleared of knee issues (as well as hip issues and other genetic problems). Have this in writing.

2) Since trauma can cause this or can be the trigger for a knee that is weak, never allow your Shih Tzu to jump a distance that is any higher than the dog is tall. For example, if your Shih Tzu is 10 inches tall (from floor to withers [shoulders], he should not jump down from more than 10 inches. This means that a Shih Tzu should not be allowed to jump out of many types of cars, off of chairs or even your bed. You may want to think about getting indoor canine steps or ramps to place against any furniture that your Shih Tzu loves to go up onto such as the sofa.

3) Make sure to routinely exercise your Shih Tzu. Walking is the best activity for your dog and at least a daily walk should be part of your normal routine. Two shorter walks are even better.

4) Early treatment is important in regard to how well a dog will heal. Look for signs of limping, if a dog is running or playing around and suddenly stops and sits down, or is favoring a leg. If you suspect a problem, have your Shih Tzu checked out. It's much easier to treat a 'grade one' condition than a grade 2, 3 or 4.

5) All Shih Tzu should have their knees checked every 2 years, even if they seem fine.

6) A Shih Tzu that has a history of a luxating patella should be kept as trim and lean as possible by eating a diet consisting of freshly cooked foods that contain plenty of vitamin C, as well as having regular moderate exercise. Foods that a Shih Tzu can eat that provide a good amount of vitamin C are: Potatoes, blueberries, cranberries, raspberries, blackberries, and strawberries. You can mix any of the listed foods into a Shih Tzu's normal food. And if you home cook for your Shih Tzu, you can certainly be creative by putting any of these ingredients into meals.

Here is a great recipe that offers fresh cooked food and vitamin C:

The Ingredients You Will Need:

• 2 cups of white chicken breast meat, cooked and cut into cubes – You can cut it into cubes and bake it at 425 for approximately 20 minutes or you can steam the pieces.
• 3/4 cup potatoes, cubed and boiled until just soft
• 3/4 cup fresh blueberries
• 1/2 cup plain whole white yogurt or sour cream
• 1 tbsp. apple cider vinegar
• 1 tbsp. pineapple juice

How to Prepare It- 1. Toss the chicken, potatoes, and blueberries together in a bowl; don't mash them up too much. **2.** Mix the yogurt or sour cream, apple cider vinegar and pineapple juice together and pour this over the chicken/potatoes/blueberry mixture. **3.** Just mix it up a bit more and serve it to your Shih Tzu. **Tip:** You can keep any leftovers in the fridge for 5 days. This is actually pretty yummy and you may find that you enjoy eating it too!

Skin Problems

Please note: This is an extremely short section, though you will still have all the information you are looking for. As you may remember from this book's Introduction, in order to make it possible for you to have this AllShihTzu - Print Edition book, we needed to make some smart decisions regarding length. We have tried very hard to not repeat text unless necessary. We have been so completely thorough in our information, that just about every topic regarding skin issues has already been covered under other sections in this book. If your Shih Tzu has dry skin, please refer to the 'Grooming', 'Choosing Your Products' section for complete details (page 76). If your Shih Tzu has scaly skin with hair loss, since skin & coat go hand-in-hand, please refer to 'Hair & Coat' (page 91) If there are hot spots and/or irritated skin, since this is *almost always* related to allergies, look to 'Allergies' page 215. If your Shih Tzu has issues with his paws, refer to the 'Health – Body Part Specific', 'Paws' section, page 191. If there is flaky/ flaky & oily skin, look to 'Hair & Coat', Dandruff, page 95. For round, hairless regions, this may be parasites, look to 'Worms', page 249. And for very smelly skin, look to 'Smells & Odors', page 241. The only skin topic not covered elsewhere is Demodectic Mange.

Demodectic Mange – This is also known as red mange, follicular mange, or puppy mange & is a particular type of skin disease. There is conflicting information around the web, so we hope that we can clear up any confusion for you. This is most often seen in puppies, although it can develop in an older dog. It is caused by a mite, called the Demodex mite. You may wish we did not tell you this, however the microscopic Demodex mite lives on all humans and all dogs.

They are extremely tiny, just 1/4 of one mm, residing inside the hair follicles of both hominids & canines alike (and other animals too!). Again, you may not want to read this, however on humans, they also live on our skin, eyelids and in the crease of our nose. There is never a time that these mites are not on a dog; they spend their entire lives there, reproduce there and new generations take over. The life cycle of any one particular mite is about 1 month. So, a mange infection is not the assault of 'new' creatures on a dog. This all has to do with how a dog's body responds to the mites that are always there. Or, trouble can arise if the normal mite population increases beyond what a dog can handle. Certain situations (such as very dirty living conditions like unethical kennels) or a dog's weakened immune system can cause his body to react badly to these ever-present mites.

This affects a dog's skin first and then the coat. Patches of the coat may fall out; this can happen in just one particular location or several across the body. As the hairs fall out and areas become thinner, you will often notice that the skin underneath is pink. There may also be an odd, unpleasant odor. There may be one spot or countless spots. The skin may or may not be itchy. The lesions themselves are red and often crusty. The skin may also look moist and/or greasy. These lesions that cause pink/red skin and hair loss can be anywhere on the body, but often start on the head (around the muzzle or eyes). With very young puppies (3 to 6 months old), the spots may tend to start off on the legs.

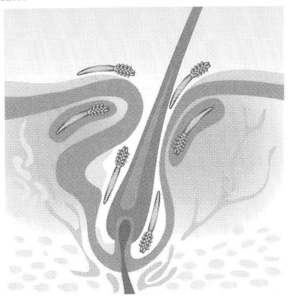

If this is suspected, the veterinarian should do what is called a deep skin scraping that takes a sample that can then be observed under strong microscopes. If it is found to be demodectic mange, it can be treated with prescription medication.

Common misperceptions: These cannot be inherited, because all dogs have them to some degree. One issue that can happen however, is if a female who just gave birth to a litter has a larger than normal number of mites on her (and has thereby most likely been diagnosed with Demodectic Mange, these mites can travel to the newborn puppies (who had none on them, since they were just born). Those pups may or may not show a reaction to this. If a female has a known case of Demodectic Mange, she should not be bred.

Smells & Odors

There are many different reasons why a Shih Tzu might have a bad smell and this section is going to go over the various causes along with steps you can immediately take to resolve the problem. Some owners may have noticed a slight odor that worsened over time and others will see (or rather, smell) a problem that seemingly popped up overnight. There is always a reason why a particular odor is emitting from a dog and there is really no smell that is considered normal, other than the very brief noxious fumes that will surround the dog due to flatulence.

Mouth: There are several reasons why a bad smell may be coming from the mouth. As to not repeat text, please refer to the 'Health', "Bad Breath' section, page 221.

Ears: A bad smell may be due to excess ear wax and/or infection. As to not repeat text, please refer to the 'Health – Body Part Specific', 'Ears' section, page 187.

All-over Body Odor: There are some cases where you either cannot pinpoint where the smell is coming from or it really does appear to be coming from the dog's entire body. These issue will be covered here.

Shih Tzu smells after going outside: This is not all that uncommon. The skin is constantly producing body oils. These work to keep both skin and coat healthy. However, over time these oils accumulate since oil does not evaporate. It is recommended to give a Shih Tzu a bath every 3 weeks since this seems to be the tipping point when too much oil is trapped beneath the coat and needs to be cleansed away. If a Shih Tzu goes outside and smells bad after being in the rain or even if there is some humidity in the air, the moisture mixes with the oils in the coat and this can produce a really bad smell that some refer to as 'dog odor'. Therefore, this most commonly occurs when a Shih Tzu is one week or less away from his scheduled bath time.

Another possible reason could be if the dog rolled in feces or other sticky matter, however since most owners are keeping a close eye on their puppy or dog, this is less likely to be the cause of a mystery smell.

Prevention and treatment: If the smell is really bad, you can give your Shih Tzu a bath a bit early as long as you are

using quality products that will not dry out the skin or coat. Be sure to do a full body brush beforehand. If your Shih Tzu has just recently had a bath (within the past 2 weeks), you can give the coat a good brushing. This will do two things: It will lift the hairs on the dense coat, allowing the moisture to air dry as you brush. In addition, the brushing will pull out dead hairs that are trapped close to the skin, which will be covered in the water/oil combination. Removing these hairs will often remove the odor.

Shih Tzu smells after going to the bathroom:

There are actually several different reasons for this odor problem. In regard to urinating, there can be some splash-back, particularly if a male Shih Tzu pees on a tree or other object that may cause the urine to splatter back onto his genital area and/or underbelly. Female dogs can have some splash-back as well, depending on their positioning when urinating. This can cause a Shih Tzu to reek of urine.

In regard to bowel movements, there are a couple of odor causing possibilities. When a dog pushes out a stool - and especially if that feces is large and/or hard - it can cause the anal glands to secrete more scent oil than normal. The oil from anal glands is often referred to as one of the worst smells possible. It is usually quite overpowering and can just about knock you over. Additionally, if there are any feces that have become stuck to the fine hairs around the anus, this will cause a Shih Tzu to smell like poop long after he has gone to the bathroom.

Prevention and treatment: If there is a urine smell due to some being on the body, both genders can be wiped with a quality canine wipe. If there is fecal matter stuck to the hairs, a small amount that is still moist can be cleaned up with a canine wipe or a canine 'tushie wipe'. Take care to only wipe out and not toward the genital area. While females are more prone to the issue, both genders can develop a UTI if feces travels to the urinal opening. If the poop is dried, this can be scrubbed clean with a full or partial bath.

If the origin of the smell is anal gland oil, the area should be inspected to look for any possible tears in the skin. If an anal sac tore open when the Shih Tzu was going to the bathroom, this broken skin will now be vulnerable to infection. It can be washed with warm water and a dab of antibiotic gel can be applied. You'll want to keep a close eye on this, however, since it can become infected. If there is any redness, swelling, signs of discomfort and/or if the tear has not healed within 3 days it should be treated by a veterinarian. You may also wish to refer to 'Health -Body Part Specific', 'Anal Glands', page 186.

My Shih Tzu smells bad even after a bath: A couple of things may be at play if a Shih Tzu has a bad odor even when he has just been scrubbed clean:

1) Scrubbing was not done deep enough. During a bath, it is not just the coat that needs to be cleansed, it is the skin. You may find it helpful to use a small canine bath scrub brush; the bristles will reach down through the coat and also this method of cleaning a Shih Tzu works well because it massages the skin which is super healthy for stimulating blood flow and cleaning out skin pores. As a side note, do be sure to rinse out the bubbles very well and to follow with both conditioner and a leave-in spray to protect the coat and add a nice scent.

2) Low-grade products were used. For shampoo to actually clean away oils and wash away bad smells, it needs to have both the right amount of surfactants (the cleansing agents) & emulsifiers (this enables the water to mix with the oil to then wash it away). Cheap products will either be lacking this or will have subpar ingredients. You'll want to take care to have top-notch grooming products. ** *If neither of these tips help, look ahead to 'Smells Bad all the Time'.*

Female Shih Tzu Smells Bad During Heat: During heat, discharge is a mixture of blood, endometrial tissue and watery body fluids. While blood does not have much of an odor, when it dries it can emit a smell that may be described as musty. Minuscule dried pieces of endometrial tissue can also start to emit a stinky smell if they have dried and become crusted on the dog. While this is not usually an overpowering odor, some owners who may be sensitive to this particular odor will notice it more than others.

You can give partial or full baths during this time. Also, if you place a doggie diaper on your Shih Tzu (which is highly recommended so that discharge does not accumulate on furniture, bedding, carpeting, etc.) you may want to change these more often. Depending on how heavy the flow is, a new diaper may need to be placed on every 4 to 12 hours.

Female Shih Tzu Has Vaginal Smell: First reassess if this is a urine or feces smell, if so see previous advice for
'smells after going to the bathroom'. If this is not the cause (and since even if your female is in heat, this does not normally cause an odor), this may point to an issue such as a yeast infection, a UTI (urinary tract infection) or another health issue that should be diagnosed by the veterinarian.

If a Shih Tzu Smells Really Bad All the Time – Skin Infection: While the listed causes for odors are most often to blame for bad odors, if a Shih Tzu has a constant smell, this may point to a skin infection. Just a small infection can cause a bad odor, so if there is a full body yeast, bacterial or fungal infection, this will not often go away with baths even if you are using good products and cleaning your Shih Tzu on a regular schedule. Signs of this include flaking and/or oily skin and itching. The skin may have a musty or sour-like smell. While it is recommended to have a veterinarian diagnose this, you may want to speak with your vet about treating this at home with a quality medicated shampoo for fungus or bacterial skin infection. While the names of the ingredients may throw you off, those with Coal Tar, Salicylic Acid & Micronized Sulfur are safe for dogs short-term (2 to 3 weeks) and can also help with scaling issues. *To treat yeast, fungal or bacterial skin infections at home, we suggest (with vet approval), SynergyLabs Richard's Organics Anti-Bacterial Shampoo with Tea Tree Oil and Neem Oil.*

If a Shih Tzu's Paws Smell: The most common reason for a bad smell coming from the paws is the previously mentioned yeast infection. Since a dog's paws may pick up moisture every day from the grass and other outside surfaces, it is not easy to keep them dry. The area between the toes, like the wrinkles, is damp, dark and warm which makes the feet an attractive area for yeast growth. A vet can diagnose this. The treatment is often a medicated wash, with the paws being soaped up and cleaned 3 times per week for 2 weeks. Ask your vet if you can use a medicated shampoo for yeast (see previous).

How to Keep a Shih Tzu Smelling Nice- There are many things that you can do to keep your Shih Tzu smelling fresh and clean.

1) Time the baths. Once every 3 weeks works well for most Shih Tzu since this is the time lapse in which oils are just accumulating enough that if you wait another week, the dog will start to smell bad.
2) Brush often. Do a good brushing at least 2 times per week. While a slew of people like to say that the Shih Tzu (or other breeds with hair instead of fur) do not shed, this is not true. All dogs lose hair on a continual basis, just like we humans do. Dead hairs can fall back into the coat, fall down to the skin level and mix with body oils. This can cause a really bad musty and stinky smell. By keeping the coat free of these dead hairs and by distributing oils with the brush, it can help keep a Shih Tzu smelling nice.
3) Use a nice smelling leave-in spray. There are some great canine spritzes that have two benefits: they give off a fresh, clean smell and they protect the hairs from contact friction, the rays of the sun and from drying effects of arid air. Most will need to be applied every other day and be sure to not use a lot; all you need is a light spritz over the body with a quick brush down in the direction of the hair growth.

Spaying & Neutering

With a female Shih Tzu, spaying refers to when the dog's uterus and the ovaries are surgically removed. For the male Shih Tzu, neutering means that the testicles are surgically removed. It is a common belief that this is only done to stop dogs from mating. While this is one of the end results, there are also other important ways in which this will help your Shih Tzu live a healthier and longer life.

When a female Shih Tzu is spayed, all benefits to the dog include:

• Stops the chance of her of getting pregnant. Without proper pre-pregnancy testing (including measuring pelvic width), carrying a litter and giving birth can be exceedingly stressful and even dangerous for a dog. And since dogs do not enter the human equivalent of menopause, females of any age can get accidentally pregnant.
• Eliminates her chances of developing ovarian cancer and greatly reduces her chances for developing mammary cancer. This will also decrease her odds of developing ovarian infections. The younger she is when being spayed, the better the chances.
• Cuts down on urges to run away when in heat (some females will actively pursue males)
• Stops possible hormone related mood swings
• Helps with marking issues (90% of the time if a female is spayed before the first heat); keep in mind that territorial females mark just as males do.

When a male Shih Tzu is neutered, the benefits to the dog include:

• Eliminates the chance that he could impregnate a female.
• Eliminates the possibility of testicular tumors
• Reduces the risk of prostate disease – This is a very common and serious health issue for male dogs. Roughly 60% of male dogs, that are older than 5 years old and not neutered, show symptoms of an enlarged prostate.
• Cuts down on territorial marking
• Cuts down on urges to run away (males can smell a female in heat 1 to 3 miles away)

Sorting out the Facts

1) Neutering a dog will not automatically make him depressed, lose strength or decrease his activity level. Studies have shown that male dogs do not act out any mating behavior unless they are moved by their own hormones in reaction to a female dog that is in heat. When neutered, it does not trouble a dog that he cannot mate. When a male dog is neutered, his body can then use its energy for other things besides mating. A male dog will behave normally in all regards of activity and in having endurance to exercise.

2) A female dog will not automatically become overweight and/or lazy. When given the appropriate amount of food and exercised properly, female dogs will not have any noticeable changes in weight or activity.

The Age this is Typically Done - The younger a dog is, the better it is for their health. Studies show that a female's best chance of good health is to be spayed before her first heat. The odds of developing mammary cancer increases even if the dog goes through one heat and increases as each future heat cycle is allowed to happen. To offer her the best chance, a female Shih Tzu should be spayed by 3 or 4 months old. However, even if an owner waits, having this done at any age will have benefits. With a male, this is typically done before he reaches puberty. This way, there is not a chance for habits such as marking to be established. The age of puberty will be from between 4 and 6 months old.

How the Procedure of Spaying and Neutering is Performed -Spaying females is performed by giving the dog general anesthesia. A small incision is made in the abdomen. The uterus is then removed from that small incision. The ovarian ligaments and blood vessels are securely tied. The abdominal tissues are stitched back together in layers (internally). Outside (external) stitches are put in place as well. Neutering a male is performed by

making an incision in front of the dog's scrotum. The testicles are then removed through this small incision. The blood vessels are tied off and cut. The incision will either have stitches that dissolve or ones which will need to be removed 10 days after the surgery.

What to Expect Afterwards- For both female and male dogs, water should not be given for 1 hour after the procedure. For the female Shih Tzu, it is important that she be allowed to completely rest for 10 days. Though rare, if she shows any signs of vomiting, tremors, pale gums or bleeding, this indicates complications and the dog should be brought to the veterinarian immediately. A female may try to lick her stitches and this can cause infection; therefore steps can be taken to prevent her from doing so. In about 2 weeks, she will have a checkup to make sure all is well and stitches will be removed at that time. For a male, there is usually swelling for about 3 days. There may be some light bruising. Discomfort is usually low and most dogs do not need pain medication. The majority of male dogs are ready to play, exercise and run around as normal even just days later; however to make sure that the incision heals correctly, it is recommended to limit these activities for 2 weeks.

Spaying/ Neutering Senior Dogs - Some owners do not see the point of spaying or neutering an older, senior dog. However, doing so may help to extend a dog's life span. There are several reasons why including:

• **A female may have heat cycles for her entire life.** Dogs do not have the canine equivalent of menopause. Since a female can conceive during heat, there is always the chance of an accidental pregnancy. Having puppies in the senior years can be very dangerous for both the female dog and impending puppies.
• **It still decreases chances of cancer.** Having this done, even to a senior dog, can be very helpful in allowing him/her to live as long as possible.
• **When a female is spayed, this reduces hormone changes in her body.** These changes can affect other health conditions a dog may have including diabetes and epilepsy.

Swallowed Something - Rocks, Bones, Batteries, Coins

Hopefully you've puppy-proofed your house, no matter how old your Shih Tzu is, to prevent your dog from mouthing, chewing and potentially swallowing something that he shouldn't. However, even the most diligent of owners can mistakenly leave out an item or a very clever Shih Tzu can latch onto something that was thought of as safe and off limits. So, unfortunately, there may very well be a time that your Shih Tzu ingests a non-food item. It's important to know what to do and how to react if your Shih Tzu does this. Some objects may pass right through however others may cause a partial or full blockage that can take up to several days to manifest and with other swallowed things, quick action from owners can save the dog's life. We are going to look at some of the most common items swallowed by Shih Tzu and exactly what you should do if this happens.

Rocks - It may seem odd that a puppy or dog would purposely swallow a pebble or rock, however this does happen. This may occur while the Shih Tzu is nibbling on some grass, although some dogs will lick and mouth stones and end up ingesting them in one gulp. It is theorized that one reason canines even bother to mouth rocks is due to the salty taste. River or ocean rocks that have been smoothed by water are rather easy for dogs to swallow, though if a Shih Tzu is chewing down a mouthful of grass, he may accidentally ingest some rough-edged pebbles as well. Some owners do not even notice this at all and only realize that it happened after the fact when they see small rocks in the dog's stool. What you do if your Shih Tzu swallows a rock will really depend on the size of the stone vs the size of the dog. If you know that the pebble was approximately the size of a pill that the dog could hypothetically gulp down, there is a good chance that it will pass through. However, in some cases a Shih Tzu may end up with 5, 10 or even more rocks in his stomach. Some may pass through and others may not.

You will want to seek help immediately if the dog is showing any signs of distress, alert the veterinarian as to what happened (it's also important to make contact so that you can be given instructions regarding what to do if your Shih Tzu shows signs of distress when the office is closed). If the Shih Tzu is not showing any symptoms of blockage, most owners will be instructed to take a 'wait and see' approach. As with other non-food objects, it will be important for someone to be watching the dog for several days since obstruction can occur at any time as the rock moves through the body's digestive system. Even if you are not sure how many rocks your Shih Tzu ate, it's best to check the stool and count how many are expelled.

Chicken bone - Bones and particularly cooked bones should not be given to puppies or dogs due to their tendency to splinter. Chicken bones are the biggest cause for concern, although any small bone such as those from spare ribs, turkey, fish and beef can be dangerous as well. Cooked bones can cause much more damage than raw since the cooking process causes an evaporation of both moisture and calcium deposits within the marrow that makes the bones very brittle. This can cause injury to the soft tissue in the mouth, bone fragments can become lodged between teeth and the tongue, esophagus, stomach, intestines and/or rectal areas are all vulnerable to being punctured. If your

Shih Tzu swallows a chicken bone or other meat bone that is apt to splinter, here is what you can do:

1) Inspect your dog's mouth for any signs of injury. You'll want to carefully look at the tongue, inner cheek tissue and between all teeth. Small bone fragments are similar to needles and can pierce the skin quite deeply; the piece may be imbedded. **2) It is often not recommended to induce vomiting** since the bone can cause quite a bit of damage on the way up. If it made its way to the stomach, it's best to allow it to remain there and take the next step. **3) Feeding your Shih Tzu certain foods** after he eats a chicken bone can help offer a cushion around it, and this can help it pass through the body. Some good choices are rice and bread. You'll want to make this as tempting to your dog as possible, so adding some warm chicken or beef broth over the food can tempt an otherwise not-so-hungry Shih Tzu to ingest a bit of the mixture. **4) You'll want to keep a very close eye on your puppy or dog for at least 3 days.** And as with rocks and other objects that can possibly cause obstruction, it is really best for someone to remain home with the dog even if this means calling in friends, family members and/or taking time off from work. You'll be looking for any signs of distress including: vomiting, dry heaving, straining when going to the bathroom, a hunched over posture or odd positioning (if the bone is poking into the stomach lining a dog may twist his body into strange positions in an attempt to lessen the pain), breathing issues, weakness and/or reluctance to eat.

Battery, Chewed or Swallowed - While it will generally be smaller watch batteries that a Shih Tzu may swallow, any size can be chewed and cause serious issues; All cases of battery ingestion or chewing must be taken very seriously. AAA, AA, C, D and 9 volt all have corrosive properties. If a Shih Tzu swallows a tiny disc shaped battery, while smaller these are actually just as dangerous. If the battery case is punctured, burns to the mouth can occur immediately, though signs of this can take up to 12 hours to manifest. These can be very serious tissue burns that manifest as painful ulcers on the tongue, lips and inside the mouth. And even if a Shih Tzu swallows a battery whole, there are still dangers since the casing may have been punctured by a sharp tooth before being gulped down. Finally, depending on the size of the battery, stomach or intestinal blockage is always a concern. If your Shih Tzu swallows a battery of any kind or if a battery is missing and you suspect that your puppy or dog may have ingested it, here is what to do:

1) Bring your Shih Tzu to the veterinarian or closest animal hospital ASAP. While there are some steps that may be taken at home and even if your Shih Tzu appears to be fine, internal burns can take hours to appear and it will be imperative to have x-rays taken to determine where the battery is located in the body.

Crazy Things that Dogs Have Swallowed, Confirmed Via X-Ray & Removed Via Surgery
6 inch corn dog stick
Rubber duck
Metal shish-kabob skewers
43 socks (swallowed by a Great Dane, all were removed at one time)
Light bulb (it remained intact; small A15 series swallowed by a Golden Retriever)
Fishing hook (done by many dogs; one was a Shih Tzu that gobbled down a mackeral with the hook still in it)
9 sewing needles (swallowed by a Chihuahua)
2 cups of gravel from turtle tank
A quarter and 104 pennies (swallowed by a Pug)
Pocket knife
Hacky Sack ball
Matchbox car
Mini headphones
Arrowhead
Tube of antibiotic cream
Candy wrapper
Engagement ring
Metal fork
Phone charger
10 inch bread knife (swallowed by a Jack Russell Terrier)
Bra (swallowed by a 3 month old Rat Terrier)

2) Do not induce vomiting. This can cause serious burns to the throat.
3) You may be instructed to first rinse your Shih Tzu's mouth with lukewarm water or small amounts of milk for 10 to 15 minutes (your vet will tell you how much, based on your dog's weight, since too much can cause diarrhea).

4) At the clinic, the mouth and esophagus will be examined to look for potential chemical burns and treated accordingly. Medications to help try and protect the gastrointestinal tract will be given; this may be given at the office and if blockage is ruled out, you may be instructed to continue giving this to your Shih Tzu at home. X-rays will be taken to determine the location of the battery and decision will be made regarding surgical removal. If it is suspected that the battery is leaking fluid in the stomach, it will need to be removed ASAP.

The full extent of burns from a dog eating a battery can take up to 12 hours to appear. For this reason, a Shih Tzu may be kept at the clinic or may be sent home where owners will need to keep a super close eye on the dog. Signs to look for include developing lesions in the mouth and/or lips, drooling, weakness, reluctance to eat, vomiting and/or any signs of pain or distress. Battery burns on dogs are often treated with strong pain medication and antibiotics to help prevent infection. Those with oral injury are often fed soft wet foods until the burns have healed.

Coin - If a Shih Tzu swallows a penny, this can cause life-threatening toxicity. This is because pennies that were minted from 1982 and on are predominantly zinc (97.5 % zinc, 2.5% copper) which is considered to be highly toxic to canines. Pennies made from 1962 to 1982 contain smaller levels of zinc alloy (5%). The time that it takes for a dog's stomach acid to dissolve the penny enough to release the zinc into a dog's bloodstream can range from just minutes to several hours; though the rate of speed at which this occurs will vary and how much food a Shih Tzu has in his stomach is just one element that will have an effect on this.

Signs of zinc poisoning include weakness, lack of appetite, vomiting, diarrhea, a yellowing of the eyes and/or dark urine. If your Shih Tzu swallowed a penny or got into some coins and you are not sure if a penny was included with that, you will want to call the vet right away and bring your dog to the office ASAP. When you call you may be instructed to induce vomiting, which is typically done by giving a dog 1 teaspoon of hydrogen peroxide per 10 pounds of body weight. Even if the penny does come back up, it will be important to have x-rays taken to make sure that there are no more in the stomach. If one or more are found to be in a dog's stomach, these can often be removed via endoscopy. In addition, the chemical reaction between the zinc and stomach acid (hydrochloric acid) can be caustic to the stomach lining and the vet will treat for this as well.

If a Shih Tzu swallows a nickel and/or dime and an owner is 100% positive that a penny was not eaten, the vet may recommend the "wait and see' approach to see if the coin(s) pass, often assisted with a high fiber diet (added green beans and/or pumpkin) or if more than one coin was swallowed, may recommend x-rays to determine how many are present and if intervention is recommended to prevent blockage.

Please Remember - There is no limit to what a Shih Tzu can swallow other than what cannot physically fit into his mouth after being chewed. Whether due to boredom, curiosity or a combination of both, there are endless items that a Shih Tzu may mouth, chew and/or ingest. This includes shoe laces, jewelry, plastic bottle caps and tiny children's toys. There are documented cases of larger dogs actually swallowing whole miniature light bulbs, metal knitting needles, gravel from a turtle tank and even fishing hooks.

While puppies are more apt to mouth things than older dogs, this is not an age related issue and a Shih Tzu of any age (even one that never did anything like this before) can end up swallowing something that he should not. We encourage you to routinely 'puppy proof' your home, no matter how old your Shih Tzu is. Never think that this is something that 'happens to someone else' and let's all try to create the safest environment possible for our incredible canine family members.

Worms

It's important to understand how serious worms are.

Tapeworms - Tapeworms are flat worms with segments across the body. The head usually has suckers or muscular grooves that enable the tapeworm to attach itself to an animal's intestine. An adult tapeworm living inside a dog can be as large as 20 inches (50 cm) long. The tapeworm stays alive by sucking nutrients from a dog through its skin. Especially in puppies, tapeworms can cause lack of growth, anemia and intestinal blockage. *Image Attribution: By CDC [Public domain], via Wikimedia Commons*

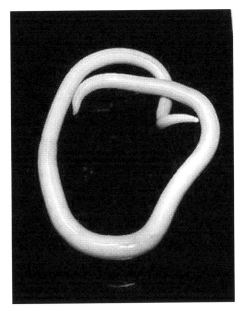

How a Dog Gets Tapeworms - A dog can get tapeworms by swallowing a flea. Fleas can contain tapeworm eggs. In rare cases, a dog that gains access to a rodent or lizard may get tapeworms from these animals also.

Signs - You may see dried segments of the tapeworm around your dog's anus. These will be about as small as a grain of rice. Because this parasite causes irritation, your dog may scoot his rear across the ground. Full worms may actually be present in a dog's bowel movement; these worms can sometimes be seen moving.

Prevention - A Shih Tzu puppy should have a feces analysis performed by a veterinarian at the age of 20 days. This is done because a puppy can be born with tapeworms. If found, the dog should be de-wormed, which is done with medication given by a veterinarian. After that, de-wormings, which begin at the age of 6 weeks, will help prevent this.

Treatment - If you suspect that your Shih Tzu has tapeworms, your veterinarian will most likely want to examine a stool sample. Once confirmed, this is very treatable with medication.

Hookworms - Hookworms are a nasty little worm! This parasite hooks onto a dog's intestine with its sharp teeth and then it pokes a hole in a blood vessel. It will then begin to suck blood from the dog. If a Shih Tzu was infested with 300 hookworms, the dog would lose 5 to 10% of his blood supply each day. For this reason, hookworms can be fatal if not treated.

How a Dog Gets Hookworms - There are 3 ways that a dog may get hookworms. A puppy may be born with them, a puppy may get them when drinking mom's milk or a Shih Tzu may swallow a hookworm larva. These microscopic larvae can be found on anything from blades of grass to infected dog food dishes.

Signs - Once infected, the symptoms can mimic other health conditions: Diarrhea (often very black or bloody), vomiting, loss of appetite, pale colored mucous membranes may appear in the dog's mouth, weakness, emaciation and/or slowed growth.

Prevention - Preventing hookworms is done via several methods. Good hygiene is very important. The dog's feces should not be left in the yard outside. Having human family members wash their hands often is helpful as well as keeping your Shih Tzu well-groomed and clean. Because hookworms can travel from one dog, to an environment and then on to another dog, it is best to keep away from unclean dog parks. In addition, if you ever feed your Shih Tzu homemade food, be sure that the meat is cooked well. When cleaning your home, using bleach on hard surface floors can kill hookworm larvae. The most important prevention is to have your Shih Tzu receive regular checkups and bring your dog to the veterinarian at the first signs of any symptoms.

Treatment – Once confirmed by a veterinarian, this is very treatable via prescribed oral medications.

Roundworms
Roundworms are one of the most common parasites found in dogs. They are rather big, 4 inches (10.1 cm) long. They are usually a white color and resemble a strand of cooked spaghetti. These worms can live inside a dog's intestine and live off of partial digested food.

How a Dog Gets Roundworms - A puppy may be born with Roundworms if the dam was infected. The puppy may also become infected from its mother's milk. Even if the mother dog has tested negative for roundworms, she may still be infected if the larvae have not fully developed. A dog may also pick up this parasite by eating soil that contains eggs or by eating or chewing on small rodents.

Signs - In the beginning stages of a roundworm infestation, there are no symptoms; therefore regular de-worming is very important. Follow the schedule that your puppy's veterinarian gives to you. If not checked and a dog becomes severely infected with roundworms signs may include: The dog may vomit up the worms (you will know that it is a roundworm because its body will not be segmented as a tapeworm is), the dog may have a swollen stomach and the dog may show signs of pneumonia as the worms migrate through the dog's body into the lungs and other areas.

Prevention - Keeping regular vet checkups and not allowing your dog to chew at outside elements such as soil or rodents will help to keep this at bay.

Treatment - Medication will work to get rid of these worms. It will cause the worms to let go of the dog's body and pass out through bowel movements. A dog may need many treatments. Prognosis is good, if this is caught in enough time before too much damage to the dog's body is done.

Heartworms
Heartworms are about the same size as the Roundworm and Tapeworm. A case of Heartworm disease can be fatal. This worm lives inside of a dog's right ventricle of the heart and nearby blood vessels. A dog may catch heartworms if an infected mosquito bites him. It is hard to believe that something as small as a mosquito can be so dangerous to a dog! Heartworm larvae will enter into the dog and grow. Within about 3 months, they will complete their travel to their destination: the dog's heart. Growing up to 14 inches (35.5 cm) these worms can overtake a dog's body. After 6 months, they are reproducing.

Signs - Many dogs do not show signs until later stages at which time it may be too late for treatment. If a dog does show early signs, this includes one or all of the following: Trouble breathing, vomiting, weight loss, coughing and/or weakness. Late stages of this canine disease are exercise intolerance and/or fainting.

Prevention - Prevention is done by giving your Shih Tzu heartworm prevention medication. Choosing to forgo doing this can lead to death. Many owners are concerned about heartworm medications making their Shih Tzu sick and for good reason! Some that are just fine for other breeds cannot be tolerated by Shih Tzu. We believe topical Advantage Multi to be the one most tolerated by Shih Tzu. Cydectin is also a very good one that works very well and is considered safe for toy breeds. We do NOT like Comfortis or Trifexis! Ivermectin is 'okay' and only sometimes tolerated.

Treatment - Once a dog is badly infected, treatment can be very tricky. Arsenic-based drugs are used to kill adult heartworms and the dog must be very carefully watched by the veterinarian. Usually a dog will need to have in-patient care for at least several days. As the adult heartworms are rid from the dog's body, they may block blood vessels to the dog's lungs, causing a pulmonary embolism, which can be fatal. To help reduce the chance of this happening, the dog must be kept very calm and quiet for 4 weeks following treatment. In the most severe cases, surgery is performed to remove the worms. Both of these treatments are not always successful. In some cases, a dog needs to be euthanized.

Ring Worms
Contrary to its name, ringworm is not a worm at all, it is a fungus called Dermatophytes. Dermaphtytes means 'plants that live on the skin'. In the past, because of the circular lesions made by the fungi they were thought to be caused by worms, hence the name ringworm. The fungi live on the surface of the skin and in the skin follicles, feeding on dead skin tissue and hair. There are three different types of fungus that can cause ringworm but the most predominant ones found on dogs is called: Microsporum canis.

How Dogs Get Ringworm - Transmission can happen by direct contact with another infected animal or a person. It can be passed from dogs to cats and vice versa and from pets to humans and from humans to pets. It is very contagious. You can catch this from your Shih Tzu or you can give it to your Shih Tzu. Ringworm can spread while petting or grooming dogs. You can also get ringworm from other animals such as cats, cows, goats, pigs and horses.

Image Attribution: By Norman Purvis Walker [Public domain], via Wikimedia Commons

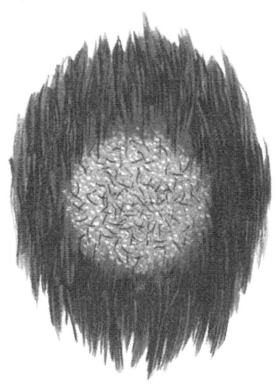

The fungal spores can live in the environment for a long time and can be found in carpets, bedding, grooming equipment, etc. and can infect your Shih Tzu if he comes into contact with them. The incubation period is 10-12 days. This means that following exposure to the fungus, about 10-12 days will pass before any lesions will be seen. In rare cases ringworm can be spread by contact with infected soil. The fungus can live for months in soil if the nutrients are right. Fortunately, the spores are easily killed with a solution of bleach and water (500 milliliters of bleach to 4 liters of water).

Are all Dogs Susceptible to Ringworm? Healthy adult dogs usually have a resistance to ringworm. Young dogs and puppies are more susceptible because their immune system hasn't fully developed. Many dogs are carriers of ringworm but show no symptoms. They can, however, infect other pets or humans.

Signs - The usual symptom is a round hairless lesion. This means that in many cases there will be balding on the coat in the area that the ringworm appears. The ringworm may also be clearly seen on the belly of a dog. The characteristic 'ring' (the circle of red *within* the circle of the lesion) that we see on humans doesn't always appear as a ring on dogs. This lesion will grow in size and often become irregular in shape. The fungi cause the hair shafts to break off and this results in patches of coat loss. Ringworm is commonly is found on the face, ears, tail and paws, as well as other areas. The lesions are scaly and may or may not be itchy and often the skin is red and swollen.

Diagnosis of Ringworm - It is not possible to make a proper diagnosis visually. The vet will need to do one of the following tests.
• Wood's Lamp - This is an ultra violet lamp also known as a black light. At least 50% will glow under the lamp.
• Microscopic diagnosis- A hair or skin sample is observed under a microscope.
• Culture – A scraping is taken from the lesion and sent to a laboratory to see what the culture grows.

Treatment - If no treatment is carried out, ringworm will usually run its course in 2 to 4 months and the symptoms will resolve themselves. However, you may want to have this treated to stop him from suffering any longer than necessary and to cut down the period of time he is contagious. Treatment includes:
• Griseofulvin - This is an anti-fungal medication that is used for dogs with ringworm but it does have some side effects so be sure to consult your vet before using this.
• Shampoos and Dips - Lime sulfur dips are often recommended. Dips should be given twice a week and can be performed either by your vet or at home. Please be aware that Lime Sulfur will stain clothing and may cause temporary yellowing of a dog's coat. It also has a strong, overpowering smell.

De-Worming Schedule - Puppies should be dewormed at 2, 4, 6, & 8 weeks of age, then again at 3 months old and then 4 months old.

Female Issues

Heat

Heat is the term that is used to describe the time during a female dog's cycle of menstruation. This is also referred to as a dog 'entering into season'. During part of the cycle, she is able to conceive and become pregnant. This cycle will be very different than a human female cycle and an owner should be informed about all of the aspects.

Age - This will begin sooner than many owners expect. The age a female has her first cycle is generally between the young ages of 4 and 6 months old. However, this can vary quite a bit. Some dogs enter the cycle early and some enter as late as 15 months. If your female has not been spayed & is over 15 months and you have not noticed that she has entered into heat yet, she should be brought to the vet for a full checkup to see what is delaying this natural process.

The 4 Stages of the Cycle - Technically there are four stages of a dog's cycle; however most owners will only notice one of them; the one in which there is discharge and possible mood changes:

1 - Proestrus - During this 1st stage, estrogen levels rise for an average of 9 days. The body is preparing for the next stage. While there are hormonal changes, a female is not yet able to conceive and will not be receptive to a male's advances.

* 2- Estrus - It is this 2nd stage that owners will notice and is the stage that is often referred to as the 'heat cycle'. Estrogen levels drop while progesterone levels rise. Typically, signs of heat will be obvious. This stage lasts from 14 to 21 days; though there is a smaller window of time within these 2 to 3 weeks that a female will be receptive to a male. That 'window' typically ranges from 7 to 10 days within this time frame.

3- Diestrus - Once a dog comes out of estrus, she enters this 3rd stage that lasts roughly 2 months. Her progesterone levels are still elevated however she will not be receptive to a male.

4- Anestrus - This 4th stage simply refers to the 'resting' stage once hormone levels are completely back to normal and lasts until the 1st stage starts again.

The Signs - The signs of a Shih Tzu in heat include the following:

• **Her vulva will become swollen and this is often very noticeable.** It's a good idea for first-time puppy owners to take note of the size of a female dog's vulva so that when it swells, owners will know for sure that heat has begun.

• **A small amount of blood will be discharged.** It may be mixed with other fluids and therefore the color will range from light to dark pink to red. The amount of blood may be a lot less than one may expect; toy breed dogs often have very negligible amounts. However, with this said, a small discharge over the course of 2 to 3 weeks can make for one big mess. Discharge can build up on a dog's bedding and on your furniture and carpeting. We'll discuss hygiene ahead.

• **Male dogs may seem overly interested in her;** stray male dogs may hang around your yard. Males that have not been neutered will be able to detect that your dog is in heat from as much as 3 miles away. When a female is in heat and urinates outside, blood will exit along with the urine. This sends a strong signal out to any un-fixed males in the area and male dogs have been known to 'stake out' the yards that females are brought outside to. When a female is in heat, males may try to approach her if you take her out for a walk. It is recommended to keep a female indoors as much as possible during the heat cycle and to take a very good look around before you bring her outside to go to the bathroom.

Confusing Heat with Anal Gland Secretion - Some first time owners can become confused between blood discharge due to the heat cycle and discharge due to burst anal glands. Essentially, oil from anal glands has an overpowering odor and the color of the oil is typically a very dark red to almost a brown/black. For more about anal glands, please refer to the 'Health-Body Part Specific', 'Anal Glands' section, page 186.

Pain and Behavioral Changes During Heat - While no one can say for sure, it is suggested from studies that a female's behavior shows that she is aware of her cycle and may indeed feel some cramping or discomfort. Many females may "nest", they will want more rest in a comfortable area, sometimes appearing to want to be alone and arranging blankets and other soft items around her. Some - but not all - female dogs will become moody during a heat. She may either distance herself or do the opposite and stay closer than ever. She may have less tolerance for others, appear restless and/or have more attention-seeking behaviors.

How Long Heat Last For - The average time a Shih Tzu's heat cycle lasts is 2 to 3 weeks and it will happen about 2 times per year (spaced approximately 4 to 6 months apart). Unless you have your Shih Tzu spayed, she may continue to have this for the rest of her life. It is not healthy for dogs of a senior age to go through this twice a year phase as it puts both physical and emotional stress on a dog.

Split Heats - While most dogs will have normal heat cycles, once in a while a dog can have a 'split heat' in which there is a spacing issue. Quite simply, this means that the cycle will begin, it will stop for days (or a few weeks in some cases) and then begin again. This does not mean that your dog is having 2 heat cycles; it is technically 1 heat cycle that is disrupted and then begins again. It is thought that this occurs due to changing hormone levels.

Silent Heats - While a Shih Tzu may clean herself quickly and often enough that the owner does not notice any discharge and other symptoms may be negligible, a silent heat refers to when a dog does indeed go through the estrus cycle but does not show any of the typical signs. There is no discharge, no swelling of the vulva or any other signs. Do note that this is a different event than a missed heat and it can be difficult for an owner to know the difference. Completely skipping the entire cycle may be due to a medical issue, some which are quite serious. This includes:

• Hypothyroidism- Other signs are hair loss, dulling coat, black patches of skin, cold intolerance and/or weight gain.
• Cushing's Disease - Other signs are increased thirst, bloated stomach, increased appetite and/or thinning coat.
• Diabetes - Other signs include increase in both thirst and urination, being hungrier than normal and/or weight gain even if extra food is not ingested.

Because of this, if your Shih Tzu appears to miss her heat cycle and shows any clinical signs of a possible health problem, it is best to have her evaluated by the veterinarian as soon as possible.

Spaying and Why This May Be a Good Idea - All experienced veterinarians, breeders and clinical researchers are in agreement: Spaying your female Shih Tzu will give her a better chance for a healthy life. Unless you have serious plans to breed your Shih Tzu and if you know that you *do* want to have her spayed, you'll strongly want to consider having it done sooner than later. Many vets recommend having a female spayed even before she enters her first heat. While spaying will reduce a female dog's risk of developing certain cancers, it is most beneficial when done early. Studies have shown that if it is done after the 2nd cycle, the risk for mammary tumors increases. If a female enters in and out of 4 seasons before the procedure, she will have a 1 in 4 chance of this type of cancer.

Hygiene - The amount of discharge that you see will vary; smaller dogs like the Shih Tzu often have much less discharge that larger dogs. In addition, the discharge may vary from white to pink to red at different times of the heat cycle. Even if you do not clearly see much discharge, a small amount that comes out over the course of a week or two is going to add up to a considerable amount. This discharge will soak into bedding, blankets, pillows, furniture and more. For these reason, you may wish to have your female wear a doggie diaper during the cycle. Many owners slip a cotton canine panty over the diaper just so that the dog looks cute.

Breeding

Essentially, when it comes to the many aspects of breeding information, there is only one way to word it. The information does not vary nor is it up for interpretation. For that reason, when it comes to this breeding chapter, the majority of what you want to know is readily available on the AKC website. If we repeated all of the things that you can also easily learn *there*, that would add 45 pages to this book, which would needlessly add bulk to this book. It makes more sense to let you know exactly where to read all of the needed breeding information.

To Begin – To familiarize yourself with all needed information to start off, please refer to the AKC's 'Responsible Breeding' section of their website. The URL address is http://www.akc.org/dog-breeders/responsible-breeding, however you can find it very easily simply by searching for 'AKC breeding'.

You can watch the AKC's video of: 'Planning Breedings: Are you ready to breed a litter?' And then read all of their pages, which include: 'Prepare Yourself for Breeding a Litter',' Breed to Improve', 'Understand the Commitment', 'Choose A Suitable Mate', 'Know Your Genetics', 'Finalize Stud Contract', 'Perform Pre-Breeding Health Checks', 'Mating', 'Pregnancy and Whelping Preparation', 'Puppies Are Born', 'Consult Your Veterinarian if Complications Arise',' Keep Your Puppies Warm, Fed and Clean', 'Register Your Litter with the AKC Soon After Whelping', 'Wean Puppies from their Mother', 'Sending Your Pups to Their New Homes' and finally 'Encourage New Owners to Register Their Puppy with the AKC'.

The AKC did a fantastic job with all of their breeding information, so please make use of it; You will find that it covers a lot!

10 Breeding Elements to Keep in Mind

Deciding to breed a Shih Tzu is an enormous responsibility and much time should be spent deciding if you are prepared for all that will be needed. Breeding is a lot more complicated than just allowing two Shih Tzu to mate. Too many owners rush to think, "My Shih Tzu is so beautiful, I should have puppies!" Rushing into this without understanding all that is involved can lead to overwhelming responsibility and risking your dog's health and the health of future litters.

"Breeding is not the mating together of two AKC registered dogs to produce puppies. That has been the downfall of many breeds. It's a creative art that requires the study of genetics, conformation, and bloodlines and veterinary procedures. The responsibilities for the future generations lie with a breeder" ~ AKC

Before you decide to breed your Shih Tzu, you will want to keep the following 10 elements in mind:

1) It is important to study the genetics and the backgrounds of the dogs in question. You will want to feel confident that this will be a sound breeding, i.e. that the puppies will be free of any serious genetic defect and will be good quality examples of the breed. Both sire and dam should meet the AKC standards so that you are breeding to improve the breed standard; any defects will continue those flaws in the potential litter.

2) Appropriate size of the dam. It's important that the dam is of appropriate size and has pelvic breadth and good tuck up to carry puppies and deliver them. You will usually want the female to be larger than the male. For example, a 15 pound female to a 10 pound male (whose parents are also similar in size). She must have a thorough veterinarian checkup to make sure that she has the correct proportions to carry and deliver.

3) Both dam and sire should be at the appropriate age. The AKC states that a dam must not be younger than 8 months and the sire not less than 7 months. Personally, we feel that this is much too young. We recommend a breeding age of 2 to 3 years old for the dam; she will be physically mature yet still have enough youthful flexibility. A male's sperm will be viable at about 4 months old, however we suggest waiting until the 1 year mark to ensure sperm is strong. Additionally, dogs must be placed in 'retirement' at the correct age; it is particularly dangerous to have an older female carrying and delivering litters. In general, a female should be retired from breeding at 7. However, this will vary greatly depending on her health, how quickly she recovers, if a cesarean section was needed, the size of her litters and so much more.

4) Have your breeding goal clearly defined. Will you focus on a certain color? Will you aim for the low or high end of the weight standard? What sort of registration will you provide? AKC? CKC? Will you keep show quality dogs? How will you handle the sale and follow-up?

5) Never over-breed. While each dog should be individually evaluated, in general, most veterinarians recommend breeding twice in a row and then allowing a rest. Alternatively, you may wish to breed every other heat cycle. The most important element is that the female be evaluated after each litter to see if she is even able to handle having a future litter. When a Shih Tzu must have a cesarean section, in many cases she should not have any more litters.

6) Be very aware of the cost that are involved. Breeding is a huge undertaking and is expensive. When close to delivery, the dam should not be left home alone. You will need to be there and this may mean taking time out of work. The litter of newborn puppies will need 24 hour, around the clock care, you will need to be there every moment. You will also need money for:

- Cesarean sections –Careful pairing of dogs can help lessen the chances of a cesarean section, but it is always a possibility.
- Veterinarian checkups for all dogs and all future puppies
- Shots and de-worming
- High quality puppy food and dog food
- Blankets, doggie beds, play pens, toys, food dishes, gates, cleaning supplies, grooming tools, etc.

7) You will have to be emotionally prepared for loss. Ethical loving breeders have a huge weight on their shoulders. While their devotion is to breed happy, well socialized, healthy puppies, even the most careful breeder will most likely experience the loss of newborn pups over any long period of time.

8) Ethical breeding requires dedication to shaping the pups' personalities. The breeder plays a huge role in shaping the personality of a puppy; the interaction between breeder and pup is essential. One should be able to provide excellent socialization, including handling the pups, grooming and having one-on-one interaction. If puppies are not socialized enough, they will not develop needed socialization skills to transition well into their new homes.

9) Be prepared for medical issues and emergencies. A breeder should have an outstanding veterinarian and should be aware of the signs and symptoms of all possible health issues. The life of the dogs and puppies are in the breeder's hands.

10) This is a long-term commitment. You will need to commit to keeping puppies that are not able to be sold for any reason, including medical issues. And you will need to commit to keeping adults that are not able to be re-homed once retired. Finally, you will be expected to honor your contract that a puppy may be returned to you for any reason.

Pregnancy
Important Facts to Know

1) A female can become pregnant during the first heat cycle, even if there is hardly any discharge. As soon as a female enters puberty - which will be her first heat cycle - she is able to conceive. For toy breed dogs, this can be at a very young age; usually between the ages of 4 and 6 months old. It is during the estrus phase of the cycle, which lasts between 2 and 3 weeks that the female is generally receptive to a male. Within this time, there is a smaller window - usually between days 10 to 15 (starting to count from day 1 that discharge began) that eggs will drop and the female can become pregnant.

2) Pregnancy can occur even if a tie does not appear successful. Many owners may believe that they stopped a mounting before anything happened, it may actually be too late.

3) A Shih Tzu can become pregnant by two different dogs. This is known as a multi-sired litter. The reason that this is possible is because with female canines, more than one ova (the eggs produced by the ovaries) remain available for several days. Hypothetically, a female may be mounted on day 1, with an egg being fertilized and then if mounted on day 3 by a different male, another egg may become fertilized.

4) A Shih Tzu can become pregnant by a much larger dog. This would make for a very dangerous pregnancy and delivery. When owners bring their female Shih Tzu outside for bathroom needs, the area should be scanned for any stray dogs. Never allow an un-spayed female and an un-neutered male alone together, even for a second, if there is any possibility she is even *near* her heat cycle.

5) A dog can have a false pregnancy. This is also referred to as pseudopregnancy and is thought to occur due to hormonal imbalances of progesterone and prolactin. The belly can enlarge, there may be enlarged breast tissue and in rare cases, milk production. Your vet may suggest warm or cold packs to be placed on mammary tissue to reduce uncomfortable swelling. This normally ebbs away within 3 weeks. If it persists, hormonal supplements may need to be given.

6) The average sized litter for Shih Tzu is 1 to 5 puppies.

SIZE OF LITTER	1	2	3	4	5	6
PERCENTAGE	10%	25%	30%	20%	10%	5%

How to Know Your Shih Tzu is Pregnant — Whether you look for visible signs or have pregnancy confirmed by a veterinarian, the earliest this can be confirmed is Day 22. Let's take a look (this is counting out from the day of mating):

- A blood test can confirm pregnancy as early as Day 22
- An ultrasound can confirm pregnancy as early as Day 28
- Palpation can also confirm pregnancy as early as Day 28
- An x-ray can confirm pregnancy as early as Day 42, however it is suggested to wait until Day 55 for an accurate reading of how many puppies to expect.

Without any of these things done to confirm pregnancy, you will not know for sure, until about Week 4 (Day 28 and on), due to the visibly enlarged stomach.

Why It's Important to See the Vet - With a planned breeding, both male and female dogs have extensive testing *before* a pairing, to ensure their health and to rule out the possibility of passing on any hereditary conditions to a potential litter. In addition, the female's pelvic width is checked to see if she can naturally birth puppies. With unplanned pregnancies, it is very important to bring the female to the vet right away, as both of these elements are of great concern.

Signs of Pregnancy

Week 1 - At this early stage, there will usually be no signs. Towards the end of Week 1, some dogs may have slight nausea that causes a decreased appetite.

Weeks 2 and 3 - Signs will begin to emerge. Some will be minimal. The dam may be more tired than usual, the stomach may seem *slightly* swollen, she may clean herself much more than normal and/or her nipples on her tummy seem slightly larger than before. During Week 2 there may still be some 'morning sickness' that causes nausea. The nausea is often short-lived with a heartier appetite emerging as she transitions into Week 3.

Week 4 - Signs are now very clear: The stomach will be distended to the point that there is no doubt she is carrying a litter, nipples will be enlarged and darkened as her body prepares for nursing. Some that were previously flush with the skin will now be popped out. For those that have been bred before, nipples may hang down as they fill with colostrum. She may also have nesting tendencies and her appetite should be strong.

Weeks 5 and 6: As she approaches the end of the gestation period, the dam may tire much more easily, may prefer to remain at home resting in a quiet spot and will usually be less social. *Photo courtesy of High Point Shih Tzu*

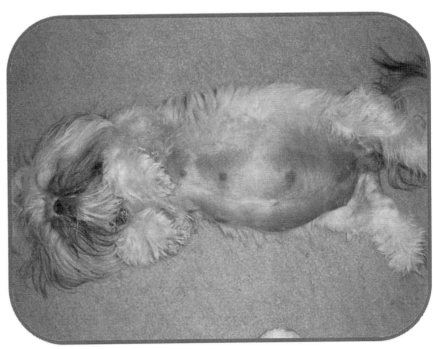

Pregnancy lasts for 63 Days – This is a general figure. It can vary from Day 58 to Day 65 and be considered normal.

Morning Sickness - This type of nausea, as you probably know, can happen at any time of the day or night. If there is vomiting, change to a very bland diet for 2-3 days (plain white chicken meat and plain steamed white rice and/or cooked sweet potato). If vomiting persists (dehydration is just one risk of repeated vomiting), speak to your veterinarian about the possibility of providing anti-nausea medication.

Feeding Overview – While you do not need to have things be 'exact', it is not good to over or under-feed. A dam does not need an increase in food for the first few weeks; calorie needs increase as she moves into Week 3. Many vets suggest a change to puppy food. If possible, stay with the same brand, choosing the 'puppy' variety. Do NOT give any calcium rich foods. By the end of Week 3, calories should be approximately 25% more than normal. She may do best with more frequent meals as opposed to larger portions. Just before delivery, a dog may refuse food; this is a sign that labor will soon begin.

Expected Weight Gain- During the entire course of pregnancy, a Shih Tzu will gain *about* 20% of her normal body weight. For example, a 15 lb. Shih Tzu will gain about 3 lbs., ending at 18 lbs. at the time of delivery. An 9 lb. Shih Tzu will gain about 1.8 lbs., for an ending weight of 10.8 lbs. Check with your vet if you suspect too little or too much weight gain. Weight gain will be comprised of not just the pups but also fluids (water, amniotic fluids) and tissue (amniotic sacs that surround each fetus).

Supplements - In most cases, a pregnant dog should not be given ANY extra vitamins or supplements. Doing so can be detrimental to both dam and litter! This is particularly true of calcium; do NOT give any extra; it is linked to eclampsia, difficult deliveries, soft tissue calcium deposits in the puppies, and certain joint abnormalities in the pups. HOWEVER, she WILL need extra calcium right before labor (this helps with contractions) and during whelping (needed for proper lactation and whelping).

Care • **Activity** - Unless there are any exercise restrictions set in place by the veterinarian, you will want to continue to walk your Shih Tzu daily at a nice pace; albeit perhaps a bit slower. This will allow her to stay fit and keep her healthy for labor. Do not allow her to jump down from the sofa or any other height that would cause a jarring (this should be the rule for all Shih Tzu). During the final 2 weeks - depending on how many pups she is carrying - she may have trouble maneuvering around and walks can be put on pause at this time.
• **Comfort** - If your Shih Tzu has been sleeping in your bed, prepare a bed for her as nesting instincts are often strong. This can be a playpen or gated off area with a quality canine bed. She should NOT be isolated; have this in a quiet corner of a room that the family uses.
• **Other Dogs** - If your pregnant Shih Tzu becomes nervous by the presence of other dogs in the house (male or female), surround her resting spot with portable baby gates. If the sire is in the house, separate the two dogs starting at the beginning of Week 5. He can re-join her when the pups are 4 weeks old - with your supervision. Once they are fully weaned, he can have full access.

Pregnancy Step-by-Step Care- Week by Week - It is important to make changes from the 1st day that you believe your Shih Tzu is pregnant.
•   On a calendar, count ahead 56 days from the first breeding and mark that day. Day 56 is the day you should be 100% ready.
•   If at all possible, plan to take a break from work beginning on Day 56 and ideally for 2 weeks from that point. After Day 56 she should not be left alone unless regular temperature checks prove she is not close to labor.
•   Immediately restrict calcium rich foods.

Pregnancy Week 1 through 3: Mild morning sickness and slight moodiness is normal. There may be a light pink discharge. *Care during this time:*
•   Keep exercising her as usual (ideally she is used to 1 to 2 walks per day).
•   Do not give any medications without vet approval.
•   Do not use flea treatment without vet approval.
•   She cannot be given any live vaccinations.

Pregnancy Week 4 (Days 21 to 28): The dam is clearly pregnant, with a swollen stomach and nipples are really beginning to develop (this is usually when you will notice the 'extra' ones that 'pop' out). By now, the veterinarian should have confirmed pregnancy. The dam may have a clear, odorless vaginal discharge; this is normal. The fetuses are most susceptible to defects due to the dam eating something toxic. Therefore, perform an extra 'puppy-proofing' of the house and outside area that she has access to. *Care at this time:*
•   Limit long walks, but continue short daily walks.
•   Per vet instruction, switch to puppy food, do not give any calcium rich foods.
•   Feed extra to comply with any increased appetite.

Pregnancy Week 5 (Days 28 to 35): At this time the fetuses begin to look like puppies; their toes and nails are developing. Eyes that were open, now close (when eyes are developing in the uterus, the eyes are developed in an open position and then they close and remain closed until about 10 days old or so after birth). Fetuses are much more resistant to development problems. *Care during this time:*
•   Remain limiting long walks, but continue short daily walks.
•   Increase her food as needed.

• Speak to your vet about now offering small daily amounts of whole white yogurt and/or whole cottage cheese.

Pregnancy Week 6 (Days 35 to 42): Puppies become colored (skin pigment develops) the Shih Tzu's nipples will continue to darken and grow. *Care during this time:*
• It is time to prepare and put up the whelping box in a quiet area. Encourage (but not force) her to sleep there.
• As always, never let your dam outdoors without 100% supervision. Sometimes, pregnant dogs have an urge to run away to give birth.

Pregnancy Week 7 (Days 42 to 49): A Shih Tzu may start shedding some stomach hair. *Care during this time:*
• Increase her food as needed.
• Stop any rough playing and all jumping.

Pregnancy Week 8 (Days 49 to 57): When your Shih Tzu is resting you can sometimes see and feel the pups moving. Now is the time to be prepared in case the puppies come early. The production of breast milk (colostrum) may begin as early as day 45. *Care during this time:*

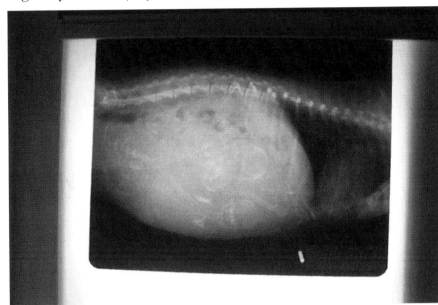

• Call your veterinarian to schedule x-rays to determine the size and number of pups. Days 55 or 56 are the best days to do this.
• Have your whelping area and all supplies ready. Have a plan in place if an emergency trip to the clinic is needed.
• It will be normal for your Shih Tzu to be fussy with food this week.
• Speak to your vet about starting calcium supplements at this time.

Pregnancy Week 9 (Days 57 to 65): Nesting behavior may start or increase. *Care during this time:*
• Appetite may decrease
• Start taking her temperature 3 to 5 times a day

Take her temperature as follows: On **Day 57**: 3 times a day, **Day 58:** 4 times a day, **Day 59:** 5 times a day, and once in the middle of the night, **Day 60:** Every 2 hours during the day and every 4 hours at night. Make sure that the thermometer is inserted at least 1.5 to 2 inches into the rectum, using Vaseline as a lubricant.

The Mucus Plug – There will be a mucus plug in the vaginal area that develops during pregnancy. As the dam approaches full term, this will begin to shed. It usually sheds off into dry pieces, most commonly 4 to 7 days before labor.

Preparing the Birthing Area/ Whelping Box - While you can find impressive construction plans for all kinds of whelping boxes that are very elaborate, there are two easy methods: **1) Use a sturdy cardboard box.** These work well since aside from being free of cost, they are portable, easy to discard of and can be cut to create an entrance/exit flap. The box should be lined with an abundance of clean newspaper. During the birthing process, as the paper becomes drenched, you can slip out a layer to expose clean and dry paper, quickly throwing away a soaked layer into a leak-proof trash bag. **2) A Perla dog bed.** These are plastic dog beds that keep a Shih Tzu feeling safe and secure. Layers of cloth and paper can be laid down and easily removed as they become soaked.

You will want to place the birthing box or Perla bed in a quiet room of your home where there will be no disturbances, no phones ringing, no people running in and out…just a nice quiet area for the dam to give birth, with your assistance. A heating pad will need to be placed nearby after the puppies are born, so be sure to choose a spot where the cord of a heat pad will easily reach. With the whelping box, you can place the heating pad under a blanket. With the Perla bed, you can place the heating pad right under the Perla.

Giving Birth

Items You Will Need to Prepare for Labor and Birthing

1) Infant's Nasal Aspirator (bulb syringe) **2)** Towels **3)** Dental Floss **4)** Sterilized scissors **5)** Iodine **6)** Sterilized cups

Signs that Labor Will Begin. You will know that your Shih Tzu is going to have puppies within 24 hours by taking note of when her internal temperature drops below normal. Have your Shih Tzu in an area where she feels safe and comfortable. Use a canine rectal thermometer. You should lubricate it well and insert it about 1.5 to 2 inches. Leave it for three minutes. Your dog's normal temperature should be between 101 and 102.5° Fahrenheit (38.3 to 39.17 Celsius). When your Shih Tzu's temperature drops below 100° F (37.77 C), she should deliver the Shih Tzu pups in less than twenty-four hours.

Call the vet ASAP if:
*   She has been pregnant for more than 70 days
*   It has been 24 hours since her temperature dropped and she is vomiting and/or crying but puppies have not been birthed
*   1 puppy came out, but it has been more than 2 hours without any more coming out (and you know there are more)
*   If her temperature has risen
*   If discharge fluids have a foul smell

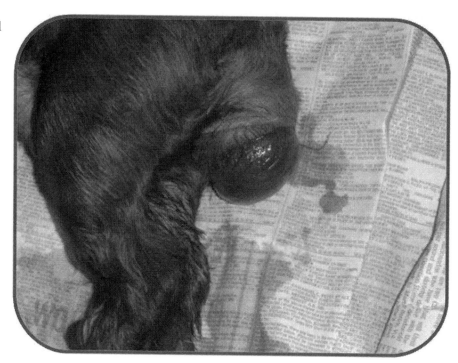

Giving Birth   Stage 1 of Labor: When you know she is about to give birth, make sure she is in her whelping box. If the sire or other males are in the house, block access.

During the first stage of labor the cervix will dilate and contractions begin. This can be extremely painful for a dog. She may be uncomfortable, restless, quite possibly pacing, shivering, panting and may cry. She may not want to eat and she may even vomit. This is the longest stage of labor, typically lasting 6 to 18 hours.

Photo courtesy of High Point Shih Tzu

Stage 2 of Labor: Each puppy is born in his/her own individual amniotic sac. This may break right before the puppy is pushed out or simultaneously. Puppies will usually be pushed out every 10 to 30 minutes of forceful straining. It is normal for many puppies to be born feet first or sideways. If you see the rear legs of a puppy protruding but the pup is not coming out, you can gently pull the puppy in a downward and rearward arcing motion. *Photo courtesy of High Point Shih Tzu*

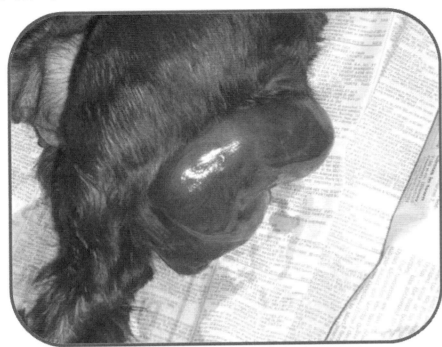

As the pups emerge, the dam will lick the puppy clean and bite off the umbilical cord. It is important to let the dam do this. The rough licking of the mother stimulates the puppies to breathe and it gets their circulation going. It is normal for the mother to eat the afterbirth tissues, including the amniotic sacs.

If the dam does not bite the umbilical cord, you will need to cut it. Please note that you will need to tie it before you cut it:

1- Tie a piece of dental floss around the puppy's umbilical cord. This first piece should be about 1 inch (2.5 centimeters) away from the puppy's belly. A second piece of thread should be tied 0.25 inch (0.64 centimeters) away from the first piece, toward the placenta.

2- Using sterilized scissors, cut the umbilical cord between the two pieces of thread.

3- Iodine should be applied to the cut end of the puppy's umbilical cord. It is best to dip the end of the cord into iodine. This can be done by pouring some iodine into a sterilized cup. The umbilical cord will then usually fall off within a few days to a week.

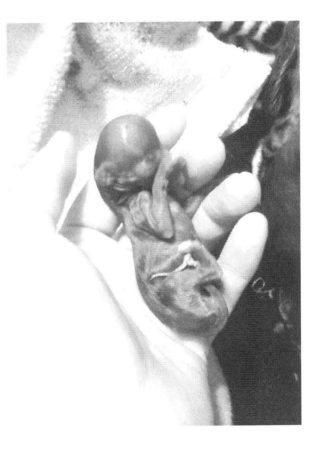

Stage 3 of Labor: Once all the puppies have been born the dog enters this third stage of labor during which time the uterus contracts fully, expelling any remaining placenta, blood and fluid. Just let your Shih Tzu stay close to her puppies as you clean up.

Bleeding- A female will have some bleeding and discharge for up to 10 days after giving birth. This is normal if the bleeding/discharge lessens each day and if there are no signs of a health issue. By day 12, all bleeding and/or discharge should have stopped. Take your Shih Tzu to the vet ASAP if:
- Bleeding is excessive
- Bleeding increases as the days go by

- There is a foul odor coming from the blood or discharge
- Your Shih Tzu seems to be very weak and/or will not eat
- The Shih Tzu has a fever
- There are any signs of ill health

After the Birth - Newspapers should be taken away and soft, clean baby blankets put down. Clean the surrounding area with soap and bleach. In the whelping box, *under* the blankets, a heating pad should be placed. With a Perla bed the heating pad can go under a blanket or under the Perla bed. There should be areas in the box/bed that are a warm 80-85°F, so that the puppies may move from a warm area to a bit cooler area as they wish. With a whelping box, the flap of the box should be closed, so that the dam and puppies feel safe and secure. Clean the dam her with a warm, soapy sponge, patting her dry afterward.

You will want to keep a very close eye on all puppies. If a puppy is not able to receive enough milk from the dam, you will probably need to bottle feed the pup. Some puppies will need to be gently moved over to nurse. Be sure to weigh the puppies each day. Every day there should be a weight increase. You can use a kitchen scale to weigh the pups. It will work best to place a soft cloth on the scale and then place the puppy inside. If the coloring of the puppies is very similar, you may find it helpful to mark the pups. This can be done by using 'White-Out' and putting a small dot on each puppy in a different area that you will easily be able to identify. *Photo courtesy of High Point Shih Tzu*

Tips:

• The newborn pups should be gaining weight EACH DAY. If not, contact the vet ASAP.
• Look for any signs of hypoglycemia with the puppies (weakness, very inactive). This can develop very, very quickly. Therefore, a check on the puppies should be done each hour for the 1st week, every other hour for the 2nd and 3rd week and every 3 hours on the 4th week.

• By Week 4, the dam will begin to need a bit of time away from the puppies; it is suggested to add another box to the whelping box.
• Cut away a section so that the puppies may begin to roam from dam to the 2nd 'room' to play and begin to learn about toys, etc.

Is There Something Wrong with the Dam? If you need to ask if something is wrong, most likely this means yes; something *is* wrong. If she is displaying any behavioral changes or any physical changes that makes you question things or be concerned about her, this is your immediate signal to take her to the veterinarian or closest animal hospital right away. Aside from the mentioned bleeding that can occur as the uterus is being cleaned out, there are **no** health issues that are 'normal'.

It is not normal for her to be vomiting… It is not normal for her to be in pain… It is not normal for her to have discharging pus… It is not normal for her to be aggressive or to bite… It is not normal for her to be limping. Signs of dehydration (sunken in eyes, dizziness, refusal to eat) is not normal. We are saddened by the amount of owners who write to us, asking if this or that is normal, when they should instead be taking their Shih Tzu to the vet. Please do not write to us or ask questions on online communities if your dam that just gave birth is obviously ill or in pain. Take her to the vet. If you wait for an email response (we receive hundreds each day and cannot answer all of them) or for someone with varying experience to answer your questions in online forums, you are taking away precious time that she could have been being helped.

Eclampsia

Eclampsia is also called 'milk fever' or 'puerperal tetany'. This is an acute, life-threatening disease that happens most often with lactating dogs. Some dogs cannot keep up with the increased demands for calcium. As calcium is being moved to a dam's milk supply, her own body becomes depleted. Both pregnant dogs and nursing dogs are at risk. Eclampsia most commonly occurs 1-3 weeks after giving birth, but it can even occur during pregnancy. Toy breeds, such as the Shih Tzu, are at higher risk for eclampsia. The puppies themselves are not affected as the mother's milk appears to be normal during this period.

The Symptoms - Eclampsia is a very serious disorder but fortunately the signs are fairly easy to recognize, especially when coupled with late term pregnancy and/or milk production. Initially, the affected dog will be restlessness and nervousness. Shortly thereafter, signs will include walking with a stiff gait, wobbly walking, disorientation. Eventually, there may be inability to walk, rigid limbs, high fever (over 105° F) and/or increased respiration rate. At this point, death can occur if no treatment is given.

Treatment - If you suspect your pregnant or post-pregnant Shih Tzu has eclampsia, seek veterinary attention immediately and prevent the puppies from nursing for at least 24 hours. Feed them with a commercial milk replacer. A veterinarian can confirm eclampsia with a blood test to determine blood calcium levels. Eclampsia is treated via IV calcium supplementation. Oral calcium supplements may be given once she has recovered. If a dog responds well to treatment, in some cases, the puppies *may* be gradually allowed to nurse again. If your Shih Tzu has had eclampsia, be sure to consult with your veterinarian before allowing the puppies to nurse.

Prevention - Too much calcium during the pregnancy can increase the odds of a female Shih Tzu developing eclampsia. This is usually due to an owner giving calcium supplements. Calcium is regulated by a hormone called the parathyroid hormone. If pregnant dogs are given extra calcium, levels of the parathyroid hormone decrease. When calcium needs suddenly develop (giving birth triggers the need), that lack of proper parathyroid hormone makes it impossible. Blood calcium levels drop and this is when eclampsia can develop. Once a dog has had eclampsia, there is a higher chance that she will also have it with future litters if preventative steps are not taken which include working very closely with your vet in regard to *exact* feeding during and after pregnancy.

Mastitis

Mastitis refers to two different conditions: An infection of the milk ducts and/or a blocked milk duct in which dangerous toxins can build up. Mastitis can also occur with dogs that have just had a false pregnancy or those that are nursing. It is a serious condition which can come on quickly. In some cases, it can only take ½ day for symptoms to progress.

Symptoms-

- Her milk glands feel hot to the touch
- Her milk glands may be very hard
- There may be pain when milk glands are touched

- Her milk will quite often also be off colored and puppies could show signs of malnutrition (they will not be gaining weight each day)
- She may not eat as much or may stop eating completely
- She may be extremely thirsty
- Her body temperature may rise to as high as 105° Fahrenheit (40.5°C)
- She may vomit
- She may become aggressive toward the puppies

Treatment - Bring your Shih Tzu to the vet ASAP. This is considered to be a medical emergency. If you cannot get to the veterinarian immediately, (if it is 2 AM and there are no after-office hours, etc.) there are some steps you should immediately take: Each hour, apply a warm compress to her milk glands and/or try to gently remove any contaminated milk by squeezing her teat between your forefinger and thumb. By doing this you are enabling her milk to flow freely and helping to stop the toxin produced by Mastitis from absorbing into her blood stream. A method (untested by us) is to use a compress of hot clothes soaked in vinegar. Though again, she must be seen by the vet ASAP.

Pyometra

Pyometra is the most common uterus disease seen in female dogs that have not been spayed. It is an important disease to be aware of because it can come on very quickly and can be fatal when not treated. Pyometra is a result of bacteria traveling into the uterus. This can happen at any age, whether a female has been bred or not, and whether it is her 1st or 10th heat (although it becomes more common as the dog gets older). The main risk period for a female is for eight weeks after heat has ended. Normally as the heat cycle ends, the cervix (which opens during her heat), starts to close and the inner lining begins to transition back to normal. During this time, if bacteria (often E. Coli) sets in, there can be an infection. If the cervix is still open, the infected tissue can leave the body, and this is easier and safer to treat. This is known as open pyometra. If the cervix is fully closed, there is no discharge from the vulva, and like in appendicitis, the uterus may rupture. This causes pus to escape into the abdomen, causing severe inflammation and possible rapid death. This is known as closed pyometra.

Symptoms - The most obvious symptom of open pyometra is a discharge of pus from the vulva in a female dog that has recently been in heat. However, symptoms of closed pyometra are less obvious. Symptoms of both types include: Vomiting, lack of appetite, depression (moping around and not wanting to participate in normal activities), increased drinking and urinating and/or fever (which is seen in less than a third of females with pyometra). Closed pyometra is a more serious condition than open pyometra not only because there is no outlet for the infection but also because a diagnosis of closed pyometra can easily be missed.

Diagnosis – If you notice any of the signs, bring your Shih Tzu to the veterinarian right away. The vet should perform several tests:
- Blood tests – This will show any dehydration, increased white blood cell count and increased alkaline phosphatase.
- X-rays – Done to look for an enlarged uterus.
- Ultrasound - This will confirm the presence of a fluid filled uterus.

Treatment - The most important aspect of treatment of pyometra is quick action. Females are often septic and in shock. Intravenous fluids and antibiotics should be given immediately. The best treatment is an emergency spay to remove the infected uterus. Spaying completely and swiftly eliminates the infection, prevents uterine rupture and prevents recurrence, in most cases. Spayed dogs seldom develop pyometra in the uterine stump (more ahead).

Alternative Treatments - There is another treatment option for females if the owner wishes to breed. We personally **do not** recommend this and feel that the dog's life should not be compromised at all simply for the sake of breeding. Prostaglandin F2-alpha (PGF2-α) and long-term antibiotics can be used to expel the pus from the uterus and treat the infection. PGF2-α stimulates the uterus to contract, and requires at least 3-5 days to completely remove the infected material. It's only used with open pyometra, otherwise uterine rupture could occur. This only works on less than 30% of dogs. Once bred one last time, they should then be spayed because the chances of developing pyometra again is 70%.

Stump Pyometra - Stump pyometra is a serious condition in females that underwent the spaying but the remaining stump of the uterus becomes infected and filled with fluid. The symptoms are similar to those of true pyometra. To prevent this, when having your dog spayed, speak to the vet regarding what is done to ensure the stump is removed. With stump pyometra, a second surgery would be performed to remove the stump.

Newborn Care

Weaning

Weaning is the interim stage of transitioning a puppy from a liquid diet (the dam's milk) to a diet of solid food. This usually starts at about the 4 week mark. The dam does not have as much milk and the puppies are therefore not drinking as much. Weaning properly is vital to the pup's health and in essence, his ability to survive.

A pup that is weaned too early and does not have a smooth transition from dam's milk to solid food can develop food allergies and/or intestinal distress. Allergies can become a big issue for the owners of the dog; as they must be extremely vigilant in regards to what the dog eats, most likely for the rest of his life.

How to Wean - The goal will be to offer gradual steps to solid food. It should begin as a wet, mushy soup-type food and over the course of a couple of weeks, contain less and less liquid. It is suggested to use the food that the dam has been eating as the 'base'. In this way, no new ingredients are added that could cause any stomach upset. You'll need a blender, puppy milk replacer such as Esbilac Powder Milk Replacer and hot water (bottled, spring or filtered water).

1- Place 2 cups of the dam's dog food into a blender.
2- Add 12.5 ounces of liquid puppy milk replacer.
3- Top the blender off with the hot water.
4- Blend until it has the consistency of baby food.

Offer this in small, shallow stainless steel or ceramic bowls, 3 to 4 times per day. The pups will need some time to learn to sense the food and lap at it. Pay attention to when the puppies go to the dam to nurse. You will want to politely interrupt this to offer the blended food. Once they are done, they may go back to the dam for a bit of nursing to 'top off their tummies'. Each week, decrease the amount of liquid, continuing to use the blender so that the food is 'mushy'. The goal is to have the pups used to eating solid food - with no milk replacer or water added to it - by the end of the 6 week mark.

While you are paying attention to feeding the puppies, this will give their mother a good opportunity to leave for a bit. By this time, she will appreciate some time away from the litter. As time goes by, the weaning puppies will get used to having their mother gone for a longer and longer period of time. Simultaneously, the weaning pups will become more adjusted to your presence. This will continue on like a domino effect, until they are completely ready to move out on their own.

Note: It is not normal for pups to maintain or lose weight during weaning; appetite should be robust. If a pup struggles, you should seek immediate help from the veterinarian. There is a syndrome called 'Fading Puppy Syndrome' which one could equate to the human 'Sudden Infant Death' syndrome. This affects pups 12 weeks and under. A major sign is weakening, a deterioration and under-eating.

Milestones for the Newborn

Here you see the very same newborn Shih Tzu at 1 week, then 2 weeks, then at 3 weeks old. This pup's coat lightened dramatically and went from eyes closed & sleeping 'round the clock to being alert & curious about his new world. *Photos courtesy of Silky Silhouette Shih Tzu*

Newborn Overview – Newborn puppies still have developing nervous systems, yet have basic reflexes: **1)** Burrowing; this causes a pup to seek warmth by snuggling close to dam and littermates **2)** Suckling; this instinct allows him to nurse **3)** Perineal reflex; this is in regard to urination and stool elimination; the dam often triggers this by licking the pup's belly and under the tail. **4)** Carrying reflex; this allows the pup to automatically tense and stiffen if the dam grabs him by the scuff to move him.

Puppies should be gaining weight every day. 2 to 20 grams on the first day is expected and a gain for all additional days. Using a digital kitchen scale is the easiest method to do daily weigh-ins. By Day 10, weight should be doubled from Day 1. In the first 3 weeks, the dam will be the sole caretaker for the puppies. She will feed them and clean them. They should all be together in an area (canine playpen, fresh whelping box, etc.) so that they are all together and neither pups nor dam can leave.

If a Shih Tzu puppy is having a hard time getting to the dam for milk or is constantly pushed away by its litter mates, you can remove the other pups for a little while to a close by area (with blankets with a heating pad underneath) or to another section within the same box and allow that puppy to be alone with the dam. The dam can be lifted out of the pen/box to go to the bathroom and when the puppies are 3-4 weeks old, be taken out for breaks to play with you, etc. Keep an eye on the puppies' nails; it is not uncommon for nails to grow quickly and need to be trimmed. This is important so that the pups cannot scratch each other or the dam. Pups are sleeping 90% of the time.

2 Weeks – Eye lids are *beginning* to open. Hearing is *starting* to come in. Milk teeth may be just starting to come in. Tails are wagging. The 2 week old newborn is still crawling but may make some short-lived attempts at walking. The newborns are very close to the dramatic transition stage of Week 3.

3 Weeks - The 3 week mark is an exciting one. By 3 weeks, puppies can hear. And eyes are now fully open. At this age, the pups are becoming more active and able to walk around. It's something that many people do not think about, however puppies need to learn to walk, just like human babies do; though the process happens much more quickly. When a pup makes his first attempts, he may be very wobbly and this can be quite amusing! Within just 1 to 3 days, he will have it down pat and be able to run around. The door from the whelping box should now lead into another box where the puppies can walk around and play. Be sure to line the boxes with newspaper. Do not allow the newborns to be able to leave the boxes and roam the house.

The 1st de-worming should be done by now; do keep in mind that this must be approved by your veterinarian, even if you plan to do the de-worming yourself. The veterinarian should evaluate each puppy to see if he/she is big enough, strong enough and healthy enough for the de-worming.

4 Weeks Old - If you have not already done so, the entire house should be puppy-proofed. Please refer to 'Bringing a Puppy Home', 'Puppy Proofing', page 19. The puppies can begin to venture out of the whelping box to begin exploring the home. It is important to keep the bedding in the whelping box clean and smelling fresh, however, only change the newspaper once in a while. A puppy will learn by the scent on the paper that it is the area in which they should urinate and eliminate (as they are still too young to go outdoors).

Usually by week 3 or 4, puppies have developed their sense of smell, and will start to understand where to go. At this age, the puppies are beginning to play with their littermates, are becoming more aware of their environment, and slightly vocal. A pup at this age may try to bark a bit. At this time, you can begin to offer toys, as the pup will notice and play with them. Milk teeth are erupting and weaning should begin. If a de-worming was not done at 3 weeks, it should be done at 4 weeks. However, since the exact timing depends on a pup's weight and health status, do check with the vet.

5 Weeks Old - The puppy is now doing well with weaning and is for the most part eating the soft blend of food and milk replacer. He is almost on a completely solid diet. At this point, you may want to work to keep the whelping box clean of urine and feces and encourage the pups to either use newspaper placed outside of the box or in many cases, pups will follow the dam to her designated bathroom area and mimic her. Be careful that if they go outside, that the area is not one that any other dogs or animals can have access to at all. The puppies should all be held and touched each day. This is very important socialization that allows a puppy to become used to human touch. You'll want a 5 week old puppy to start to get used to human noises, being washed down with a warm soft washcloth, hearing regular household noises and being stroked. This allows that puppy to then go on to be a happy, well socialized family member in its new home.

6 Weeks Old - The puppy has fully developed its sight and hearing. The puppy is however, a bit too young to respond to his name. A Shih Tzu of this age will be very curious and want to explore his "world". Weaning will be just about complete and you can use 'feeding time' as a time that the dam has some time away. A 6 week old Shih Tzu should be encouraged to walk around the home, investigating new sights, sounds and smells. The puppy should still be cleaned by the owner with a soft & warm wash cloth. Although, it is almost time to begin giving regular baths. At 6 weeks, most puppies are given their first round of puppy shots. This will be a combination vaccine without leptospirosis (unless the pup is at risk) and coronavirus where coronavirus is a concern.

8 Weeks Old - The Shih Tzu puppy is, in most US states, allowed to go to his new home. When raised correctly, the 8 week old Shih Tzu is happy, healthy and ready to meet his new family.

Age

We've all heard it before, that a dog ages 7 years for each human year. However, this is such a general statement that it does not hold true for any breed. Dogs will age at varying rates depending on their breed; with their size playing a big role in maturity rates. You may be interested to know the 'human age equivalent' of your Shih Tzu so that you can

AGE OF YORKIE	HUMAN AGE EQUIVALENT
6 MONTHS	5
1 YEAR	15
2 YEARS	23
3 YEARS	28
4 YEARS	31
5 YEARS	35
6 YEARS	38
7 YEARS	42
8 YEARS	45
9 YEARS	49
10 YEARS	52
11 YEARS	56
12 YEARS	59
13 YEARS	63
14 YEARS	66
15 YEARS	70
16 YEARS	74

adjust such things as feeding and exercise and know what to expect. An energetic adolescent will have much different needs than a senior. In addition, an older dog will have a higher risk for certain health ailments and diseases. As a responsible owner, you can keep an eye out for certain symptoms that would point to an impending health issue.

The rate at which a dog matures is not equal at all stages of his life. If you have had your Shih Tzu for a while, it may be hard to believe that your 12 year old dog is the equivalent age of 59 human years; however this is a guideline that refers to the breakdown of the body's ability to fend off disease, level of exercise a dog is able to handle and so forth. A Shih Tzu owner can have a dog that is in his teens that still loves to run around the park!

Aging Milestones

8 Weeks - A puppy is ready for his new, loving home. Growth is going to be rapid. Meals should be 'free-fed', meaning that fresh food is left out at all times. Do not take a young puppy out to public places until he has had all of his puppy shots. House training can start now.

3 to 4 months – At 3 months old, a puppy can start having 3 meals per day. Any snacks should be given as reward for good behavior. House training is still underway but the pup should be making progress. Though he will be filled with energy and curiosity – bouncing from one thing to another, he should be able to focus enough to being progressing with command training as well. Walks should be twice per day, for 20 minute durations and at a pace that is brisk for the puppy. A Shih Tzu starts teething at this age; it will last several months.

4 to 7 months – With teething in full swing at 4 and 5 months old, this is perhaps the most trying age, but rest assured it will be over with soon. Be sure you have an excellent supply of teething toys. Importantly, puberty normally begins at this time. Un-spayed females have their first heat. Un-neutered males have viable sperm. The adult coat is coming in; it will be thicker, be able to grow longer and you may notice some color changes.

9 months - Growth slows. Some Shih Tzu puppies will stop growing by the age of 9, 10 or 11 months. For others, just a bit of weight will be gained from now until 12 or 15 months. The typical puppy will now be fully housebroken. Even if all commands were taught, continue to reinforce them. Teething toys are no longer needed, but do be sure to have lots of 'stay busy', chew and companion toys.

1 Year - A Shih Tzu is deemed an adult, although he or she may still display puppy-like tendencies. Adult weight and height is just about set at this time. Meals are now twice per day. The 1 year old Shih Tzu is a lot calmer than when he was a pup.

1.5 Years to 9 Years - The Shih Tzu is in his or her prime.

10+ Years - There is no exact age that a dog is declared to be a senior and it varies from breed to breed. Toys age much slower than large breeds and tend to have longer lives. The declaration that any dog is a senior is done by the veterinarian who is familiar with the dog's health history. Many vets will classify a Shih Tzu as a senior by age 10.

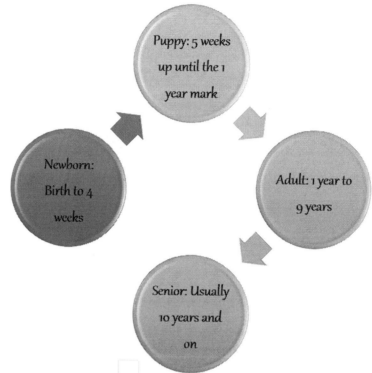

Senior Care

It's never easy to accept the fact that our dogs age so much quicker than we do. In general, Shih Tzu live 10 to 16 years, with 13 years being the average.

There is not an official age that a dog becomes a senior; it is the veterinarian who will make the call. However, in general it is 10 years old and it is almost certainly always by the teens. Declaring a dog to be a senior is an important element, since those once-per-year health checks will increase to twice-per-year. This is because the dog's risk for many health problems increases with age and you'll want to catch issues early for the best possible chance of quick recovery.

As your Shih Tzu grows older, it is best to keep an eye out for changes and to make some adjustments to keep your dog happy and comfortable.

Changes to Expect as Your Shih Tzu Becomes a Senior - These are the signs to look out for, that will let you know that your Shih Tzu is growing older and his needs will be changing.

How Activity Levels may Change - As the senior dog ages, he gradually loses muscle tone, his energy level decreases and for many, arthritis may settle in. The overall result is a slowing down. Sometimes this happens so gradually, that owners may not notice until there is such a huge change that it can't be denied. Changes will be subtle at first; there may be some hesitation in movement or signs of stiffness. Arthritis related stiffness, like humans, often is worse if the weather is rainy and/or cold. Arthritis can occur just about anywhere, but is most commonly seen in the legs, hips and spine. If a Shih Tzu previously had luxating patella, he will be more prone to having arthritis in those areas. As to not repeat text, you may wish to refer to 'Health Issues', 'Arthritis', page 219.

What you can do to help: Lower activity expectations, making walks both slower and taking a break or two to rest and have a drink. Do keep up with exercise unless your veterinarian tells you otherwise. The older dog that does not leave the house can take a turn for the worse quite quickly. Some seniors will still want to run around and play! So, do allow this and even encourage it, however stop things when he appears to be getting tired and offer plenty of water breaks.

How Sleep may change: The number of hours a dog sleeps will increase as he transitions from adult to senior. Nighttime sleep may be restless and fitful. Whether or not a senior Shih Tzu sleeps less, more or the same at night, most will need more naps or longer naps during the day. Many older dogs will insist on lying in doorways and hallways to keep tabs on you, unless you encourage them to choose better spots.

What you can do to help: An older dog must be able to rest undisturbed, so any young children should be supervised as to not disturb a senior's naps. Help a senior have a better night's sleep with a quality orthopedic canine

bed and for some, a self-heating pad. This will be beneficial for arthritis issues as well. Senior dogs will not often do well with 'full day outings'. Even if given plenty of breaks to rest, a senior may have trouble napping or sleeping anywhere but his own area that he is accustomed to. If you will be bringing your Shih Tzu to someone's house for a visit, do bring along his bed and other supplies to help him be comfortable. Make sure your Shih Tzu's resting area is in a spot where he feels most comfortable; this may change as he ages (window view vs non-window view, close to a heating source, further away from the TV, etc.)

How Appetite may Change: As dogs age, their metabolism slows down; a senior does not need to ingest as many calories as his adult counterpart. This, in turn, can cause the dog to self-regulate and eat less. There are also many health issues that can cause a decreased appetite, so if your senior is losing weight, this is your sign to bring him to the vet for a full checkup. Tooth loss and/or intolerance for hard foods can cause a senior to have trouble eating.

What you can do to help: If you offer a manufactured food, transition to the senior variety. Older dogs need a different amount of carbs, proteins, nutrients and minerals. Senior dogs generally do better with more fiber; adding bran, apple slices (no core, no seeds, no peel) or pumpkin (real pumpkin, not the pumpkin pie filling) to meals can be a good method to do this. Adding low-sodium chicken or beef broth to foods and well as warming meals in the microwave and help the older Shih Tzu chew and eat his food.

There may be Weight Gain: Due to decreased metabolism combined with less exercise (due to the senior walking slower and often less often), a Shih Tzu may gain some weight. With this breed, excess weight often shows on the abdomen. Even just a pound or so can affect Shih Tzu with knee, hip or back issues, so for this reason, you'll want to be careful about letting a Shih Tzu gain too much.

How to help: You should be switching to a senior brand dog food (more ahead), however swap out some of his 'regular' food for lower calorie options (mixed well into the food). Good additions include baby carrots, peas and green beans. Fruits can be added as well, including blueberries (which are high in antioxidants), raspberries, banana and mango.

Skin and Coat may Change: Both skin and coat can be much more prone to dryness. This can cause itching and the coat may become very brittle.

How to help with this: If you are not already, do use high quality shampoo, conditioner and a really good leave-in coat spray (you may also wish to refer to 'Grooming', 'Choosing Your Products', page 76). Dry paws and nose can be helped with an effective paw wax and a quality nose butter. Omega-3 or Omega-3, 6, 9 canine supplements can be very helpful.

Eyes may Become Cloudy or Hazed - As they age, dog's eyes often show a bluish transparent 'haze' in the pupil area. In some cases, it will be an issue of lenticular sclerosis which does not affect vision. In other cases, it may point to cataracts. Some dogs can live with mild cataracts (under 30 % opacity). Those that are due to diabetes or that are over 60% opacity should be treated with surgery. It will be important to have any eye clouding to be checked by the veterinarian since cataracts are a progressive disorder that may lead to blindness.

Other Changes that May or May Not Occur

Cognitive Dysfunction - Dogs, like people, can experience age-related dementia. Like humans, it is caused by physical changes in the brain and its chemicals. This can affect a senior dog's ability to think, focus, learn new things and remember. A senior dog with CCD will display a number of the following behaviors:

- Appears confused in familiar places around the home or backyard
- Becomes trapped behind familiar furniture or in room corners
- Has trouble finding and/or using doors and negotiating hallways
- Does not respond to his name or familiar commands
- Is withdrawn and unwilling to play, go for walks, or even go outside
- Does not recognize or is startled by family members
- Paces or wanders aimlessly throughout the house
- Has difficulty learning new tasks, commands, or routes
- Frequently has accidents in the house
- Sleeps more during the day but less during the night
- Stares at walls or into space
- Appears startled when lights or the television are turned on or off
- A decreasing need for your attention, praise, and play
- Is hesitant to take treats, drink water, or eat

Though both a physical and neurological exam, a veterinarian can rule out other causes such as hearing loss, vision loss, UTI and kidney disease. There is no cure for CCD, however some medications may help for some dogs. The most popular one (though rather expensive) is selegiline (brand name Anipryl). It is the only FDA approved drug to treat canine senility and 70% of dogs have improvement after one month of treatment.

 Caring for a senior with CCD

- Do not change the layout of the home
- Declutter the house
- Know your senior's limits when introducing new toys, food, people, or other animals
- Keep commands short & simple
- Encourage short sessions of quiet play with you (easy games, puzzle games, etc.) to stimulate the mind and help a dog focus

It works by increasing the amount of dopamine in a dog's brain, as this is linked to nerve impulses and brain function.

Allergic reactions are rare but do include loss of appetite, vomiting, diarrhea, drooling, restlessness, itching and/or shaking).

Reduced hearing – Some seniors may have reduced hearing to some degree. This may occur in one ear or both. Some signs to look for include not responding when called and/or acting startled when you approach or wake him (due to not hearing your footsteps). A vet exam should be done first to rule out other medical problems, such as an infection, growth, or foreign body in the ear. If there is age-related hearing loss, it cannot be reversed however there are steps that you can take to keep him safe and make him comfortable. (See image next page)

Reduced Vision - As like humans, dogs can have reduced vision due to aging. If you notice that your older Shih Tzu seems to have trouble seeing, you will want the veterinarian to first rule out glaucoma, cataracts and other conditions. Signs of trouble seeing include: General clumsiness, bumping into walls and furniture, startling easily, apprehensive behavior, inability to easily find toys and/or reluctance to go out at night.

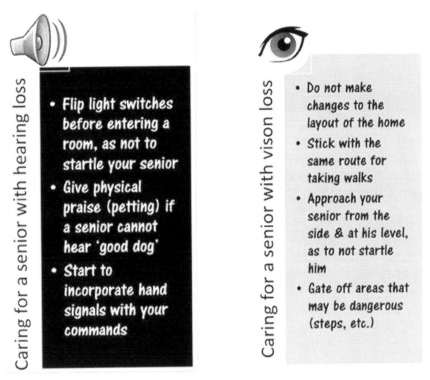

Caring for a senior with hearing loss
- Flip light switches before entering a room, as not to startle your senior
- Give physical praise (petting) if a senior cannot hear 'good dog'
- Start to incorporate hand signals with your commands

Caring for a senior with vison loss
- Do not make changes to the layout of the home
- Stick with the same route for taking walks
- Approach your senior from the side & at his level, as to not startle him
- Gate off areas that may be dangerous (steps, etc.)

Leading Causes of Death for the Shih Tzu Breed

The life expectancy of the Shih Tzu is between 10 to 16 years with a median age of 13 years. Female Shih Tzu live - on average - 1.5 years longer than males. While the median age of 13 is not considered an exceptionally long life expectancy, it is a tad longer than the average age that domesticated canines live in general, which is 12.67 years in the United States and 11.08 years in the UK. It should be noted that the figure of 12.67 years in the US is death by natural causes. When death by trauma and other means are factored in the number goes down to 11.1 years.

There are 2 main reasons why this breed has a slightly longer life span than the national average:

1) Toy breeds generally live longer than medium and large breed dogs.

2) The Shih Tzu is a rather healthy breed. The majority of health issues that Shih Tzu contend with are not fatal.

Leading causes of death for the Shih Tzu Breed - A very helpful study was conducted by the University of Georgia that lasted over two decades to record the top causes of death of dogs. They documented 82 purebred dogs along with mixed breeds. There were 74,556 dogs in all and within this study group, several hundred were of the Shih Tzu breed.

Their goal during this 20 year study was to find mortality patterns that would lead to better health-maintenance practices that may allow dogs to live longer lives. The findings give us a good understanding of what Shih Tzu die of and surprisingly some of the causes of death are preventable.

Results are divided into two groups: Puppies which are dogs under the age of 1 year old and adults which are 1 year and older.

The Top Leading Cause of Death for Shih Tzu Puppies

#1 Infection - Sadly, the top cause of death seen in Shih Tzu puppies is infection. This includes a variety of diseases including:

- Parvovirus - This is also known simply as 'Parvo' and it is a scary disease that attacks the gastrointestinal tract and immune system of a puppy. At that point, there is intense vomiting and diarrhea that can quickly cause fatal dehydration. It is very contagious for any Shih Tzu that is not properly vaccinated. Some pups catch this during a 'window of vulnerability' when antibodies from the dam's milk have waned off but the vaccine has not yet had time to completely offer appropriate protection. This virus lives on infected dogs and also in the feces from those dogs; it can travel among a litter or a group of dogs in a kennel extremely fast. Keeping puppies vaccinated on schedule and also applying proper cleaning methods to all areas of a kennel are vital to stop the spread of Parvo. **Note:** At the time of this writing, there is an experimental new treatment for Parvo, parvoONE, which shows great promise, curing approximately 90% of cases. If released, it can be offered at home for a rather low estimated cost of under $500. Hopefully, this will be approved soon; maybe by the time you are reading this book, many more puppies will be able to survive this terrible disease.

- Distemper - There is a vaccine for this deadly disease as well. This is a highly contagious infection of the respiratory and/or gastrointestinal tract. Early signs are coughing and weakness. It progresses into bouts of diarrhea that drain a dog of electrolytes and hydration. The fatal phase occurs when it spreads to the spinal cord and brain of the puppy. Being diligent with immunizations and refraining from bringing a puppy out in public until the entire rounds of puppy shots are complete can prevent a puppy from catching this.

- Leptospirosis - Despite this being a deadly canine disease, in many areas the inoculation for this is voluntary. While there are many forms of leptospirosis, the lethal strain causes liver and kidney damage. It is contracted via the infected urine of wild life. For this reason, only dogs deemed at risk will receive protection. This would include any Shih Tzu that live on property that abuts wildlife habitats. Wildlife includes small woodland creatures such as skunks and raccoons.

#2 Trauma - This is a concern for adult Shih Tzu as well. Many cases of trauma are preventable. Death by trauma included fatal injury to the head, body or both. This included completely avertable injury including:

- Being stepped on
- Being tripped over
- Being accidently knocked down a staircase
- Being dropped
- Being hit by a car

The average life span of this breed would increase dramatically if fatal injury were taken out of the equation.

The 4 Top Causes of Death for Shih Tzu Adults

#1 Cancer – 15.1% of Shih Tzu succumb to cancer. Even though cancer is not among the leading causes of death for many toy breeds (Chihuahua is only 7.5 % and Pekingese is only 7.8%), it is the top cause of death for the Shih Tzu. This includes a wide variety of cancers including lymphoma (a tumor of the lymph nodes), mast cell tumors (a form of skin cancer), mammary gland tumors, soft tissue sarcomas (these occur on the surface of the body and within body organs, then slowly grow and metastasize in the lungs and liver) and bone cancer. It is important to note that 50% of all cancers are curable if caught early and that the risk of developing mammary cancer can be decreased dramatically if a female is spayed. Therefore, in regard to this cause of death, some cases are preventable.

#2 Urogenital – 13.9% of Shih Tzu died due to urogenital disease which includes kidney disease, urinary stones, pyometra (infection of the uterus), and prostate disease. It occurs more often with toy breeds than with larger breeds. Out of all dog breeds, the Shih Tzu is among the 12 breeds in which this occurs most often.

#3 Infection. This is the 1st leading cause of death for Shih Tzu puppies and the 3rd top cause of death for adult Shih Tzu, with 7.9% of adult Shih Tzu dying from some type of infection. This includes the diseases as discussed previously with puppies but with adults there are more cases of fungal infections (such as blastomycosis and histoplasmosis) and protozoal disease (such as babesiosis and leishmaniasis). Additionally, this includes anaerobic bacterial infection, which can develop around a wound, such as bone fractures and breaks (which again, brings in the issue of trauma, the 2nd cause of death for puppies, but certainly a concern for adult Shih Tzu as well). Finally, this includes sepsis, which is a full body infection that can stem from an untreated dental infection.

Extending the Life Expectancy of Your Shih Tzu - There are many things that you can do to help your Shih Tzu live as long as possible. Care that you give from the day you bring home your puppy, through adulthood and into the senior years will have a great impact on your dog's health and his or her life span.

1) Vaccinations – A dog can be immunized against many of the diseases that are fatal to this breed. Never believe that a dog that is kept inside the majority of the time does not need inoculations. It only takes a moment of sniffing infected urine or a brief period of contact with an infected dog for disease to spread. In addition, protecting your Shih Tzu does not end with the round of puppy shots. Adults need boosters and this should be discussed with your dog's veterinarian.

2) Safety First - Since trauma is the 2nd leading cause of death for puppies and comes into play as well with adult Shih Tzu (both the issue of traumatic injury and possible subsequent infection from that), life span can be drastically increased if safety precautions are put into place and followed by everyone in the household. Here are some tips for keeping your Shih Tzu safe:

- There should be a leash rule that dictates the Shih Tzu is never off leash when outdoors. Even the most well trained dogs can suddenly dart off without warning. An otherwise obedient male may run away if he smells a female in heat (and he can sense this from miles away) and a female in heat may escape to find a mate. Enclosed yards are deceptively unsafe. There is risk of another animal entering, the Shih Tzu finding a hole to escape, poisonous plants, chance of insect swarms, ingestion of such things as pebbles and risk of disease such as leptospirosis in any areas of wildlife such as raccoon and skunk.

- Have a rule in place for the door. All it takes is a blink of an eye for a dog to dart outside when someone opens a door either to exit or enter the home. It can help to have household members knock before entering in order for someone to make sure the Shih Tzu is not close enough to run out when the door is ajar.

- Teaching your Shih Tzu all basic commands can save his life. If running away, some dogs may be too focused on their goal to listen, however many dogs can be stopped in their tracks with a loud and firm "Sit!" or "Come!". Shouting out a command to stop a dog from crossing the street may very well prevent that dog from being hit by a car.

- Since being dropped or stepped on is a major concern, it is important for all members of the family to understand that this is an 'under-the-foot' dog. It only takes a moment for a distracted owner to step backward onto a Shih Tzu that was lying or sitting quietly behind him/her.

- Children should be taught proper methods of picking up the dog and youngsters should be only allowed to carry the dog if they can handle this important task.

- Always look around before walking, switch on dimmer lights at night if the Shih Tzu has reign of the house and never hold your Shih Tzu if you will be balancing and holding other things in your arms. This breed is a pro at wiggling out of his human's grasp.

- Always make sure that your Shih Tzu is safely in a certified canine car seat that is appropriately sized. This should be the rule whether you are taking a long drive or just going around the corner to grab some milk.

3) Provide proper dental care- When a tooth becomes infected and there is decay in the mouth, infection can travel into the body reaching the heart and/or brain. Dogs with decayed teeth suffer in pain which puts stress on the entire body and older, senior Shih Tzu with missing teeth have trouble eating. For all of these reasons, proper cleaning of the teeth is so important and can be a step that you can take to increase the life span of your Shih Tzu. A good 4 to 5 minute brushing each day along with once a year professional checkups can keep a Shih Tzu's teeth healthy and strong. Use a quality paste and supplement this with dental treats that promote good oral hygiene.

4) Spay/neuter -Males that are neutered before the age of 6 months old live 20% longer than their unfixed counterparts. Females that are spayed before the age of 6 months old (it should be done before her first heat cycle) live 25% longer lives than their un-spayed counterparts. When a female is correctly spayed, it eliminates the odds of developing ovarian cancer. This type of canine cancer is fatal in 50% of all cases. Spaying also reduces her risks of mammary cancer. With males, it eliminates the chances of having testicular cancer (when done before the 6 month mark) and decreases the odds of developing prostate cancer.

5) Avoid chemicals; both food and water - What your dog eats day after day, month after month and year after year has a huge impact on his overall health and therefore his lifespan. Only offer high quality commercial brands or home cooked food. Avoid brightly colored manufactured treats. Use a filtering device on your kitchen tap to avoid giving straight tap water to your puppy or dog and be sure that your dog is meeting water requirements to stay properly hydrated.

6) Be diligent about exercise- In conjunction with a healthy diet, regular exercise throughout your Shih Tzu's life will keep him healthy. It is good for the heart, keeps muscles toned and contributes to the emotional health of a dog. Many owners find themselves doing well during the spring and summer; however, exercise is cutback in the colder autumn and winter months. It is important to allow your Shih Tzu to receive the benefits of activity all year round.

While you can take a day off during blizzard or sub-zero days, if you properly clothe your Shih Tzu (and yourself so that you don't want to run right back inside) your dog will do just find in the cold and snow if kept to 20 minutes twice per day.

7) Do not delay vet visits - Many serious conditions have favorable prognosis if caught early. This is particularly relevant in regard to both urogenital disease (2nd leading cause of death for adult Shih Tzu) and cancer (top leading cause of death for adult Shih Tzu). Never put off yearly health examinations. And be sure to budget for unexpected medical issues. It is such a shame when owners hesitate to bring their dog to the vet due to the financial burden of a visit when the expense could have been factored into an owner's monthly budget. You may also want to consider pet insurance; though most do not cover congenital defects and pre-existing conditions. Many plans do cover: infections, eye problems, allergies, stomach ailments, ulcers, arthritis, skin problems including skin cancer, bladder problems, nail issues, abrasions, thyroid conditions, kidney disease, tooth removal, trauma care, lung infections, diabetes and more.

The bottom line is if you have to wonder if your Shih Tzu needs to see a vet, chances are that he does. Adults should have exams each year, seniors twice per year and a Shih Tzu of any age should be brought to the vet if there are ANY signs of illness. Catching problems early is important for successful recovery and receiving proper treatment can stop small issues from turning into larger, more serious issues that can be life threatening.

8) Accept the age of your dog - Time slips by quickly and many owners do not want to admit that their Shih Tzu is becoming a senior and is in his or her last stage of life. However, being keenly aware of this breed's typical life span and making changes to care as the Shih Tzu ages will aid in quality of life. Older dogs should be given proper orthopedic beds for age related arthritis. Exercise and food may need to be adjusted. Supplements for the coat and more focused grooming techniques can help with problems of aging such as dry coat and skin.

Knowing When to Let Go - We receive a lot of email from owners who have senior dogs with health problems and want to know "when it is time to let go?" As your Shih Tzu ages, there may very well come a time when you must make a decision regarding letting your Shih Tzu pass on. This most often happens when an older, senior dog is diagnosed with a health issue that causes pain or distress that no medication or treatment can relieve. In any case such as this, we highly recommend getting a 2nd opinion, no matter how long you have had the same vet or how much you admire/trust him or her. This will put your mind at ease that the diagnosis and prognosis is absolutely correct. There is always a chance that a different vet or specialist may have a different diagnosis.

Once you are at the point of needing to make a decision, we can only say that loving your Shih Tzu means putting his or her needs ahead of your own. We feel that this decision should be based on the amount of pain the dog is in and the discomfort he is feeling. If your Shih Tzu is in pain or distress the majority of the time, you may opt to give yourself the emotional pain of saying goodbye in order to give your Shih Tzu the gift of being free from the pain. This is the most unselfish, loving thing that you can do.

Extra - Keeping Your Shih Tzu Safe & Happy

Traveling with Your Shih Tzu

Your Shih Tzu in a Car

It is common for dogs to have trouble being in a car. The most typical issues involve:

• **Car sickness** - A Shih Tzu puppy or dog may develop a terribly upset stomach, dizziness and nausea. This feeling can evoke panic (trying to escape, whining) and can result in vomiting. While this can happen to people as well, with dogs it is often very pronounced and happens more easily. When the inner ears sense movement (the car is driving) but the dog does not see movement (he is not moving in relation to the inside of the car) this is often what creates the feeling of being ill. (More ahead on this)

• **Fear** - Many dogs are afraid of the car; for those not used to it (and double for those with bad experiences) it can be an overwhelming event, stressful enough that the Shih Tzu will bark, whine, become restless, shake and even try to escape.

• **Barking** - Though this is often related to either the queasiness, fear, or a combination of both, it is not uncommon for owners to avoid traveling with their Shih Tzu in the car simply because the barking is non-stop, causing a distraction and being a stressor.

Here are some tips: It is possible to make car rides with your Shih Tzu much more enjoyable. It does take some planning and in cases of a phobia, it can take some time. However, it is well worth it when you have the freedom to bring your Shih Tzu with you as opposed to leaving your dog at home.

1) Practice. Just like many other elements, a Shih Tzu often needs to be desensitized. This involves a gradual introduction and experience within the car. Very few dogs will do well if placed in a vehicle and taken for an hour drive the first time. And one issue is that an owner may have taken their Shih Tzu for a ride without realizing the effect it would have, but now feels it's too late to 'start over'. However, whether you have a puppy that you now want to start driving around or you have an older dog that never did well, starting from the beginning can help out quite a bit.

Here is a Training Schedule:

• **Step 1** - Secure your Shih Tzu (more ahead on the best car seats) and sit behind the wheel. Turn the car on. Do not drive anywhere. That's right, the goal is to sit in the driveway with the engine on. This allows your Shih Tzu to get accustomed to his car seat, the sound of the motor and the general overall feeling of being in the confined space. Be sure to have your supply of toys (more ahead). Start off with 5 minutes and work your way up to 15. Do this for 7 to 10 days, at least once per day if you are able.

• **Step 2** - With everything in place, this will be slow movement back and forth in the driveway. Take care when applying the brakes, making the transition as easy as possible. If you have a very short drive, you can jump to the next step. It is best to do this for 1 week, with 5 to 10 minute sessions.

• **Step 3** - Short drives. This is a short drive of 15 minutes in a thinly settled district where you can safely drive 35 mph or under.

• **Step 4** - Now you are ready to take longer rides in the car. It is best for you to make the destination be a fun one such as a visit with a doggie friend or a trip to the park. However, in any case, a reward when exiting should be given. Even if your Shih Tzu appears to be doing fine, take a rest stop every 30 minutes. This is vital, as most owners keep driving if the dog seems to be okay. However, without a break, that can change very quickly. It is much easier to avoid upset stomach or restlessness than try to fix it once it happens. Pull over somewhere safe and with your Shih Tzu on

leash and harness, allow him to walk around, have a drink and a snack and 'find his legs' again.

2) Prevent Motion Sickness- If the nausea can be kept at bay, this is a huge hurdle to being able to bring your Shih Tzu in the car. **Here are some tips:**

1. Food & meals. Any extreme, an empty stomach or a full stomach should be avoided. Offer a small snack; dry biscuits are best. Many dogs respond well to a bit of sugar. This can be a jelly bean or a small teaspoon of white sugar. Do not overdo this (it can cause a high sugar spike that results in the Shih Tzu having too much energy), be sure it is real sugar, as fake sugar is toxic and of course, do not give anything with chocolate.

2. Calming remedies. There are some herbal calming remedies that can help a Shih Tzu feel better when traveling in the car. The ones that seem to work best are those containing natural pheromones. These can also be used for other times of severe stress. You do not spray this directly onto the dog; it can be sprayed onto the car seat before you place your dog into his spot.

3. Inside car adjustments. Dogs often do best if it is just a tad cooler than owners would assume is a comfortable temperature. While you don't want to freeze your Shih Tzu, keep the heat a bit lower than you would otherwise or the AC down one notch. You'll also want to have one or two windows open a bit. When there is a cross breeze (your driver's window and the rear passenger window both open) this creates a good amount of air movement. Do note that having windows open all the way is often too much wind for a Shih Tzu. Experiment in regard to how much they are lowered depending on the speed. Soon you will learn what your dog likes best.

4. The car seat. Not only is this nonnegotiable for safety, it also helps a dog endure travel. You may wish to refer to the 'Care Items – Shih Tzu of All Ages', 'Car Seats' section, page 40.

3) Keep your Shih Tzu Calm - The elements that will help during car travel that we already went over (but also help with reducing stress) are: A gradual desensitizing, prevention of motion sickness, taking breaks at least every 30 minutes. Other tips that will help include: Have special car toys that are only given inside the vehicle. With your dog safe and free from nausea, this alone can quickly train a Shih Tzu to actually look forward to traveling. Experiment with music - Some dogs will calm down with certain music; easily listening is often best, however experiment with genre and volume.

Taxis and Uber - It is best to make sure that your Shih Tzu is very familiar with cars before trying to take him into a taxi or other car service. Not all taxis and Uber accept dogs; in most cities, this is the driver's discretion. What they fear most is the dog soiling the car or vomiting. Since it will be difficult to drag a car seat along with you if you are jumping into taxis and you'll want to put the driver at ease, it is often best to have your Shih Tzu in a sling (best if he is under 10 lbs.) or in a canine carry case.

Buses and Trains - There is not one blanket rule for pets for this type of transportation. Each bus and train line has different guidelines. Some only allow dogs if they are checked as luggage, in a crate. We suggest avoiding this at all costs. Others will allow small dogs if they are in canine travel bags and yet others will allow a dog if on leash. You may want to look over the Pet Travel Guide http://www.pettravel.com/passports_pubtrans.cfm that lists out rules by city and even covers traveling by ferry.

Flying on an Airplane with your Shih Tzu - If you are traveling far and the plan is to fly there, a lot of preparation will need to be done. Not all airlines allow pets in the passenger cabin; they have dogs go into the cargo compartment with luggage and this can be risky, if not fatal. It can be overwhelmingly stressful, not to mention the extreme temperature changes. Here is a list of the 6 things to do & know:

1. Call an airline ahead to find out their exact rules and guidelines. You'll want to choose a flight that allows your Shih Tzu to travel with you, in a carrier.

2. Choose the travel carrier wisely. For those airlines that do allow pets to travel with owners, they will need to be in a travel carrier. Luckily, since the Shih Tzu is a toy breed dog, this can be accomplished. However, rules on the size of the carrier are strict. You'll want to take measurements to be absolutely sure that it meets the regulations.
Also, be sure to train your Shih Tzu to become used to the carrier. Even if he does well in a car seat and is happy to be in a sling… canine travel crates are much different.

3. Book a direct flight. Changing planes is stressful enough without having to worry about your Shih Tzu too.

4. Health-check papers. Many flights want you to produce papers stating that your dog is in good health and up-to-date on shots. In most cases, this must be dated within 10 days of travel. So, you'll want to plan ahead to obtain this from the veterinarian. If you will be traveling overseas, there may be much stricter regulations, so you'll want to inquire about this. Do you remember when Johnny Depp's dogs were put in a quarantine facility in Australia for not having proper documentation? You don't want that to happen to your Shih Tzu.

5. Dealing with bathroom needs. Unless the flight is very short, traveling on a plane will no doubt involve your dog needing to go to the bathroom at some point. If allowed to do this in the crate, it can be uncomfortable for your dog, not to mention the noses of every other passenger. This is where doggie diapers can come in handy. While you'll have some cleaning up to do once you land (via quality canine body wipes), keeping urine and feces contained makes for more comfortable travel.

6. Calming remedies - If you know that your Shih Tzu doesn't do well with planes, you can start this before takeoff (see previous). However, if you are not sure, you can bring some along or apply a small dose to his travel carrier just in case. It is not recommended to use prescribed tranquilizers unless there is a strong, valid reason. Many are not tested to see how animals respond when at high altitude and if a dog were to have an allergic reaction, tens of thousands of feet in the sky is not where you want to be.

Arriving at Your Travel Destination
- While you may have been looking forward to vacation for quite a while, your Shih Tzu may not share your excitement. The 2 biggest mistakes that owners make when traveling are not having a plan for their dog in regards to lots of walking and assuming that their dog will be fine staying at a new house or in a hotel. Let's look at these issues:

• **Walking** - As with many things, the fact that a Shih Tzu is a toy breed dog makes life a bit easier. If you'll be doing a lot of walking or sightseeing, you'll want to take steps so that your Shih Tzu **1)** does not tire out and **2)** is not overwhelmed being walked among a bunch of people in a new setting. While it's just fine to let your dog explore a bit (safe on leash and collar) having a sling or body-carrier for your dog can be a great help. These are much different than carry cases; a quality sling is an open-air cloth sling bag that keeps your Shih Tzu against your body (similar to a pocket book or 'man purse'). A canine body-carrier is similar to a baby carrier, a sort of 'pet backpack' that has leg and head openings, keeping your Shih Tzu secure on your front. If you have *tons* of walking to do or if it is hot & sunny and you want to allow your Shih Tzu to be in the shade, you may wish to try a pet stroller; these are fantastic for these situations. To see some great choices for slings, carriers & the top recommended stroller, look to 'Carriers & Slings' in the Shih Tzu Specialty Shoppe.

• **New environment** - While you can't take everything with you when traveling, if possible do bring your Shih Tzu's bed. This can really help a dog settle into a new place. It can also help to bring along his food and water bowls. Pets can get attached to these and may be finicky about eating if the food is not served in the dish that they are familiar with. And of course, bring along favorite toys.

Traveling can be exciting, but not always for dogs. If you are planning a long trip, do put some thought into what will make your Shih Tzu happier: Staying at home (with friends or family) or being somewhere new with you. It's not always an easy decision. If you do take your puppy or dog with you, with a bit of planning, you can both enjoy the getaway.

First Aid Kits

Overview Not everyone has a first aid kit for themselves, let alone their pets. So do you really need one for your Shih Tzu? It is really worth the time to assemble one? Will you ever need to use it? The answers may surprise you. Having a few things put together is the wise move; it can save you the stress of running around looking for things, get your Shih Tzu immediate help and in some cases, it can even save his life.

Also, if you're traveling or heading out on an excursion with your dog, it's a good idea to bring the kit along with you. You never know and it's really best to prepare. No worries, the kit is rather small and easy to tuck into your travel bag.

One issue with lists of first aid items recommended for dogs is that about half of the items aren't really needed for a basic kit. Since most of us don't have extra money to assemble a kit with things that'll never be touched, let's go over what you actually may need at some point in your Shih Tzu's life.

What you Really Need

1. Betadine Solution - This is for washing out cuts. It is a fast-acting, broad-spectrum antiseptic to clean wounds and reduce bacteria that can cause serious infection. When you use it, you water it down until it has the color of iced tea. Why use this? Veterinarians do NOT recommend using soap, rubbing alcohol or hydrogen peroxide. Alcohol can actually damage tissue, soap is not effective and hydrogen peroxide is best used if infection has already set in.

2. Gauze pads - Sterile gauze pads are used to apply the betadine. You'll want to wash your hands first. Some betadine can be poured over the injury (or use a syringe - see ahead) and then using some gauze pads, dab at the edges of the wound. These are also used to apply pressure to a wound that is actively bleeding. You'll want to apply pressure, stopping every 10 minutes to see if the bleeding has stopped.

3. Paw bandages - While a cut is healing or when transporting your Shih Tzu to the veterinarian, it's important to keep the site clean. If a Shih Tzu receives a nasty cut or injury to one of his paws, you'll find it really hard to wrap it up without these. These can really come in handy with Shih Tzu that are too big to carry and need to walk when brought to the vet with a paw injury. These slip over the paw and are secured via a Velcro piece that wraps around the ankle. This disposable paw bandages are really a great idea.

Tip - For puncture wounds, keep a damp compress on the injury as your dog is being brought to the vet; the goal is to delay the formation of any scabbing which can lock infection under the skin.

4. Canine rectal thermometer - It's really important to have one of these to properly take your Shih Tzu's temperature. You'll need to do this if there is question of heat stroke or fever. We highly recommend one with a flexible rubber tip and a quick, digital readout. The normal body temperature for all puppies and dogs is 101 to 102.5 degrees Fahrenheit.

5. Petroleum jelly - You'll want to have this to use in conjunction with the thermometer. When you take your Shih Tzu's temperature, use this to lubricate the thermometer, which is then inserted into the anus 1/2 inch for puppies and 1 inch for adult Shih Tzu.

6. Hydrogen Peroxide - In case of poisoning, you may be instructed to immediately induce vomiting. Please note that this is dependent on what a Shih Tzu ingested; with some toxins more damage can occur if the dog throws up and with others, it can be lifesaving to induce vomiting. If you are instructed to induce vomiting with your Shih Tzu, one of the most effective methods is to give the dog hydrogen peroxide. Check with your vet; however the recommended dose is 1 teaspoon for each 5 pounds of body weight with another dose given after 10 minutes if the dog does not vomit.

7. Activated charcoal tablets - This is used - in some cases, to absorb toxins. If your Shih Tzu is poisoned, you should call the vet ASAP for instructions. It is best to have both this and the hydrogen peroxide in case your Shih Tzu eats or swallows something toxic, you know what it was and the vet tells you do administer either of these. Time is of the essence in these cases.

8. Medicine syringe - If your dog takes liquid medicine, most likely it came with a syringe; however, in cases of emergency if you need to get your Shih Tzu to swallow hydrogen peroxide, you'll want one of these. An effective method (and best if you have a helper) is to pull back the skin to create a small pocket and deposit the liquid between the cheek and the teeth.

9. Thermal blanket - You might never need to use this, but if your Shih Tzu is severely injured (hit by a car, etc.) this can be lifesaving. Wrapping a dog in a thermal blanket can stop him from going into shock while you transport him to the animal hospital.

Tip: Unfortunately, ambulances will not come to help a dog that is hit by a car or otherwise severely injured; you will need to transport your Shih Tzu to the closest animal hospital. An appropriately sized blanket is one of the best methods to move a puppy or dog that is injured in this way and of course, you'll want a helper to two. The blanket should be used as a sort of stretcher and kept under the Shih Tzu during transport so that he can be removed from the vehicle in the same way.

10. Eye wash - This is needed to flush a dog's eyes of any contaminants if such an event occurs. If you are alone with your Shih Tzu, it is best done by holding the bottle above the dog's head (where he cannot see it) and letting the drops drip down into the eye. In emergency cases, if you have a helper, one can hold the bottom lid out a bit, and drops are put into the pocket of the bottom lid.

Tip - Please note that the eye wash is completely different products than eye tear staining liquid or any type of cleaner like that. Those are grooming items and this is a first aid item formulated to clean and flush the eyes.

11. Artificial tears - If you have to flush out your Shih Tzu's eyes, you'll want to use an artificial tears product afterward to help soothe them.

12. Benadryl - While you may have this for yourself or others in your household in tablet form, you'll want to have liquid Benadryl for your Shih Tzu. This is given in cases of moderate to severe allergic reaction to an insect bite including bees, hornets and wasps. You'll want to use plain Benadryl (no flavoring, etc.). The recommended dose is 1 mg/ for each pound of body weight, given every 8 hours; but can be doubled to 2mg for each pound of body weight, if needed. **Note:** Most liquid formulations of Benadryl will have a concentration listed on them, usually 5mg per teaspoon, so be sure to read the label before giving any to your puppy or dog.

13. Baking soda - If your Shih Tzu has been stung by a bee and yellow jacket, a paste made of water and baking soda should be applied to the skin for 15 minutes. If you have this in your kitchen, there no need to add to the kit unless you are traveling or out hiking around, etc.

Tip: If a wasp or hornet has stung your Shih Tzu, a small piece of cloth soaked in vinegar should be applied to the bite for 15 minutes. This will help neutralize the alkaline in the venom.

What You May Not Need- If you look up lists of things to have in an emergency kit or first aid kit for pets, you'll see a long list. And we certainly wouldn't discourage anyone from obtaining most of the items, if they have the budget to do so. The more you have, the more you'll be prepared. However, some of these things you either already have in your house or really don't need at all (and some are downright ridiculous). For some, it's recommended only if you are traveling with your dog. And finally, for some of these the advice to use them is flat-out wrong and can make things worse.

5 inch hemostat - Sometimes seen on lists as a tool to use to clamp for blood vessels to stem bleeding - If you know how to clamp a blood vessel, that's great. If not (and really, who does other than vets and doctors), the vet will do this if needed. Even attempting this without training could kill a dog, not help him.

Bandanna and/or nylon stocking - This item is suggested by some to tie up a dog's muzzle so that he doesn't bite after being injured; some dogs do bite when hurt as it is canine instinct to be defensive when feeling vulnerable. However, this is rare and can impede the dog's breathing. While we certainly don't want anyone to get bit from a dog that's acting out of instinct, do use this with caution and only if absolutely necessary.

Cotton balls - For applying antiseptic or topical medications; not bad to have but sterile gauze works better.

Credit card - To remove stingers from bee stings, etc. It'd be hard to imagine that someone doesn't have some sort of plastic card (bank card, license, etc.) and would need to put one in the kit.

Dishwashing liquid - Not only is there a 100% chance you already have this, it's not recommend to flush wounds.

Mixing water with betadine is best but if you don't have any, just water is the next best thing.

Disposable safety razor - Some suggest this for shaving the coat back from around a wound; as with the scissors, this is something the vet will do, so there is no need for this.

Eyedropper - Meant to apply the saline solution and artificial tears; however those usually are already in a bottle that dispenses the fluid as needed.

Ice pack - Never use this for heat stroke! You'll want to bring your Shih Tzu to a shady area and lay wet, cool towels over him. If inside, have a fan blowing close to him. Once his temp goes down, bring him to the vet. Packing the dog with ice will make things much worse. While some say this should also be used to reduce swelling on injuries, if your Shih Tzu is injured enough to have swelling, he's injured enough to be brought to the vet. This is good to have in the house for afterwards, though most likely you already have some in your freezer.

Nexaban - Do not use this. This is skin glue that holds wounds closed; this is not recommended at all. The vet will determine how the cut should be closed and the worst thing you can do is glue it shut, possibility trapping infection under the closure.

Phone numbers of the vet and closest animal hospital - Not needed for an at-home kit (since you no doubt already have this). However, if you're traveling with your Shih Tzu or taking him out for a walk that is a bit off the beaten path, it's good to have. If your phone dies, you'll be happy you have the numbers written out on paper. Also, if you're far from home, obtain the number of the closest vet from where you are staying.

Rolled gauze - This is on a lot of lists meant to stabilize joints and such. If a Shih Tzu were to suffer a broken limb, you don't want to be wrapping it up. You can do more damage and it can cut off blood circulation.

Rubber gloves - If you wash your hands before assisting your Shih Tzu with an injury, you really don't need gloves. The betadine can stain a bit, so some owners may want these.

Rubbing alcohol – One suggested (from sources other than us) is to use this to cool down a dog's body in case of heat stress. This is NOT recommended by us. A cool, shaded area (if outside) or near a fan (if inside) and the use of cool, wet towels placed over the dog's body is best, while you are waiting for his temperature to go down in order to safely transport him to the vet. The other possible use would be for wound care and again, this is not recommended as it can damage a dog's skin.

Scissors - Meant to trim hair around an injury, this is not really needed since any cut or wound will be flushed and compressed while you head to the vet. The vet will shave the area if stitches need to be given.

First Aid

How to Treat a Cut

1. Apply pressure to stop the blood. It's best to use sterile gauze pads. Do this for about 10 minutes, then check. During those 10 minutes, if the blood goes through the gauze, don't lift it off, just add more. If it's still bleeding when you check it, do another 10 minutes. If blood is still flowing after that, the cut most likely needs to stitched by the vet.

2. Once the bleeding has stopped, gently flush the cut using betadine mixed with water (until it is watered down to look like the color of iced tea) and a plastic syringe. If you don't have this, you can dab it (not wipe) with gauze pads and betadine.

3. Apply a thin strip of antibacterial ointment. If the cut is on an area that the Shih Tzu can lick, it is best if this is reapplied each night, just as the puppy or dog has fallen asleep.

4. If it oozes any pus, if the skin is raised or red or if it is not showing any signs of healing after 3 days, you'll want the vet to take a look. It may need to be butterfly bandaged, it may need stitches and/or medication for infection may need to be given.

Stung by a Bee, Wasp or Other Stinging Insect

Facts to Know About the Dangers of Bees - Dogs, and especially toy breeds like the Shih Tzu, are targets for stinging insects. Many of the offenders will hover in places that a Shih Tzu may innocently be walking over or near. Since these insects can move very fast, it may not be clear if the attacker was a honeybee, other type of bee, wasp, hornet or yellow jacket.

- Bees - Only the honey bee dies after stinging; all other varieties can sting a dog (or you) numerous times. There are over 20,000 species of bees and 70% live underground or at ground level.
- Wasps- A wasp rarely strings once and will typically attack a dog or human several times. The pain can last a long time since elements in the venom slow down blood flow that would otherwise dilute the venom. Some types, such as the Ground Digger Wasp live near the ground in gardens and other such places.
- Yellow jackets - These are exceeding dangerous. They not only sting, they can bite as well and often do so completely unprovoked. Swarms can be found at ground level since they often make their nests in abandoned rodent holes.
- Hornets - They can sting a dog repeatedly since the stingers are not pulled out of the body. They can have nests in shrubs and on the ground. Stings are more painful than wasps due to a high level of venom.

What to Do if Your Shih Tzu is Being Attacked by Bees or Other Stinging Insects - Whether just a single wasp is attacking your dog or your Shih Tzu is being swarmed by bees, you should react in the same way since you may have no idea if your puppy or dog is allergic to the venom or how many times a single insect may inject his stinger. The only real way to help your Shih Tzu escape being attacked by bees or other insects is to pick up your Shih Tzu and run. Do not try and swat the bug(s) or flail your arms in an attempt to make them go away, since this can be interpreted as an aggressive action that triggers a stronger attack.

- Pick up your Shih Tzu securely so that he is not jostled and run as quickly as possible.

- The main areas that a Shih Tzu will be stung are those that are not covered with hair; this means that the Shih Tzu's face, belly and paws are going to be attacked more than the main body. If possible, tuck your Shih Tzu under your shirt and then pull up the top of your shirt over your face while not obscuring your view. While a bee can still sting through clothing, it does offer somewhat of a barrier.

- Your goal will be to seek a sheltered area such as a house, building or even your car, though do keep in mind that depending on the size of the swarm that was attacking your Shih Tzu, some may follow you inside.

- If bees or wasps enter into the house, you can flea to another room and close the door or in some cases, running into the bathroom and jumping into the shower with your Shih Tzu can make them fly away. If you can run into a well-lit building, these venomous pests can get temporary confused and be attracted to the windows.

What to Do After Your Shih Tzu Has Been Stung - The most important element is to remove the stingers since many types will continue to release venom until they are removed. However, if they are pulled out by fingers or even tweezers, this can also release venom into your dog's bloodstream. The best method is to grab a driver's license or credit card and use a scraping motion over the skin to pull them out. Carefully part the coat in 1/2 inch sections, looking for stingers. Be sure to check all areas of the body including the tail and under the chin.

You may wonder if you need to bring your Shih Tzu to the vet. The elements to keep in mind with this is that:

- Any puppy or dog can have an allergic reaction to any stinging insect such as wasps, hornets, yellow jackets and bees.
- Not having an allergic response in the past does not mean it cannot happen the next time; some dogs may have been okay with one previous sting but will react badly with two.
- Even if a Shih Tzu has proven to not be allergic to a bee, he may have a response to a wasp and vice-versa. This holds true for just about any insect bite, though most dogs that are allergic to wasps are also allergic to hornets.
- While signs of an allergic attack can begin almost immediately, it can take up to 45 minutes for symptoms to appear... and if a Shih Tzu is indeed allergic, you will want him already at the vet as opposed to waiting and being too late to respond.
- A **huge** concern with toy breeds like the Shih Tzu is the concern of a buildup of toxins, which is a separate problem from allergic reactions. For dogs, 10 stings per 2.2 pounds of body weight can be fatal and 5 stings per 2.2 pounds of body weight can cause a dog's system to be overwhelmed, causing acute illness. And for young puppies, it may be even fewer than this. These are numbers easy to reach should a swarm of bees attack your Shih Tzu. For example, with a 5 pound Shih Tzu pup, 25 stings can cause the body to be overloaded with venom and 50 stings could be deadly. Please note that with multiple stings of bee or wasps, serious issues can occur *days after* a bee attack. Proteins in the venom break down and can damage cells in the body. The kidneys can then become clogged, causing kidney failure.

Therefore, if you have any concerns, you should bring your Shih Tzu to the veterinarian. At the vets, he can be checked for stingers that you may have missed, be treated for the pain if necessary, receive treatment for possible swelling and be given either precautionary allergy medication such as Dexamethasone or should there be signs of anaphylactic shock, the reactionary treatment of epinephrine.

At-Home Treatment for a Shih Tzu that Was Stung by a Bee - If the previous does not apply to your Shih Tzu and you feel safe in keeping him at home and being treated at home, there are some things that you can do to help with discomfort and swelling.

1) Be sure that all stingers have been properly removed by scraping them out

2) Clean the injection site on your Shih Tzu with warm water and soap to remove body oils that may impede further treatment.

3) If a wasp or hornet has stung your Shih Tzu, a small piece of cloth soaked in vinegar should be applied to the bite for 15 minutes. This will help neutralize the alkaline in the venom. If a bee and yellow jacket has attacked your Shih Tzu, a paste made of water and baking soda should be applied to the skin for 15 minutes. For each of these, treatment may be repeated if the puppy or dog is still showing signs of discomfort or if the area is very red.

4) Once this is done, it can help to apply a small ice pack to help with the swelling.

5) Anything other than a very minor case of an allergic reaction MUST be treated at the veterinarians where a powerful drug such as epinephrine may need to be used. With this said, for very minor cases, Benadryl may be given. Benadryl is given based on the weight of the dog, regardless of age. The recommended dose is 1 mg/ for each pound of body weight, given every 8 hours; but can be doubled to 2mg for each pound of body weight, if needed. **Note:** Most liquid formulations of Benadryl will have a concentration listed on them, usually 5mg per teaspoon, so be sure to read the label before giving any to your puppy or dog.

6) Keep a very close eye on your Shih Tzu to look for any signs of an allergic reaction. This can come on quickly and it can take up to 45 minutes to develop.

Signs and Symptoms that a Shih Tzu is Allergic to a Bee - While rare, a dog can have Anaphylaxis, which is a life-threatening allergic reaction. Without treatment, it can lead to shock, cardiac arrest and death. The most common signs include:

- Swelling of the face - Even if the dog was not stung on the face, areas of the face may swell. This includes one or both eyes, around the lips or any other area.
- Severe swelling at the sting site - If red, irritated skin does not fade down and/or if the bump does not recede.
- Weakness - This includes any out of the ordinary behavior including acting overly tired, confused or having marked lethargy.
- Trouble breathing - This includes raspy breathing, making gagging noises, heavy or shallow breathing.
- Other possible signs include:
- Rash - This is not always present, however this includes red bumps or hives
- Vomiting - While this is not always a symptom, a dog that is having an allergic response to insect stings may dry heave or throw up.
- Pale gums - Gums may appear white, light blue, light gray or very pale pink.
- Cold limbs - A dog's legs may be colder to the touch than other parts of the body.
- Drooling - There may be excessive salivation

Emergency Treatment for Bee Stings - Just like humans, a dog that is having an Anaphylaxis response needs immediate treatment with Epinephrine. When given quickly enough, it will stop the things in their tracks. In some cases, this will need to be administered literally within minutes, and for this reason keep a close eye on your Shih Tzu or bring him to the vet after being stung.

Poisoning and Exposure to Toxins

Ingested Toxins - The list of things that are toxic to dogs includes literally countless elements that are also toxic to humans, along with:

- Alcohol
- Caffeine (any food/drink with caffeine)
- Cherries
- Chocolate
- Currents
- Garlic (a bit of garlic powder is not toxic; pieces of garlic are)
- Grapes – One of the most toxic foods in the world for canines. Very poisonous and can be fatal.
- Grapefruit
- Mushrooms (not all types; but it is better to be safe than sorry)
- Onions
- Potatoes (when raw or green)
- Raisins – Like grapes can be fatal if eaten.
- Rhubarb

Note: There are so many other things that can be toxic to a dog; if you are even in doubt, call your vet.

What to do: If you know your Shih Tzu has ingested something that may be harmful, or your dog is showing signs of poisoning such as seizures, drooling or trouble breathing, call the vet ASAP. Do not delay. Depending on what may have been ingested, you may be instructed to induce vomiting (by giving the dog hydrogen peroxide; 1 teaspoon for each 5 pounds of body weight with another dose given after 10 minutes if the dog does not vomit), give him milk **OR** rush him to the clinic.

Note: If your Shih Tzu has vomited, bring as large of a sample as possible with you to the clinic.

You may also want to phone the Animal Poison Control Center hotline (888.426.4435 – available 365 days/year, 24 hours/day) or the or the Pet Poison Helpline at 1-855-213-6680. Do keep in mind that there is a fee for both of these.

Chemical Exposure – This would be any airborne chemical that the Shih Tzu inhaled or any chemical that the dog touched. This includes but is not limited to cleaning products, poison for rodent control, pesticides and anti-freeze.

If Skin is Exposed to a Chemical – Read the label and follow the instructions; in many cases you will flush with water.

If a Chemical Has Been Inhaled – Bring your dog outside, if possible, for fresh air. Then, call the vet or the Animal Poison Control Center hotline (888.426.4435 – available 365 days/year, 24 hours/day) or the or the Pet Poison Helpline at 1-855-213-6680. Do keep in mind that there is a fee for both of these.

If a Dog Has Stopped Breathing/ Is Choking

1) Stay calm. If you panic, it will be very hard to follow through with what you need to do.
2) If possible, have another person call the veterinarian while you help your dog.
3) You will need to open the airway. This is done by gently pulling the tongue out of the mouth until it is flat. If you are able, look to see if you can spot any foreign objects in the mouth or the back of the throat.
4) If you DO see an object, try to remove it with a tweezers or pliers. Do not spend a lot of time doing this; 30 seconds at the most.
5) If you do see an object but cannot remove it, place your Shih Tzu in your lap, with his back to you. Place both hands on the sides of his ribcage. Apply a quick, firm pressure 3 times in a row. If this does not work, lie your Shih Tzu down and using the palm of your hand, strike the rib cage firmly 3 times.
6) If you do not see an object OR if your Shih Tzu is not breathing (and you do not know why), perform rescue breathing. This is done by closing the dog's mouth with your hand and breathing directly into the dog's nose. The chest should expand outward when you do this. Perform every 4 seconds (count out 'one Mississippi, two Mississippi, etc.) until you arrive at the clinic.

Why Vet Visits are So Important

At Home Vs the Veterinarian – It must be noted to Shih Tzu owners everywhere, that while home remedies can be very effective in many cases of minor problems, there will be times throughout a Shih Tzu's life that going to the vet is necessary. And it is important to be firm about how long you will wait and to admit when professional veterinary care is needed. We live in a modern world where access to professional veterinary care is within reach of all owners. To deny a dog veterinary care while the dog suffers is nothing short of neglect. Responsible dog ownership includes budgeting for unexpected vet visits.

Wellness Checks – Aside from bringing your Shih Tzu to the vet when ill, yearly wellness checks are very important as well. For a 'regular' physical examination, the cost is usually under $75, so this is really something that can be worked into a budget; putting away less than $7 a month is all you need to do. Once a puppy has all of his puppy shots and up until the Shih Tzu is declared to be a senior, he should see the veterinarian 1 time per year and seniors should be seen 2 times per year (because the chance of developing health issues increases).

Please know that even if a dog seems perfectly fine, he may not be. And catching issues early is your best chance for a good prognosis and the best chance for recovery. A dog of any age may catch worms from a flea (it only takes one and that can be one from another dog outside of your household) or from eating feces. Even with parasite prevention, sometimes parasites slip through and some, such as heartworms (nicknamed a 'silent killer') is deadly. Even if you brush your Shih Tzu's teeth at home (and we really hope you do!), dental issues often do develop. Catch this early, and it will typically be easy to treat; catch this late and the consequences can be severe. Dental infection can spread up into the sinuses and it can also travel into the bloodstream and then to organs all over the body. Diabetes, kidney disease, liver issues…thyroid disease, vision and hearing issues… these are all things that may not have immediate symptoms.

What will Happen at the Vet Office –Your puppy or dog will receive a full physical examination, a stool sample will be checked and blood testing will be run. The vet will take his vitals (temperature, pulse rate, respiratory rate) and weigh him. The head will be checked (eyes, ears, mouth). The coat and the skin will be examined to look for any signs of concern including skin bumps that owners may have not noticed. Using a stethoscope, the vet will not just be listening to your Shih Tzu's heartbeat, he will also alter your dog's breathing (slightly) by touching the nose and mouth, to check for breathing and heart issues.

Your dog will be checked for proper posture; knees and hips will be checked as well (which is very important for this breed, since Shih Tzu are prone to patella and hip issues). Lymph nodes will be checked, as well as reflexes. Veterinarians also know how to access a dog in regard to 'intangibles' such as how a dog is responding and his level of alertness.

The vet will speak to you about prevention steps that he/she feels is necessary for some 'borderline' issues that may have been detected. You will discuss your Shih Tzu's diet and his exercise routine. This is also your opportunity to ask any questions; you are not expected to just sit quietly; a good owner is an involved owner!

Please remember – Vet visits are not that expensive, relatively speaking, and it can (and probably will) extend your Shih Tzu's life span. Every day, thousands of dog owners are reeling from the death of their dog. However, many early deaths could have been avoided if the dog was properly cared for and taken to the vet annually or biannually for early detection and prevention. When you decide to bring a dog into your life, you are taking on a huge responsibility. It is akin to raising a child. There are very few parents who would avoid taking their child to the doctor for well-visits and this same mindset should be in place for your canine family member(s).

If you purposefully do everything possible to keep your Shih Tzu happy and healthy, you will be a loving and caring owner… which is the type of person that your Shih Tzu deserves!

Bonding with Your Shih Tzu

You might think that bonding should be a natural process; however there are many elements that can come in the way of a strong relationship taking place. Perhaps your Shih Tzu is very young and just doesn't seem interested in much… owners of puppies can feel as if they are being ignored and wonder if their dog doesn't like them. Even older dogs may seem distant and not overly fond of cuddling or showing affection. The truth is that all dogs are capable of having very strong feelings toward their owners, but in some cases this needs to be cultivated and for many Shih Tzu, there needs to be regular interaction that not only holds together the relationship that you have established, but also works to increase the bond.

If this issue is ignored, very little will change. Dogs, and particularly Shih Tzu, often do not engage first… they will not make the first move to have an exchange… they take cues from their owners and will only bond well if the owner is in charge of the process. However this is good news, since it means you can take purposeful steps to grow the relationship.

Signs of Weak Bonding - The following are signs that there can be some improvement in regard to the bond that you have with your Shih Tzu. The more that you can agree to, the more effort and work that will need to go into improving the relationship. Do keep in mind, that if there is not a strong bond, this is not a personal reflection of either your or your dog… even loving owners may find that somehow important bonding rituals were not done often enough or there were extenuating circumstances that prevented spending enough time together.

• Little or no desire to play • Little or no eye contact • Not wanting to cuddle or be petted • Attempts to run off when being picked up • Not listening to commands • Aggression such as baring the teeth or growling

How Much Bonding to Expect - A Shih Tzu is 100% capable of feeling and expressing love. This is a very sensitive and affectionate breed. However as touched on earlier, many Shih Tzu do not make the first move. A Shih Tzu left to his own defenses will not typically 'extend a hand' to form a friendship with a human. He craves it. He will relish it once it is established and once a bond is strong a Shih Tzu will be your best and most loving friend to the end… but many need the owner to do things, say things and create an environment that is conducive to this.

It has been proven that canines do have a wide range of emotions. Science has proven that canines have many of the same brain structures that we do, that are responsible for emotion. And it has been determined that dogs have the emotional development of a 2.5 year old human child. Well, if you have been around a toddler, you know that this is quite something! Dogs will feel sad, happy, excited, jealous and feel strong affection which has been equated to feeling love. And when dogs love their human, unless there is neglect or trauma this love is for life. Dogs do not 'break up' with an owner or ever become angry enough to call it quits! So, once you have a good foundation and you work to grow the bond between you and your Shih Tzu, you will have a dog that is as close to you emotionally as possible. Your Shih Tzu will be your best friend and your closest confident (even if he or she cannot verbalize this back to you).

Uninterested Puppies - If you have a very young Shih Tzu puppy that does not seem interested in your or essentially ignores you, it's important to not take this personally. Puppies can have a hard time focusing on any one thing…and it takes time for a puppy to realize just who you are and what an important role you play in his life. If you follow all of the upcoming advice for bonding, the attachment that your puppy will have with you, will grow over time.

Issues that May Masquerade as Emotional Distance - One thing to keep in mind is that many of the signs of what we would classify as a dog not caring or not wanting to be close, may actually be a symptom of a health problem. Any time that a dog is feeling discomfort or pain, he may retreat and want to be alone. Why? When a canine is ill or injured, he feels vulnerable - even with loving owners - his instinct may tell him to retreat and keep his distance. So, if your Shih Tzu has suddenly started acting odd and keeping away or is a puppy and despite the steps listed here, just does not respond, this is a reason to have him be brought for a full veterinary examination.

Another element is that when a dog is afraid, this can really alter his personality. A Shih Tzu that is scared may cower on his bed, try to hide under the bed or look for a safe spot in a closet. He may be wary of coming close, may shake and/or have trouble eating. There are cases of acute issues such as a dog getting startled by lightning or a loud noise. However, there can be ongoing issues of a Shih Tzu experiencing some sort of emotional stress that is preventing normal interaction and therefore, any bonding.

A common reason is separation anxiety; some Shih Tzu get so nervous and stressed that it is difficult to 'go back to normal' even after an owner arrives back home. Less common but certainly something to keep in mind are two issues that we have helped owners with lately. The first problem may be a Shih Tzu that is harassed and bothered by another pet. If owners are not home, they may not see this happening. However, it can cause a Shih Tzu to be very upset at all times... not wanting to play or interact…and some may be so 'bullied' that it affects everything from eating to sleeping.

Another rare but possible issue is that another human is mistreating the dog. Sadly, this was the case recently with a young woman whose boyfriend was jealous of her Shih Tzu and took this out on the dog when she was not looking. It is shocking and not something that one would want to think about, however since this can happen, it is something to consider if things appear that this may possibly be the case.

Shih Tzu or any other dogs for that reason, just cannot act normal and have a close bond with their owner if they are living under stress and experiencing problems on a constant basis. As long as the home environment IS one of peace, love and happiness, you can move on to learn how to bond with your Shih Tzu…. And if there are issues that need looking at, certainly do this before going any further.

Another element that can be mistaken for a bonding problem is actually play, believe it or not. We recently met an owner who was troubled that her Shih Tzu would only come to her halfway and then would lie down, seemingly act afraid and refuse to come any closer. In response, she would pick up the Shih Tzu and once settled on the sofa with her, the Shih Tzu was happy, content and loving. Why would her dog do this? It was determined that her Shih Tzu was actually playing a game and was essentially 'trained' to act this way. He would lie down and act as he did, knowing that the next step 'should be' that the owner came over and scooped him up.

Finally, a chaotic household that has frequent yelling, overcrowding, loud music and other elements that strip away a sense of peace and security will often affect a dog negatively and to the point that he is too overwhelmed to relax and even try to enjoy any interaction. In order to have a close bond with a dog, the dog needs to first feel safe and content in a safe, warm, peaceful, happy home. Without this, it is an uphill battle and if these elements are not offered, it could be considered neglect.

Elements that Encourage Bonding
- There is not one magic remedy for close bonding. Rather, to have a great relationship with your Shih Tzu, it is a matter of many things all working together that combine to create a great friendship and one of respect.

1) Establish yourself as the leader. If you want to bond with your Shih Tzu, you probably are thinking that you want your dog to be your best friend… and this can happen, but respect must be there first. We must remember that the canine to human relationship is different than human to human bonds. Canines without structure…without a real leader… without the safety of a true 'pack' and clear hierarchy are often confused, will try to take over as leader themselves and will certainly not have the right foundation to listen or properly interact. This cannot be achieved in one day and owners should follow these rules at all times. Once a Shih Tzu learns this, it needs to continue to be reinforced. In addition, every human in the house should also follow these guidelines, since problems can arise if only one or some humans do this and others ignore this. You may wish to refer to 'Teaching Proper Hierarchy', page 108.

2) Teach your Shih Tzu an agility exercise. While this breed can do well with short bars for jumping, pole weaving is typically the easiest and one of the most fun agility activities your dog could do. These can be set up indoors or outdoors. While you can use just about any objects, both of you will have more fun if you use actual weaving poles which are colorful and are sized appropriately for toy breeds.

3) Train your Shih Tzu for a new command or trick. When a dog and an owner are working hard toward a goal, this itself is a great bonding experience, regardless of how long it takes. As long as you have tons of enthusiasm and your Shih Tzu enjoys this time due to being rewarded for trying hard, that is all that matters. And of course, a great added benefit is that your Shih Tzu will be a well-trained dog. Whether you aim for a simple 'Sit' or a more complicated 'Shake Hands', this is a great method to feel that you've achieved something together.

4) Have your Shih Tzu help you with household chores. When we are rushing around cleaning and trying to get things done in the house, it's easy to place our Shih Tzu in his area and go about our chores; however this is a huge missed opportunity to bond. Slow down the pace a bit and allow your Shih Tzu to be your assistant. While a task may need to be moved to another day, the enjoyment that you receive far outweighs the extra time needed. Though your dog may be confused on the first day, if this is done on a regular basis, you might be surprised just how much bonding can take place and how good a Shih Tzu can get at certain tasks. One of the best chores to take on together is sorting clean laundry. Teaching a Shih Tzu to give you socks or small wash clothes, gives him a job that he can be proud of. It takes a while to teach a dog which items to mouth and 'hand over'; however with consistent practice this

can easily be accomplished. After a while, a Shih Tzu will get very excited that it is 'laundry time' and will rush over to help. Be sure to always end with a super tasty reward for the good work.

5) Bring your Shih Tzu with you as often as you can. There are several things that prevent an owner from bringing their Shih Tzu along with them to run errands and whatnot. First, some owners worry that if they spend too much time together, this will increase the dog's separation anxiety as he will be 'too used' to being with the owner. However, this is not true and having a full and happy life outside of those times of being home alone can only increase a dog's overall happiness. The second issue is that owners may just want to rush out to get things done as quickly as possible, rationalizing that they will just leave their Shih Tzu home since they will be back soon. However this is also a huge missed opportunity to bond. Whether you're dashing off to grab milk at the corner store or need to explore a hardware store for just the right item, bring your Shih Tzu when at all possible.

The last issue that gets in the way is excuses…. My Shih Tzu doesn't like the car…. That store may not allow dogs…. What fun will he have at the garden shop? …and it goes on. It must be remembered that if a dog does not like the car, riding in the car is the very thing that will allow him to become accustomed to it (& our advice for car sickness will help). And there are a zillion stores that do allow toy sized breeds if they are in a carry bag or sling. Slings for dogs are great simply because they are so easy; they go around you similar to a pocketbook, but are sized and have support for a dog to feel comfortable, with his head out and able to look around. Many Shih Tzu find the rhythmic motion of being in one while you walk to be quite relaxing.

And last but not least, a dog enjoys being with his owner no matter what and no matter where. A dog home alone is certainly going to be more bored than along with you, even if you don't think the event is interesting. If you want your Shih Tzu to be your little buddy, you need to let him be one… and that is done by doing things together.

6) Be silly. Dogs do have their own personalities, however with this said, they mimic owners a LOT. If an owner is depressed, moody and sad, their dog may be as well. If an owner dances when a song comes on the TV, sings when it's raining and makes silly faces for no reason other than to be silly, a dog will learn to have a sense of humor too. When you are outside in your yard in the summer heat, turn on the water hose and see if your Shih Tzu wants to play in the stream…. When you want your Shih Tzu to check out a new toy and he's not interested, roll around on the floor, wave it in the air and let out a "Whahhhhttt?" in a silly voice! Play with your Shih Tzu as if you are trying to amuse a baby… act engaging… have enthusiasm… smile! The vibe of the house should be light, fun and filled with happiness… and a dog in that environment will thrive and be much more prone to want to bond.

7) Take on a new challenge. Whether this is getting your Shih Tzu a life vest, dabbing sunscreen on his nose and taking him out on a canoe… or waking up early to finally go see that sunrise over the ocean… or choosing an 'easy' hiking trail that will lead you both to new sights and sounds…. Choose something new to do with your Shih Tzu. Many owners hesitate to explore like this because they are alone; but when you have a dog you truly are never alone!

Please remember - When you want to have a really great bond with a dog, it's important to not focus on what may be missing and move forward in a direction of growth with tons of enthusiasm. Whether your Shih Tzu is shy or is young and needs time to learn about the world… or needs a nudge each day to interact… it is you who needs to engage your Shih Tzu. Very rarely will a dog all on his own suddenly pick up a toy and ask to play when there is not a history of playing.

And since our dogs can't speak in the traditional way, just assume that your Shi Tzu *does* want to help with things in the house, would love to go to a store and would be super happy to be brought somewhere new or to try and learn a new command or trick. It's so easy to get stuck in our ways, that we don't make changes… but to limit yourself and the relationship with your dog in that way is such a shame. Dogs are so capable of offering us a rich and loving friendship; for some it just takes a bit of purposeful effort.

We hope that you enjoyed reading your AllShihTzu Book and that you find it to be a great resource for years. Please be sure to keep visiting the AllShihTzu website; just about every month, we write a new article... and it's always something helpful and interesting, in regard to your Shih Tzu's care and happiness.

If you are not yet a free AllShihTzu Member, be sure to sign up (a button is at the top of all pages of the AllShihTzu site). When you are a Member, this allows you to receive a friendly notice when a new page of info is added to the site.

Loves, Hugs & Shih Tzu Kisses,

The AllShihTzu Team

Made in the USA
Charleston, SC
25 October 2016